Two Decades of Market Reform in India

India and Asia in the Global Economy

In the last few decades a 'new' India has surfaced – an India that is socially confident, globally active, economically visible, technologically suave, and youthfully smart. Its expatriate professionals, students, and computer engineers and its entertainment industry have placed India in the global economy in profound ways, while its regional engagement with Asia, quiet collaboration with China, and growing bilateral relationship with the US is realigning the global political architecture. Yet India still faces numerous challenges, including its large absolute poverty level, social injustices and inequalities, political fragmentation and uneven development.

Anthem's **India and Asia in the Global Economy** series invites scholars and researchers to undertake bold projects exploring the internal and external dimensions of a 'new' India, and its economic and political interactions with contemporary global systems. Titles in this series examine India's economic development and social change in global and Asian contexts, with topics including the politics of globalization, Indian middle class revolution, the politics of caste, India–US relations, India in Asia, emigrants and diaspora, economic policy and poverty, and changing gender relations.

Two Decades of Market Reform in India

Some Dissenting Views

Edited by
Sudipta Bhattacharyya

ANTHEM PRESS
LONDON · NEW YORK · DELHI

Anthem Press India
An imprint of Wimbledon Publishing Company India Private Limited (WPCIPL)
WPCIPL is a subsidiary of Wimbledon Publishing Company Limited (UK)

This edition first published in India 2014
by ANTHEM PRESS INDIA
www.anthempress.co.in

First published in UK and USA 2013
by ANTHEM PRESS
www.anthempress.com

Cover photo courtesy of Rik Rudra Mandal.

ISBN-13: 978 93 80601 84 7 (Hbk)
ISBN-10: 93 80601 84 0 (Hbk)

Dedicated to two great dissenting economists, the
late Professors Krishna Bharadwaj and Ashok Rudra, who were pioneers
in interpreting the Indian economy from alternative perspectives.

CONTENTS

LIST OF TABLES AND FIGURES

Tables

Figures

FOREWORD

The economics profession in the country has never been as sharply divided as it has been on the issue of 'liberalization' and 'globalization'. The moment we step outside of the economics profession and take cognizance of the views of other social scientists the disquiet among them over the implications of 'liberalization' and 'globalization' appears even greater than among the economists. And of course if we look at the wider circle of social activists and intellectuals, this disquiet is even greater. Much of this disquiet does not get adequately reflected in the popular print or electronic media. Besides, linguistic subterfuge is disingenuously used by the defenders of neoliberal policies to claim a consensus for it: 'Everybody is for reforms', goes the refrain, without mentioning the fact that everybody is *not for the neoliberal* reforms. The sleight-of-hand appropriation of the term 'reform' exclusively for the neoliberal agenda has the desired effect of misleading the unwary into a belief in the universal acceptance of neoliberalism. As a matter of fact, however, we have to honestly accept that we are sharply divided over the desirability of the neoliberal agenda and over the implications of our pursuit of it since the beginning of the '90s.

To be sure, the disquiet over the pursuit of this agenda has grown over time. In the beginning many believed that it would provide a way out of the impasse that the dirigiste strategy had got the economy into, that it would introduce a rule-governed system, admittedly the rules of the market, in the place of rampant cronyism, arbitrariness and corruption of the dirigiste era, and that it would enable us to achieve the remarkable growth rates that China and the other economies of East and Southeast Asia were achieving. This euphoria has now come to an end. Far from there being any kind of a 'retreat of state', what we have had is a different, and in many ways even more aggressive, kind of intervention by the state. Far from there being an end to cronyism, we have had a real efflorescence of it, noticeable in particular in the 'privatization' drive for public enterprises and in the Enron deal. Far from our following in the footsteps of East and Southeast Asia, those economies have themselves come to grief as a direct consequence of their 'financial liberalization' agenda. And far from these 'reforms' being a panacea for the travails of a poverty-stricken backward economy, we now have deprivation on a massive scale where per capita availability of foodgrains in the country as a whole (in 2002–2003) has fallen to the average levels that prevailed during the Second World War (years that saw the terrible Bengal famine), even as food stocks with the government have burgeoned.

Now that the euphoria, the hype and the hoopla are over, the time has come to recognize that there were divisions within the profession all along, to listen to what the dissenting voices have to say and to undertake a dispassionate assessment of what the neoliberal agenda entails and has achieved. Dr Sudipta Bhattacharyya's effort in bringing together this collection of articles, written from diverse points of view, is welcome in this context. It is imperative that we make up our minds on this, the most burning, issue of our time; and for doing so this volume should be a useful aid.

Prabhat Patnaik

ACKNOWLEDGEMENTS

The global community looks at India's liberalization experience with interest as it involves a transformation from a strong interventionist to a neoliberal regime. Much of the writings on the contemporary Indian economy tend to be uncritical and sometimes blindly glowing about India's economic growth rates. This book has come out to meet the aspiration for a volume which looks at the present experience of liberalization in India critically and challenges conventional wisdom.

At the outset I would like to express my gratitude to all contributors to this volume who extended their cooperation. At the same time I am grateful to two anonymous referees of Anthem Press for very useful feedback on the previous version of this volume. I would like to express my gratitude to my teachers at the Centre for Economic Studies and Planning, Jawaharlal Nehru University, particularly Professors Utsa and Prabhat Patnaik who always inspired me to publish this volume. I always received encouragement from Barbara Harriss-White at various stages. I prepared the blueprint of this volume during my visit to the Asia Research Centre, Copenhagen Business School, Denmark as ICCR-CBS Visiting Chair Professor for 2009–10. I received feedback and cooperation from time to time from Professor Anthony D'Costa, Professor of Indian Studies and Research Director at the Asia Research Centre, Copenhagen Business School. I presented an initial draft of the introductory chapter of this volume at the internal seminar of Asia Research Centre, Copenhagen Business School, held on 25 February 2010. I am indebted to the participants of that seminar. In particular I am grateful to Kjeld Erik Brødsgaard, Peter Ping Li, Bente Faurby and Xin Li for their extremely useful feedback.

Back in India I received thorough technical assistance from my beloved students Saswati Acharya, Paushali Bhattacharya, Amit Mandal and Gouriprasad Nanda during the preparation of the final manuscript. I am also grateful to Swapna Eleswarapu for bearing the pain of copyediting. I received continuous support from Maumita and Titir as well.

Sudipta Bhattacharyya
Santiniketan
27 March 2013

ACKNOWLEDGEMENTS

Chapter 1

INTRODUCTION: A CRITICAL LOOK AT TWO DECADES OF MARKET REFORM IN INDIA

Sudipta Bhattacharyya

Introduction

India adopted neoliberal policies in 1991 and broke away from its tradition of state interventionist economic planning since independence. India's new journey coincided with the global ideological and economic hegemony of neoliberalism and the collapse of the Soviet Union and East European socialism. Globally, capitalism was freed from the clutches of Keynesianism and reached a new consensus which was captured under the umbrella of the Washington Consensus.[1] The corporate-dominated Indian media hailed India's transformation from Keynesian state interventionism to neoliberalism. India's policy makers agreed to the Washington Consensus and joined the tide of globalization.

This book would like to point out that the neoliberal policy reform was not based on any political and economic consensus. It was launched in India by a minority government led by the then prime minister P. V. Narasimha Rao and finance minister Dr Manmohan Singh, who is now the country's prime minister. Neither did the Congress Party manifesto during the 1991 parliamentary election promise any neoliberal policy reform,[2] nor was any referendum held on the issue of whether India should go ahead with globalization. Ironically, the neoliberal reform was introduced as a compulsion of the loan conditionality of the International Monetary Fund (IMF).[3] While the Indian government time and again explained its compulsion of borrowing from the IMF, it has not explicitly acknowledged the fact that its transition towards neoliberal reform was due to the loan conditionality. According to the government of India the compulsion of borrowing was due to the drying up of its erstwhile stable export market in the Soviet Union, stopping of foreign currency inflows from the Gulf due to the first Gulf War and bad harvest.[4] A group of 35 leftist and progressive economists in a collective memorandum pointed out that in spite of these reasons, borrowing from IMF was not inevitable and could be avoided (J. M. 1992). However, it is evident that the 'New Economic Policies' since 1991 have been identical with the policies of the Structural Adjustment Program of the IMF–World Bank and the Washington Consensus. These policies include devaluation, reduction of fiscal deficit by means of reduction of subsidies for the poor, denationalization or privatization/disinvestment from PSUs, trade liberalization, tax reform – that is, reduction of corporate tax rate – and so on.

The neoliberal policy reform coincided with a high degree of political instability in India accompanied by the highest frequency of changes in ruling parties and prime ministers. Needless to say, such changes in government were not merely by accident. Instead, this represented the Indian people's clear mandate against neoliberal reform. It was the misfortune of the Indian people that there was no viable political alliance in India that could pursue alternative economic policies in opposition to neoliberalism. At election time, almost all political parties contested the election on an antiliberalization platform. But once voted to power they followed the same neoliberal policy reforms as their predecessors.[5] Each time, the media proposed inadequate reform as the root cause for the electoral debacle. Finally, since 2004 the government led by the United Progressive Alliance (UPA) under the pressure of left-wing parties had to distance itself from some policies of neoliberal reform[6] (e.g. privatization of nationalized commercial banks and insurance companies) and adopted some pro-poor economic policies (e.g. a national rural employment guarantee scheme, expansion and writing off loans for the poor and a midday meal scheme for schoolchildren). As a result, the UPA government was voted to power again in 2009. However, the postelectoral formation allowed the UPA-II government to continue in power without the support of the Left. As a result, initially some policies of neoliberal reform regained importance. But soon the non-Congress parties within the UPA-II, particularly the second largest allies, the Trinamul Congress (TMC), realized that they would lose popular support if they allowed the central government to go ahead with neoliberal reform; they started to oppose these policies tooth and nail with the opposition parties. After some failed attempts, the ultimate success of the government in passing a bill in the parliament related to FDI in retail turned out very costly. The government's main ally TMC withdrew their support from UPA-II following the controversy related to FDI in retail.[7]

The objective of this volume is to challenge the conventional wisdom of market reforms in India by demolishing the myriad myths that surround the beneficial effects of neoliberal policies. The contributors of this volume take a closer look at the outcomes of past neoliberal reforms on the current performance of the economy. Dominant interests in India such as big business and media have fabricated various myths in support of neoliberal policy reform in India.

Myth 1: Past reforms have created a flexible, dynamic economy which is expected to weather the crisis and benefits from high rates of growth. This volume demolishes this myth by showing that the growth process has been uneven and vulnerable to crisis. It accompanied poor employment generation and agrarian crisis (see Bhaduri, Chapter 3 in this volume, and Ghosh and Chandrasekhar, Chapter 5).

Myth 2: High economic growth in recent decades has a trickledown effect on the Indian economy, and therefore, no state-interventionist policy is required. This has been reflected in substantial expansion of IT sector and global corporations in India. As a result, a new middle class has been developed. This volume has demolished the myth by showing that the trickledown mechanism was empirically unfounded in India. The period with high-level state intervention in the 1970s and 1980s had the highest level of reduction in poverty (see Byres, Chapter 2 in this volume, D'Costa, Chapter 7, and McCartney, Chapter 14).

Myth 3: High fiscal deficit is the root of all evil, since it raises the rate of interest and therefore dampens investment. Similarly, a rise in fiscal deficit raises inflation. According to this volume, the real rate of interest is high because global finance capital needs a high real rate of interest for investment. The high real rate of interest in turn raises fiscal deficit and therefore the causation is the other way round. On the contrary the high fiscal deficit may cause inflation (via deficit financing) only under full employment or near full employment. In a situation of chronic unemployment, deficit financing would raise the output, instead of price level (see P. Patnaik, Chapter 4 in this volume, and Das, Chapter 13).

Myth 4: Denationalization is one of the effective ways to reduce fiscal deficit. Denationalization is a must, since the public sector is less efficient than the private sector. This volume demolishes this myth by showing that loss making at a given set of arbitrary prices is not an indicator of 'inefficiency'. There is not enough empirical evidence in support of the claim that the public sector is less efficient than the private sector (see in this volume P. Patnaik, Chapter 4; Rudra, Chapter 10; and Nagaraj, Chapter 11).

Myth 5: Industrial stagnation in the 1960s and 1970s was due to the license *raj* and inefficiencies in the pre-liberalization period. Specifically, Nehru–Mahalanobis Planning was responsible for the Hindu rate of growth and industrial stagnation. This volume exposed neoliberal efforts to confuse growth rate during the Nehru–Mahalanobis plan period with the Hindu rate of growth. As a matter of fact, the former was much higher than the latter, while the latter rate (3.5 per cent) was not weak. On the contrary, the industrial growth rate was the highest during the first three plans, also known as the Nehru–Mahalanobis Plan (see Mazumdar, Chapter 12 in this volume, and Byres, Chapter 2).

Myth 6: Rural and urban poverty declines during the liberalization period as a result of the increase in income of the people below the poverty line. According to this volume, this claim is based on the indirect and faulty method of measuring poverty of Planning Commission experts. The direct estimates of poverty show a steep rise in poverty during the reform period (see U. Patnaik, Chapter 6 in this volume).

Myth 7: There is 'overproduction' of foodgrains due to 'voluntary reduction of foodgrain intake' as a result of 'increased income' and decline of poverty during the reform period. Therefore, it is necessary to diversify agriculture from food to non-food export-oriented production. This volume refutes this by showing that the 'lower foodgrain intake' is due to the 'reduced effective demand' owing to increase in poverty during the reform period. There is an inverse relationship between export-oriented agriculture and domestic availability of foodgrains (see Patnaik, Chapter 6 in this volume).

Myth 8: The rural and urban labour market reflects a positive outcome after 1999 as the proportion of self-employment in the total workforce increased and casual employment declined. This volume has refuted this myth by showing that these tendencies have not been substantiated by any increase in remunerative or productive employment. The distress of the workforce is largely feminized as well (see Bhattacharyya and Basak, Chapter 9 in this volume).

Myth 9: Trade liberalization is one of the effective ways in which the Indian economy may benefit a lot. This volume has demolished this myth and showed that during the process of industrialization and development, today's developed countries followed protectionist as well as state interventionist policies. India did not gain from the trade liberalization, as with growing exports, imports also grew at a faster rate. India gained from export of services as it served the purpose of the developed countries. The developed countries maintained high agricultural subsidies and at the same time applied various tricks to comply with the WTO rules. India, along with other developing countries, faces unfair competition from subsidized cheap exports of the developed countries (see Pal, Chapter 8 in this volume).

The essays in this volume refute and dismiss the myths systematically. A brief description of the authors' views and analyses is presented in the synopses of the chapters below. Some of the essays in this volume have been published during the various phases of economic reform and some of them are fresh contributions. It is necessary to incorporate some essays published during the early years of liberalization as they have wide contemporary relevance. Some of them analysed various aspects of the pre-liberalization period in a comparative manner to understand the liberalization period with clarity. For example, T. J. Byres systematically describes the transformation of the Indian economy from one based on economic planning and state interventionism to one based on liberalization in a comparative manner. Another two contributors, namely Ashok Rudra and R. Nagaraj, compare the performance of the public sector industries with those of the private sector in the pre-liberalization period, which is important to understand Indian liberalization in totality. It is important to compile all these papers in a single volume, as it will portray a unified vision of the shortcomings of the liberalized market regime in India.

Theoretical Framework

Market reform means conscious policy actions, where the state is voluntarily withdrawn from economic affairs in such a way that a country can align itself to the global free trade regime. The Bretton Woods institutions, particularly the IMF, advocated supply side macroeconomics, inflation targeting, monetarism and above all, the Washington Consensus. As a matter of fact these ideas have shaped the IMF (Boughton 2004). According to these theories, the important pillars of the structural adjustment programmes are the internal macroeconomic adjustment policies, namely reducing interventions and state support, which are inextricably linked with the policy of trade liberalization. The neoliberal macroeconomic schools see 'deficit' as the villain of the piece. This follows from the microfoundation of macroeconomics, that at the individual level saving is considered as a virtue and expenditure as a vice. In particular, expenditure beyond one's own means is seen as a great offence. The neoliberal microfoundationists oppose deficit financing through effective monetary policy on the grounds that it would generate inflation. The logic of the neoliberals in this context is indeed valid if the economy remains at full employment or close to it. However, it is not at all clear why in a situation of chronic unemployment, as in India, the mechanism of 'crowding-out' and not 'crowding-in' in the form of Keynesian demand management through a multiplier should be operative. One can recall the famous 'paradox of thrift' argument that if most people in an economy followed the Victorian virtue of thrift, it would reduce the income in the economy as a whole (Bhaduri 1990, 57–9). However, the IMF and the World Bank, through the loan conditionality, compel developing countries to follow a policy of reducing development expenditure (U. Patnaik, Chapter 6 in this volume). Similarly, the Fund–Bank idea of labour market reform involves incentives for an individual entrepreneur such as the right to hire and fire and a downwardly flexible real wage rate. For the macroeconomy as a whole, it creates a decline in the money income of wage-earning classes, and therefore, a decline in effective demand; that in effect would cause a decline in countries' income and employment (Bhaduri 1990, 76–7). The Washington Consensus opined that developing countries should go ahead with internal reform, which includes among others financial and labour market reform in order to integrate their economy with the global market (Rodrik 2001, Shaikh 2003).

In the declaration 'What We Do' the IMF stated,

> Marked by massive movements of capital and *abrupt shift in comparative advantage*, globalization affects countries' policy choices in many areas, including labour, trade and tax policies. Helping a country benefit from globalization while avoiding potential downslides is an important task for the IMF. (Emphasis added)[8]

Elsewhere on the IMF website,

> The growth in global markets has helped *to promote efficiency through competition and the division of labour* [...]
>
> More generally, trade enhances national competitiveness by driving workers to focus on those vocations where they, and their country, have a *competitive advantage*. (Emphasis added)[9]

The IMF, in the two statements above, used two terms to represent free trade, namely 'comparative advantage' and 'competitive advantage', that need to be investigated further. One should also analyse the IMF's view about the 'abrupt shift in comparative advantage' as a cause and/or effect of globalization. The original comparative advantage theory of David Ricardo states that two trading countries (Portugal and England in Ricardo's example) can obtain gains from trade even if absolute costs/prices of production of all commodities are initially higher in one country (Portugal) than in the other (England). The only condition required is that the relative costs/prices differ in both countries. In this sense the weaker partner in competition can also have gains from trade by availing comparative advantage. However, critics pointed out that Ricardian theory depends on the necessary condition that each country produce two goods at the autarky without which trade is not possible on the basis of comparative advantage. This is clearly an unrealistic assumption (Subasat 2002, 277–8). In the original example of Ricardo, England has no endowment for production of wine. Thus, the comparative cost of textiles remains undefined in England. The same thing is true when we consider the trade between agricultural goods of any tropical country and industrial goods of the advanced capitalist country (Patnaik 1996). This was the logical fallacy that Ricardian theory could not overcome. England and Portugal were not two stray examples. Ricardo had an agenda to give theoretical support to colonialism. Production of clothes augmented the level of industrialization in England while the production of wine did not make any structural change in Portugal. In other words, the suggestion that arose from the Comparative Cost Theory of Ricardo was that the less developed countries should not go ahead with industrialization, but export food and raw materials to fulfil the industrial needs of the North. England, along with today's advanced capitalist countries, industrialized directly at the cost of de-industrialization and underdevelopment of the non-white colonies in the South (Bagchi 1982, Frank 1967, 1975).

According to the Hecksher–Ohlin–Samuelson (HOS) theory, the explanation of comparative advantage lies in the difference in factor proportions. In the HOS theory, intensive application of abundant factors makes it possible for a country to reduce its cost of production and have comparative advantage (Findlay 1987). In other words, a country with capital-intensive factor endowments can have lower comparative costs in capital-intensive goods, and therefore, this country must have comparative advantage in the production of such goods. Therefore, this version of comparative advantage theory similarly supports the existing structure of the North–South divide.

However, the North–South divide has far more implications in the New Trade Theory advocated by the IMF than in Ricardian or HOS comparative advantage theory. In the era of globalization it is indeed immaterial whether any country has abundant endowment in intensive factors of production to produce its export goods. The IMF-propounded 'abrupt shift in comparative advantage' and 'efficiency through competition' is nothing but an indefinite rat race among nations (developed or developing) to specialize in certain commodities that have high demand in the international market. The 'comparative advantage' has now been replaced by 'competitive advantage'. According to Shaikh, not only 'the very principle of comparative costs is wrong even under competitive condition' but the 'competitive advantage rejects the standard theory [comparative advantage] altogether' (Shaikh 2003, 8). The competition in 'classical competitive advantage' means 'real competition' in the business sense, which is far from perfect competition (Shaikh 2003, 8–9). Global competitiveness is determined by differentials in real wage and technology across nations. (Shaikh 2003, 9). In other words, international competition becomes a price war among nations in the global market. Every country tries to meet the global demand for goods and services at the lowest possible price. The developed countries try to lower prices using superior technology, while the developing countries try to reduce price by using a lower real wage. Breaking the old paradigm of comparative advantage, globalization makes it possible for developing countries to specialize according to global competitiveness and 'abrupt shift' in division of labour. But this changing trade pattern must take place in initial factor intensity and factor price. However, the process of development involves a shift in both factor intensity and factor price. For example, through the process of development a labour-intensive country may transform to a capital-intensive country and a steep increase in the real wage is likely to happen. Therefore, the idea of global competitiveness is against the development process altogether 'by reinforcing the initial conditions' and therefore, by reinforcing 'underdevelopment itself' (Sanyal 1993, 1327). However, paradoxically, Northern countries started to fear that by using cheap labour and even child labour the developing countries might be a potential threat in competition in certain commodities like Indian garments and Bangladeshi carpets. They used the World Trade Organization (WTO) as a platform to raise their voice for labour standards as a weapon against competition of cheaper goods from the South. This is nothing but shedding crocodile tears on behalf of child labour in developing countries with the sole objective of erecting non-trade barriers against the South (Sanyal 1993, Patnaik 1999). At the end of the day, however, developing countries, which find themselves with competitive disadvantage, cannot push their exports in the global market, leaving their markets for the product originating in low-cost developed countries. This leads to trade deficit and job losses and, therefore, further imports, foreign aid and further trade deficit. Foreign direct investors generally displace more jobs than they create.[10] A typical Third-World country with competitive disadvantage is trapped in a cycle of persistent trade deficit, ineffective devaluation and eventual debt crisis (Shaikh 2003, 9–10). That was precisely what happened under the structural adjustment programme of the IMF in Latin American countries in the 1980s and to some extent in India in the 1990s.

Rise of Structural Adjustment Lending and New World Order

With the end of the Second World War in Europe (July 1944), the Northern countries, particularly the UK and the US, met at a conference at Bretton Woods, New Hampshire. Three institutions, namely the International Monetary Fund (IMF), the World Bank and the General Agreement on Trade and Tariffs (GATT) were formed from that conference. These three institutions were supposed to frame the world economy for the remaining years of the twentieth century. The objective of the Fund was stabilization from short-run fluctuations and assisting countries in temporary but deep liquidity constraint (Ray 1998, 701–5). On the other hand, the Bank was to address the long-run objectives, namely reconstruction and development. These institutions were not strong enough in the 1950s, 1960s and 1970s. The IMF really gained some space with the emergence of the world debt crisis as described below. GATT found immense strength to dominate the global trade in the 1990s since the collapse of the Soviet Union, and it transformed into the WTO in 1995.

The history of the current phase of globalization has to be traced to the global debt crisis of the 1980s. It is evident that the current phase of globalization did not drop from the clear sky of free trade. Rather, it evolved from the desperate urge of the Northern countries in the wake of the global debt crisis during the 1980s. That crisis stemmed from a rise in petroleum prices in 1973–74 from $3 per barrel to $15 per barrel. As a result, oil-exporting countries accumulated a huge amount of foreign exchange reserve. The Gulf countries could not find an outlet to invest this huge reserve in their own countries. Instead, they preferred to deposit this amount into commercial banks in the US. The US banks now faced a big dilemma. This huge amount of reserve had to be reinvested as credit; otherwise the bank would have faced bankruptcy in meeting interest obligations.

The US commercial banks, therefore, decided that they would extend loans to various Latin American countries. The Latin American countries, on the other hand, were willing to pay at least 2 per cent in excess of interest rates on US government bonds (Ray 1998, 685). As inflation eroded the value of debt, it was apparently logical policy for the Latin American countries to embark on a 'deliberate development strategy designed to foster import substitution: foreign loans poured in to finance these investments' (Ray 1998). The Latin American countries therefore borrowed a huge amount of development loans from the US commercial banks. These countries faced absolutely no problems until 1979. The only obvious outcome was that with the rise in imports the deficit in the current account of balance of payments increased, although the dollar value of exports was growing and interest rates on the debt were low. The debt–export ratio during this period remained steady or even fell.

In 1979, the oil prices increased sharply once more to $80 per barrel. The same process was repeated. The oil exporter countries further accumulated huge foreign exchange reserves. This meant the oil importers faced a large deficit. Accordingly, this huge fund floated the US commercial banks, which were in search of potential borrowers. The US government started to realize that the completion of the same process would mean a big blow to their banking system as a whole. In 1979, the US central bank announced a unilateral rise in interest rates. The real rate of interest increased further in 1980–81 to an exceptionally high level. The monetary policy of the US was guided by a naïve conservative idea that the increase in interest rates implied a fall in money supply, which implied a halt in inflation. However, in reality there was no halt in inflation. But a sudden rise in interest rates triggered a recession in the world market. The rise in the real rate of interest went hand in hand with a fall in commodity prices. The average export prices of non-oil developing countries fell significantly and had very adverse impact on debtor countries. As a result, the Latin American states found it extremely difficult to export their products in the world market. In fact, worldwide recession also caused a drop in export earnings, largely induced by a sharp fall in export prices. As a result, the debt–export ratio started to soar. The Latin American countries had to stop their on-going developmental projects. Instead, they were compelled to borrow from global financial institutions to meet their debt and interest obligations. Ultimately, in 1982, Mexico declared that it was not in a position to repay its debt. Brazil also followed the same path by expressing its inability to repay the debt. The US wasted no time in politicizing the entire issue by stating that non-payment amounted to a breach of normal international relations.

At this juncture the IMF and the World Bank came to the rescue. Until the late 1970s, the IMF and the World Bank authorities advocated the globalization policy only at the level of debate and persuasion. But since 1980 when Structural Adjustment Lending (SAL) was introduced, globalization became a major conditionality for getting a fresh loan. It is evident from the above discussion that SAL was introduced in the context of the severe recession in the North in the late 1970s, which led the Northern countries to raise tariff and trade barriers against their imports on the one hand and on the other hand to promote their exports to the South by means of hardening the conditionality in the world capital and money market. The conditionalities are mainly to maintain market forces in the product and foreign exchange market, the decline in the real wage rate and above all privatization or the abolition of state intervention.

Structural Adjustment Policy, Globalization and the Indian Economy

India entered the neoliberal regime in 1991 when it borrowed from the IMF and as a part of loan conditionality had to adopt the structural adjustment programme. The conditionalities are mainly to maintain market forces in the product and foreign exchange markets and to be competent in the international market through the policy of devaluation, the decline in the real wage rate and the abolition of state intervention. The New Economic Policy (NEP) was announced, which was framed in line with the structural adjustment programme of the IMF. According to the NEP, the Indian economy could liberate itself from the clutches of state intervention in three inter-related ways. First of all, a process of 'globalization', where the closed domestic economy could be adapted to the current tide of the world economy. Second, a process of 'stabilization', which means some internal adjustment of the economy to remove certain perpetual constraints. And third, a process of 'privatization', which seems to be a must for the improved efficiency of the domestic production process. For the first objective of globalization, the Indian economy followed the policy of trade liberalization; in particular, all the barriers against import were removed. To achieve the second goal, it was attempted to minimize the fiscal deficit by lowering subsidies at the highest level. The fiscal deficit was reduced primarily to reduce the price level on the one hand and to lower interest rates on the other. The third policy objective is related to the second one in the sense that disinvestment is required for the purpose of curbing the fiscal deficit. By adopting these policies India would achieve take-off like the Asian tiger economies such as Korea and Taiwan. Two decades have passed since the NEP was introduced, and now the time has come to reassess its achievements and failures.

First, we have already discussed how the free trade theory at the hands of David Ricardo extended support for colonialism. We have also discussed how the World Bank/IMF version of the free trade theory turned out to be far more naïve and dangerous than the original version. The IMF–World Bank theorists would have us believe that a developing country like India may achieve take-off like Korea or Taiwan by liberalizing its trade front (export-led growth) without bothering much about internal macroeconomic transformation. We have already seen the problems related to theoretical arguments in support of trade-led growth. Thus, they tried to prove it through the example of model countries such as Korea and Taiwan. First of all, before opening their trade fronts, Korea and Taiwan made some remarkable progress in land reform and literacy. Second, while the advocates of the IMF–World Bank project multiparty democracy as the ideal nation state, they often suppress the fact that there was no democracy in Korea and Taiwan during the postwar period of so-called 'export-led transformation'. Taking advantage of market autocracy, they could suppress the wage rate as much as possible in the name of 'labour market reform'. Third, geopolitics acted in their favour, as their proximity to North Korea and China drew the economic and political attention of the contemporary imperialist countries, particularly the US, to develop South Korea and Taiwan as models of development in order to compete with socialist models. In the absence of the socialist Soviet Union and East Europe, hardly any developing country such as India can obtain the advantage of geopolitics at present. Fourth, the market size or population of South Korea or Taiwan is nothing compared to today's vastly populated developing countries such as India and Brazil. How far these countries can develop themselves only on the basis of export-led growth is not at all clear. Chakravarty (1984) argued against a so-called export-led growth strategy for India on the grounds of, first, the existence of a very big non-tradable sector in India; second, downward rigidity of efficiency wage to meet the criterion of competitiveness; and third, uncertainty regarding the newly emerging international division of labour in the face of new technological changes in the world market. M. Narasimham, who headed the committee that recommended financial liberalization in India, confessed:

> We need growth-led export and not a strategy of export-led growth. The example of Korea and Taiwan, so often cited, has little relevance for us. The size of their domestic economies is small. The international trading environment in the period of their most rapid export expansion in the '60s and '70s was also conducive to the adoption of the strategy. The international trading environment is now increasingly being affected by the spreading contagion of protectionism. Export-led growth seems to be an idea of the past. (Narasimham 1988, xvi–xvii)

Back to the Structural Adjustment Policy: we would like to explore first the policy of devaluation. In our view, devaluation cannot be an effective weapon for an export boom. First, devaluation cannot be a sole weapon in the hands of a particular country. The devaluation could have a positive impact on exports of a particular country if other countries do not devalue their currency. At this phase of growing international competition it is difficult for a particular country to get mileage in exports. The Southern countries, in particular, face steep protectionism against their exports imposed by the Northern countries. The most important factor is that even if a developing country can expand its exports, it can hardly cut its imports simultaneously, especially in the environment of import liberalization. India's imports are by and large price inelastic, as the major share includes essential items like petroleum and capital goods. Any policy including devaluation can hardly affect it. (Bhattacharyya 1995, 2004). Any export augmenting policy including devaluation can hardly affect it.

The explicit goals of the economic reform strategy with respect to the external sector were to create a major shift in the momentum of export growth, and to attract very large inflows of foreign capital (particularly FDI) to augment domestic savings and therefore allow much higher rates of gross domestic investment; that in turn may generate a high rate of economic growth. In actual fact, the reform process accomplished neither of these objectives by the end of two decades. Instead, it involved rates of export expansion more or less similar to those of the past, caused much greater import penetration in manufacturing and therefore particular pressure on employment-intensive small-scale industries, and made the economy as a whole much more dependent upon volatile short-term capital inflows without really increasing the total inflow of foreign capital in relation to GDP. The situation became worse in the face of the global economic and financial crisis. In spite of an increase in India's share of world exports during the last decade, it was as low as 1.5 per cent by 2010 (Government of India 2012, 155). Though the first half of the 2000s shows a relatively impressive performance, we have witnessed a steady decline in the growth of export value in terms of US$ from 29 per cent in 2007–08 to 13.6 per cent in 2008–09 and ultimately to (–)3.5 per cent in 2009–10 (Government of India 2012, 152). The growth rate of volume of exports declined from 9 per cent in 2008–09 to (–)1.1 per cent in 2009–10 (Government of India 2012). The global recession hit the employment-intensive export-oriented sector in India, and the already established pattern of jobless growth during the reform period gained momentum. There has been an export recovery in 2010–11 following the record depreciation of the Indian rupee. Given the world economic environment of prolonged recession, it is difficult to believe that this recovery will be sustainable. As in the past, this time too India does not gain from the export boom as India's imports have also been substantially increased. Presently, with the depreciation of the rupee, India has to pay a higher import bill for its inelastic imports like petroleum, capital goods or jewellery, which in turn creates inflation as the cost of production increases. Particularly with the global recession, Indian investors' preference for imported gold is quite clear as they think that the purchase of the latter is relatively safe. It is ironic that though the theory of globalization advocates the idea of export-led growth, during the period of the market economic reform India experienced a persistent trade deficit. The trade deficit increased by 56 per cent ($185 billion in 2011–12) between 2010–11 and 2011–12. Now it is 10 per cent of GDP. The mounting trade deficit eats up a lion's share of India's revenue earning from services exports and remittances by non-resident Indians (NRIs). As a consequence, foreign exchange reserves are rapidly depleting. The foreign exchange reserves declined from $315.7 billion to $294.4 billion between June 2011 and March 2012 (Chandrasekhar and Ghosh 2012). It should be noted that the FDI increased massively with the advent of the global economic crisis. But these FDI are less export-intensive, and more import-intensive. As a result, the net balance of payments impact of FDI flows has been negative (Chandrasekhar and Ghosh 2010). Last but not least, India's high growth story has ultimately been shattered. India's GDP growth was only 5 per cent during 2012–13, which was the lowest in the decade. However, if we consider only the material producing sector such as agriculture and industry, the performance was even poorer. The agricultural sector's growth rate declined from 3.6 per cent in 2011–12 to 1.8 per cent in 2012–13, and the decline of the manufacturing sector's growth rate was from 2.7 to 1.9 per cent (Government of India 2013). As a matter of fact, the growth bubble in the Indian economy had always been service-led and jobless (Bhaduri, Chapter 3 in this volume). While the so-called high growth rate was 'tenuous', the stimulus of this growth was always 'domestic' (Chandrasekhar 2012). With the spread of the global economic and financial crisis, foreign capital started to intrude into India and other 'emerging markets', but as India's investment in the material producing sector had already stagnated, it remained confined to real estate and debt-financed purchase of automobiles and durables (Chandrasekhar 2012). Following the government's decision of 100 per cent FDI in the construction business in 2005, FDI in real estate jumped from $0.39 billion in 2004–05 to $2.12 in 2006–07 (Nachane 2009). In fact, the housing space of the big cities moved out of reach of the lower and middle class to the 'upper crust of Indian society (comprising a motley group of multinational executives, corrupt politicians, businessmen and criminals)' (Nachane 2009).

Fiscal Deficit and Policy of Stabilization

Since India entered the phase of 'liberalization', the government steadily denied that the IMF's Structural Adjustment Program has influenced its macroeconomic policies. But the macroeconomic management policy of the government remained miraculously identical with that of the Fund–Bank. One such policy prescription is reducing fiscal deficits relentlessly. The Fund–Bank theorists would have us believe that the key to controlling inflation is to curb the fiscal deficit. However, this proposed causal link between fiscal deficit and inflation is quite vague. First, deficit financing can raise the price level only when the economy is in full employment and all capacities are fully utilized. In the face of widespread unemployment and huge excess capacity (as it exists in India) the deficit financing would lead to *quantity adjustment* by raising the output level, rather than *price adjustment* (Bhaduri 1986). Second, even if we consider the case of full employment, the proposed link between fiscal deficit and inflation is difficult to understand, because it is not the fiscal deficit but budget deficits that create inflation via a process of deficit financing. Rakshit (1991) showed the empirical invalidity of the proposed causal link between fiscal deficit and inflation in the Indian economy during the 1980s. Mody (1992), in another study, took 28 countries with double-digit inflation and 18 countries with high fiscal deficits and showed that fiscal deficit has no relationship with inflation. The data suggest that there is no correlation between fiscal deficit and inflation, though during this period all the governments in India took steps to reduce the fiscal deficit on the basis of a misconceived notion of a positive relation between inflation and fiscal deficit (Goyal 2004, Chakraborty 2002, Das, Chapter 13 in this volume).

By definition,

Fiscal Deficit = (Revenue Expenditure – Revenue Receipts) + (Capital Expenditure – Recovery of Loans) – Non-Debt Capital Receipts

In a developing country such as India, the most desirable way of curbing the fiscal deficit is by raising revenue receipts, which means an increase in resource mobilization, which includes tax and non-tax revenue of the government. But the 20 years of the post-liberalization period experienced no substantial increase in the tax–GDP ratio.[11] There are several reasons for the low tax–GDP ratio. First, the indirect tax revenue reached saturation, and because of the income deflation for the vast majority of the Indian population during the liberalization period, it has no capacity to increase further. Second, the government was directed by the blind logic of the Laffer curve argument of the neoliberals that there is an inverse relationship between the tax rate and tax revenue.[12] The government lowered the tax rate to give incentive to the corporate sector, and as a result there was a decline in tax revenue and tax–GDP ratio. Third, the government had lowered custom duties as part of the trade liberalization policy, and subsequently lowered excise duty to compensate the domestic producers and to save them from de-industrialization. In all advanced capitalist countries, as well as in Korea and Taiwan, the share of direct tax to total tax revenue is very high, but it is extremely low in India. In fact, the essential feature of neoliberalism is to give subsidy to the rich, particularly corporate capitalists. Thus, in India the prime route through which the fiscal deficit is being lowered is reduction of revenue expenditure. Among the different components of revenue expenditure the interest payment to GDP ratio was comparatively high during the liberalization era.[13] It fluctuated from 3.7 per cent to 4.8 per cent during the liberalization period. Defence expenditure, another important component of revenue expenditure, cannot be cut for geopolitical reasons. Therefore, the remaining item 'subsidy' had been the prime target for lowering fiscal deficit. The proportion of subsidy reduced from 1.7 per cent in 1990–91 to 1.3 per cent in 2008–09 (BE). The adverse impact of the withdrawal of food, fertilizer and credit subsidy we have already discussed. Capital expenditure as a proportion of GDP has been drastically reduced to 1.6 per cent in 2008–09 from its pre-liberalization level of 4.4 per cent, which directly hit the industry and called forth a recession. Similarly, recovery of loans reduced from its pre-reform rate 1 to 0.1 per cent of GDP during the late 1980s. On the other hand, non-debt capital receipt, which was mainly PSU disinvestments, nil in pre-liberalization period, constitutes 0.8 per cent in 2007–08. For the last two (election) years, that is, 2008–09 and 2009–10, it declined to zero. The inclusion of this item is nothing but an accounting fallacy of reducing fiscal deficit. It resembles raising one's income by selling durable assets of the household. Despite all that, the fiscal deficit to GDP ratio remained at 5.9 and 6.5 per cent in the years 2008–09 and 2009–10 respectively, which is quite high in relation to the Fund–Bank's dictum.

The government claimed that there was a cause-and-effect relation between high fiscal deficit and high real rate of interest. The Finance Ministry proposed a policy of a cut in fiscal deficit with the aim of lowering the real rate of interest. According to Prabhat Patnaik in this volume, the causation is the other way round as the interest payment is an essential component of the fiscal deficit. On the other hand, the real rate of interest was high in India and elsewhere because of globalization. In other words, the real rate of interest became high in order to attract speculative finance capital.

Chapter Outlines

In Chapter 2, Terence J. Byres dissects the growth performance of the Indian economy in the pre-liberalization period. He refutes the neoliberal argument that the 'Hindu rate of growth' is synonymous with the 'Nehru–Mahalanobis rate of growth'. In fact, the former growth rate was much less than the latter. Byres points out that even the Hindu rate of growth of 3.5 per cent was 'respectable' if not 'impressive', but not at all 'weak'. Byres claims that the rate of growth of GDP increased above the 'Hindu rate of growth' during 1980–85, which was indeed the pre-liberalization period. The neoliberal economists have described the stagnation of Indian industries in the 1960s and 1970s as an example of the inefficiency of the pre-liberalization period. However, the neoliberals overlooked the industrial recovery in the late 1970s and early 1980s, which was, according to Byres, due to the legacy of the Nehru–Mahalanobis era. Byres also refutes the trickledown theory advocated by the neoliberal economists that opposes state intervention. This theory proposes that economic growth automatically ensures poverty alleviation through a process of trickledown. However, the protagonists of economic reform could not provide any empirical evidence in support of this trickledown mechanism. On the contrary, Byres shows the prevalence of poverty due to the adoption of new technology in agriculture. In fact, in the post–Green Revolution years, from 1960–61 to 1973–74, rural poverty increased, contradicting all the plausible hypotheses of the trickledown theory. On the other hand, poverty massively reduced during the period 1970–73 to 1988–89, when there was substantial state intervention in the form of anti-poverty or employment generation programmes such as the Integrated Rural Development Programme (IRDP), National Rural Employment Programme (NREP) etc. The post-1991 period registered a sharp increase in poverty due to the suspension of these state intervention measures. In particular, the rise in foodgrain prices had a negative impact on poverty owing to the reduction of the food subsidy.

In Chapter 3, Amit Bhaduri unfolds the hidden truth behind the recent high economic growth in India. Bhaduri dismisses the 'hyped story' about the high growth rate, first on the grounds that it is accompanied by increasing economic inequality. According to Bhaduri, there is no possibility of 'trickling down' of growth, as the market mechanism is that 'growing inequality drives growth, and growth fuels further inequality'. Second, according to Bhaduri this is 'jobless growth'. India grew at 7–8 per cent in recent years, but the regular employment growth remained around 1 per cent. By adopting labour-saving and capital-intensive technology, labour productivity increases at the expense of employment, which gives rise to an 'enormous source of profit' at the expense of the masses. Bhaduri observes that more than three-fifths of Indians have income less than $2, and this huge population are left out of the growing market in India based on luxury goods. With rapid growth of income for the 'privileged', the market for luxury goods grows even faster following the operation of 'income elasticities of demand'. This in turn raises the income of the richest much faster than that of the rest of the society. According to Bhaduri, 'market-driven high growth' gives rise to a 'production structure' which has 'blatant biases' against the poor. The demand for basic necessities of life hardly expands as a result of restricted purchasing power of the poor and decline in welfare expenditure by the state. This anti-poor production structure becomes irreversible over time because it is difficult to convert investment from luxury goods production to basic necessities. Bhaduri points out that the liberalized market system, by grabbing agricultural land from peasants, making corporate investment in big dams and investing in production-intensive and non-reproducible resources, caused 'unacceptable violence to the environment' at the price of 'heightened misery of the poor'. The demand for output generated by the rich can hardly be filled by village artisans or small producers. The latter find no place either as producers or consumers, and all the economic activities are captured by big corporate entities, which Bhaduri terms the 'destructive creation of corporate wealth'.

Prabhat Patnaik in Chapter 4 gives a macro-theoretic critique against liberalization policy with a particular reference to India. This essay is divided into several parts. In the first part, Patnaik deals with the question of efficiency and inefficiency of the public sector. According to Patnaik, loss making at a given set of arbitrary (shadow) prices is not any indicator of 'inefficiency', and such a loss-making enterprise does not necessarily warrant closure or privatization. The subsidy, which is integrated with loss making, is nothing but a negative tax. If a tax cut or a negative movement in the tax rate is allowed, the subsidy elimination cannot have any theoretical ground. Patnaik sharply refutes the apparent causality of fiscal deficit on the real rate of interest. According to Patnaik, the real rate of interest in India and other Third-World countries is high, particularly in the post-liberalization period, precisely because it is kept high in order to attract finance capital (which is highly volatile). Global finance capital would not be interested in investing in the Third World if the real rate of interest were not at least higher than that prevailing in their safe First-World home countries. This is why the real rate of interest is high in most of the Third-World countries in the post-liberalization period. Patnaik gives examples of many countries where even negative fiscal deficit prevailed in an environment of a high real rate of interest. According to Patnaik, if any causality exists at all, it is the other way round. Since interest payment is an integral part of the fiscal deficit, the high real rate of interest raises the fiscal deficit. Patnaik points out that hitherto the state governments had to raise loans from the Centre. But against the backdrop of the Fiscal Responsibility and Budget Management (FRBM) Act, the 12th Finance Commission suggested that the government had to raise loans from the market. According to Patnaik, this is nothing but an obsession of the so-called 'financial sector reform' to make the state governments 'creditworthy' in the eyes of international finance capital. This has been reflected in the replacement of the Sales Tax by uniform VAT. In the latter, the state governments have no power to fix the rate. This has undermined the federal spirit of our country and would give rise to 'Balkanization' on the one hand, and would impose a uniform set of policies on the state governments on the other.

In Chapter 5, Jayati Ghosh and C. P. Chandrasekhar refute the essential decoupling hypothesis that growth in Asia was driven by domestic factors and is not only unaffected by the global economic crisis but may serve as a shock absorber for Western economies. According to Ghosh and Chandrasekhar, the high growth of GDP is due to factors like demographic change, large market size and 'favourable' factor environment rather than some stimulus generated through global integration. Despite the recent growth, both China and India remain far behind the developed countries in per capita income and levels of productivity. This calls for a huge catch-up process to continue. China and India protect themselves from crises because of their 'prudent' policies related to some capital controls and limited convertibility of the currency for capital account transactions. According to the authors, this growth process has been more uneven and vulnerable to internally and externally generated crises. This growth is the consequence of the financial deregulation which is associated with retail credit boom and fiscal concessions to the richest quintile of the population. As a result, along with the high growth rates the Indian economy witnessed poor employment generation and prolonged agrarian crises. The share of profit goes up and that of wages declines. According to the authors, it is a similar story of speculative bubble-led expansion that other developed and developing countries experienced.

Utsa Patnaik in Chapter 6 observes that since 1991 India strongly pursued deflationary macroeconomic policies even at the cost of a high unemployment rate. This is precisely the logic of global finance capital where international creditors wish to maintain the high real value of their financial assets and high real interest rates (inflation would erode both). Public planned development expenditures are curtailed as part of this policy and as a result private investment also declines, given the complementarities of both. It has high negative impact on irrigation, rural infrastructure and above all agricultural output and employment. The manufacturing sector is also in stagnation. The ballooning of service sector growth primarily based on IT cannot be sustainable. After the liberalization policy, eight million hectares of food-growing land were converted to exportable crops, leading to a fall in the domestic per capita food availabilities. The exporting farmers, on the other hand, face steeply falling global primary prices, which has plunged them into spiralling farm debt leading to the suicide of nearly 0.3 million farmers in India.[14] According to Patnaik, this is just the tip of the iceberg. There is an unprecedented agrarian crisis reflected in steep decline in domestic foodgrain absorption to the levels prevalent 50 years ago and a fall in calorie intake in rural India. The Planning Commission interprets this crisis as 'overproduction' in relation to an allegedly 'voluntary reduction of food grain intake' so that the former prescribes that foodgrain output should be further cut back. In order to justify itselves, the Planning Commission shows a massive reduction in poverty, which, according to Patnaik, is based on spurious data and methodology. The Planning Commission's methodology for estimating the poverty line (2400 kcal per capita in rural areas and 2100 kcal in urban areas) is based on NSSO estimates of 1973–74. In the years since 1973–74 they just deflate the same estimates with price level. According to Patnaik, a direct estimation of poverty would show 74.25 per cent of people below the poverty line, which according to ('indirect') official estimates is only 27.09 per cent.

In Chapter 7, Anthony P. D'Costa theoretically links the Indian middle class to the general process of globalization and empirically investigates the relationship between the globalized new economy sector, namely the Indian information technology (IT) industry, and the transformation of the state. He shows that India's new middle class, constituted of students, professionals, entrepreneurs and white collar bureaucrats, have ideologically absorbed globalization, while the state has extended its support to the IT industry in its internationalization. The confluence of these two developments has contributed to the state's neoliberal turn resulting in the state's abdication of its earlier role in social transformation. According to D'Costa, the state has been transformed by two constituencies – the Indian middle class (internal constituency) and transnational forces (external constituency). He argues that the internal constituency, which is a creature of the state and a product of an earlier state-led capitalist development process, pulls in transnational forces just as global economic forces find the liberalization of the Indian economy highly attractive. The Indian middle class, according to D'Costa, was able to alter the functioning of the state ideologically in a 'cumulative, path dependent way' by establishing extensive links with the world economy. This is an acknowledgement of the selective success of the state in creating a globally linked Indian capitalist class and the relative weakness of the state in managing social and economic change. He further indicates that one result of the transformation of the state has been a polarized society where the cost of internalization of neoliberalism has been substantially borne by India's impoverished masses, namely the non-internationalized, non-glamorous sectors.

Parthapratim Pal in Chapter 8 points out that the WTO largely fails to ensure a significant welfare benefit to developing countries through fair trade, and poorer countries are increasingly getting marginalized. India did not gain much benefit from trade liberalization because with the growing exports, imports too grew faster in recent years. However, India performs remarkably well in the exports of services, as it serves the interest of developed countries in the sectors like telecommunication, banking and insurance. India has agreed to liberalize its agriculture following the Agreement on Agriculture (AoA) under the WTO, which aims at elimination of distortions in world agricultural trade. However, the trade liberalization in agriculture contributed to a marginal increase in the market share in agriculture of the developing countries since the formation of the WTO. Agriculture still remains a distorted sector. The developed countries managed to comply with the WTO rules and yet maintain high agricultural subsidies. The farming communities of the developing countries are now facing unfair competition from subsidized and artificially cheap exports from developed countries. However, agriculture and primary commodities are still dominating India's export market. According to Pal, given the international volatility of commodity prices and prolonged agrarian crisis in recent years, India should not make any commitments that might threaten the livelihood and food security of the millions of small farmers. The author further shows that today's developed countries followed protectionist as well as state interventionist policies during the initial phase of their industrialization rather than WTO-recommended tariff reduction. These countries have progressed by evolving comparative advantage in high technology areas rather than being stuck in a static framework of comparative advantage implicitly adopted by the WTO. In the earlier rounds of multilateral trade talks, negotiations were essentially done by developed countries. The welcome development of the Doha round is that 60 or 70 countries are actively involved in negotiation, where every member has potential veto power. With the economic recession, countries (particularly the developed countries) are more interested in preventing economic slowdown or job losses, rather than further trade liberalization. As multilateral trade talks are not progressing well, most countries are opting to increase trade through bilateral channels such as Regional Trade Agreements (RTAs). The developed countries, through North–South RTAs, are trying to push aggressively the WTO plus clauses that hurt the interests of developing countries. In these circumstances South–South trade blocks may emerge as a viable alternative. The idea of a South Asian trade block should also be explored.

In Chapter 9, Sudipta Bhattacharyya and Uma Basak compare the employment scenario on the basis of NSSO data between pre- and post-liberalization periods and different phases within the post-liberalization period – the first (1993–94 to 1999–2000), the second (1999–2000 to 2004–05) and the third (2004–05 to 2009–10) phases of economic reform for the rural and urban sectors. This chapter looks critically at the trend of NSSO data that the casualization declined and diversification increased in the second phase of the reform compared to the first, when the opposite happened, although the casualization increased again in the third phase of reform. The labour force participation rate (LFPR) during the reform period showed a downfall in the first reform period (1990s), a recovery in the second phase (1999–2000 to 2004–05) and remained more or less unchanged in the third phase (2004–05 to 2009–10). The protagonists of economic reform explained this tendency with a 'withdrawal hypothesis', where the decline in LFPR reflects a welcome tendency as age-specific LFPR indicates a decline in labour force participation by the younger (school-going) age group (Chadha and Sahu 2002). There was a continuous decline in child work participation for the 5–14 age group from 1987–88 to 2009–10 for both male and female workers in rural and urban areas. This is no doubt an achievement. But the withdrawal hypothesis cannot be substantiated by the fact that the participation rate increased particularly for the old age group (60 years and above). The so-called welcome tendencies have not been substantiated by any development of remunerative or productive employment. Agricultural workers, without any gainful job in agriculture, are compelled to engage in non-agricultural 'jobs'. Since there is no job available in the nonagricultural sector, again they have no other alternative but to divert into non-remunerative and less productive self-employed activities in a hand-to-mouth situation. The distress of the workforce during the liberalization era is largely feminized, as female participation in domestic activity increased in recent years; it dominates vigorously other activities such as education (where the male population dominates), and female participation in the old age group increased during the second and third reform period compared to the first. The proportion of casual employment is also substantially high for females.

In Chapter 10, Ashok Rudra provides two hypotheses: One, the performance of an industry does not have any necessary links with the forms of ownership of the means of production – private or public. Two, some degree of protectionism is essential for making industries competitive, withdrawal of which would give rise to a disaster in the economy. Rudra refutes the common wisdom that the public sector enterprises are inefficient and private sector ones are efficient. That the public enterprises in India are bad does not imply that the private enterprises are necessarily better – they could be even worse. This is not a matter of logic but of empirical facts. The basic fallacy in comparison between the two sectors is that when the private sector starts to make losses they go out of business. But the sick industries belonging to the public sector are allowed to survive. The loss making public sector units cannot be compared with the profit making private sector units but with those that went bankrupt or survive with subsidies. The losses of the private sector have to be accounted for in the form of assets that have to be written off. The second error arises out of the fact that the public sector enterprises are assigned to running public utilities on a non-profit basis, and therefore they cannot be branded as inefficient for not making profit. The third error is to assume that the public sector enterprises cannot engage in competition. According to Rudra, the history of the now developed capitalist countries is a history of protectionism. Rudra lays bare the hypocrisy and double standard in Fund–Bank arguments. First, the Fund–Bank always advocates in favour of privatization of industries but not the privatization of financial institutions like banks. The public sector mobilizes resources but is not allowed to utilize them. Second, the IMF as a banking institution imposes a 'peculiar English conditionality' on the loan recipient countries in the name of creditworthiness. But when state enterprises provide loans to industry, any kind of conditionality, including licenses, is opposed. According to Rudra, 'regulation by the IMF–World Bank is good but regulation by the government of India is bad – is nothing but a double standard'. Third, America and other leading capitalist countries practise protectionism and trade discrimination while India and other Third-World countries are deprived of benefits of competition between loan-giving countries and international agencies. In a good society there is an economic order where every person can cooperate and not compete with the other. The 'competition' and the associated phenomenon of consumerism (or 'commodity fetishism') is characteristic of the law of the jungle under capitalism.

In Chapter 11, R. Nagaraj starts with the statement of the industrial policy of the government of India that public sector enterprises register a low rate of return and become a burden on the government. Therefore, the Structural Adjustment Program put emphasis on greater reliance on the private sector in order to reduce 'public sector saving gap and fiscal deficit'. Nagaraj (1991) in an earlier study already showed that the problem of declining investment in public sector and fiscal deficit imbalances occurred since the mid-1970s due to the growing subsidization of administrative departments and not on account of the public sector enterprises. The 1980s registered a reversed trend as operating surplus as a proportion of value added in non-departmental financial enterprises increased. Nagaraj shows that though fiscal deficit and the overall deficit of PSEs both deteriorated during the 1970s and 1980s, the trend of the latter is significantly less sharp than that of the fiscal deficit. Rather, the divergent trends in the two series reveal that 'the growing fiscal deficit is perhaps not attributable to the overall deficit of the public enterprise sector.' Nagaraj then shows that the PSEs' budgetary burden (as a proportion of GDP and PSEs gross expenditure) significantly declined in the 1970s–80s. He also points out that the self-financing ratio of PSEs showed a 'generally upward trend, especially in the '80s', while the private corporate sector showed a declining trend so that the two ratios converged to the same level of around 40 per cent towards the end of the decade. Nagaraj questions the basis for the IMF-styled reform policy that put greater reliance on the private corporate sector. Finally, Nagaraj shows 'a statistically significant improvement in capacity utilization' during the late 1970s to the early 1990s as an indication of an improvement in resource mobilization of PSEs. Similar to Rudra, Nagaraj's study also proves no positive association between the nature of ownership and performance, which seriously calls into question the reform policy of 'diluting public ownership'.

Surajit Mazumdar, in Chapter 12, argues that two decades of reform policies, namely industrial deregulation and trade liberalization, failed to resolve the jeopardy in India's stunted liberalization. Mazumdar refutes the neoliberal assertion that India's industrial backwardness is mainly the legacy of the interventionist policies after independence (Bhagwati 1993, Lal 2008) and argues that it is essentially a colonial legacy. Mazumdar points out that even after freeing itself from the shackles of intervention in 1991, the Indian economy could not achieve a secular and sustained momentum of industrialization. Instead, post-liberalization industrial growth was extremely unstable in nature. He showed that the first 15 years after independence (that is, the Nehruvian period), characterized by interventionism, had the most significant and the highest industrial growth. The share of the industrial sector in aggregate GDP achieved a peak (25.01 per cent) in 1966–67 from 16.1 per cent in 1950–51 and thereafter went up very slowly, and 'even this has ceased after liberalization'. Mazumdar observes an unwelcome transformation from industry-led growth after independence to service-led growth after liberalization. During the mid-1960s, slow growing and unstable agriculture was the largest sector in the economy, which was replaced by the service sector after 1991, which in turn contributed nothing to industrial growth except instability. Though the organized sector constitutes 61 per cent and 71 per cent of the industrial and manufacturing sector's output respectively, there was a substantial shift of industrial employment from the organized to the unorganized sector. While technological modernization determines the employment trend in the organized sector, the unorganized sector's employment is distress driven. Even within the organized sector there was a functional distribution of income from wage to profit. According to Mazumdar, the prime reason for this development is the narrowness of the market. Liberalization has aggravated income inequality and sharpened the already existing narrowness of the market. As a result, the share of manufactured goods in GDP declined and the share of services increased since the mid-1990s, which created a double squeeze on industrial demand. At the same time, India failed miserably to increase manufacturing exports following trade liberalization, though services exports increased successfully, which partially counteracted the growing trade deficit. There had been a dramatic increase in private corporate savings in the post-liberalization period, reflecting the tilt in the distribution of growing income in favour of profits. At the same time, private corporate investment exhibited extreme instability, which again has adversely affected industrial growth. After the eruption of the global crisis, both corporate and manufacturing investment growth collapsed and industrial growth declined. Though the global crisis has aggravated the situation, both investment and industrial growth started slowing down even before the global crisis erupted, signifying the root of the present industrial slowdown lies not in the global crisis but primarily in the depressed demand in the domestic market.

In Chapter 13, Surajit Das dismisses the conventional wisdom that the expansionary government policy, even under a demand-constrained situation, would be detrimental because the higher fiscal deficit would crowd out private investment by increasing the real rate of interest in the economy. In this chapter, Das discusses the chronological and sequential development of this widely believed theory and its problematic aspects. Das analyses the available empirical evidence from the Indian economy on the relationship between the fiscal deficit to GDP ratio and the real interest rate, for the period 1980–81 to 2006–07, considering various interest rates such as deposit rates of different maturity periods, lending rates and yields on government bonds deflated by the GDP deflator of the respective years. He does a similar kind of data analysis for 82 countries, considering five kinds of interest rates, namely real government bond yields, treasury bill rates, deposit rates, lending rates and the money market rate of interest for the period 1981– 2005. Finally, this work ends with the conclusion that real interest rates do not necessarily depend on the fiscal deficit as a proportion of GDP. There is absolutely no theoretical reason or empirical basis, either in India or in other countries around the world, to believe that higher fiscal deficit to GDP ratio necessarily causes interest rates to go up and results in crowding-out of private investment.

In Chapter 14, Matthew McCartney analyses the crisis in the Indian liberalization period in a theoretical framework of intermediate regime and intermediate classes.

Kalecki (1972) developed the original theoretical framework in a general form relevant for developing countries. According to Kalecki, the intermediate regime forms as an alliance between the intermediary classes (IC) as a middle class and rich peasants/ middle peasants. During the 1990s, the intermediate regime came to an end, though the intermediate classes have not disappeared. The middle class, backward castes and agrarian communities have exerted influence, but could not succeed to be part of policy making and implementation. McCartney shows that between 1989–90 and 1999–2000, the share of the self-employed among the non-manual middle class remained stable around 24 per cent. The penetration of FDI remains low during the liberalization period and domestic small-scale firms continue to dominate, and the level of concentration is also relatively stable. This is an indication of the domination of intermediate class capital. Similarly, the process of subcontracting allows small firms to coexist with large firms in the liberalization period. McCartney observes a rise and growth of a new middle class in India, similar to the observation of D'Costa in this volume. This middle class is structurally linked with corporate capital as D'Costa also observes. This middle class is therefore quite distinct from intermediate classes. However, a big proportion of middle class did not benefit from economic reform characterized by jobless growth and casualization of white-collar jobs. McCartney cites Kalecki's important observation that under an intermediate regime, state capitalism creates employment for the sons of intermediate classes. However, with the demise of the intermediate regime, the state has progressively withdrawn from creating employment for the middle class.

Conclusion

India, one of the largest state interventionist economies in the world, adopted neoliberal reforms by weakening the state since 1991. A minority government, without any pre-electoral promises, adopted neoliberal reform specifically because of the conditionalities of the IMF loan that India borrowed. The acute political instability during the decade following economic reform showed the people's mandate against neoliberal reform where almost all political parties breached promises to fight neoliberalism once voted to power.

This volume would like to challenge the myriad myths that surround the beneficial effects of neoliberal policies. These myths are, first, that the high growth rate of the Indian economy is able to weather the crisis – external and internal. Bhaduri (Chapter 3 in this volume) and Ghosh and Chandrasekhar (Chapter 5 in this volume) demolish the myth by showing that the growth process has been uneven and vulnerable to crisis. Further, this is a jobless growth and accompanied an agrarian crisis. Second, neoliberalism broadcasts that the growth automatically trickles down; therefore, state interventionist policy like an 'anti-poverty programme' is not required. This 'trickledown effect' is reflected in the development of a huge IT sector and global corporate institutions in India and a population of a new prosperous middle class dependent on this sector. Byres (Chapter 2 in this volume) demolishes this myth by showing that the trickledown mechanism was empirically unfounded in India. Byres quotes neoliberal Indian scholars at the policy level who showed that there was no trickledown in India. He also exposes neoliberal efforts to confuse the growth rate during the Nehru–Mahalanobis plan period with the Hindu rate of growth. As a matter of fact, the former was much higher than the latter, while the latter rate (3.5 per cent) was not weak. He also shows that, contrary to the trickledown mechanism, there was a substantial decline in rural poverty in the period of the anti-poverty programme and there was a big increase in poverty during the liberalization period. D'Costa (Chapter 7 in this volume) and McCartney (Chapter 14 in this volume) points out the rise and growth of a prosperous new middle class who are linked with corporate capital and/or transnational forces. While McCartney observes this phenomenon as a demise of the intermediate regime, D'Costa views this process as 'internalization' at the cost of non-internalized as well as impoverished masses. Third, Prabhat Patnaik (Chapter 4 in this volume) and Das (Chapter 13 in this volume) demoslish the myth that a high fiscal deficit causes a high rate of interest and inflation and therefore dampens investment. According to Patnaik and Das, the real rate of interest is high because global finance capital needs a high real rate of interest. The high real rate of interest in turn raises fiscal deficit, which has proved that the causation is the other way round. On the other hand, fiscal deficit can cause inflation via deficit financing only in the situation of full employment or near full employment. In a situation of chronic unemployment, deficit financing may create additional output and not a rise in the price level. Fourth, once the fiscal deficit is positioned as the villain of the piece by floating myths, neoliberalism further reconstructs bigger myths that suggest the way to curb the fiscal deficit. According to this myth, the public sector is less efficient than the private sector. Based on this myth, neoliberalism suggested that denationalization and privatization is the one effective way to curb the fiscal deficit. In this volume, Prabhat Patnaik refutes the myth related to private and public sector efficiency by showing that loss making at a given set of arbitrary prices is not any indicator of 'inefficiency'. Rudra (Chapter 10 in this volume) and Nagaraj (Chapter 11 in this volume) show that there is no empirical evidence that the public sector is less efficient than the private sector. Utsa Patnaik (Chapter 6) disproves the sixth myth propagated by Indian officialdom that there was a steep decline in poverty. Patnaik shows that the government's poverty estimation was based on faulty indirect methods of estimating the poverty line by deflating consumption expenditure related to the poverty line in 1973–74 with price indices in the subsequent period. The direct method of estimating the poverty line in fact shows a diametrically opposite picture of the poverty ratio (74.25 per cent) to the official one (27.09 per cent). Seventh, the 'lower foodgrain intake' in the post-liberalization period was accepted as 'increased income' (declined poverty) and subsequently policy makers encouraged the farmers to diversify their production to non-food items. Utsa Patnaik (Chapter 6 in this volume) counters this myth and shows that 'lower foodgrain intake' is related to 'demand deflation' or 'decline in effective demand' as a result of rising poverty.

The history of globalization is traced back to 1944 when three institutions, namely the IMF, the World Bank and GATT were formed at Bretton Woods. The present phase of globalization started with the petrodollar crisis of the 1980s. The Gulf countries deposited a huge accumulation of funds in American banks following the oil price hike. The American banks started to give cheap loans to Latin American countries in order to assist their development works. When there was a second hike in oil prices, the US Federal Reserve raised the interest rate and there was a big capital flight from Latin America to the US. The IMF started conditional lending in order to help with the mounting trade deficits of these nations. The loan conditionality was that the borrowing nation had to implement a structural adjustment programme. India borrowed from the IMF in 1991 and it started a structural adjustment programme which included, first of all, a process of trade liberalization or 'globalization'; second, a process of 'stabilization', which meant a cut in fiscal deficit through a cut in subsidies; and third, a process of 'privatization', which would improve the efficiency of the domestic production process.

The theoretical framework of the Bretton Woods institutions was never explicitly specified. But we have tried to trace this framework. The neoliberal supply-side macroeconomics positioned 'deficit' and 'deficit financing' as the villain of the piece without addressing the central question why, in a economy with other than near full employment, it may cause inflation. The IMF loan conditionality virtually compels the developing countries to reduce development expenditure. It is well known that the Ricardian or Hecksher–Ohlin–Samuelson theory of comparative advantage had implications for a North–South divide. But the New Trade theory advocated by the IMF involves a greater implication of a North–South divide. The IMF-propounded 'abrupt shift of comparative advantage' and 'efficiency through competition' is nothing but an indefinite rat race among nations to specialize in certain commodities that have high demand in the international market. A developing country such as India can earn global competitiveness by reducing prices through lowering real wages. The lower real wage, particularly the use of child labour, opens up a process of underdevelopment altogether. However, when the Southern countries posed a potential threat to Northern countries in competition by means of cheap labour, the latter countries used WTO as a platform to raise their voice for labour standards as a weapon against competition of cheaper goods from the South. This is nothing but shedding crocodile tears on behalf of child labour with the single agenda to put up non-trade barriers against the South. Ultimately, the developing countries face a competitive disadvantage with drying-up of exports, joblessness, mounting trade deficit and debt crisis.

Notes

1 According to Serra, Spiegel and Stiglitz (2008) the Washington Consensus is the set of views about effective development strategies that have come to be associated with the Washington-based institutions: the IMF, the World Bank, and the US treasury. John Williamson first introduced the term. Williamson's Washington Consensus is based on ten reforms: (1) fiscal discipline (2) change in public spending from subsidies to health and education, (3) tax reform, (4) market-determined rate of interest, (5) market-determined exchange rate, (6) trade liberalization, (7) no restriction in foreign direct investment (FDI), (8) privatization, (9) deregulation and (10) solid private property rights (Williamson 1993).

2 Instead, state interventionist reforms were promised in the area of the anti-poverty programme, agriculture, women's and child welfare, education, and science and technology (www.congress.org.in/salient-point.php).

3 'The decline in [foreign exchange] would have been still larger if the Government did not resort to borrowing from IMF' (Government of India, *Economic Survey 1990–91*, ch. 1, 3: http://indiabudget.nic.in/es1990-91/esmain.htm).

4 Government of India, *Economic Survey 1990–91* (http://indiabudget.nic.in/es1990-91/esmain.htm).

5 For example, the Bharatiya Janata Party in their Election Manifesto 1998 opposed the 'phoney liberalization' of the Congress that made the economy '*more* impoverished' (emphasis added). 'More' signifies prolonged '50 years' of Congress rule before liberalization. The BJP vehemently opposed the Congress Government's 'surrender' to 'IMF conditionalities'. Against such 'phoney liberalization' BJP 'advocated the reinstatement of the *Swadeshi* idea particularly because of the heavily one-sided pro-West WTO in the offing' (www.bjp.org/content/view/2628/376/).

6 The Finance Minister of UPA-I, P. Chidambaram admitted recently: 'For example, in UPA-I we had the red line we could not disinvest. We managed to cross the red line once in the NTPC disinvestment but then again they drew a thicker red line and said no you can't disinvest [...] So we did only NTPC and we did not do anything thereafter.' 'Red lines not obvious in UPA-II unlike UPA-I: Chidambaram', *Hindustan Times* 10th July, 2012 (http://www.hindustantimes.com/India-news/Bangalore/Red-lines-not-obvious-in-UPA-II-unlike-UPA-I-Chidambaram/Article1-886502.aspx).

7 According to Chidambaram: 'In UPA-II frankly the red lines are not so obvious. Suddenly some new red line emerges that is the difference between UPA-I and UPA-II.' (ibid.) Kaushik Basu, the Chief Economic Advisor to the Indian Prime Minister, appealed to TMC leader Mamata Banerjee, who is supposed to have 'an intuitive intelligence' to understand that FDI in retail is 'actually a win-win situation for the people of Bengal'. However, the TMC leader summarily rejected this appeal (http://www.thehindubusinessline.com/industry-and-economy/marketing/article3613463.ece?homepage=true&ref=wl_home).

8 See IMF, 'What We Do' (http://www.imf.org/external/about/whatwedo.htm).

9 See IMF Staff, *Globalization: A Brief Review* (www.imf.org/external/np/exr/ib/2008/pdf/053008.htm).

10 According to one estimate, for each job Wal-Mart creates in India, 17–18 local traders and their employees would be displaced (Ghosh 2011).

11 Government of India, *Economic Survey*: Various Issues.

12 Government of India, *Economic Survey*: Various Issues. All subsequent data used in this section were drawn from the same source.

13 Renowned Indian economists Srinivasan and Bhagwati (2002), without giving any empirical support, indicated the falling portion of the Laffer curve with 'India currently [1991] likely to be somewhere here.'

14 According to the latest Annual Report of the National Crime Record Bureau, Government of India, 290,470 farmers committed suicide in India during the period from 1995 to 2011(http://ncrb.nic.in/).

References

Bagchi, A. K. 1982. *Political Economy of Underdevelopment.* Cambridge: Cambridge University Press.

Bhaduri, A. 1986. *Macroeconomics.* London: Macmillan.

Bhagwati, Jagdish. 1993. *India in Transition: Freeing the Economy.* Oxford: Clarendon Press.

Bharatiya Janata Party. 1998. *Election Manifesto.* Online: http://www.bjp.org/content/view/2628/376/ (accessed 20 May 2010).

Bhattacharyya, Sudipta. 1995. 'Economic Liberalization in India: One Step Forward – Two Steps Back'. *Mainstream* 33, no. 17: 7–9, 34.

______. 2004. 'Economic Development under the Neo-liberal Regime: Swadeshi Rhetoric and Hijacked Swadesh'. In *Development Alternatives: Theories and Evidence* edited by Sudipta Bhattacharyya, Mihir Kumar Pal and Purnendu Sekhar Das. New Delhi: Allied, 1–18.

Boughton, James M. 2004. *The IMF and the Forces of History: Ten Events and Ten Ideas that have Shaped the Institution*. IMF Working Paper, No. WP/04/75, IMF. Online: http://www.imf.org/external/pubs/cat/longress.cfm?sk=17199.0 (accessed 20 May 2010).

Chadha, G. K. and P. P. Sahu. 2002. 'Post-reform Setbacks in Rural Employment: Issues that Need Further Scrutiny'. *Economic and Political Weekly* 37, no. 21: 1998–2026.

Chakraborty, Lekha. 2002. 'Fiscal Deficit and Rates of Interest: An Econometric Analysis of the Decentralized Financial Regime'. *Economic and Political Weekly* 37, no. 19: 1831–8.

Chakravarty, Sukhomoy. 1984. 'Aspects of India's Development Strategy for 1980s'. *Economic and Political Weekly* 19, no. 20: 845–47, 849–52.

Chandrasekhar, C. P. 2012. 'India's Growth Story Ends'. *Macroscan*, 6th June. Online: http://www.macroscan.org (accessed 20 March 2013).

Chandrasekhar, C. P. and Jayati Ghosh. 2010. 'FDI and the Balance of Payments in the 2000s'. *Macroscan*, 10th March. Online: http://www.macroscan.org (accessed 20 May 2010).

______. 2012. 'Banking on Debt'. *Macroscan*, 10th July. Online: http://www.macroscan.org (accessed 20 March 2013).

Findlay, Ronald. 1987. 'Comparative Advantage'. In *The New Palgrave: A Dictionary of Economics* edited by John Etwell, Murray Milgate and Peter Newman. Vol. 1, London: The Macmillan Press, 514–17.

Frank, A. G. 1967. *Capitalism and Underdevelopment in Latin America*. New York: Monthly Review Press.

______. 1975. *On Capitalist Underdevelopment*, Bombay: Oxford University Press.

Ghosh, Jayati. 2011. 'Multinational Retail Firms in India'. *Macroscan*, 12th December. Online: http://www.macroscan.org (accessed 30 April 2012).

Government of India. 2012. *Economic Survey 2011–12*, New Delhi: Oxford University Press.

______. 2013. *Economic Survey*. http://indiabudget.nic.in/survey.asp (accessed 20 March 2013).

Goyal, Rajan. 2004. 'Does Higher Fiscal Deficit Lead and Rise in Interest Rates? An Empirical Investigation'. *Economic and Political Weekly* 39, no. 21: 2128–33.

IMF Staff. 2008. *Globalization: A Brief Overview*. No. 08/02, May 2008, Online: http://www.imf.org/external/np/exr/ib/2008/053008.htm (accessed 20 May 2010).

Indian National Congress. 1991. *Election Manifesto, 1991: Salient Points*. Online: http://www.congress.org.in/salient-point.php (accessed 20 May 2010).

International Monetary Fund. 2010. 'What We Do: About the IMF'. Online: http://www.imf.org/external/about/whatwedo.htm (accessed 20 May 2010).

J. M. 1992. 'An Alternative Economic Survey'. *Economic and Political Weekly* 27, no. 8: 382–4.

Kalecki, Michal. 1972. *Essays on the Economic Growth of the Socialist and the Mixed Economy*. London: Unwin.

Lal, Deepak. 2008. 'An Indian Economic Miracle?' *Cato Journal* 28 (Winter): 11–33.

Mody, R. J. 1992. 'Fiscal Deficit and Stabilisation Policy'. *Economic and Political Weekly* 27, no. 7: 325–6.

Nachane, D. M. 2009. 'The Fate of India Unincorporated'. *Economic and Political Weekly* 44, no. 13: 115–22.

Nagaraj, R. 1991. 'Increases in India's Growth Rate'. *Economic and Political Weekly* 26, no. 15: 1002–4.

Narasimham, M. 1988. *World Economic Environment and Prospects of India*. New Delhi: Sterling.

Patnaik, Prabhat. 2001. 'Ten Years of "Economic Liberalization"'. *The Marxist* 17, no. 2: 3–17.

Patnaik, Utsa. 1996. 'Export-Oriented Agriculture and Food Security in Developing Countries and India'. *Economic and Political Weekly* 31, Special Issue, no. 35–7: 2429–31, 2433–7, 2439, 2441–9.

______. 1999. 'Cost of Free Trade: The WTO Regime and the Indian Economy'. *Social Scientist* 27, no. 11–12: 3–26.

Rakshit, Mihir. 1991. 'The Macroeconomic Adjustment Programme: A Critique'. *Economic and Political Weekly* 26, no. 34: 1977–9, 1981, 1983, 1985, 1987–8.

Ray, Debraj. 1998. *Development Economics*. Delhi: Oxford University Press.

Ricardo, David. 1951. *On the Principles of Political Economy and Taxation*. Edited by Piero Sraffa. Vol. 1, New York: Cambridge University Press.

Rodrik, Dani. 2001. *The Global Governance of Trade: As if Trade Really Mattered*. United Nations Development Programme (UNDP).

Sanyal, Kalyan. 1993. 'Paradox of Competitiveness and Globalization of Underdevelopment'. *Economic and Political Weekly* 28, no. 25: 1326–30.

Serra, Narcis, Shari Spiegel and Joseph E. Stiglitz. 2008. 'Introduction'. In *The Washington Consensus Reconsidered: Towards a New Global Governance* edited by Narcis Serra and Joseph E. Stiglitz. Oxford: Oxford University Press, 1–7.

Shaikh, Anwar. 2003. 'Globalization and the Myth of Free Trade'. Paper for the Conference on Globalization and the Myths of Free Trade. New York: New School University.

Srinivasan, T. N. and J. Bhagwati. 2002. 'India's Economic Reforms'. In *Indian Economy since Independence* edited by Uma Kapila. New Delhi: Academic Foundation, 86–158.

Subasat, Turan. 2002. 'A Political Economy Critique of the Ricardian Comparative Advantage Theory'. *Ideology of Race, and Eminent Economists* 20: 253–90.

Williamson, J. 1993. 'Democracy and the "Washington Consensus"'. *World Development* 21, no. 8: 1329–36.

Chapter 2

DEVELOPMENT PLANNING AND THE INTERVENTIONIST STATE VERSUS LIBERALIZATION AND THE NEOLIBERAL STATE: INDIA, 1989–1996*

Terence J. Byres

The General Assault on Development Planning and the State as an Agent of Economic Change: Neoliberalism, the IMF and the World Bank

By 1989, development planning, and with it the state as an agent of economic change, had been under comprehensive and sustained attack, in India and elsewhere, for two decades. The most savage line of assault, which gathered strength in the 1970s and had become hegemonic among orthodox, neoclassical economists by the 1980s, was that of neoliberalism. Neoliberalism found its intellectual formation, and its major practitioners, in the United States, although its influence soon spread pervasively from there. Its intellectual centre continues to be the United States. The assault, and its relentless anti-statism, was omnivorous: it was directed at advanced capitalist countries, less developed countries and socialist countries alike. All of these, it was postulated, were infected by the virus of state intervention. It made a determined onslaught on the interventionist state, which was portrayed consistently as a predatory state and one that inevitably, through its intervention, imposed crippling inefficiencies of resource use (allocative inefficiency) and spawned pervasive rent-seeking. It presented a virulent critique of planning, which was represented as simply the institutionalized means whereby the state pursued its predation, extended and reproduced its massive inefficiencies, and gave rise to growing and deeply entrenched rent-seeking. It advocated, as essential to economic health and economic development, the unfettered operation of the market. Its detailed policy prescriptions were summed up in its watchword, liberalization.[1]

Such advocacy, in its turn, found powerful institutional support in the lending practices, with their insistent cross-conditionality, of the International Monetary Fund and the World Bank. That twin patronage of liberalization was especially intrusive from

* This chapter is reproduced, in a slightly edited version, as it was originally published in 1997 in Terence J. Byres, ed., *The State, Development Planning and Liberalisation in India*, Delhi, Oxford University Press. No attempt has been made to update it.

1980 onwards, when the World Bank's programme of structural adjustment lending was initiated. Loans were given only if appropriate programmes were accepted and implemented by borrowers. These were the programmes of *stabilization*, the Fund's description of its policy package, which was supposedly short-run in nature and sought to bring about, or restore, macroeconomic stabilization by controlling the demand side of the economy; and of *structural adjustment*, the Bank's package, supposedly long-run in its intent and designed to free the supply side by removing those microeconomic market imperfections created largely by state intervention. In practice, the two sets of programmes overlapped and reinforced one another: with the macro- and the microeconomic, the short- and the long-run, the demand and the supply side, dealt with appropriately and to their mutual benefit. Each of the packages was quintessentially neoliberal in content.[2]

Here was a close fit of ideology and practice, of ends and means. Borrowers could be forced to swallow the medicine, prescribed by the neoliberals, that would cure their ills. The way would be cleared for dynamic growth and development. 'Liberalization' and 'structural adjustment' have come to be used interchangeably. This is so in India.

Liberalization in India, its Antecedents, and 'Encouragement' by the Bank and the Fund

Development planning's final warrant appeared to have been signed when, in the wake of India's 10th General Election (of May–June 1991), P. V. Narasimha Rao's Congress (I) government, freshly elected, introduced in June 1991 a package of reforms which aimed to introduce full-blooded economic liberalization, or, in the terminology of the International Monetary Fund and World Bank, which were both closely associated with this seemingly dramatic initiative, stabilization and structural adjustment.

This was implemented by the finance minister, Manmohan Singh, a prominent economist and a former opponent of liberalization.[3] The presumed architect of the reforms was Montek S. Ahluwalia,[4] an economist who has worked for the World Bank,[5] who is the present finance secretary, Government of India. Ahluwalia, when working for the Bank, was an early and influential exponent of a central tenet of the liberalization philosophy, the notion that trickle-down mechanisms exist that will ensure that growth brings a reduction of poverty, and, therefore, that no action by the state is necessary to ensure poverty alleviation (Ahluwalia 1976 and 1978). He is a source of official exposition of the progress of the liberalization reforms (Ahluwalia 1995) – notwithstanding the disarming caution that 'the views expressed are his own and not those of the Government of India' (Ahluwalia 1995, 29). Liberalization's major popular expositor and defender has been Manmohan Singh.

What was intended was, indeed, a final overturning of the old order, and the dawning of a new era in India's political economy. According to two of the programme's most sophisticated and uncompromising defenders, Jagdish Bhagwati and T.N. Srinivasan – both distinguished émigré economists in the United States, professors, respectively, at Columbia and Yale, who have kept a close interest in the Indian economy – what we witness is the introduction of a set of policies that would bring 'a successful transition from an essentially inward-looking posture to an outward-oriented economy, exploiting foreign trade and investment opportunities fully' (Bhagwati and Srinivasan 1993, 66); a 'new policy framework which will promote greater efficiency, growth and therewith a surer and deeper attack on poverty alleviation' (Bhagwati and Srinivasan 1993, ii). Economic dynamism, growth, and development will follow, inevitably, if the reforms are pursued resolutely, and these will be sufficient, in themselves and without major state intervention, to reduce significantly, if not eliminate, poverty.[6]

The roots of the liberalization programme of June 1991 might be seen to lie in an earlier period: in, for example, the liberalization of the trade regime in the late 1970s, under the Janata government; the new regime of industrial policies of the early 1980s, initiated by Indira Gandhi, with certain other measures, after she returned to power in 1980; and the so-called New Economic Policy of Rajiv Gandhi's government, introduced in 1985.[7] Certainly, the last of these, as Ahluwalia pointed out in a paper written in 1986, were 'characterized by the catch-all phrase "economic liberalization"' (Ahluwalia 1988, 345). But those previous, successive initiatives, described by Bhagwati and Srinivasan as 'reforms by stealth' (1993, 9), arguably sought to retain some continuity with the past, albeit a continuity that was increasingly remote from purposive development planning and a strongly interventionist state. In Ahluwalia's words, at the time: 'It is [...] important to distinguish the Indian policy initiatives from the classical "liberalization packages" which are ardently advocated in many quarters' (Ahluwalia 1988, 345). From those latter he distanced himself – and the Indian government, disclaimers notwithstanding – quite firmly, in 1986.[8] Joshi and Little (1994) point, disgustedly, to the 'funereal pace' of the liberalization that took place between 1975–76 and 1984–85 (63). Thereafter, they suggest, while the reforms 'largely pointed in the right direction', they were lacking in boldness, 'lop-sided', and slow (63). On this basis, if the 1991 liberalization measures had any true roots in the past, they date from 1985, and even then they were doubtfully shallow.

The liberalization programme of the early 1990s, contrariwise, was a purposive and open attempt at root-and-branch transformation of the economy's institutions and functioning.[9] While the Indira Gandhi measures represented, it has been suggested, a 'shift from *planning* the economy to *management* of the economy' (Kurien 1996, 10, emphasis mine), to which the Rajiv Gandhi New Economic Policy added greater latitude for the purchasing power of upper income groups, the liberalization programme of the early 1990s was an effort at more fundamental change[10] at 'freeing the economy',[11] certainly from significant state intervention, if not from some minimal *management* by the state.

The details, and the full rationale, of that package may be seen in several places.[12] Here, we need only consider them in the briefest summary form. We may say that the package covered a combination of short-term stabilization measures and medium-run, or long-run, structural adjustment economic reforms, each designed to achieve the goals noted above. The two sets of measures, of course, are not mutually exclusive, and each includes action that bears upon the other set of goals. Moreover, the measures in question are seen to be highly complementary in nature: as Bhagwati and Srinivasan say of some of them, for example, 'the question of direct foreign investment [...] is related to the question of trade and industrial policy, reforms in one suggesting and even requiring reforms in the other' (1993, 44). It is part of the liberalization philosophy that piece-meal measures are not appropriate.

The stabilization measures encompassed devaluation (the rupee was devalued by 20 per cent on July 1st and 3rd, 1991), public expenditure restraint (e.g. reducing subsidies on fertilizers, food and petroleum), reduction of the fiscal deficit and removal of the restrictions on the flow of foreign capital. Thus would the immediate crisis be resolved and the economy's macroeconomic stability be secured. However, far-reaching microeconomic measures were necessary to ensure the economy's long-run health and vigour.

Those long-run structural adjustment measures covered a broad series of reforms: in trade policy (with elimination of licensing controls and partial convertibility of the rupee); industrial policy (*inter alia*, the deregulation and freeing of industry from all controls and licences); the public sector (e.g. significant narrowing of its scope by reducing reserved areas from 17 to 8, a disinvestment of public sector equity in profit making enterprises, withdrawal of support from those making losses and greater freedom in fixing prices); the financial sector (with, for example, greater freedom for both private and foreign banks to operate in the money market); the capital market; the tax system (with reforms in direct taxes and in excise and customs duties); and measures to promote the inflow of direct private foreign investment (seen as a non-debt inflow which gives access to international technology and markets). Thus would the vestiges of development planning be finally rooted out and the Indian state be rolled back in the economic sphere. Thus would rent-seeking be drastically reduced, the Indian economy integrated into the world economy and Indian industry rendered more competitive and efficient.

That package, indeed, bears a striking resemblance to the advice offered in the World Bank's October 1990 Report on the Indian Economy (World Bank 1990). It is also congruent with the conditions attached to the World Bank Structural Adjustment Loan and the IMF Stand-By Loan negotiated by India in 1991, during the external debt crisis, and to the likely conditions of the later Extended Fund Facility (EFF), for which the Narasimha Rao government was expected to apply. Some two years after its introduction, the Ministry of Finance issued a discussion paper on the economic reforms (Government of India 1993), which, it has been suggested, was 'really an attempt to prepare the ground for the far tougher conditionalities to which the country is to be subjected as the price for the EFF and ESAF (Extended Structural Adjustment Facility) borrowing from the IMF and the loan for financial sector reform from the World Bank' (EPW Research Foundation 1993, 1563). In the event, as pressure on the Indian balance of payments eased, the EFF was not negotiated and the ESAF borrowing not sought, but the influence of the Bank and the Fund, whether actual or prospective, is clear.[13]

Crisis, Foreign Pressure, and India's Neoliberals Both Past and Present

Whether the Narasimha Rao government would have embraced liberalization, in the chosen form, in the absence of the 1991 crisis and the 'encouragement' of the Bretton Wood sister organizations is, perhaps, one of history's imponderables. Two of its most distinguished, and most fervent, advocates, Bhagwati and Srinivasan,[14] have suggested that it would. It is worth considering their argument in some detail, since it raises some important issues.

Bhagwati and Srinivasan argue as follows:

> The fact that the reforms were part of the conditionality that came with multilateral assistance has [...] created the impression that they are the result of foreign pressure. In turn, there is the notion that the ideas and policies being imposed on us are foreign and also that they are ill-designed, in consequence, for us. (Bhagwati and Srinivasan 1993, 8)

Two quite separate propositions are then made. Both are expanded upon, and we may comment on the positions adopted by Bhagwati and Srinivasan.

The first proposition relates to pressure by the Bank and the Fund:

> Indeed, it is true that, without the crisis being on us, the initial adoption of the reforms may have continued to be postponed. Our earlier efforts at initiating them had been hesitant and limited at best. *Conditionality played a role, for sure, in strengthening our will to embark upon the reforms.* But the seriousness and the sweep of the reforms, and the Rao government's explicit embrace of them as against the earlier 'reforms by stealth', demonstrated that the driving force behind the reforms was equally, even overwhelmingly, our own conviction that we had lost precious time and that the reforms were finally our only option. (Bhagwati and Srinivasan 1993, 9, emphasis added)

The combination of crisis and conditionality is seen to be significant, in translating 'reforms by stealth' into decisive reforming action.

One notes that a fine line exists between 'having one's will strengthened' and 'yielding to pressure'. That the crisis created an apprehension that dramatic action was called for seems clear. But such action need not have been the liberalization package opted for. To quite what degree the will to embark upon radical liberalization existed, independently of conditionality, is not clear. The thrust of the Bhagwati and Srinivasan argument is that it did. They merely assert that, however. They produce no direct evidence in support of their assertion. They follow a different tack. In their second proposition they make a spirited attempt to argue that such a will had strong Indian intellectual roots in the past. Even if it were true, of course, it hardly disposes of the pressure argument. But is it true? Here we may scrutinize the nature of their claim.

The second proposition, then, runs as follows:

> The complaint that the ideas being implemented are extraneous does not reflect the reality either. These reforms in our, and indeed in many other developing countries' policies, were being advocated from the *early 1960s* and the proponents, *the pioneers, included Indian economists*. It is ironic, in fact, that these ideas, rejected at the time by our authorities and by many of our economists as well, have now been adopted worldwide but have come to be adopted by us only at the end of this

> revolutionary change. Indeed, these ideas have been *recycled back to us, in many cases, by the staff of the multilateral institutions who learnt them from our own pioneering economists.* The claim that the ideas are foreign and hence ill-suited to us is therefore incorrect. In any case it is surely odd and counterproductive to accept or reject ideas based on where they are coming from! (Bhagwati and Srinivasan 1993, 9, emphases added)

This is, to say the least, dubious. It is so on at least three counts: on the suggested timing, on the postulated strength of the early liberalizing arguments of Indian economists, and on the proposition that it was from 'our own pioneering economists' that the 'staff of the multilateral institutions' learnt the relevant logic.

No evidence in support of this second proposition is given in the text in question, although we are referred to Bhagwati (1993) 'for further details'. Unfortunately no page references are supplied, but if we locate the relevant passage (68–9) we find that the 'pioneering Indian economists' identified turn out to be Bhagwati and Srinivasan themselves, along with V. K. Ramaswami and Padma Desai; while the foreign economists named are Bela Belassa, Arnold Harberger, Anne Krueger and Ian Little. This is all somewhat curious. Why?

We may say that in the development field generally, and in India in particular, the neoliberal ideas in question were very much a minority view in the early 1960s – the period mentioned – to the point of being negligible in their visibility and trifling in their influence. The dominant paradigm, at that time, and probably until the end of the 1960s, was one in which the case for planning and state intervention was central. That much, presumably, would not be disputed by Bhagwati and Srinivasan. If, indeed, the Indian economists mentioned were the pioneers of neoliberalism, they were not much in evidence in the early 1960s.

The most likely Indian candidate for the role of pioneer, in fact, was B. R. Shenoy, who is not mentioned by Bhagwati, but who, in the late 1950s and early 1960s, and thereafter, was actively opposing planning and state intervention.[15] It might be more accurate, perhaps, to describe Shenoy as a voice in the wilderness at that time, rather than a pioneer. I suppose that the transition from voice in the wilderness to pioneer is made when something of the wilderness has been tamed. There is no evidence of that in Shenoy's case. His arguments are, within the neoliberal paradigm, perfectly cogent, but they were little noted at the time, and it is difficult to attribute very much *influence* to them. I have suggested above that neoliberalism had its roots essentially in the United States. That I believe to be so. It is difficult to find genuine Indian roots. This is not to say that Bhagwati and Srinivasan (or, indeed, the late V. K. Ramaswami, and Padma Desai) are other than outstanding exponents of neoliberalism. That they can be portrayed as 'pioneers', who taught the staff of the multilateral institutions their neoliberal nostrums, is, however, doubtful. I have seen no evidence to sustain that proposition. On the other hand, there is considerable evidence to the effect that in the field of planning Indian economists made substantial original contributions, and were, assuredly, true pioneers. To that I will return in the next section.

Let us stress that Bhagwati himself did not take an obvious neoliberal position until the end of the 1960s. Far from being an 'early pioneer', he was an apparently dedicated proponent of planning and state intervention, certainly until the publication, in 1966, of his *The Economics of Underdeveloped Countries* (Bhagwati 1966). There is, moreover, little trace of sympathy for neoliberal ideas in the long piece co-authored with Sukhamoy Chakravarty and finished in May 1968, 'Contributions to Indian Economic Analysis: A Survey' (Bhagwati and Chakravarty 1969). The tendencies towards neoliberalism may have been there – with, for example, his advocacy of devaluation in 1964 (Bhagwati 1964) – but, if they were, they seem to have been carefully camouflaged or severely repressed. It was not until the publication, in 1970, of the book written with Padma Desai, *India, Planning for Industrialization: Industrialization and Trade Policies Since 1951* (Bhagwati and Desai 1970), that Bhagwati's neoliberalism surfaced openly.[16] Peter Bauer – among foreign economists, the most outspoken and unremitting neoliberal in the development field throughout the 1950s and 1960s, and the author, in the early 1960s, of a book on *Indian Economic Policy and Development* (Bauer 1961), but nowhere mentioned by Bhagwati – in his review of Bhagwati's 1966 book, dismissed Bhagwati, the later exponent of liberalization, as assuming that 'development planning in the sense of state control of the direction and composition of economic activity is indispensable for development' (Anon. 1966, Bauer 1971, 525).[17] Bauer also took Bhagwati to task for his stress on the achievements of the Soviet Union that were the result of development planning. Bhagwati, no doubt, might defend himself, as Keynes once did when taxed with inconsistency: 'When someone persuades me that I am wrong, I change my mind. What do you do?'[18] That is an important intellectual principle. But it would have been interesting if Bhagwati had noted his earlier commitment, and explained why he maintained it until some point in the later 1960s.[19]

Among foreign economists Peter Bauer was more of a pioneer than any in the 1950s and 1960s. Like Shenoy, however, he had little influence, either generally or in international institutions. Ironically, his ideas and suggested policy changes, which today would be seen as neoliberal orthodoxy, were dismissed as irrelevant raving. I.M.D. Little, for example, one of Bhagwati's supposed pioneers of neoliberalism, wrote, in a review of Bauer's aforementioned book (Bauer 1961): 'One would like to dismiss this book as the obvious outpourings of a political adolescent with an economic idée fixe [... deriving] from an extreme laisser-faire position' (Little 1961, 835). Little then takes Bauer to task for advocating a strategy for India that was 'Gladstonian' in its stress upon the need for 'low taxation and rigorous finance', and observes that Bauer 'describes present policies as throttling Indian development at every turn [...] not mention[ing] that India, since independence, has probably grown three times as fast as she did under those pre-war policies which appear similar to his' (Little 1961, 835). Little has moved closer to Bauer than would have seemed likely then, but to identify him as a pioneer of neoliberalism of the early 1960s is hardly credible.

Neoliberalism in India now has a large number of adherents, both in India and abroad. Among the most conspicuous are the present finance minister, Manmohan Singh, and the present finance secretary, Montek S. Ahluwalia. There is currently available a considerable literature sympathetic to the reforms.[20]

Towards a Corrective of the Neoliberal Representation of the Pre-1991 Record

The opposition of planning and market is not, of course, a new one. It has been the object, more distantly, of a general debate, with *socialist* possibilities in mind. The Indian context is that of the state and the development of *capitalism*, although that general debate is not without significance in this respect. This is not the place, however, to rehearse either that debate or its recent resurgence, whether general or in the specific context of India.[21] Nor does it seem especially useful to attempt a serious *comparison* of India's pre-1991 experience (say, from 1950 to the mid-1980s) with the years of full-blooded liberalization. We do not have, in the five years' experience of liberalization in India, a period to compare adequately with the three decades or so of more or less seriously pursued development planning. It would, further, be inappropriate to consider here in detail the impact and significance of economic liberalization in India, or its likely future course. That has been done elsewhere, in texts both sympathetic to and critical of liberalization.[22]

It is the case, as Ahluwalia observes, that 'these changes have been accompanied by a lively debate in India and have attracted great attention abroad' (Ahluwalia 1995, 13). Indeed, they continue to attract attention and to generate debate. One cannot, however, necessarily, accept his judgement that in India 'the broad direction of reform has met with wide approval' (Ahluwalia 1995, 13). There exists a more widespread, critical sense than he is willing to allow,[23] and it may be useful to reflect briefly upon one aspect of the contending strategies of planning and liberalization.

We may hazard some observations on the wholesale dismissal by the neoliberals of the pre-1991 experience: as something of a counter to that dismissal. Such a dismissal, we may insist, simply does not stand up to careful scrutiny. One need not embrace a utopian view of development planning, or of the nature of the Indian state, to supply such a corrective. Nor need we romanticize the Nehru–Mahalanobis model, which was embraced by the Indian state and lay at the heart of Indian planning from the mid-1950s. Yet, if I may cite Ashwani Saith, 'while the failings of the Nehru–Mahalanobis model are widely known, its contributions cannot be dismissed lightly' (Saith 1995, 1). Certainly, they cannot be ignored completely, and, indeed, metamorphosed into a nightmare – a kind of Kafkaesque great insect, to be invoked with a shudder – as they are by the neoliberals. We may recall the measured defence, within a critical framework, of the Indian planning record, by the late Sukhamoy Chakravarty, in *Development Planning: The Indian Experience*, (Chakravarty 1987).[24] Let us now consider that record, with the neoliberal arguments in mind.

We may start with the virtuosity and originality of the Indian contribution to what Chakravarty and Bhagwati have termed 'planning theory and techniques' (1969, 3). Something of that may be seen in the Chakravarty and Bhagwati survey;[25] but it is, perhaps, most usefully conveyed in Ashok Rudra's *Indian Plan Models* (1975). It is not too much to say that Indian planning was remarkable in the early use that was made of planning models, the sophisticated development of those models which planning engendered, and the extensive utilization of such models with respect to plan *formulation.*

Previously, such models had been employed in the Soviet Union. But India was the first contemporary developing economy to employ them and develop them actively in its attempted planning of economic development. The late Ashok Rudra, not given to gratuitously laudatory remarks about any field of endeavour, observed:

> Planning models constitute an area in economic model making where India has the distinction of having made contributions at par with work done anywhere in the world. The development of the subject in India has been almost entirely autonomous and independent of developments on parallel or similar lines which took place in other countries. This took place in response to demands arising out of the essential problems of the society which, of course, is a precondition for the genuine and autonomous development of any branch of science. (Rudra 1985, 758)

One might go further than Rudra, indeed, and argue that India's contributions have been in advance of contributions made anywhere else. One cannot say the same of neoliberal theorizing, whose heartland, I have suggested, remains resolutely in the United States. The major Indian neoliberal theorists, whom we have mentioned, are domiciled there, and are not, anyway, in the vanguard of neoliberal theorizing in the way that those who formulated planning models were in that domain.

Of course, intellectual response to a society's demands is not enough. Theory must be joined to effective practice. It is the case that plan *implementation* in India proved to have significant deficiencies. These were partly technical, and the technical defects have been considered cogently by Sukhamoy Chakravarty (1987, chap. 4).[26] More fundamentally, however, they are the clear reflections of the nature of the Indian state and of existing class relations and class dominance. They are a manifestation of the powerful contradictions of a painfully developing capitalism. Again in Rudra's words,

> The way planning or any other instruments of social action work depends entirely on the classes that wield these instruments. The instruments can no more transform the wielder than the tail can wag the dog. (Rudra 1985, 763)

It is at that level that the deficiencies need to be considered. They cannot be seen usefully, I would submit, in neoliberal terms. Nor can one validly argue that an unfettered market or a far leaner state would have produced a superior outcome. That they were serious, and led to regular shortfalls in planning targets, is clearly the case. But, notwithstanding the contradictions in question, and without making the leap from Franz Kafka to Dr Pangloss, we may see the pre-1991 era in more positive light than do the neoliberals.

I will proceed, first, at the most general level, and consider certain macro indicators. Ideally, detailed disaggregation in sectoral terms is called for, but space forbids, and the macro exercise, anyway, is revealing enough for present purposes. A brief reference to the record of agriculture and industry will, however, be made. I will then move to some observations on poverty, with state intervention in mind, before some comments on the matter of the state. What is pursued here is not an exercise in contemporary Indian economic history. It is, rather, a limited attempt to provide a perspective on the pre-1991 era other than that of neoliberalism. We may do that, in part, by considering the neoliberal charge-sheet in the case against development planning.

The first charge of the neoliberals is one of 'slow rates of growth of income and per capita income' (Bhagwati 1993, 22). Bhagwati takes the years 1960 to 1988, and argues that we find a 'weak performance' in relation to India's 'own aspirations' (presumably those of the planners); a 'sorry performance [...] compared to the super-performers, Taiwan, South Korea and Japan' (23–4), inferior, though not so markedly, to 'the average performance of both middle-income and low-income East Asia' (24); and equivocal by comparison with the 'Latin American performance' (which was better than the Indian performance in the 1970s, but inferior in the 1980s). We may pass the irrelevance of the comparison with Japan – like not being compared with like (Japan, in the period in question, being in the ranks of advanced capitalist countries). That said, we note that a variety of possible defences of the Indian performance is rejected: whether in terms of growth now being at the expense of growth in the future (which may be the Latin American experience of the 1970s and 1980s); or of growth representing a significant break with the stagnation of pre-independence India (which is not denied, but is said to be more striking in the case of the 'super-performers'); or of any 'special' features of Far Eastern economies (24–5). Of these, I will comment only on the second, and simply note that the break with the past should not be dismissed quite so lightly – as Ian Little was at such pains to stress in the 1961 comments I have quoted above.[27] While conscious of the need to 'look beyond [...] macro indicators [...] into the nature and direction of the process of development, including its social and political consequences' (Patnaik 1995a, 157–8), let us, nevertheless, address the neoliberal charge. The important issue, of course, is that of the long-run rate of growth of the Indian economy, and whether we can usefully identify such a rate of growth. We can. In 1983, the late Raj Krishna calculated that between 1951–52 and 1982–83 the long-run rate of growth of the Indian economy – of real national income – was about 3.5 per cent per annum (Krishna 1983); which, given the rate of population growth over the period, meant a per capita growth rate of 1.4 per cent per annum. He would, with some irony, call that the 'Hindu rate of growth' – a representation which stuck, and which is much repeated. We might better replace that unfortunate term with that of the 'Nehru–Mahalanobis rate of growth', to underline the point that this was the growth achieved under the regime portrayed so unfavourably by the neoliberals. As Krishna pointed out, there were considerable year-to-year fluctuations, but the significant point is the *persistence* of this growth rate. He was at pains to point out that, when he wrote, by 1982–83, there was no evidence of *acceleration*. Equally, one might stress, there was no indication of *deceleration*. A similar exercise done in, say, the mid-1960s or the mid-1970s, would have yielded the same conclusion.[28]

The story does not, however, end there. Ironically, there is substantial evidence to suggest that even as Raj Krishna was doing the exercise in question, there *was* in process a transformation that he did not detect: what has been described as a 'marked acceleration in economic growth [...] a sharp increase in the long-term growth rate of real domestic product from less than 3.5 per cent in the earlier period to more than 5 per cent in the later period' (Dholakia 1994, 2303). Indeed, the very architect (or presumed architect) of the 1991 liberalization reforms, Montek S. Ahluwalia, stressed, in his pre-1991 manifesto, in a paper written in 1986 (1988), that by the mid-1980s the 'underlying growth rate of the economy' had accelerated from the earlier 3.5 per cent to 5 per cent per annum (347) and that by then 'the economy had gained in strength and structural maturity in many dimensions' (359). There seems now to be general agreement that there was 'an acceleration in the 1980s' (EPW Research Foundation 1995, 2958).[29] It has been the subject of sophisticated measurement, and, in the relevant literature, it is concluded that this 'break in the time trend of real income in the Indian economy' (EPW Research Foundation 1995, 2304) took place at some point in the late 1970s and early 1980s. Ganesh (1992) suggests 1981–82 as the most likely year of rupture with the past. But the 'break year' seems likely to have been earlier: Bhargava and Joshi place their money on 1980–81 but do not exclude the possibility of 1975–76 (1990, 2660), while Nagaraj (1990) identifies 1979–80 as the probable year of break. Of these, Nagaraj is, perhaps, the most convincing. But, whatever the precise timing, the acceleration has nothing to do with liberalization, since it clearly predates the liberalization era.[30] It may be seen as an outcome of the Nehru–Mahalanobis era (if we take that to stretch into the 1970s, albeit in increasingly diluted form).

Whether one can dismiss this as a 'weak' or a 'sorry' performance is surely doubtful. At worst, one might say that in the earlier period (that of the 3.5 per cent growth rate) 'growth rates were respectable, if not impressive' (Saith 1995, 1), while if one takes the whole pre-liberalization era, and takes account of the acceleration of the 1970s/1980s, it is rather more than respectable. As Chakravarty argued for the whole period 1950–85, while it would be foolish to suggest that 'India's development planning has been on the whole a great success', equally, 'it would be just as rash [...] to dismiss Indian planning as an essay in failure' (1987, 84).

Moreover, Chakravarty's invoking of Frederick List's distinction between 'production' and 'productive power' (43) is illuminating. The neoliberals have little to say about 'productive power', about the importance of investment and accumulation in establishing the productive base for future performance. That, however, may be a significant contribution made by Indian development planning to Indian capitalism as the contradictions of primitive accumulation unfolded. One might hypothesize that the aforementioned acceleration in the growth rate is the outcome of a productive base created previously.

If we turn next to savings and investment, we may shed further light on the growth performance we have identified. The neoliberal charge here is that 'the weak growth performance reflects, not a disappointing savings [and, therefore, investment] performance, but rather a disappointing productivity performance' (Bhagwati 1993, 40). This is a partial, rather than a full, charge, inasmuch as savings (and investment – or, at least, the quantum of investment) are deemed adequate. The reasons for the disappointing productivity performance are those familiar neoliberal demons: (1) extensive and stifling bureaucratic controls; (2) inward-looking trade and foreign investment policies; and (3) a large, unjustified and inefficient public sector (46–69). If, of course, there is no 'weak performance' to explain then all of this becomes somewhat superfluous. While we may doubt the productivity-inhibiting effects of trade and foreign investment policies, this is not to deny the excesses of bureaucratic controls or the problems of India's public sector. Without, then, denying the existence of serious problems, one can question vigorously the nightmare outcome postulated by the neoliberals.

Rather more needs to be said about savings and investment in the pre-liberalization, or planning, era. In fact, I would suggest a hypothesis quite the opposite of the neoliberal one. The most recent comprehensive treatment of domestic savings and capital formation, from 1950–51 to 1993–94 (EPW Research Foundation 1995b) reveals that the gross domestic savings rate rose from 10.4 per cent in 1950–51 to a peak of 23.2 per cent in 1978–79 but has shown 'relative stagnation [...] since the second half of the 1970s' (3024), while the net domestic savings rate rose from 6.8 per cent to 16.4 per cent in the first period and displayed a 'distinctly declining trend thereafter' (3024).[31] At the same time, the rate of gross domestic capital formation increased from 10.2 per cent in 1950–51 to peak at around 23 per cent in 1978–79 and showed a clear tendency to decline thereafter, while the rate of net domestic capital formation rose from 6.6 per cent in 1950–51 to a peak of 16.5 per cent in 1978–79 and showed a distinct tendency to fall in the 1980s.[32] What, then, do we make of these trends, with respect to the present argument? They sit ill with a neoliberal treatment. Neoliberals assign secondary significance to the investment ratio. Rather, they have shifted the previous emphasis of development economics from 'investment as the key to growth' to the 'efficiency of resource use' as the crucial element (Patnaik and Chandrasekhar 1996, 31).[33] We may, however, posit that the 'respectable' 3.5 per cent growth rate of the three decades from the 1950s to the late 1970s was achieved, to a significant degree, via a *doubling* (or rather more) of the domestic savings rate and investment rate; that, to use Patnaik and Chandrasekhar's formulation with respect to a far broader treatment of the growth experience across underdeveloped countries, 'it is really the investment ratio which plays the crucial role' (1996, 36). If this is so, then what would have transformed a 'respectable' into an 'impressive' growth rate was a rise in the investment ratio, made possible by a rise in the savings rate. As Patnaik points out, 'no country in the contemporary epoch has succeeded in breaking into the charmed circle of high growth economies without substantially stepping-up its investment ratio' (1995, 211). It is true that over the relevant period the incremental capital–output ratio rose: the gross ratio from 2.87 in 1951–52 to 1955–56, to 5.86 in 1969–70 to 1973–74, and the net ratio from 1.97 to 4.30 (Chakravarty 1987, 105, table 3). That, however, does not necessarily imply inefficiency of resource use (as the neoliberals argue). It has been suggested that 'if allowance is made for the stage of development, the capital–output ratios were not exceptionally high' (Saith 1995, 1). Moreover, it can be argued that an increase in the investment ratio would have lowered capital–output ratios, by 'open[ing] up larger possibilities of transforming commodities into one another through trade, and introduc[ing] greater synergy into the functioning of the economy' (Patnaik 1995b, 218).

The acceleration of the growth rate to 5 per cent or so was accompanied by *declining* rates of savings and investment. This might be taken to imply, overall, *pace* Bhagwati, an *improved* productivity performance. Indeed, the capital–output ratio clearly fell: the gross ratio to 4.45 between 1980–81 and 1983–84, and the net ratio to 3.38 (Chakravarty 1987, 105, table 3). This, again, predates liberalization. One might hypothesize that it is, in part, a function of the productive base created in the previous years, and that a more marked acceleration in the growth rate would have emerged from a rising investment ratio. This, rather than inefficiency in resource use, is what needs to be addressed.

The foregoing does suggest a problem of domestic resource mobilization, which derives, to a degree, from the 'fiscal crisis' of the Indian state stressed by Chakravarty (1987, 48–9, 51, 76–7) and Patnaik (1995b, 219). This, in turn, stems from, *inter alia*, an inability to directly tax dominant classes in the countryside. It is a problem that continues. Liberalization would do nothing to resolve such a dilemma. On the contrary, the neoliberals argue that taxation is not necessary to raise the savings rate (Bhagwati 1993, 21). A capacity to directly tax agriculture has proved, historically, to be a critical component of successful capitalist transformation. It requires, in India, not withdrawal by the state but more effective state action. It is not a matter of imperfectly functioning markets. It is one, rather, of effectively functioning dominant classes, able to resist taxation. It will be resolved not via the operation of the market, but in the arena of struggle between dominant classes. In that struggle, the state, as it has always done in the past in other historical contexts, must play a crucial role.

Before turning, briefly, to the record on poverty, it is to be stressed that there are many other features of the pre-1991 performance of the economy that are essential to a full treatment. These include the experience of the two major sectors, agriculture and industry. Curiously, amid the litany of failure, and as little more than an aside, we find, in the neoliberal account, the surprising reference to 'India's successful policies and performance [...] in transforming traditional agriculture' (Bhagwati 1993, 17n10). One might have expected rather more to be made of this in assessing the Indian experience.[34] There is no such favourable reference to industry, which is portrayed as a haven of rent-seeking and inefficiency, and whose prolonged stagnation of the 1960s and 1970s is stressed (Bhagwati 1992, 45). Indeed, India's industrial stagnation from the mid-1960s to the late 1970s is much discussed by Indian economists.[35] But Indian industry did revive in the late 1970s, and grew in the 1980s (Nayyar 1994a, 5), well before the advent of liberalization. That the neoliberals need to consider.[36] It has been argued, indeed, that an important legacy of the Nehru–Mahalanobis era is a significant industrial base: 'a good base in production technology [...] across a variety of sectors [...and] a trained labour force and managerial know-how so far as modern production methods across a wide range of reasonably sophisticated products [...] are concerned' (Vyasulu et al. 1991, 2206).[37] This made the impressive industrial growth rates of the 1980s possible.[38] Attention has been drawn, too, to the creation of 'the basic infrastructure [both physical and human] essential for rapid economic development' (Vyasulu et al. 1991, 2206).

None of this is to be taken to suggest an economy in the pre-1991 years that was smoothly functioning and consistently dynamic; or one that had yet acquired that 'elasticity [... that] capacity for sudden extension by leaps and bounds, which comes up against no barriers but those presented by the availability of raw materials and the extent of sales outlets' (Marx 1976, 579) that would signal a 'degree of [capitalist] maturity' (Marx 1976, 579). On the contrary, it was an economy riven by contradictions, some of which are identified and characterized by inefficiencies and shortcomings. It does, however, provide a perspective quite different from that of the neoliberals: one in which development planning and an interventionist state cannot be dismissed *tout court* as having been responsible for an unmitigated economic disaster. On that basis, one might argue not for the abandonment of planning and the withdrawal of the state, in favour of the neoliberal 'invisible hand', but rather, as Chakravarty insisted, that 'there is a clear need for the "visible hand" of planning, as many of [the relevant] problems involving expansion and modification of the resource base itself require far-sighted action which is beyond the decision horizon of private actors' (1987, 6). If India is now to move from the absorption and adaptation of technology imported from abroad to a capacity to generate new technology, on a basis of indigenous research and development, that will require not only 'far-sighted action' (i.e. planning) but also resources on a scale that only the state can provide. The case for development planning can still be made.

We cannot leave the pre-1991 record without some consideration of poverty, an issue that, rightly, looms large in the planning/liberalization opposition. Clearly, I cannot hope to do justice here to this vast, contentious and complex issue, and its daunting literature. There is, however, an important conclusion to be drawn.

The neoliberal charge here is straightforward enough: that 'the disappointing growth rate seriously handicapped the alleviation of poverty in India' (Bhagwati 1993, 25). The neoliberal logic is that growth, through the celebrated trickle-down mechanisms (which Bhagwati, anxious to create a more positive image, prefers to call 'pull-up' mechanisms), automatically reduces poverty: quite simply, by creating income (Bhagwati 1993 26), which is spread through 'pull[ing] people up into gainful work' (Bhagwati 1993, 32). The faster growth proceeds, the more quickly will poverty diminish. It is a fallacy to suppose that 'the removal of poverty requires "direct" anti-poverty programmes, not growth' (Bhagwati 1993 26). The state need not intervene directly to reduce the incidence of poverty. Indeed, state intervention, inasmuch as it seriously retards growth, will perpetuate poverty.

The record with respect to poverty does not bear out any of this. We may concentrate, here, on rural poverty, which has been the major focus of attention, and which, indeed, represents the great bulk of poverty in India.

There is, quite simply, no convincing evidence to support the existence of trickle-down (or 'pull-up') mechanisms in a society like that of India. The early questioning of the Ahluwalia thesis by Saith (1981) remains powerfully convincing. The earlier Ahluwalia work (1976, 1978), to which Saith responded, is noted above. Ahluwalia's later attempt to confirm the trickle-down thesis (Ahluwalia 1985) is no more persuasive. Ahluwalia, there, is at pains to stress that 'growth alone will not bring about a large reduction in the incidence of poverty in the near future' (Ahluwalia 1985, 73). Nevertheless, he maintains his position that trickle-down mechanisms do operate in India. But even T. N. Srinivasan, himself sympathetic to the trickle-down thesis, is not convinced (1985). He concludes: 'Empirical studies testing the trickle-down hypothesis are inadequate, either because they use data that do not indicate significant growth to trickle-down or because they draw inferences from cross-sectional data about dynamic processes' (Srinivasan 1985, 52). That is to say, there is no empirical basis for the trickle-down thesis.

In the earlier paper (Ahluwalia 1978), trickle-down could be shown to work, it seemed, at the all-India level, but not at the level of individual states. Ahluwalia chooses to favour the former, but it is not at all clear why one might accept the all-India rather than the state data. As Saith points out, Ahluwalia, in that earlier paper, is sufficiently unsure of the data to suggest that 'the state-level analysis [...] shows that there may be processes at work in the rural economy which tend to increase rural poverty over time' (Ahluwalia 1978, 320). Indeed, one may argue that such processes do work powerfully in rural India: that class-for-itself action by dominant rural classes is able, via the deployment of mechanisms of surplus appropriation, to appropriate the vast bulk of whatever 'gains' are associated with agricultural growth. Such action includes, very significantly, widespread labour-displacing mechanization, in those areas to which the so-called 'green revolution' spread most, which prevents Bhagwati's 'pulling of people into gainful work'. I have, myself, presented evidence to this effect, in the context of the 'new technology' (Byres 1981). If that is so, then if any dent is to be made on rural poverty substantial intervention by the state is essential.

The pre-1991 experience might be taken to bear this out. My own reading of the vast amount of measurement that now exists – over which there is immense disagreement, I hasten to add – and which I will not attempt even to list, is as follows. It is difficult to make even broad statements about the pre-1960 situation. Thereafter, however, there are two distinct phases: the first, between 1960–61, for which the first reasonable estimates exist, and, say, 1973–74; and the second between 1973–74 and 1988–89.

In the former period, the incidence of rural poverty rose substantially: from, possibly, 40 per cent to, perhaps, 56 per cent.[39] This is what Ashwani Saith has described, very accurately, as 'a dismal performance with respect to poverty' (Saith 1995, 1). It is, assuredly, not one of development planning's successes. On the contrary, the state failed palpably to intervene to moderate this most vicious of an insufficiently mediated, early capitalism's traits – a clear process of immiserization. Poverty alleviation programmes, to the extent that they existed, were miserably funded, weak and inconsequential.[40]

Now, this might be perceived to be in the interests of rural dominant classes (not least in the ranks of those classes themselves), reflecting, as it does in the immediate situation, maximum surplus appropriation. But, objectively, and in a way clear to the representatives of the state, it constituted a threatening contradiction in at least two senses. The first resided in the constriction of the home market confronted by the Indian manufacturing industry, which might be eased, if not eliminated, by some diminution of poverty.[41] Here, the interests of industrial capital needed to be represented at the possible expense of rural dominant classes. Secondly, a threat to the whole social order lay in the possibly explosive, disruptive potential of a poverty that was both deepening and changing its nature, with a severing of traditional relationships and underemployment transformed, increasingly, into a more menacing open unemployment.[42]

Thereafter, in the second period, there emerges what was to many a surprising, but what appears to be an incontrovertible, steady decline in the incidence of rural poverty (it was certainly very surprising for me, and it took much evidence to persuade me of its plausibility). The most recent figures indicate a decline from the peak of, perhaps, 56 per cent in 1973–74 (or thereabouts) to a trough of 34 per cent in 1988–89 and, maybe, 1989–90 (Chandrasekhar and Sen 1996, 101). Saith argues that 'it was largely on account of extensive targeted programmes of poverty alleviation' (Saith 1995, 1). This is a most plausible hypothesis. The sheer scale of the programmes in question – both the Integrated Rural Development Programme (IRDP) and the employment generating schemes, most recently (since April 1989) the Jawahar Rozgar Yojana (JRY), but especially the former – was unprecedented.[43] That this action was related to an awareness of the aforementioned threats posed by increasing immiserization seems likely.

Let us not get carried away. It is clear that much of the funds and effort did not reach the intended targets; that where the poor were reached it was not the 'hard-core' poor; that for those that were reached their new-found condition of non-poverty was, indeed, a precarious one that might be suddenly reversed by adverse price movements, or by a slackening of activity on the poverty alleviation front. Nevertheless, action by the state did have an appreciable effect. With respect to poverty, it is this, and not 'trickle-down', that is called for. Indeed, in the post-1991 years the sharp rise in the incidence of poverty, to 44 per cent in 1992 (Chandrasekhar and Sen 1996, 101), is clearly consequent, in part, upon a significant slackening of activity in poverty alleviation programmes, both IRDP and JRY (Nayyar 1996, 34, 39, 41). A dramatic rise in foodgrain prices, which was sufficient to set up powerful pressures towards a significant increase in the incidence of rural poverty, needed an intensification of such activity. Liberalization brought the contrary, and the incidence of rural poverty rose to levels not seen since 1983; an effect that liberalization measures have clearly brought elsewhere.[44]

Some Observations on Neoliberal Anti-statism and the Nature of the Interventionist State

We may comment, finally, on the anti-statism of the neoliberals and their call for a minimalist state. In so proceeding, we may clarify some misconceptions about the issue of the interventionist state in a context such as the Indian: that of an as yet immature capitalism.

The neoliberal imagery is one of illness, disease and pathology. As Bhagwati has it: 'The cure is defined by the diagnosis' (1993, 71). Henry Bernstein has noted of another regional setting, Africa, that a central postulate of the World Bank/neoliberal diagnosis is of states 'marked by the full misery of their own contradictions – as documented in the symptomology of irrationality, inefficiency, corruption and authoritarianism' (1990, 23). In such a view, the state and its activities represent the essential obstacle to the emergence of a vigorous, rapidly growing capitalism. The state must be 'rolled back', must be made 'leaner'. Such terms are appropriate to the neoliberal treatment of the Indian state.

Bernstein notes the curious paradox that, where World Bank structural adjustment is sought, a 'critical double contradiction' exists, whereby the very effort to push back the state has to be pursued via the state; while the necessary 'leaner state', in effect, 'is by no means a minimalist state (a continuing bourgeois illusion [...]) but one in which greater demands of technical expertise and efficient performance and macro economic management are imposed [...] as well as greater effectiveness in terms of control' (Bernstein 1990, 23). The same would be true of an Indian neoliberal state. The state, then, beneath the cloak of privatization and deregulation, would become, in particular respects, more intrusive than it was previously: and that especially with regard to control of labour.

Bhagwati and Srinivasan insist upon the need for 'a flexible labour hire-and-fire policy' (1993, 26). To implement that, in the face of opposition from organized labour, is likely to involve considerable coercive interference by the state. We may further argue that while, then, the logic of capitalist accumulation would drive a neoliberal state in specific, intrusive – and coercive – directions, a heavy price would be paid, in the Indian context, in an important sense, with respect to accumulation. The essential point is captured by Prabhat Patnaik:

> under the logic of liberalization the state begins to withdraw from the role of a principal player in the arena of production itself. As a result, 'liberalization' leaves the economy without any agency capable of transforming potentially investible resources into actual productive investment, i.e. capable of using the slack in the economy to step up its rate of growth. (1995b, 226).

How, then, has this dilemma been resolved among the 'super-performers', to use a favourite formulation of Bhagwati's? They, after all, are the exemplars to which India is urged to look.

If, indeed, we turn to these 'super-performers', regarded with such favour by the neoliberals, the 'minimalist state' is nowhere to be seen. It is a myth which surely deserves to be laid to rest. There is a strong argument, supported by abundant evidence, to the effect that 'the success of East Asian countries is primarily due to the active role of the state in formulating a vigorous economic system that promotes capital accumulation, innovation and productivity growth' (Chang 1994, 3).[45] Even the World Bank (if we may give it a collective identity), in its 1993 Policy Research Report on *The East Asian Miracle: Economic Growth and Public Policy*, prepared by a galaxy of non-radical development economists, concluded of the High-Performing Asian Economies (the HPAEs) – another acronym with which to baffle the uninitiated:

> In the past six years, the neoclassical interpretation of the sources of rapid growth has been criticised for its lack of factual validity, at least as it applies to Japan, Korea and Taiwan [...] Advocates of this view, sometimes dubbed revisionists, have systematically documented that governments in these three economies extensively and selectively promoted individual sectors. They have convincingly shown that levels of protection and the variation of protection across sectors has been greater than recognised in neoclassical interpretations [...] Indeed, governments in each of these three economies at times intervened forcefully in markets [encouraging and promoting particular industries, offering protection and financial incentives, using public investment in large-scale manufacturing enterprises...] Moreover, capital markets were not free in these three economies [...and] market failures are pervasive and [are] a justification for governments to lead the market in critical ways. In this view, the experience of Japan, Korea and Taiwan [...] provide[s] evidence that governments can foster growth by 'governing markets' and 'getting prices wrong' and by systematically distorting incentives in order to accelerate catching up – that is, to facilitate the establishment and growth of industrial centres that would not have thrived under the workings of comparative advantage. (World Bank 1993, 83–4)

One wonders why it took them so long. Let that be the obituary notice for the minimalist state. Let it rest in peace. Might one expect World Bank structural adjustment programmes, from now on, to reflect something of this 'revisionist view'? Or is the 'neoclassical view' too deeply entrenched, too ideologically hegemonic, to be dislodged?[46]

The language – protection, intervention, market failure – has more than a trace of that used in the early case for development planning in India and elsewhere.[47] Indeed, Chalmers Johnson, a decade before the World Bank's startling discovery, suggested (1982, 18–26) that the notion of 'plan rationality' was more appropriate to the experience of Japan and the other East Asian economies than that of 'market rationality'. We would seem to have come full circle.

India is not a 'super-performer' – is not an HPAE. Yet, just as the neoclassical/neoliberal view of the East Asian economies must be rejected, so that of the Indian experience of development planning and the interventionist state may be severely questioned, along with its policy/strategy prescriptions. As far as *capitalist accumulation* and the *containment of capitalist processes of immiserization* are concerned, I have contested the neoliberal view, on a basis of a reading of the pre-1991 Indian experience very different from the neoliberal one. I have also argued that a qualitative transformation of certain crucial processes requires not the abandonment of planning, but a continuing, and far more imaginative and far-sighted, development planning; and not a minimalist state, but an interventionist state capable of mobilizing, allocating and utilizing resources on the necessary scale. The evidence for the so-called HPAEs would appear to lend such a view contemporary comparative support.

As already emphasized, the interventionist state, of course, is the locus of powerful contradictions. To suggest the importance of an interventionist state to the unleashing of capitalist accumulation, and the possibility of the state moderating the excesses of capitalist immiserization, is not to deny the reality of a coercive capitalist state. That is almost a truism. The evidence is far too extensive to deny such a reality. The alternative, that of an actually functioning neoliberal state, is likely to be no less coercive. For other compelling reasons, it is not one to be contemplated with equanimity.

Notes

1 For an excellent critical treatment of the neoliberal assault, and its theoretical underpinning, with respect to advanced capitalist countries, less developed countries and socialist countries, see Chang and Rowthorn (1995, Introduction). The first major intervention with respect to less developed countries came with I. M. D. Little, T. Scitovsky and M. F. G. Scott, *Industry and Trade in Some Developing Countries*, published in 1970, with its stress upon efficiency of resource use. Cf. Patnaik and Chandrasekhar (1995, 31). Thereafter, the rent-seeking argument, with its emphasis on the creation of entry barriers by the state, consequent deadweight welfare losses, and wasteful expenditures associated with state intervention, especially in relation to import substituting industrialization, was developed by Krueger (1974) and Posner (1975). Then came the New Political Economy, with its emphasis on the operation of a predatory state in less-developed countries, which maximizes revenues rather than social welfare (North 1981, Findlay 1990). Cf. Chang and Rowthorn (1995, 10).

2 On the content and rationale of the lending programmes of the International Monetary Fund and the World Bank see, respectively, for example, Killick (1984, part 2) and Mosley, Harrigan and Toye (1995, parts 1 and 2).

3 On Manmohan Singh, cf. Kurien (1996, 8–9).

4 See Kurien (1996, 7). On this, Kurien cites Wadhva (1994, 29).

5 There he was Chief of the Income Distribution Division of the Development Research Centre.

6 Among the large number of eminent Indian émigré economists, Jagdish Bhagwati and T. N. Srinivasan have been prominent and forceful in their defence of the liberalizing reforms: Bhagwati in, for example, his Radhakrishnan Lectures (the same series in which Sukhamoy Chakravarty's book, *Development Planning: The Indian Experience* (1987) – see below – had its initial incarnation), delivered in Oxford in June 1992, and published as *India in Transition: Freeing the Economy* (Bhagwati 1993); Srinivasan in, for example, Srinivasan (1991a, 1991b, 1993); and the two together, in deadly combination, in the report cited, which is entitled *India's Economic Reforms*, and was commissioned for the Ministry of Finance by Manmohan Singh (Bhagwati and Srinivasan 1993), and is described by the latter as 'a labour of love' (Preface). In it, they congratulate the Rao government on the boldness of its reforms and urge it 'to extend them boldly in several new directions', with all speed (70).

7 These liberalizing measures, respectively, of the late 1970s, the early 1980s and 1985–86 to 1989–90 are noted in Joshi and Little (1994, 57, 62–3, 154, 269, 270). The Rajiv Gandhi liberalizing measures are usefully summarized there (62–3). For brief observations on the nature and significance of these earlier measures see, for example, Nayyar (1995, 10) and Kurien (1996, 3 and 10).

8 He was at that time additional secretary, prime minister's office, having previously been economic adviser, Ministry of Finance.

9 Cf. Kurien (1996, 3–4, 10).

10 Cf. Kurien (1996, 3–4).

11 This is the subtitle of Jagdish Bhagwati's book, *India in Transition*, already referred to (Bhagwati 1993).

12 See, for example, the Finance Ministry's own clear statement (Government of India, 1993), a document which is examined critically in J. M. (1993); and Bhagwati and Srinivasan (1993). For a very brief overview see Bhalla (1995, 10–14). I have drawn on the foregoing sources in identifying the details that follow.

13 On this paragraph and for an account of India's dealings in these various respects see Policy Watch (1991), B. M. (1991, 1993), J. M. (1993), and Kurien (1996, 6–7).

An IMF Stand-By arrangement represents the Fund's third line of credit. The first two lines – the reserve or gold tranche and the first credit tranche – carry no conditionality. A Stand-By Loan does, and requires a government to adopt a stabilization programme agreed by the Fund Management and Executive Board and includes various performance criteria. Performance is carefully monitored, and if the performance criteria are not met, access to the stand-by facility is denied until the stabilization programme is renegotiated. Such a loan is usually drawn down over a single year and is generally repayable over five years. An Extended Fund Facility (EFF) provides balance of payments support for longer periods and in larger amounts. Here tougher conditionality holds. Extended Structural Adjustment Facility (ESAF) loans are given by the World Bank and the IMF jointly. On this see Harris (1983, 19–20), Killick (1984, 183–4), and Stewart (1995, 19n11).

14 On Bhagwati and Srinivasan, see above, note 6.

15 His relevant papers may be seen in Shenoy (1963, 1968). Shenoy was a consistent and unrelenting proponent of what we have termed the neoliberal position. For a critical treatment of Shenoy (1963) see Byres (1966a).

16 It must have been bubbling away, since the then forthcoming Bhagwati–Desai text, and some of its conclusions, are signposted in the Bhagwati–Chakravarty survey noted. But the espousal of a full-blooded neoliberalism is barely hinted at. The text in question is in the same series as the Little, Scitovsky and Scott volume (1970) noted above as the first major neoliberal intervention with respect to less-developed countries.

17 The review was published initially in the *Times Literary Supplement*, when reviewers in that august weekly were still anonymous (Anon. 1966). I still have, inserted in my copy of the book, a cutting of the *TLS* review. It was later reprinted in Bauer's collected papers on the economics of development (Bauer, 1971).

18 Cited in Nolan (1988, 1).

19 Among the few hints one gets as to his earlier position is his 'confession' (to use his own formulation) that 'I was among the many who thought in the 1950s and 1960s that the public sector enterprises could be operated better' (1993, 64). His commitment, however, was rather greater than that.

20 Without attempting to be exhaustive, one notes the following. I have cited some of the relevant studies already. These include the volume by Joshi and Little (1994). This is a detailed World Bank study, which considers India's macroeconomic history from 1964 to 1991, in avowedly political economy terms, and concludes that 'India's control system was not only microeconomically inefficient [...] but also macro economically perverse' (Joshi and Little 1994, xiv). In so doing, they attempt to make a strong case for liberalization. They distance themselves from the more extreme liberalizers – the so-called 'new classical' macroeconomists – who oppose any form of government intervention, but their strong liberalizing message is clear. See the comprehensive volume, containing papers largely sympathetic to liberalization by both Indians and non-Indians, including some well-known development economists (among them, the aforementioned Joshi and Little) (Cassen and Joshi 1995). It includes a paper on 'India's Economic Reforms', by Montek S. Ahluwalia. The various writing by Bhagwati and by Srinivasan, and their joint writing, have been noted already. For vigorous defence of the liberalization reforms see also, for example, Shroff (1993); and for more cautious, even equivocal, endorsement, but endorsement nevertheless, Basu (1993).

21 The debate, in the inter-war years, between Barone (1908 and 1935), Lange (1936, 1937 and 1939) and Taylor (1929 and 1939), on the one hand, and Mises (1935 and 1936) and Hayek (1935) on the other, with the former arguing the case for central planning, and the Austrians arguing its impossibility, is well-known. Cf. Chang and Rowthorn (1995, 12). Chang and Rowthorn refer us to Lavoie (1985) for an excellent survey of that debate. The dimmest of echoes appear in Bhagwati (1993, 51, 64–5), where Hayek is briefly cited with favour. Cf. also Chakravarty (1993a, 185), who briefly argues the continuing relevance of the general debate. Chakravarty observes (1993a, 185): 'while much of development economics has been critical of the role of the market, Hayek has stated the case for the market much more convincingly than anyone else. My personal views are very different from Hayek's but that does not mean that in the famous debate with Lange [...] I subscribe to the view that victory went entirely to Lange'. See also Chakravarty (1987, 5, 91n4).

22 Some sympathetic texts are noted in footnote 20. For critical treatment of the reforms see, for example, Vyasulu et al. (1991), Rudra (1991), J. M. (1993), Nayyar (1993), Oommen (1993), and Patnaik (1994). More recently, both Nayyar and Kurien provide excellent critical treatments of economic liberalization in India, aimed at different audiences. Deepak Nayyar's work, *Economic Liberalization in India: Analytics, Experience and Lessons* (Nayyar, 1996) is an excellent 'insider's' view of the nature and impact of liberalization, written, with great clarity, for professional economists. It is based on his R. C. Dutt Lectures in Political Economy, delivered in Calcutta in 1993. Professor Nayyar was chief economic adviser to the Government of India, and permanent secretary in the Ministry of Finance, from June 1990 until he resigned in December 1991. C. T. Kurien's booklet *Economic Reforms and the People* (Kurien 1996) is, as I write, the best and clearest treatment available, in non-technical terms, of the Indian liberalization programme. It appeared originally as a series of articles in *Frontline*. The author tells us that it is 'meant for those who are not familiar with professional economics and yet are eager to know something about the current economic reforms and their impact on different sections of the population' (iii). He is excessively modest. Many with close familiarity with professional economics would gain from reading it. Currently in press is another text of great clarity on

liberalization, intended for a lay audience, which is incisive and cogent, *The Intelligent Person's Guide to Liberalisation*, by Amit Bhaduri and Deepak Nayyar (Bhaduri and Nayyar 1996). The critical literature is becoming increasingly rich.

Not all texts fall clearly into either category. Guha (1990) is a collection that appeared before the 1991 measures were introduced, in which differing views on the desirability of liberalization are expressed. Other collections include Parikh and Sudarshan (1993), which addresses human development; Bhalla (1994), which focuses upon the implications for agriculture; Rao and Linnemann (1996), on liberalization and poverty alleviation. See also Drèze and Sen (1995, especially 179–204), who, while claiming to go 'Well Beyond Liberalization' in discussing the serious absence of 'social opportunity', acknowledge the need for reforms of the liberalizing variety and side-step many of the issues discussed here (although not that of inequality and poverty) – somewhat loftily abjuring 'acrimonious debates' while granting that 'a bit of healthy mud-slinging might indeed have something to commend in making people take an interest in complex and apparently dull problems' (202).

23 The literature noted in the previous footnote represents something of that critical sense.

24 The book is an extended version of the Radhakrishnan Memorial Lectures given by Chakravarty at All Souls' College, Oxford, in 1985.

25 See Bhagwati and Chakravarty (1969, 3–29). This takes us through to the late 1960s and is apposite inasmuch as most of the outstanding work had been done by then.

26 The relevant chapter in Chakravarty's book was published in Byres (1994).

27 On this see Byres (1966b, 98–9).

28 Thus, my own efforts in this respect seemed to show just that. See Byres (1966, 92–3) and Byres and Nolan (1976, 51). In 1978, Shetty's figures for the periods 1951–52 to 1965–66 and 1966–67 to 1976–77 (Shetty 1978, 6, table 1) are remarkably close to this.

29 The evidence in question may be seen in the following sources: Nagaraj (1990, 1991), Bhargava and Joshi (1990), Ganesh (1992), Dholakia (1994), and EPW Research Foundation (1995a).

30 Somewhat bizarrely, and clearly unconvincingly, Bhargava and Joshi suggest as a 'tentative explanation' that one of the important factors in the 'improved growth performance' was 'economic liberalisation' (1990, 2660). But since the improvement dates from before any recognizable liberalization measures had been introduced, as Joshi himself, along with Little, elsewhere argues (see above, footnote 7), this is unacceptable. Unhappily, one cannot have it both ways.

31 The detailed time series for gross and net domestic savings from 1950–51 to 1993–1994 may be seen in EPW Research Foundation (1995b, 3025, table 4A).

32 The detailed time series for gross and net capital formation from 1950–51 to 1993–1994 may be seen in EPW Research Foundation (1995b, 3030, table 6B). I have quoted the adjusted figures (column 13).

33 For robust and insightful treatment of this see Patnaik and Chandrasekhar (1996) and the excellent essay by Patnaik (1995b).

34 Bhagwati (1993, 15) notes, appositely, that 'development economists with any historical sense' realize that, in agriculture, 'growth rates of 4 per cent are considered a supreme achievement'. So, the agricultural success-story in India, stressed by Bhagwati and Srinivasan, would seem to be a real one: 'agriculture has been generally successful in India with the average growth rates being 2.5% and 3.1% per annum in 1965–80 and 1981–90' (1993, 10n8).

35 See Nayyar, ed. (1994a) for an excellent collection of reprinted papers on the debate concerning industrial growth and stagnation, with a valuable introduction by the editor.

36 In a footnote, Bhagwati does note that in the first half of the 1980s total factor productivity in the manufacturing industry grew at 3.4 per cent per annum compared with no growth in the previous 15 years (1993, 45n12). But that is as much as we get.

37 India's competence is noted in basic metals, like steel and aluminium; in capital goods, like machine tools and heavy electricals; in heavy chemicals; in petroleum and petroleum products; and in 'sunrise' industries like electronics.

38 Vyasulu et al. (1991, 2206) show that the industrial growth rate, which was 4.4 per cent per annum between 1970–71 and 1980–81, grew to 7 per cent in 1981–82 to 1984–85 and 8.5 per cent in 1985–86 to 1989–90.

39 I would base such a conclusion on the data presented in the following: for 1960–61 Dandekar and Rath (1971, 6, 8, 24–8), Bardhan (1974, 272–8), and Ahluwalia (1985); and for 1973–74, Dandekar (1986) and Chandrasekhar and Sen (1996, 101) and Sen (1997). Note that I do not, necessarily, happen upon the precise figures arrived at by these scholars, but opt, rather, for a likely broad figure. Space forbids a detailed account of the reasons why some estimates seem more likely than others.

40 For a brief treatment see Byres and Nolan (1976, 80–81).

41 On the constriction of the home market, in relation to the industrial stagnation experienced between the mid-1960s and the late 1970s, see, for example, Chakravarty (1994, 262), Nayyar (1994b, 232–6), and Sau (1994, 38).

42 On this see Byres (1976).

43 On poverty alleviation schemes in India generally see Bandyopadhyay (1985) and Rao (1994, Part 2, 83–156); on IRDP, Copestake (1992); and on the employment generating schemes, especially JRY, Neelakantan (1994) and Chathukulam and Kurien (1995).

44 For a comprehensive treatment of the undeniable increase in levels of poverty consequent upon the imposition of IMF and World Bank stabilization and structural adjustment programmes in Latin America and Africa see Stewart (1995).

45 For detailed documentation see Deyo (1987), White (1988), Amsden (1985 and 1989), Wade (1990), Jones and Sakong (1980), Appelbaum and Henderson (1992) and Chang (1994, ch. 4).

46 The report draws on some of the sources noted in the previous footnote, especially Amsden (1989) and Wade (1990). Other sources drawn upon are: Pack and Westphal (1986); Westphal, Ree and Pursell (1988); McKinnon (1973). It was prepared by a team led by John Page, which comprised Nancy Birdsall, Ed Campos, W. Max Corden, Chang-Shik Kim, Howard Pack, Richard Sabot, Joseph E. Stiglitz and Marilou Uy.

47 For a rigorous statement of that case see Chakravarty (1993b).

References

Ahluwalia, Montek S. 1976. 'Inequality, Poverty and Development'. *Journal of Development Economics* 3, no. 4: 307–42. Reprinted in *Development Economics and Policy: Readings* edited by I. Livingstone. London: Allen and Unwin. 1981.

_______. 1978. 'Rural Poverty and Agricultural Performance in India'. *Journal of Development Studies* 14, no. 3: 298–323.

_______. 1985. 'Rural Poverty, Agricultural Production and Prices'. In *Agricultural Change and Rural Poverty: Variations on a Theme by Dharm Narain* edited by John W. Mellor and Gunvant M. Desai. Baltimore and London: Johns Hopkins University Press.

_______. 1988. 'India's Economic Performance'. In *The Indian Economy: Recent Developments and Future Prospects* edited by Robert E. B. Lucas and Gustav F. Papanek. Boulder, CO and London: Westview Press.

_______. 1995. 'India's Economic Reforms'. In *India: The Future of Economic Reform* edited by Robert Cassen and Vijay Joshi. New Delhi: Oxford University Press.

Amsden, Alice. 1985. 'The State and Taiwan's Economic Development'. In *Bringing the State Back In* edited by P. Evans, D. Rueschemeyer and T. Skocpol. Cambridge: Cambridge University Press.

_______. 1989. *Asia's Next Giant.* New York: Oxford University Press.

Anon. 1966. 'Purposeful Economics'. *Times Literary Supplement*, December 8. In 1966 reviews in the *Times Literary Supplement* were still anonymous. This one, in fact, was by Peter Bauer and is reprinted in Bauer (1971), with the same title.

Appelbaum, Richard P. and Jeffrey Henderson, eds. 1992. *States and Development in the Asian Pacific Rim.* London and New Delhi: Sage Publications.

Bandyopadhyay, D. 1985. 'An Evaluation of Policies and Programmes for the Alleviation of Rural Poverty in India'. In *Strategies for Alleviating Poverty in Rural Asia* edited by Rizwanul Islam. Dhaka and Bangkok: Bangladesh Institute of Development Studies and International Labour Organization.

Bardhan, Pranab. 1974. 'On the Incidence of Poverty in Rural India in the Sixties'. In *Poverty and Income Distribution in India* edited by T. N. Srinivasan and P. K. Bardhan. Calcutta: Statistical Publishing Society. This is a revised version of a paper originally published in *Economic and Political Weekly* 8, nos. 4–6: 245–7, 249, 251, 253–4.

Barone, Enrico. 1908. 'Il ministerio della produzione nello stato collettivista'. *Giornali degli Economist.* Translated into English and reprinted in *Collectivist Economic Planning: Critical Studies on the Possibilities of Socialism* edited by F. A. von Hayek. London: Routledge.

______. 1935. 'The Ministry of Production in the Collectivist State'. In *Collectivist Economic Planning: Critical Studies on the Possibilities of Socialism* edited by F. A. von Hayek. London: Routledge. This is a translation of Barone (1908).

Bauer, Peter. 1961. *Indian Economic Policy and Development.* London: Allen and Unwin.

______. 1971. *Dissent on Development: Studies and Debates in Development Economics.* London: Weidenfeld and Nicolson.

Basu, Kaushik. 1993. 'Structural Reform in India, 1991–93. Experience and Agenda'. *Economic and Political Weekly* 28, no. 48: 2599–2605.

Bernstein, Henry. 1990. 'Agricultural "Modernisation" and the Era of Structural Adjustment: Observations on Sub-Saharan Africa'. *Journal of Peasant Studies* 18, no. 1: 3–35.

Bhaduri, Amit and Deepak Nayyar. 1996. *The Intelligent Reader's Guide to Liberalisation.* New Delhi: Penguin Books.

Bhagwati, Jagdish. 1964. 'The Case for Devaluation'. *Economic Weekly* 14, no. 31: 1263–6.

______. 1966. *The Economics of Underdeveloped Countries.* London: Weidenfeld and Nicolson.

______. 1993. *India in Transition: Freeing the Economy.* Oxford: Clarendon Press.

Bhagwati, Jagdish and Sukhamoy Chakravarty. 1969. 'Contributions to Indian Economic Analysis: A Survey'. *American Economic Review* 59, no. 4: 1–73.

Bhagwati, Jagdish and Padma Desai. 1970. *India, Planning for Industrialization: Industrialization and Trade Policies Since 1951.* London: Oxford University Press for the Development Centre of the Organization for Economic Co-Operation and Development.

Bhagwati, Jagdish and T. N. Srinivasan. 1993. *India's Economic Reforms.* New Delhi: Ministry of Finance, Government of India.

Bhalla, S., ed. 1994. *Economic Liberalization and Indian Agriculture.* New Delhi: Institute for Studies in Industrial Development.

______. 1995. 'New Economic Policy – A Tentative Evaluation'. *Studies in Humanities and Social Sciences* 2, no. 1.

Bhargava, S. and V. Joshi. 1990. 'Increase in India's Growth Rate: Facts and Tentative Explanations'. *Economic and Political Weekly* 25, nos. 48–9: 2657–61.

B. M. 1991. 'Towards Neo-Colonial Dependency'. *Economic and Political Weekly* 26, nos. 31–2: 1837–9.

______. 1993. 'Double-Talk on EFF'. *Economic and Political Weekly* 28, no. 21: 1015–16.

Byres, Terence J. 1966a. 'The Political Economy of Indian Planning'. *Journal of Development Studies* 2, no. 2: 189–207.

______. 1966b. 'Indian Planning on the Eve of the Fourth Five Year Plan'. *The World Today* 22, no. 3: 92–9.

______. 1976. 'The Exploiters of Fate'. *Ceres. FAO Review on Agriculture and Development* 9, no. 5: 45–8.

______. 1981. 'The New Technology, Class Formation and Class Action in the Indian Countryside'. *Journal of Peasant Studies* 8, no. 4: 405–54.

Byres, Terence J., and Peter Nolan. 1976. *Inequality: India and China Compared, 1950–70.* Milton Keynes: Open University Press.

Cassen, Robert and Vijay Joshi, eds. 1995. *India: The Future of Economic Reform*. New Delhi: Oxford University Press.

Chakravarty, Sukhamoy. 1987. *Development Planning: The Indian Experience*. Oxford: Clarendon Press.

_______. 1993a. 'The State of Development Economics'. In his *Selected Economic Writings*. Delhi: Oxford University Press. This is an essay based on a lecture delivered at Manchester University Department of Economics on 18 March, 1985.

_______. 1993b. 'Theory of Development Planning: An Appraisal'. In his *Selected Economic Writings*. Delhi: Oxford University Press. This was first published in *Economic Structure and Development* edited by H. C. Bos, H. Linnemann and P. de Wolff. Amsterdam: North Holland, 1973.

_______. 1994. 'On the Question of Home Market and Prospects for Indian Growth': In *Industrial Growth and Stagnation: The Debate in India* edited by Deepak Nayyar. Bombay: Oxford University Press for the Sameeksha Trust. First published in *Economic and Political Weekly* 14, nos. 30–32: 1229–31, 1233, 1235, 1237–9, 1241–2. This is also reprinted in his *Selected Economic Writings*, Delhi: Oxford University Press.

Chandrasekhar, C. P. and Abhijit Sen. 1996. 'Statistical Truths: Economic Reform and Poverty'. *Frontline* 13, no. 3.

Chang, Ha-Joon. 1994. *The Political Economy of Industrial Policy*. Basingstoke and London: Macmillan.

Chang, Ha-Joon and Robert Rowthorn, eds. 1995. *The Role of the State in Economic Change*. Oxford: Clarendon Press. Papers presented at a seminar held in April 1993 at King's College, Cambridge.

Chathukulam, Jos and V. K. Kurien. 1995. 'Jawahar Rozgar Yojana: An Assessment'. *Economic and Political Weekly* 30, no. 6: 343–4.

Copestake, James G. 1992. 'The Integrated Rural Development Programme: Performance During the Sixth Plan, Policy Responses and Proposals for Reform'. In *Poverty in India: Research and Policy* edited by Barbara Harriss, S. Guhan and R. H. Cassen. Bombay: Oxford University Press.

Dandekar, V. M. 1986. 'Agricultural Employment and Poverty'. *Economic and Political Weekly* 25, nos. 38–9: A90–A100.

Dandekar, V. M. and Nilakantha Rath. 1971. *Poverty in India*. Bombay: Indian School of Political Economy. Published originally in *Economic and Political Weekly* 6, nos. 1–2: 25–7, 29–48, 106–46.

Deyo, F, ed. 1987. *The Political Economy of the New Asian Industrialism*. Ithaca and London: Cornell University Press.

Dholakia, Ravinder H. 1994. 'Spatial Dimensions of Acceleration of Economic Growth in India'. *Economic and Political Weekly* 29, no. 35: 2303–9.

Drèze, Jean and Amartya Sen. 1995. *Economic Development and Social Opportunity*. Delhi: Oxford University Press.

EPW Research Foundation. 1993. 'Sugar Coating for Tougher Conditionalities to Come'. *Economic and Political Weekly* 28, no. 31: 1563–7.

_______. 1994. 'What Has Gone Wrong with the Economic Reforms?' *Economic and Political Weekly* 29, no. 18: 1049–53.

_______. 1995a. 'National Accounts Statistics of India – 1: Macro-Aggregates'. *Economic and Political Weekly* 30, no. 46: 2955–64.

_______. 1995b. 'National Accounts Statistics of India – 2: Domestic Savings and Capital Formation'. *Economic and Political Weekly* 30, no. 47: 3021–36.

Findlay, R. 1990. 'The New Political Economy: Its Explanatory Power for LDCs'. *Economics and Politics* 2, no. 2: 193–221.

Ganesh, Kumar N. 1992. 'Some Comments on the Debate on India's Economic Growth in the 1980s'. *Indian Economic Journal* 39, no. 4: 102–11.

Government of India. 1993. June. *Economic Reforms: Two Years After and the Task Ahead*, Discussion Paper. New Delhi: Ministry of Finance.

Guha, Ashok, ed. 1990. *Economic Liberalization, Industrial Structure and Growth in India.* New Delhi: Oxford University Press.

Harris, Laurence. 1983. *Banking on the Fund: The IMF*, Open University Third World Studies, U204, Case Study 9. Milton Keynes: Open University Press.

Hayek, F. A. von., ed. 1935. *Collectivist Economic Planning: Critical Studies on the Possibilities of Socialism.* London: Routledge.

_______. 1935. 'The Nature and History of the Problem'. Introduction to *Collectivist Economic Planning: Critical Studies on the Possibilities of Socialism.* London: Routledge.

Johnson, Chalmers. 1982. *MITI and the Japanese Miracle.* Stanford: Stanford University Press.

Jones, L. and I. Sakong. 1980. *Government, Business and Entrepreneurship in Economic Development: The Korean Case.* Cambridge, MA: Harvard University Press.

Joshi, Vijay and I. M. D. Little. 1994. *India: Macroeconomics and Political Economy, 1964–1991.* Delhi: Oxford University Press.

J. M. 1993. 'Discussing Economic Reforms: Achievements and Future Intent'. *Economic and Political Weekly* 28, no. 31: 1556–60.

Killick, Tony, ed. 1984. *The Quest for Economic Stabilisation: The IMF and the Third World.* London: Gower in association with the Overseas Development Institute.

Krueger, A. 1974. 'The Political Economy of the Rent-Seeking Society'. *American Economic Review* 64, no. 3: 291–303.

Krishna, Raj. 1983. 'Growth, Investment and Poverty in Mid-Term Appraisal of Sixth Plan'. *Economic and Political Weekly* 28, no. 47: 1972–3, 1975–7.

Kurien, C. T. 1996. *Economic Reforms and the People.* Delhi: Madhyam Books. A series of articles that originally appeared in *Frontline*, and written between November 1995 and January 1996.

Lange, Oscar. 1936 and 1937. 'On the Economic Theory of Socialism'. *Review of Economic Studies* 4, no. 1: 53–71 and 2: 123–42. Reprinted in Lange and Taylor (1939).

Lange, Oscar and Fred Taylor. 1939. *On the Economic Theory of Socialism.* Minneapolis: University of Minnesota Press. Edited, with an Introduction by Benjamin E. Lippincot. This is a reprint of Lange (1936 and 1937) and Taylor (1929). It was reprinted in 1970 by Augustus M. Kelley, New York.

Lavoie, D. 1985. *Rivalry and Central Planning.* Cambridge: Cambridge University Press.

Little, I. M. D. 1961. Review of Bauer (1961). *Economic Journal* 71, no. 284: 835–8.

Little, I. M. D., T. Scitovsky and M. F. G. Scott. 1970. *Industry and Trade in Some Developing Countries: A Comparative Study.* London: Oxford University Press for the Development Centre of the Organization for Economic Co-Operation and Development.

Lucas, Robert E. B. and Gustav F. Papanek, eds. 1988. *The Indian Economy. Recent Developments and Future Prospects.* Boulder, CO and London: Westview Press.

McKinnon, Ronald I. 1973. *Money and Capital in Economic Development.* Washington, DC: Brookings Institution.

Marx, Karl. 1976. *Capital, Volume 1.* Harmondsworth, Middlesex and London: Penguin Books and New Left Review.

Mellor, John W. and Gunvant M. Desai, eds. 1985. *Agricultural Change and Rural Poverty: Variations on a Theme by Dharm Narain.* Baltimore and London: Johns Hopkins University Press.

Mises, Ludwig von. 1920. 'Die Wirtschaftsrechnung im sozialistischen Gemeinwesen'. *Archiv fur Sozialwissenschaften* 47 S.86–121. Reprinted in Hayek (ed.) (1935).

_______. 1935. 'Economic Calculation in the Socialist Commonwealth'. In Hayek (ed.) (1935). A reprint of Mises (1920).

_______. 1936. *Socialism: An Economic and Sociological Analysis.* London: Cape. Translated by J. Kahane from the revised 1932 edition of *Die Gemeinwirtschaft*, which was first published in 1922. A new and enlarged edition was published in 1959, by Yale University Press, New Haven.

Mosley, Paul, Jane Harrigan and John Toye. 1995. *Aid and Power: The World Bank and Policy-Based Lending*, vol. 1. London and New York: Routledge. Second edition.

Nagaraj, R. 1990. 'Growth Rate of India's GDP, 1950–51 to 1987–88: Examination of an Alternative Hypothesis'. *Economic and Political Weekly* 25, no. 26: 1396–1403.

______. 1991. 'Increase in India's Growth Rate'. *Economic and Political Weekly* 26, no. 15: 1002–4.

Nayyar, Deepak. 1993. 'Indian Economy at the Crossroads: Illusions and Realities'. *Economic and Political Weekly* 28, no. 15: 639–41, 643, 645, 647, 649, 651, 653.

______, ed. 1994a. *Industrial Growth and Stagnation: The Debate in India*. Bombay: Oxford University Press for the Sameeksha Trust.

______. 1994b. 'Industrial Development in India. Some Reflections on Growth and Stagnation'. in Nayyar (ed.) (1994). First published in *Economic and Political Weekly* 13, nos. 31–3: 1265–7, 1269, 1271, 1273, 1275–8.

______. 1996. *Economic Liberalization in India. Analytics, Experience and Lessons*. Hyderabad: Orient Longman. This is an essay based on the R. C. Dutt Lectures on Political Economy, delivered in 1993, in Calcutta.

Neelakantan, M. 1994. 'Jawahar Rozgar Yojana. An Assessment through Concurrent Evaluation'. *Economic and Political Weekly* 29, no. 49: 3091–7.

Nolan, Peter. 1988. *The Political Economy of Collective Farms*. Cambridge: Polity Press.

North, Douglas C. 1981. 'A Neoclassical Theory of the State' in his *Structure and Change in Economic History*. New York: W. W. Norton and Co.

Oommen, M. A. 1993. 'Bhagwati–Srinivasan Report on Economic Reforms'. *Economic and Political Weekly* 28, no. 40: 2116–18.

Pack, Howard and Larry E. Westphal. 1986. 'Industrial Strategy and Technological Change: Theory vs Reality'. *Journal of Development Economics* 22, no. 1: 87–128.

Parikh, Kirit S. and R. Sudarshan, eds. 1993. *Human Development and Structural Adjustment*. Madras: Macmillan. Papers and Proceedings of the UNDP Symposium on Economic Growth, Sustainable Development and Poverty Alleviation in India (3–6 January, 1992, Bombay).

Patnaik, Prabhat. 1994. 'International Capital and National Economic Policy. A Critique of India's Economic Reforms'. *Economic and Political Weekly* 29, no. 12: 683–9.

______. 1995a. 'A Perspective on the Recent Phase of India's Economic Development'. In his *Whatever Happened to Imperialism and Other Essays*. New Delhi: Tulika. This was first published in *Social Scientist* 16, no. 2: 3–16.

______. 1995b. 'Investment and Growth in a Liberalized Economy'. In his *Whatever Happened to Imperialism and Other Essays*. New Delhi: Tulika. This is the text of the Gokhale Endowment Lectures, delivered at the Department of Economics, University of Madras, in April 1994.

Patnaik, Prabhat and C. P. Chandrasekhar. 1995. 'Indian Economy under Structural Adjustment'. *Economic and Political Weekly* 30, no. 47: 3001–13.

______. 1996. 'Investment, Exports and Growth. A Cross-Country Analysis'. *Economic and Political Weekly* 31, no. 1: 31–6.

Policy Watch. 1991. 'IMF Stand-By Loan Conditions'. *Economic and Political Weekly* 26, no. 52.

Posner, R. 1975. 'The Social Costs of Monopoly and Regulation'. *Journal of Political Economy* 83, no. 4: 807–28.

Rao, Hanumantha C. H. 1994. *Agricultural Growth, Rural Poverty and Environmental Degradation in India*. Delhi: Oxford University Press.

Rao, Hanumantha C. H. and Hans Linnemann, eds. 1996. *Economic Reforms and Poverty Alleviation in India*. New Delhi: Sage Publications. Based on papers presented at a seminar in The Hague, on 29 and 30 November, 1994.

Rudra, Ashok. 1975. *Indian Plan Models*. Bombay: Allied Publishers.

______. 1985. 'Planning in India: An Evaluation in Terms of its Models'. *Economic and Political Weekly* 20, no. 17: 758–64.

______. 1991. 'Privatisation and Deregulation'. *Economic and Political Weekly* 26, no. 51: 1100.

Saith, Ashwani. 1981. 'Production, Prices and Poverty in Rural India'. *Journal of Development Studies* 17, no. 2: 196–213.

______. 1995. 'Some Reflections on the Indian Experience of Re-Structuring'. Unpublished manuscript, dated 13th January.

Sau, Ranjit. 1994. 'Some Aspects of Inter-Sectoral Resource Flow'. In Nayyar (ed.) (1994). First published in *Economic and Political Weekly* 9, nos. 32–4: 1277, 1279, 1281, 1283–4.

Sen, Abhijit. 1997. 'Rural Poverty in India. A Re-Examination of Issues in the Context of Economic Reforms'. Unpublished manuscript.

Shenoy, B. R. 1963. *Indian Planning and Economic Development.* Bombay: Asia Publishing House.

______. 1968. *Indian Economic Policy*. Bombay: Popular Prakashan.

Shetty, S. L. 1978. *Structural Retrogression in the Indian Economy Since the Mid-Sixties*. Bombay: Economic and Political Weekly. This is an enlarged and updated reprint of a paper that first appeared in *Economic and Political Weekly* 13, nos. 6–7: 185–7, 189, 191–3, 195, 197–9, 201–2, 204–5, 207–19, 221–5, 227–44.

Shroff, Manu. 1993. 'Indian Economy at the Crossroads'. *Economic and Political Weekly* 28, no. 19: 943–4.

Srinivasan, T. N. 1985. 'Agricultural Production, Relative Prices, Entitlements, and Poverty'. In *Agricultural Change and Rural Poverty: Variations on a Theme by Dharm Narain* edited by John W. Mellor and Gunvant M. Desai. Baltimore and London: Johns Hopkins University Press.

______. 1991a. 'Indian Development Strategy: An Exchange of Views'. *Economic and Political Weekly* 26, nos. 31–2: 1850–52.

______. 1991b. 'Reform of Industrial and Trade Policies'. *Economic and Political Weekly* 26, no. 37: 2143–5.

______. 1993. 'Indian Economic Reforms: Background, Rationale and Next Steps'. Mimeo. Economic Growth Center. Yale University.

Srinivasan, T. N. and P. K. Bardhan, eds. 1974. *Poverty and Income Distribution in India.* Calcutta: Statistical Publishing Society.

Stewart, Frances. 1995. *Adjustment and Poverty: Options and Choices.* London and New York: Routledge.

Taylor, Fred. 1929. 'The Guidance of Production in a Socialist State'. *American Economic Review* 19, no. 1: 1–8. This is reprinted in Lange and Taylor (1939).

______. 1939. A reprint of Taylor (1929) in Lange and Taylor (1939).

Vyasulu, Vinod, Sukhpal Singh, D. Rajasekhar, Pooja Kaushik and A. Indira. 1991. 'Towards a Political Economy of the Economic Policy Changes'. *Economic and Political Weekly* 26, no. 38: 2205–11.

Wadhva, Charan D. 1994. *Economic Reforms in India and the Market Economy.* New Delhi: Allied Publishers.

Wade, Robert, 1990. *Governing the Market. Economic Theory and the Role of Government in East Asian Industrialization.* Princeton, NJ: Princeton University Press.

Westphal, Larry E., Yung Whee Ree and Garry Pursell. 1988. *Korean Industrial Competence: Where It Came From,* World Bank Staff Working Paper 469, Washington, DC.

White, Gordon, ed. 1988. *Developmental States in East Asia.* London and Basingstoke: Macmillan.

World Bank. 1990. *India: Trends, Issues and Options.* Country Economic Memorandum 1.

______. 1993. *The East Asian Miracle: Economic Growth and Public Policy.* Oxford: Oxford University Press for the World Bank.

Chapter 3

PREDATORY GROWTH*

Amit Bhaduri

Over the last two decades or so, the two most populous large countries in the world, China and India, have been growing at rates considerably higher than the world average. In recent years the growth rate of the national product of China has been about three times, and that of India approximately two times, that of the world average. This has led to a clever defence of globalization by a former chief economist of the International Monetary Fund (IMF) (Fisher 2003). Although China and India feature as only two among some 150 countries for which data are available, he reminds us that together they account for the majority of the poor in the world. This means that even if the rich and the poor countries of the world are not converging in terms of per capita income, the well above world average rate of growth of these two large countries implies that the current phase of globalization is reducing global inequality and poverty at a rate like never before.

Statistical half truths can be more misleading at times than untruths. And this might be one of them, insofar as the experiences of ordinary Indians contradict such statistical artefacts. Since citizens in India can reasonably freely express their views at least at the time of elections, their electoral verdicts on the regime of high growth should be indicative. They have invariably been negative. Not only did the 'shining India' image crash badly in the last general election, even the present prime minister, widely presented as the 'guru' of India's economic liberalization in the media, could never personally win an election in his life. As a result, come election time, and all parties talk not of economic reform, liberalization and globalization, but of greater welfare measures to be initiated by the state; gone election times, and the reform agenda is back. Something clearly needs to be deciphered from such predictable swings in political pronouncement.

Lived Experiences

Politicians know that ordinary people are not persuaded by statistical mirages and numbers, but by their daily experiences. They do not accept high growth at its face value as unambiguously beneficial. If the distribution of income turns viciously against them and the opportunities for reasonable employment and livelihood do not expand with high growth,

* This chapter is reproduced from the original version of the article published in *Economic and Political Weekly* 43, no. 16 (19 April 2008): 10–14.

the purpose of higher growth will be widely questioned in a democracy. This is indeed what is happening, and it might even appear to some as paradoxical. The festive mood generated by high growth is marinated in popular dissent and despair, turning often into repressed anger. Like a malignant malaise, a sense of political unease is spreading insidiously along with the near double-digit growth. And, no major political party, irrespective of their right or left label, is escaping it because they all subscribe to an ideology of growth at any cost.

Unequal Growth

What exactly is the nature of this paradoxical growth that increases output and popular anger at the same time? India has long been accustomed to extensive poverty coexisting with growth, with or without its 'socialist pattern'. It continues to have anywhere between one-third and one-fourth of its population living in subhuman, absolute poverty. The number of people condemned to absolute poverty declined very slowly in India over the last two decades, leaving some 303 million people still in utter misery. In contrast China did better with the number of absolutely poor declining from 53 per cent to 8 per cent, that is, a reduction of some 45 percentage points, quite an achievement compared to India's 17 percentage points. However, while China grew faster, inequality or relative poverty also grew, so that the increasing gap between the richer and the poorer sections in Chinese society during the recent period has been one of the worst in recorded economic history, perhaps with the exception of some former socialist countries immediately after the collapse of the Soviet Union.

The share in national income of the poorest 20 per cent of the population in contemporary China is 5.9 per cent, compared to 8.2 per cent in India (Radhakrishna 2008). This implies that the lowest 20 per cent income group in China and in India receives about 30 and 40 per cent of the per capita average income of their respective countries. However, since China has over two times the average per capita income of India in terms of both purchasing power parity and dollar income, the poorest 20 per cent in India are better off in relative terms but worse off in absolute terms.

The Gini coefficient, lying between zero and one, measures inequality, and increases in value with the degree of inequality. In China, it had a value close to 0.50 in 2006, one of the highest in the world. Inequality has grown also in India, but less sharply. Between 1993–94 and 2004–05, the coefficient rose from 0.25 to 0.27 in urban areas, and from 0.31 to 0.35 in rural areas. Every dimension of inequality, among the regions, among the professions and sectors, and in particular between urban and rural areas has also grown rapidly in both countries, even faster in China than in India. In short, China has done better than India in reducing absolute poverty, but worse in allowing the gap to grow rapidly between the rich and the poor during the recent period of high growth. A central fact stands out. Despite vast differences in the political systems of the two countries, the common factor has been increasing inequality accompanying higher growth.

What is not usually realized is that the growth in output and in inequality are not two isolated phenomena. One frequently comes across the platitude that high growth will soon be trickling down to the poor, or that redistributive action by the state through fiscal measures could decrease inequality while keeping up the growth rate. These statements are comfortable but unworkable, because they miss the main characteristic of the growth process underway. This pattern of growth is propelled by a powerful reinforcing mechanism, which the economist Gunner Myrdal once described as 'cumulative causation'. The mechanism by which growing inequality drives growth, and growth fuels further inequality has its origin in two different factors, both related to some extent to globalization.

Jobless Growth

First, in contrast to earlier times when less than 4 per cent growth on an average was associated with 2 per cent growth in employment, India is experiencing a growth rate of some 7–8 per cent in recent years, but the growth in regular employment has hardly exceeded 1 per cent. This means most of the growth, some 5–6 per cent of the GDP, is the result not of employment expansion but of higher output per worker. This high growth of output has its source in the growth of labour productivity. According to official statistics, between 1991 and 2004 employment fell in the organized public sector, and the organized private sector hardly compensated for it. In the corporate sector, and in some organized industries, productivity growth comes from mechanization and longer hours of work. Edward Luce of the *Financial Times* (London) reported that the Jamshedpur steel plant of the Tatas employed 85,000 workers in 1991 to produce one million tonnes of steel worth $0.8 million. In 2005, the production rose to five million tonnes, worth about $5 million, while employment fell to 44,000. In short, output increased approximately by a factor of five, while employment dropped by a factor of half, implying an increase in labour productivity by a factor of 10.

Similarly, Tata Motors in Pune reduced the number of workers from 35,000 to 21,000 but increased the production of vehicles from 129,000 to 311,500 between 1999 and 2004, implying a labour productivity increase by a factor of four. Stephen Roach, chief economist of Morgan Stanley, reports a similar case at the Bajaj motorcycle factory in Pune. In the mid-1990s the factory employed 24,000 workers to produce one million units of two-wheelers. Aided by Japanese robotics and Indian information technology, in 2004, 10,500 workers turned out 2.4 million units – more than double the output with less than half the labour force, an increase in labour productivity by a factor of nearly 6.[1] One could multiply such examples, but this is broadly the name of the game everywhere in the private corporate sector.

Augmented Profit and Misery

The manifold increase in labour productivity, without a corresponding increase in wages and salaries, becomes an enormous source of profit, and also a source of international price competitiveness in a globalizing world. Nevertheless, this is not the entire story, perhaps not even the most important part of the story. The whole organized sector to which the corporate sector belongs accounts for less than a tenth of the labour force. Simply by the arithmetic of weighted averages, a 5–6 per cent annual growth in labour productivity in the entire economy is possible only if the unorganized sector accounting for the remaining 90 per cent of the labour force also contributes to the growth in labour productivity. Direct information is not available on this count, but several micro-studies and surveys show the broad pattern. Growth of labour productivity in the unorganized sector, which includes most of agriculture, comes from lengthening the hours of work to a significant extent, as this sector has no labour laws worth the name, or social security to protect workers. Subcontracting to the unorganized sector along with casualization of labour on a large scale becomes a convenient device to ensure longer hours of work without higher pay. Self-employed workers, totalling 260 million, expanded fastest during the high growth regime, providing an invisible source of labour productivity growth (the data in Rangarajan et al. 2007 could be interpreted this way). Ruthless self-exploitation by many of these workers in a desperate attempt to survive by doing long hours of work with very little extra earning adds both to productivity growth, often augmenting corporate profit, and to human misery.

However, inequality is increasing for another reason. Its ideology, often described as neoliberalism, is easily visible at one level; but the underlying deeper reason is seldom discussed. The increasing openness of the Indian economy to international finance and capital flows, rather than to trades in goods and services, has had the consequence of paralysing many pro-poor public policies. Despite the fact that we continue to import more than we export (unlike China), India's comfortable foreign reserves position is mostly the result of accumulated portfolio investments and short-term capital inflows from various financial institutions. To keep the show going in this way, the fiscal and the monetary policies of the government need to comply with the interests of the financial markets. That is the reason why successive Indian governments have willingly accepted the Fiscal Responsibility and Budget Management Act (2003) restricting deficit spending. Similarly, the idea has gained support that the government should raise resources through privatization and so-called public–private partnership, but not through raising fiscal deficit or imposing a significant turnover tax on transactions of securities. These measures rattle the 'sentiment' of the financial markets, so governments remain wary of them.

The hidden agenda vigorously pursued by governments of all colour has been to keep the large private players in the financial markets in a happy mood. Since the private banks and financial institutions usually take their lead from the IMF and the World Bank, this bestows on these multilateral agencies considerable power over the formulation of government policies. However, the burden of such policies is borne largely by the poor of this country. This has had a crippling effect on policies for expanding public expenditure for the poor in the social sector. Inequality and distress grow as the state rolls back public expenditure in social services like basic health, education and public distribution and neglects the poor, while the discipline imposed by the financial markets serves the rich and the corporations. This process of high growth traps roughly one in three citizens of India in extreme poverty with no possibility of escape through either regular employment growth or relief through state expenditure on social services. The high growth scene of India appears to them like a wasteland leading to the hell described by the great Italian poet Dante. On the gate of his imagined hell is written, 'Abandon all hope, ye who enter here'. Extremely slow growth in employment and feeble public action exacerbates inequality, as a disproportionately large share of the increasing output and income from growth goes to the richer section of the population, not more than, say, the top 20 per cent of the income receivers in India. At the extreme ends of income distribution the picture that emerges is one of striking contrasts. According to the *Forbes* magazine list for 2007, the number of Indian billionaires rose from nine in 2004 to 40 in 2007: much richer countries like Japan had only 24, France 14 and Italy 14. Even China, despite its sharply increasing inequality, had only 17 billionaires. The combined wealth of Indian billionaires increased from $106 billion to $170 billion in the single year 2006–07 (information from *Forbes* quoted in Jain and Gupta 2008). This 60 per cent increase in wealth would not have been possible except through transfer of land from the state and central governments to the private corporations in the name of 'public purpose', for mining, industrialization and special economic zones (SEZs). Estimates based on corporate profits suggest that, since 2000–01, each additional per cent growth of GDP has led to an average of some 2.5 per cent growth in corporate profits. India's high growth has certainly benefited the corporations more than anyone else.

After several years of high growth along these lines, India of the twenty-first century has the distinction of being second only to the US in terms of the combined total wealth of its corporate billionaires coexisting with the largest number of homeless, ill-fed and illiterates in the world. Not surprisingly, for ordinary Indians at the receiving end, this growth process is devoid of all hope for escape. Nearly half of Indian children under six years are underweight or suffer from malnutrition, nearly 80 per cent from anaemia, while some 40 per cent of Indian adults suffer from chronic energy deficit. Destitution, chronic hunger and poverty silently kill and cripple thousands, systematically picking on the more vulnerable. The problem is more acute in rural India, among small children, pregnant females, dalits and adivasis, especially in the poorer states (Radhakrishna 2008), while market-oriented policies and reforms continue to widen the gap between the rich and the poor, as well as among regions.

Income Elasticities of Demand

The growth dynamics in operation are being fed continuously by growing inequality. With their income rapidly growing, the richer group of Indians demand a set of goods which lie outside the reach of the rest in the society (think of air-conditioned malls, luxury hotels, restaurants and apartments, private cars, world-class cities where the poor would be made invisible). The market for these goods expands rapidly. For instance, we are told that more than three in four Indians do not have a daily income of $2. They can hardly be a part of this growing market. However, the logic of the market now takes over, as the market is dictated by purchasing power. Its logic is to produce those goods for which there is enough demand backed by money, so that high prices can be charged and handsome profits can be made. As the income of the privileged grows rapidly, the market for the luxury goods they demand grows even faster through the operation of the 'income elasticities of demand'. These elasticities roughly measure the per cent growth in the demand for particular goods due to 1 per cent growth in income (at unchanged prices). Typically, goods consumed by the rich have income elasticities greater than unity, implying that the demand for a whole range of luxury goods consumed by the rich expands even faster than the growth in their income. Thus, the pattern of production is dictated by this process of growth through raising the income of the rich faster than that of the rest of the society, and also because the income elasticities operate to increase even faster than income the demand for luxuries.

Anti-poor

The production structure resulting from this market-driven high growth is heavily biased against the poor. While demand expands rapidly for various upmarket goods, demand for the basic necessities of life hardly expands. Not only is there little growth in the purchasing power of the poor, but reduction in welfare expenditures by the state stunts the growth in demand for necessities. The rapid shift in the output composition in favour of services might be indicative of this process at the macro level (Rakshit 2007). But specific examples abound. We have state-of-the-art corporate-run expensive hospitals, nursing homes and spas for the rich, but not enough money to control malaria and tuberculosis, which require inexpensive treatment. So these diseases continue to kill the largest numbers. Lack of sanitation and clean drinking water transmit deadly diseases, especially to small children, which could be prevented at little cost, while various brands of bottled water multiply for those who can afford them. Private schools for rich kids often have monthly fees that are higher than the annual income of an average unskilled Indian worker, while the poor often have to be satisfied with schools without teachers, or classrooms.

Over time an increasingly irreversible production structure in favour of the rich begins to consolidate itself, because the investments embodied in the specific capital goods created to produce luxuries cannot easily be converted to producing basic necessities. (The luxury hotel or spa cannot be converted easily to a primary health centre in a village, etc.) And yet, it is the logic of the market to direct investments towards the most productive and profitable sectors for 'the efficient allocation of resources'. The price mechanism sends signals to guide this allocation, but the prices that rule are largely a consequence of the growing unequal distribution of income in the society. The market becomes a bad master when the distribution of income is bad.

Heightened Misery for the Poor

There are insidious consequences of such a composition of output biased in favour of the rich that our liberalized market system produces. It is highly energy, water and other nonreproducible resources intensive, and often does unacceptable violence to the environment. We only have to think of the energy and material content of air-conditioned malls, luxury hotels and apartments, air travel, or private cars as means of transport. These are no doubt symbols of 'world-class' cities in a poor country, diverting resources from the countryside where most live. They create a black hole of urbanization with a giant appetite for primary nonreproducible resources. Many are forced to migrate to cities as fertile land is diverted to nonagricultural use, water and electricity are taken away from farms in critical agricultural seasons to supply cities, and developmental projects displace thousands. Hydroelectric power from the big dams is transmitted mostly to corporate industries and a few posh urban localities, while the nearby villages are left in darkness. Peasants even close to the cities do not get electricity or water to irrigate their land as urban India increasingly gobbles up these resources. Take the pattern of water use. According to the Comptroller and Auditor General report released to the public on March 30, 2007, Gujarat increased the allocation of Narmada waters to industry fivefold during 2006, eating into the share of drought-affected villages. Despite many promises made to villagers, water allocation stagnated at 0.86 million acres feet (MAF), and even this is being cut.

Water companies and soft drink giants like Coca-Cola sink deeper to take out pure groundwater as free raw material for their products. Peasants in surrounding areas pay, because they cannot match the technology or capital cost. Iron ore is mined out in Jharkhand, Chhattisgarh and Orissa leaving tribals without home or livelihood. Common lands which traditionally provided supplementary income to the poor in villages are encroached upon systematically by the local rich and the corporations, with the active connivance of the government. The manifest crisis engulfing Indian agriculture with more than a hundred thousand suicides by farmers over the last decade, according to official statistics, is a pointer to this process of pampering the rich, who use their growing economic power to increasingly dominate the multitude of poor.

No Place for the Poorest

The composition of output demanded by the rich is hardly producible by village artisans or the small producers. They find no place either as producers or as consumers; instead, economic activities catering to the rich have to be handed over to large corporations who can now enter in a big way into the scene. The combination of accelerating growth and rising inequality begins to work in unison. The corporations are needed to produce goods for the rich, and in the process they make their high profits and provide well-paid employment for the rich in a poor country who provide a part of the growing market. It becomes a process of destructive creation of corporate wealth, with a new coalition cutting across traditional right and left political divisions formed in the course of this road to high growth. The signboard of this road is 'progress through industrialization'.

The middle-class opinion makers and the media persons unite, and occasionally offer palliatives of 'fair compensation' to the dispossessed. Yet they are at a loss as to how to create alternative dignified livelihoods for those affected by large-scale displacement and destruction in the name of industrialization. Talks of compensation tend to be one-sided, as they focus usually on ownership and, at best, use rights for the landed. However, the multitude of the poor who eke out a living without any ownership or use right to landed property, such as agricultural labourers, fishermen or cart-drivers in rural areas, or illegal squatters and small hawkers in cities, seldom figure in this discussion about compensation. And yet, they are usually the poorest of the poor, outnumbering by far, perhaps in the ratio of 3 to 1, those who have some title to landed property. Ignoring them altogether, the state acquires with single-minded devotion land, water and resources for the private corporations for mining, industrialization or SEZs in the name of public interest.

With some tribal land that can be acquired according to the PESA (1996) Act only through the consent of the community (gram sabha), consent is frequently manufactured at gunpoint by the law and order machinery of the state, if the money power of the corporations to bribe and intimidate proves to be insufficient. The vocal supporters of industrialization never stop to ask why the very poor, who are least able, should bear the burden of the 'economic progress' of the rich.

It amounts to a process of internal colonization of the poor, mostly dalits and adivasis and other marginalized groups, through forcible dispossession and subjugation. It has set in motion a social process not altogether unknown between the imperialist 'master race' and the colonized 'natives'. As the privileged thin layer of the society distance themselves from the poor, the speed at which the secession takes place comes to be celebrated as a measure of the rapid growth of the country. Thus, India is said to be poised to become a global power in the twenty-first century, with the largest number of homeless, undernourished, illiterate children coexisting with billionaires created by this rapid growth.

An unbridled market whose rules are fixed by the corporations aided by state power shapes this process. The ideology of progress through dispossession of the poor, preached relentlessly by the united power of the rich, the middle class and the corporations, colonizes the poor directly, and indirectly it has begun to colonize our minds. The result is a sort of uniform industrialization of the mind, a standardization of thoughts which sees no other alternative. And yet, there is a fatal flaw. No matter how powerful this united campaign by the rich corporations, the media and the politicians is, even their combined power remains defenceless against the actual life experiences of the poor. If this process of growth continues for long, it will produce its own demons. No society, not even our malfunctioning democratic system, can withstand beyond a point the increasing inequality that nurtures this high growth. The rising dissent of the poor must either be suppressed with increasing state violence flouting every norm of democracy, and violence will be met with counter-violence to engulf the whole society; or, an alternative path to development that depends on deepening our democracy with popular participation has to be found. Neither the rulers nor the ruled can escape for long this challenge thrown up by the recent high growth of India.

Note

1 Data collected by Aseem Srivastava, 'Why This Growth Can Never Trickle Down'. Srivastava can be reached at aseem62@yahoo.com.

References

Alternative Survey Group. 2012. *Alternative Economic Survey, India (2006–07): Pampering Corporates, Pauperizing Masses.* New Delhi: Daanish Books.

Dev, S. Mahendra. 2008. *Inclusive Growth in India.* New Delhi: Oxford University Press.

Fisher, S. 2003. 'Globalization and Its Challenges'. *American Economic Review* 93, no. 2: 1–30.

Government of India. 2007. *Economic Survey (2006–07).* New Delhi: Ministry of Finance. *Green Left Weekly.* No. 710.

Rakshit, Mihir. 2007. 'Service-Led Growth'. *Money and Finance* 3, no. 1: 91–125.

Radhakrishna, R., ed. 2008. *India Development Report.* New Delhi: Oxford University Press.

Rangarajan, C. et al. 2007. 'Revisiting Employment and Growth'. *Money and Finance* 3, no. 2: 57–68.

Jain, Anil Kumar and Parul Gupta. 2008. 'Globalisation: The Indian Experience'. *Mainstream* 46, no. 8: 13–16.

Chapter 4

ON SOME CURRENTLY FASHIONABLE PROPOSITIONS IN PUBLIC FINANCE*

Prabhat Patnaik

It is a real honour for me that I have been asked to deliver the I. S. Gulati Memorial Lecture for 2005. Iqbal Gulati was not only an outstanding economist but also a person of the highest level of integrity. He was not one to change his views for convenience. He would not bend with the wind. He remained true to his basic humane values and made common cause with all those who shared these values. It is a symptom of this integrity that while many who began their careers being far more radical than Iqbal Gulati in their political convictions and academic views drifted into anti-Leftism and propagated the currently dominant IMF–World Bank positions, Iqbal Gulati moved in the opposite direction, coming closer and closer to the Left, and was even writing a regular column for *Deshabhimani* on economic matters until his failing health prevented it.

Today's occasion is particularly poignant for me since Iqbal was a close personal friend of mine, warm-hearted and generous to a fault. His company and the warm hospitality that he and Leela showered on me over the years were a source of much joy for me. I am grateful that this lecture offers me the opportunity to pay my tribute to this extraordinary man whom I had the privilege of knowing for well over a quarter century.

Iqbal had varied interests in economics, but the one area that claimed his passion was public finance. I have therefore decided to devote this lecture to an examination of certain currently fashionable propositions in public finance. It is in my view important to do so since the fashionableness of these propositions derives not from their theoretical worth but from the fact of their being assiduously promoted by the Bretton Woods institutions, and by international finance capital in general. They serve, as I hope to show in the course of this lecture, the interests of international finance capital, while being inimical to those of the vast mass of the Indian poor. They are aggressively pushed by the media, which not only are wedded to the neoliberal agenda, but also have no qualms about substituting the serious discipline of economics with fatuous formulae. Let us look at some of these formulae.

A very common formula is the following: public sector enterprises which make losses are *ipso facto* 'inefficient' and hence should be either closed down or made 'efficient'

* This chapter is based on the I. S. Gulati Memorial Lecture, 2005. An earlier version was published in *Social Scientist* 33, no. 7/8 (Jul–Aug, 2005).

through being 'privatized'. The government, in other words, must *never* subsidize loss-making public sector units, since that entails subsidizing 'inefficiency'.[1] What this formula misses is the fact that the concept of 'efficiency' in economics is a complex one.[2] Any enterprise, or more generally any 'activity', is considered 'inefficient' if at a set of *shadow prices* derived from an optimal programme, as a *dual* of the optimization exercise reflecting the social priorities, it makes losses, since, in such a case, its discontinuation or substitution by some other activity would be socially more desirable. This is absolute bread-and-butter economics which all of us had to learn in our student days.

In a market economy, of course, there is no explicit social optimization exercise possible. For such an economy an extension of the above proposition is often used. And this states that since the competitive market, *as an ideal entity*, carries out an implicit optimization exercise, where, *for a given distribution of initial endowments among economic agents*, it achieves a social optimum in a sense defined by Vilfredo Pareto (where nobody can be made better off without someone else becoming worse off), a loss-making unit *under perfect competition*, that is, at the prices prevailing in a competitive equilibrium, is 'inefficient' *in the context of this particular social optimization exercise.*

But of course this particular social optimization exercise has no special sanction; Pareto-optimality is perfectly compatible with vast inequalities in wealth distribution. And a society wishing to avoid such vast inequalities need not do so solely through lump sum (non-price-distorting) transfers of the sort that an enthusiast for perfect competition would suggest; it could very well *use the price mechanism* itself for transfers.[3] For example, in a society that is exercised not just over inequalities *per se* but over the fact that such inequalities cause deprivations for a large number of children, a better way of dealing with inequalities would be to subsidize schooling and introduce free midday meals, rather than just to ensure the payment of a lump sum amount to the parents for covering children's school and meal expenditures. Such a society in other words may choose deliberately to have prices different from the competitive prices, and at these prices there would be loss-making enterprises.

Putting the matter differently, the price system plays multiple roles: it acts as a signal for the use of available resources for producing at any particular point on the Production Possibility Frontier, and it also acts as a means of distributing a given produced bundle of goods among the economic agents. There are plenty of cases where it is worth society's while to have not just one set of prices fulfilling both these roles (as under a conventional competitive equilibrium), but to combine two different sets of prices derived from these two different roles; it is worthwhile, for instance, to make departures from the competitive prices in distributing a bundle of produced goods, in the interests of a social optimality transcending Pareto. (The amounts produced, to be sure, would be influenced by such departures). Any such combining would necessarily entail loss-making and hence subsidies.

Let me recapitulate the argument. Loss-making can at all be a matter of concern only in a world where prices derived from a social optimizing exercise prevail. In a market economy where no explicit social optimization takes place, loss-making can at all be a matter of concern only if perfectly competitive prices prevail, which are based, theoretically, on an *implicit* social optimization exercise. But even in this latter case, there are perfectly legitimate reasons for the continuance of loss-making enterprises which charge prices that are deliberately kept different from the competitive prices, insofar as the social objective is different from what the implicit optimization of a competitive market achieves. Loss-making sustained through subsidies therefore, even in a competitive market, need not be avoided and is certainly not synonymous with 'inefficiency'.

But when we are not in a competitive market, the fact of an enterprise making losses signifies absolutely nothing about its efficiency. If an enterprise makes a loss at some *arbitrarily determined* prices (i.e. prices different from those that are obtained in a perfectly competitive equilibrium), then to call such an enterprise *ipso facto* 'inefficient' is a travesty of economics. And yet this is precisely what constitutes an accepted proposition in the media-promoted, Fund–Bank-approved public discourse in India. To be sure, any such loss-making has to be investigated; the 'efficiency' or otherwise of such enterprises, defined *independently* of loss-making *per se* and in some objective fashion (such as in terms of physical indicators like the vector of physical inputs per unit of output) has to be explored; and if such an enterprise is found to be 'inefficient' by such an independent criterion, then the course of action, *if any*, that should be adopted with regard to it has to be decided upon; and even if the enterprise is found to be 'efficient' on the specified criteria, whether it should persist in making losses or whether it should adopt measures to cut down losses, and if so what measures, has to be pondered over. But these are all a separate matter, not germane to the present discussion. The point at issue here is this: loss-making at a given set of arbitrary prices is no indicator of 'inefficiency', and such loss-making does not necessarily warrant either closure or 'privatization'.

The question is often asked, even by those who see the obvious merit of this last argument: even assuming that loss-making is no indicator of 'inefficiency', how can the government keep meeting these losses year after year? Is such a course of action *fiscally* sustainable? This question merges with another currently fashionable general proposition, namely that subsidies must be eliminated as far as possible, on purely fiscal grounds. Let us consider its merit.

What is often not appreciated is that subsidies, whether on commodities or whether earmarked for individuals, are simply a negative form of taxation. A tax system consists of an entire vector of taxes and subsidies, that is, of negative and positive taxes. To say that subsidies must always be eliminated (or whittled down as far as possible) is the same as saying that a tax system must always have only positive rates. There is absolutely no justification for such an assertion under any principles of economics. What is more, if we start from some given tax system then any *reduction* of tax rates is analogous to a *negative movement* in the tax rate, and hence is tantamount to the offer of a subsidy *relative to the original situation.* Anyone opposed to subsidies must therefore, to be logically consistent, be opposed to such a reduction in tax rates.

To take a simple example, if we have a tax system to start with where we have Rs. 200 of taxes and Rs. 100 of subsidies, giving a net revenue of Rs. 100, then there are two ways of raising the net revenue to Rs. 200: eliminate subsidies or raise tax revenue to Rs. 300. Not only is it the case that no principle of economics exists which establishes the first as a superior option compared to the second, but the pursuit of the first option would not even achieve this end if *simultaneously* tax revenue gets lowered to Rs. 100. Thus the advocates of subsidy elimination not only have no theoretical argument in their favour, but are actually inconsistent if, while demanding subsidy elimination, they close their eyes to tax cuts. And yet this is precisely what has been happening in India. Precisely under the neoliberal dispensation when the demands for subsidy cuts have been the most strident and have fructified significantly, there has been a substantial cut in the central government's tax revenue to GDP that has been applauded by the very same subsidy eliminators.[4]

Clearly underlying the demand for subsidy elimination, therefore, is not any fiscal concern as is claimed, but simply a desire to alter the distribution of the fiscal burden, away from the well-to-do, who have been the greatest beneficiaries of the tax cuts, to the poor, who have borne the brunt of the subsidy cuts. This is entirely in keeping with the pattern elsewhere in the world where exactly the same propositions have been advanced and implemented.

But the poor have not suffered merely through the subsidy cuts; they have been the victims of public expenditure cuts more generally. And these latter cuts have been sustained by yet another currently fashionable proposition of public finance, namely that the fiscal deficit must always be severely curtailed. This is so fashionable that the central government has even enacted a law designed to put a cap on its fiscal deficit under all circumstances. And interestingly this law passed under the NDA government was notified under the UPA dispensation: its merits are presumably so overwhelming that their appreciation is all pervasive. Let us turn to an examination of these merits.

It is noteworthy that there is no proper published theoretical justification within India for curtailing the fiscal deficit. The only place where one gets a brief theoretical defence of this position (apart from the wisdom imparted by sundry visitors from the IMF, the World Bank and credit-rating agencies in their interactions with the media) is the report of the prime minister's Economic Advisory Council under the NDA. And that is as follows: a fiscal deficit (barring presumably a small magnitude) must always be eschewed, since, if it is monetized, it gives rise to inflation; while if it is not monetized, it raises the interest rate and crowds out private investment.

Even though this set of assertions appears in a document signed by some of the most distinguished senior economists of the country, *every single one of these assertions is plain wrong.*[5] Barring cost-push factors, whether there is inflation or not depends upon the magnitude of aggregate demand relative to the state of potential supply: in a demand-constrained situation where there are substantial unutilized capacities and unsold foodgrain stocks, a fiscal deficit, whether it is monetized or not, can have no impact whatsoever on inflation. A monetized fiscal deficit raises the magnitude of reserve money in the economy, and hence *the potential money supply*. But even if this potential money supply gets translated into actual money supply, it can have no impact on inflation as long as the aggregate demand for goods does not exceed their potential supply. (*Monetarism which holds otherwise is invariably based on the assumption of full employment.*)[6]

Likewise, if the fiscal deficit is not monetized, then it does not follow that it would necessarily give rise to a higher interest rate. The standard argument in favour of the assertion that there would be a rise in the interest rate runs as follows: if the government borrows from the 'market' then there is an increase in the supply of government securities, and hence by implication of the sum total of securities. This lowers the prices of securities and hence raises the interest rate. The problem with this argument, however, is that as government expenditure increases through the fiscal deficit, it raises the level of income and hence the level of private savings, which in turn increases the demand for securities, where such savings can be 'placed'. The fiscal deficit, in other words, acts not just on the supply of securities but also on the demand for securities. Indeed a fiscal deficit necessarily finances itself *at any given interest rate*: in a closed economy it does so by generating an excess of private savings over private investment that is exactly equal to itself. (This is but another way of saying that in a closed economy investment generates an amount of savings that is exactly equal to itself at any given interest rate). The question of a fiscal deficit increasing the interest rate therefore simply does not arise.

The interest rate is not determined by savings–investment equality, that is, exclusively through the flow equilibrium. Its determination involves the stock equilibrium, that is, the demand and supply of money (though flow elements may influence the demand and supply of money, as the IS–LM analysis famously made clear).

Thus, if a fiscal deficit raises the interest rate then that can be only because the increase in income it gives rise to creates a demand for money that is not satisfied by money supply at the existing interest rate. But there is no reason why this should happen. If banks have unutilized lending capacity, which is typically the case in a demand-constrained system, then money supply would increase in response to demand without occasioning an increase in the interest rate. And if perchance banks do not have unutilized lending capacity, so that the interest rate does increase in response to the increased demand for money, then the blame for it has to be laid at the door of monetary policy rather than the fiscal deficit: after all the interest rate is what it is because monetary policy keeps it there. Finally, if the interest rate does increase with a fiscal deficit because of non-accommodating monetary policy, then exactly the same *denouement* would follow *any* increase in the level of aggregate demand, even an increase not caused by a fiscal deficit. Thus there is no direct connection whatsoever between the interest rate and a fiscal deficit.

This proposition had been established three quarters of a century ago and constitutes bread-and-butter macroeconomics. Indeed, it is almost embarrassing to repeat it in this day and age, but one is constrained to do so because of the immense success of the IMF–World Bank ideology in giving a counter-impression. What this ideology asserts today is nothing new. In 1929 when Lloyd George advocated a public works programme financed by government borrowing as a means of overcoming unemployment in Britain, the British treasury put out a White Paper arguing precisely along these very lines: public works financed by a fiscal deficit would raise interest rates and crowd out private investment, so that there would be little net expansion in employment in the economy. It is against this view that Kahn (1931) wrote his celebrated article on the 'multiplier', which was to form the core of the Keynesian Revolution. Kahn's argument, as pertinent today as it was at the time, was simple: the level of savings, it is undeniable, depends on the level of income; if the interest rate is determined by savings–investment equality, then this can be the case *only if income is already given; that is, only if employment is already given.* There is in short an implicit assumption of full employment underlying the treasury view, which is neither theoretically justified nor, in the context of the Depression that had already set in by 1929, empirically warranted.[7]

Once we stop *assuming* that a capitalist market economy is always at full employment, it is clear that something else must be entering the picture to determine both income and the interest rate, and that something else can only be the fact of the stock equilibrium. The validity of Kahn's argument, and hence by implication the invalidity of the treasury view, arises from the elementary fact that in an economy where all economic agents, including the banking system and the plethora of financial institutions, are forever engaged in making portfolio choices based *inter alia* upon their expectations about the future, money too can be held as an asset. The interest rate is the outcome of such choices, which is enshrined in a stock equilibrium.

Or, putting the matter differently, the recognition of a stock equilibrium based on choice between assets (including money) necessarily precludes the assumption of perpetual full employment that underlies the treasury view of 1929, the 'crowding-out' theory, the view of the prime minister's Economic Advisory Council, and monetarism generally.[8] (It is a separate matter, which need not detain us here, *that these theories would be equally invalid even if full employment actually prevailed*, since a fiscal deficit in such a case would still finance itself without crowding out private investment, by generating, in a closed economy, an equivalent amount of additional 'forced savings' through a process of 'profit inflation', that is, through a process of increase in prices relative to money wages, a phenomenon with which we in India have been very familiar for a long time.)

The indiscriminate hostility to fiscal deficit, therefore, has absolutely no theoretical basis. What is more, it is a harmful doctrine. In a country like India where the public sector is in charge of supplying a variety of capital goods and even foodgrains, a fiscal deficit would in most cases not even increase the government's net indebtedness to the private sector – its impact would be to create additional incomes and hence savings within the public sector itself, though outside of the arena that is within the ken of the budget. To perpetuate unemployment in such a situation, to perpetuate hunger and malnutrition in the midst of burgeoning foodgrain stocks *within the public sector itself*, to perpetuate unutilized capacity within the equipment-producing segment of the public sector itself (and then use it as a justification for privatizing this public sector segment) even while inviting MNCs, on the basis of guaranteed rates of return, to set up units with imported equipment, *all in the name of keeping down the fiscal deficit*, underscores the extraordinary harm that false theories can do. Not surprisingly, Professor Joan Robinson (1962) called this obsession with curtailing the fiscal deficit the 'humbug of finance'.

But the irony does not end there. Let us for argument's sake assume for a moment that the prime minister's Economic Advisory Council is right, and that a fiscal deficit, if monetized, would cause inflation. But the inflow of speculative finance capital such as is occurring of late through FII investments in India has *exactly the same effect on money supply as a monetized fiscal deficit has*. Those opposed to a monetized fiscal deficit should logically therefore be opposed to the free inflow of finance into the economy. But not one voice from among those who cry hoarse over the baneful effects of fiscal deficit has been raised against the free inflows of finance capital, in favour of capital controls! This is duplicity *par excellence*.

But even the duplicity does not stop here. While fiscal deficit is supposed to be a wrong way for the government to raise resources, selling public sector equity is supposed to be perfectly harmless, while in fact there is no difference between the two. If a fiscal deficit crowds out private investment, it defies reason why disinvestment should not have the same effect. After all the only difference between the two is that one adds to the supply of bonds while the other adds to the supply of equity. If private savings are diverted from investment in the first case, they should be equally diverted in the second case as well. But government economists, while running down fiscal deficits, enthusiastically welcome disinvestment as a way of resource mobilization.

The combined effect of reduction in the tax–GDP ratio, which the IMF itself has now informed us is a pervasive phenomenon under 'liberalization', and curtailment of fiscal deficit, is a cut in government expenditure as a proportion of GDP, and a deflation triggered by it. The deflation not only contributes towards making the economy demand-constrained but also entails cuts in social expenditure and development expenditure, which have a particularly adverse effect on the poor and which compound the inegalitarian thrust of the fiscal policy noted earlier. There is, however, an additional phenomenon. Not content with the Fiscal Responsibility and Budget Management Act (FRBM) enacted at the central level, the Twelfth Finance Commission has now suggested that similar acts should be passed at the level of the states. In addition, it has now made the state governments go to the 'market' for raising loans instead of obtaining loans from the centre. FRBMs enacted at state level would, needless to say, compound the problem of deflation. In addition, making state governments go to the 'market' is a euphemism for forcing them to be obsessed with the need to remain 'creditworthy' *in the eyes of finance capital*, which, in the current era of 'financial sector reforms', means, in effect, an obsession with 'creditworthiness' in the eyes of *international finance capital.*

The implications of this obsession have to be seen in the context of the particular kind of VAT that has been introduced recently. It entails uniform rates, fixed through the instrumentality of an Empowered Committee of state finance ministers, for all states, with no freedom given to any state to fix rates of its choice. Since the sales tax had been the main instrument of resource mobilization for state governments, the replacement of the sales tax by a uniform VAT meant that state governments would henceforth have little control over the amount of revenue they could raise. Since the amounts they could borrow would depend upon how well they appeased international finance capital, which has a marked preference for a particular set of policies, *all state governments would from now on willy-nilly pursue these very policies.* The overall implication is not just to undermine in a formal sense the federal nature of the polity[9] but to impose actually a necessary uniformity on the set of economic policies pursued by the state governments.

There is something more at stake. If all state governments dealt directly with international finance capital, then the political entity called India would cease to have much relevance. And a fallout of this would be individual states handing over control over their mineral resources to multinational corporations. There would thus be an inevitable tendency towards the 'Balkanization' of the country, with mineral-rich but economically poorer states (the two tend to go together) making particular efforts to appease international finance capital by making available their mineral resources for exploitation by the latter on favourable terms. In such a case the gains of independence which had meant above all national control over mineral resources would have been 'rolled back'.

'Balkanization' of large developing countries and control over their natural resources are the twin phenomena which the major capitalist powers, especially the leading imperial power of our times, favour. This is because countries like China and India represent a potential challenge for them. The importance of using the fiscal instrument to snuff out that challenge should not be underestimated.

Let me recapitulate the argument till now. The net effect of the currently fashionable propositions in public finance is to impose a deflation on the economy, to encourage the privatization of public sector assets, to alter the distribution of the fiscal burden in the economy in an inegalitarian direction and to impose a uniform set of policies on the state governments which are neoliberal in character and which, by reducing the relevance of the centre in the economic lives of the states and bringing the latter into a direct relationship with international finance capital, pave the way for a Balkanization of the economy. The fact that these policies are theoretically untenable was argued above. The fact that these policies are immensely harmful for the nation can be denied only by those who choose to put blinkers over their eyes. But the question arises: whose interests do these policies serve? I shall now argue that these policies are in conformity with the class interests of international finance capital (including MNCs who are intimately linked with it) and its local collaborators, and against the interests of the vast mass of the people of the Third World.

Deflation promotes centralization of capital, where small producers are expropriated by large ones, including MNCs and those 'fronting' for international financial interests. The privatization of public sector assets is an obvious case of expropriation, which indeed falls under the rubric of what Marx called 'primitive accumulation of capital'. When assets built up on the basis of tax revenue collected largely at the expense of millions of common people (since they are the ones who pay the bulk of tax revenue) are given away to a few rich private buyers at throwaway prices, then we have a classic case of 'primitive accumulation'; that is, the use of the intermediary role of the State to filch resources from millions of people to build up private fortunes. Likewise, when MNCs are invited to set up power plants because the government, despite the existence of unutilized capacity in power equipment production within the public sector itself, does not increase the fiscal deficit owing to its faith in the 'humbug of finance', and when these MNCs cause an increase in power tariff to millions of peasants because the rate-of-return-guarantee they obtain encourages 'over-pricing' of imported equipment, then we are having in effect the filching of resources from millions of peasants by a few MNCs, which again is a classic case of 'primitive accumulation of capital'. Similarly, when the pervasiveness of deflation in the world economy results in a shift in the terms of trade against agriculture, as has been happening of late, we have a classic case of 'primitive accumulation of capital'. And the same is true when the fiscal burden is shifted against the poor and in favour of the rich. Expropriation, centralization and primitive accumulation are the essence of the neoliberal strategy, of which neoliberal public finance is an integral element.

This process of 'expropriation' that the neoliberal policies unleash is different from 'exploitation' as is commonly understood and as was defined by Marx. *The process of filching under the neoliberal dispensation that we have been talking about does not occur within the process of production, which is the site of 'exploitation' as Marx defined it.* The expropriation under neoliberalism is extraneous to the process of production and can increase in magnitude even in an economy where the productive forces are stagnant or retrogressing.

An implication of this distinction deserves notice. There is much talk these days that the 'trickle-down' effect of growth will improve the lot of the poor. In fact, however, the trend rate of growth since the introduction of neoliberal policies in the '90s has been no higher than the corresponding figure for the decade of the '80s. If on top of this there has been a pervasive process of expropriation and primitive accumulation of capital in the later period, then the extent of poverty at the end of this later period must be higher than at the end of the earlier period. But there is an additional point. *Even if the growth rate in the later period had been somewhat higher than in the preceding period, insofar as the growth process is accompanied by pervasive expropriation, the magnitude of poverty is still likely to have increased rather than decreased.* It follows that concentrating on growth rates, as government economists do, as a panacea for poverty eradication, is fundamentally fallacious. The pertinent issue is not the *rate* of growth but the *nature* of growth. And growth under the neoliberal dispensation, *no matter how rapid it is* (within realistic limits), would never eradicate poverty but would rather accentuate it, since such growth is invariably accompanied by a process of pervasive expropriation.[10]

One corollary of this is that the official figures on poverty, which show a decline, are really without any worth.[11] Time does not permit me to go into this issue here but I shall discuss only one aspect of it. The definition of poverty in India is in terms of a calorie norm, which, for rural India, is 2400 calories per person per day. One may not like this definition but it is the definition underlying official pronouncements. If we use this definition today then 75 per cent of the population of rural India is 'poor', which is higher than the figure (56 per cent) in 1970–71 when the poverty estimates began. Per capita foodgrain absorption in the country as a whole, which had stood at around 200 kg per annum at the beginning of the twentieth century, had gone down to around 150 kg at the time of independence; it recovered, with much effort in the post-independence years, to around 180 kg by the end of the 1980s. Significantly, it once again declined during the '90s, and particularly precipitously during the latter half of the decade, to reach 157 kg for the quinquennium ending 2002–03. This is about the same level as on the eve of the Second World War.

While no one can deny the fact of a sharp decline in foodgrain absorption, many argue that this is because of a change of taste and does not signify growing deprivation. Such an assertion is odd since per capita foodgrain absorption, *taking both direct and indirect modes of absorption together*, is always positively associated with per capita income. The US and continental Europe, for instance, have far higher per capita foodgrain absorption in this inclusive sense than Third-World countries, including India. The change of taste argument, *for the population as a whole*, appears therefore to lack substance. What is more, it also seems to be the case that according to the latest NSS round there are as many as eight states in India where rural per capita foodgrain absorption has fallen below 1800 calories per day, which is the absolutely minimum necessary nutritional intake according to the WHO. It is significant that in 1999–2000 there were only three states where the average figure for rural areas had fallen below 1800 calories.

The symptoms of growing food deprivation, and hence by inference growing deprivation in general, are quite striking, especially in rural India. Paradoxically, while this growing food deprivation was occurring the country was saddled with unprecedented surplus foodgrain stocks. By July 2002 the magnitude of stocks stood at 63 million tonnes, of which nearly 45 million represented surplus stocks. The coexistence of surplus stocks with acute and growing deprivation is indicative of a massive squeeze on the purchasing power in the hands of the rural poor, and one obvious reason for this is the curtailment in rural developmental expenditure by the government, which leads us back to the false and motivated theories of public finance that have become currently fashionable.

It follows that if the government undertook a large-scale employment generation programme, such as was visualized for instance in the Rural Employment Guarantee Scheme promised in the Common Minimum Programme, and even financed the bulk of it through deficit financing, then in a situation of foodgrain stock surpluses, it would be killing several birds with one stone: feeding the hungry, reducing unemployment, reducing the foodgrain stockpile, and, if the programme were well-conceived, building up some rural assets in the process. But successive governments under thraldom to international finance capital have refused to do this. The UPA has introduced an extremely diluted version of the Rural Employment Guarantee Programme it promised, so diluted in fact that it amounts to nothing short of reneging on its election promise. And the NDA actually sold 19 million tonnes of surplus stocks in the international market at prices below those charged to the APL population, and reportedly even below those charged to the BPL population. Much of these exports would have gone to feed pigs and cattle in richer countries. The fact that foodgrains taken from the mouths of the hungry rural poor of our own country are used to feed cattle and pigs in the richer countries shows the utter absurdity of the 'humbug of finance' which currently hegemonizes our intellectual discourse.

Notes

1 Even the Common Minimum Programme of the UPA government promises not to privatize profit-making public sector units, the clear implication being that loss-making public sector units should be privatized.

2 I have discussed this concept at length in my Kanta Ranadive Memorial Lecture. See Patnaik (1997).

3 The argument which follows is based on Dobb (1969).

4 Chandrasekhar and Ghosh (2002) discuss at length the decline in tax–GDP ratio.

5 For a detailed critique of the PMEAC's views see P. Patnaik (2001).

6 For the theoretical underpinnings of monetarism see Frank Hahn (1984).

7 A simple exposition of the issues involved is contained in my V. P. Chintan Memorial Lecture, 'The Humbug of Finance' (P. Patnaik 2003).

8 There is a view that monetarism would be validated in a world where money wages and prices were flexible. This is wrong. In a world with inherited payment commitments, wage-price flexibility, far from creating full employment, would actually create havoc, as Kalecki argued long ago (see Kalecki 1967). Besides, since even transactions' demand for money entails holding money as a store of value for a certain period, a world where there is complete flexibility of money wages and prices would actually be a money-less world.

9 On the issue of the undermining of the federal structure through a uniform VAT see Bagchi (2005).

10 This is because even if the growth rate is high enough to ensure that all expropriated find employment, since the average wage in their new employment is typically lower than their average income prior to expropriation, it would still mean a worsening of the condition of the vast expropriated mass. Breman (2003) in his Sukhamoy Chakravarty Memorial Lecture argued, much along these lines, about rising poverty in Ahmedabad owing to the collapse of the textile industry.

11 The discussion that follows borrow heavily from the work of Utsa Patnaik. See in particular U. Patnaik (2004) and (2005).

References

Bagchi, A. 2005. 'VAT and State Autonomy'. *Economic and Political Weekly* 40, no. 18: 1806–7.

Breman, J. 2003. *Observations on Labour Conditions in Ahmedabad.* Mimeo. Sukhamoy Chakravarty Memorial Lecture, Delhi School of Economics.

Chandrasekhar, C. P. and Jayati Ghosh. 2002. *The Market That Failed.* New Delhi: LeftWord.

Dobb, M. H. 1969. *Welfare Economics and the Economics of Socialism.* Cambridge: Cambridge University Press.

Hahn, Frank 1984. *Equilibrium and Macroeconomics.* Oxford: Oxford University Press.

Kahn, R. F. 1931. 'The Relation of Home Investment to Unemployment'. *Economic Journal* 41, no. 162: 173–98.

Kalecki, M. 1967. 'Money and Real Wages I'. *Studies in the Theory of Business Cycles, 1933–1939.* Oxford: Basil Blackwell.

Patnaik, P. 1997. 'On the Concept of Efficiency'. *Economic and Political Weekly* 32, no. 43: 2807–13.

______. 2001. 'On Fiscal Deficits and Real Interest Rates'. *Economic and Political Weekly* 36, nos. 14–15: 1160–63.

______. 2003. The Humbug of Finance. In *Retreat to Unfreedom* by Prabhat Patnaik. New Delhi: Tulika.

Patnaik, U. 2004. 'The Republic of Hunger'. *Social Scientist* 32, nos. 9–10: 9–35.

______. 2005. 'Theorizing Food Security and Poverty'. Mimeo. Public lecture delivered at IIC, New Delhi.

Robinson, J. 1962. *Economic Philosophy.* London: C. A. Watts and Co.

Chapter 5

THE COSTS OF 'COUPLING': THE GLOBAL CRISIS AND THE INDIAN ECONOMY*

Jayati Ghosh and C. P. Chandrasekhar

Introduction

A noteworthy feature of the current global crisis has been the failure of most mainstream analysts (unlike heterodox economists such as Patnaik 2008 and Kregel 1998 and 2008, among others) to predict its onset, estimate its duration and severity or lay bare the mechanisms that contributed to its unfolding. This weakness of telescopic and analytical faculty has been most evident with respect to developing Asia, especially China and India. Even as the global crisis and its effects were being recognized with a lag, Asian developing countries – and these two countries in particular – were seen as the potential shock absorbers in the global system, with predictions that their persisting expansion and relatively high rates of growth would prevent the global downturn from becoming a meltdown (Bergsten 2008; Kohn 2008). Such arguments were reinforced by econometric studies (e.g. Kose et al. 2008), which found evidence of divergence of business cycles across developed and emerging market economies in the period of globalization.

Three features of the economic performance of China and India were seen to warrant this assessment. The first was the superior performance in gross domestic product (GDP) and productivity growth over more than a decade of these two economies, especially China, as compared to developed countries such as the USA (Table 5.1). It was argued that this higher growth must have resulted from mechanisms other than just stimuli linked to global integration. Demographic features, potentially large domestic markets and 'favourable' policy environments were typically offered as alternative forces driving growth (Goldman Sachs 2007). Second, these countries are large in terms of geography and population, but despite recent growth they remain far behind the developed world in terms of per capita income and levels of productivity, so the scope for the 'catch-up' process to continue was estimated to be large. Lower per capita incomes also implied that their growth would generate demands for food, natural resources and manufactures from the rest of the world that would contribute to growth in a wide range of economies.

* A previous version of this chapter appeared in the *Cambridge Journal of Economics* 33: 725–39 (2009); it has not been extensively updated.

Decoupled giants driven by internal stimuli were seen to be obvious buffers against a global recession.

The third feature that was noted was the ability of China and India to avoid major financial crises such as have affected a number of other emerging markets, along with their rapid accumulation of foreign exchange reserves. It was argued that these features were the consequences of a 'prudent' even if extensive programme of global economic integration and domestic deregulation, which involved substantial financial liberalization but included some capital controls and limited convertibility of the currency for capital account transactions. Such prudence was seen to have ensured that China and India remained unaffected by the contagion unleashed by the East Asian financial crisis in 1997 and subsequently kept them protected from crises that could have cut short their high growth episodes (Cornia 2006).

However, recent events have exposed the fallacy of 'decoupling'. In this chapter, we argue that the presumption that the Indian economy was on a robust growth trajectory decoupled in important ways from the international system is wrong. Rather, the recent boom was fundamentally dependent upon greater global integration, which also made the growth process more uneven and more vulnerable to internally and externally generated crises (Chandrasekhar and Ghosh 2004 and 2006). It is commonly perceived that this reflected the impact of trade liberalization, but in fact changes in finance were probably more significant, in ways elaborated below. Essentially, recent growth was related to financial deregulation that sparked a retail credit boom and combined with fiscal concessions to spur consumption among the richest quintile of the population. This led to rapid increases in aggregate GDP growth, even as deflationary fiscal policies, poor employment generation and persistent agrarian crisis reduced wage shares in national income and kept mass consumption demand low (Chandrasekhar and Ghosh 2007). The substantial rise in profit shares in the economy and the proliferation of financial activities (which together with real estate accounted for nearly 15 per cent of GDP in 2007–08) combined with rising asset values to enable a credit-financed consumption splurge among the rich and the middle classes, especially in urban areas, which in turn generated higher rates of investment and output over the upswing. The earlier emphasis on public spending as the principal stimulus for growth was thus substituted in the 1990s with debt-financed housing investment and private consumption of the elite and burgeoning middle classes. The recent Indian growth story in its essentials was therefore not unlike the story of speculative bubble-led expansion that marked the experience of several other developed and developing countries in the same period.

By the middle of 2008, this process too was reaching its limits. The dependence of GDP growth upon largely debt-fuelled consumption of a relatively small segment of the population rather than mass demand meant a more limited and ultimately more fragile domestic market. Export growth (in software, information technology–enabled services and some manufactures) remained high but exports were not large enough to counter domestic decelerating tendencies. High rates of investment were driven by expectations of rapid growth of the domestic market as well as very substantial fiscal sops in the form of tax incentives and implicit subsidies, but the latter could not increase beyond a certain point. As a result, Indian economic growth started decelerating early in 2008, even before

Table 5.1. Selected economic and productivity indicators for the USA, China and India: 1995–2004

Country	GDP 2004 (US$)	Productivity Growth (% average annual change)			Productivity Levels GDP (US$)	
		1995–2004	1995–2000	2000–04	Per employee 2004	Per capita 2004
USA	100	2	2.3	1.7	100	100
China	71	5.5	3.1	8.6	13	16
India	28	4.2	4	4.4	10	8

Note: Productivity growth is measured on the basis of GDP per employee. GDP is in US dollars converted at 1990 purchasing power parities. China does not include Hong Kong.
Source: Conference Board and Groningen Growth and Development Centre, Total Economy Database (September 2006), quoted in National Science Board 2008 and available online (http://www.nsf.gov/statistics/).

the effects of global slowdown were transmitted through sharply declining exports. Real GDP growth, which was 9 per cent in the financial year April 2007 to March 2008, decelerated to 7.6 per cent in both the subsequent quarters. Industrial production peaked in December 2007, fell by 6.5 per cent in April 2008 and remained well below the earlier peak until January 2009. So the internal bubble-generated growth process had already begun to slacken when the impact of the global crisis created further adverse pressures.

The Export Slowdown

With the onset of the crisis, growing trade integration implied that one of the routes through which the real economy was affected was a deceleration in exports of goods and services, which had contributed significantly to the earlier boom. Trade to GDP ratios in India increased from 11 per cent in 1995 to 23 per cent in 2006. However, unlike China, where much of the export expansion was on account of manufactures, export growth in India was principally due to services. In the merchandise trade area, India's export success was restricted to a few sectors such as garments, chemicals, pharmaceuticals, and metals and engineering goods. While the first three categories of exports grew because of dynamism in the global market, the latter two were largely driven by increased demand from China in the period since 2002.

In services, however, India emerged as the largest exporter of computer and information services in the international economy in 2005, and its share in world exports of computer and information services was 17 per cent in 2006 (World Trade Organization, quoted in Reserve Bank of India 2009f). Services in general have come to dominate the Indian economy, accounting for more than half its GDP, contributing an overwhelming share to its recent relatively high rate of growth and even giving rise to arguments about services emerging as the Kaldorian growth sector in India (Dasgupta and Singh 2006). Services (excluding construction) accounted for 56 per cent of the increment in GDP at factor cost over the period 1996–97 to 2006–07 (computed from National Accounts Statistics data, available at Reserve Bank of India 2008).

Within services, the share of software and IT-enabled services in the incremental GDP generated from services had been rising, with a significant share coming from exports. Gross exports of software, business, financial and communication services amounted to 5.3 per cent of GDP at market prices in 2007–08, with software services exports touching 3.4 per cent of GDP, compared with 14.2 per cent for merchandise exports.[1] Service exports were therefore important sources not just of growth but also of foreign exchange earnings, supporting the balance of payments and making up for the fact that liberalization did not really trigger a merchandise export boom from the country. However, dependence on such service export-led growth was also a source of potential vulnerability, given the high degree of concentration of exports to a few developed countries: the USA accounted for 61 per cent and the UK for 18 per cent of India's IT-business process outsourcing (BPO) export revenues in 2006–07 (NASSCOM figures quoted in Reserve Bank of India 2009f). Moreover, since the mid-1990s, a rising share of remittances, which was the other major contributor to inflows on the current account of the balance of payments, came from the USA, reflecting the growing number of short-term migrants on H1-B visas offering software and IT-enabled services on location. This too could be seen as a form of income from trade in services, largely earned in the USA and a few other developed industrial countries.

Given these forms of integration through trade, it was only to be expected that the global slowdown would directly affect exports and economic activity in India. Merchandise trade was the first to be affected. Merchandise exports in October–December 2008 were more than 10 per cent lower than their value a year earlier. Import values on the other hand continued to increase, albeit at a slower rate because of falling world oil prices. As a result, the trade deficit for the period from October to December 2008 widened to $36.3 billion, 40 per cent higher than a year earlier and estimated to be as much as 12.6 per cent of GDP (calculated from data in Reserve Bank of India 2009a).

To some extent the implications of the widening trade deficit were mitigated by the neutralizing effects of exports of services and remittance inflows, which continued to increase in this period. Therefore the current account deficit was significantly lower than the trade deficit, but even so it increased to 5.1 per cent of GDP for October–December 2008, more than double the ratio for the same months in the previous year (Central Statistical Organisation 2009; Reserve Bank of India 2009a).

A lag in the effects of the global crisis on net services exports from India was to be expected, given that contracts in software and BPO services are typically signed for long periods such as two to three years. The effect of the crisis would be on the renewal of contracts and the signing of new contracts, and the initial impact on aggregate revenues would be proportionately lower according to the weight of legacy contracts in total. The lag was likely to be even longer in the case of remittances because workers who lose their jobs abroad and return home tend to bring their accumulated savings, and this windfall effect initially more than compensates for the fall in the remittance flows resulting from lower overseas employment. In addition, rupee depreciation over 2008 accompanied by growing interest rate differentials was likely to have encouraged larger remittances through rupee denominated non-resident accounts.

However, by early 2009 it was evident that these lags had been covered as several software and IT services firms in India predicted lower revenue growth, cut back on recruitment and even started laying off workers (*Business Intelligence* 2009; Indiatimes Infotech 2009; Lakshman 2009; *Economic Times* 2009). Meanwhile, since North America accounted for nearly 44 per cent of the total remittances to India (followed by the Middle East with 24 per cent and Europe with 13 per cent), the severity of the recession in the USA and developments with regard to use of H1-B workers and issue of H1-B visas would continue to affect remittance inflows. The World Bank (2008) estimated that remittance inflows to South Asia would be flat with zero growth in 2009, compared with the 16 per cent growth experienced in 2008.

Also, by early 2009 the adverse employment effects of the merchandise export decline were evident despite the absence of large survey data on employment. Official surveys have indicated rapid and accelerating job losses in sectors such as textiles and garments, metals and metal products, automobiles, gems and jewellery, construction, transport and the IT/BPO industry (Labour Bureau, Ministry of Labour and Employment 2009). While employment declines were predictably higher in the export-oriented sectors, it is noteworthy that these surveys have found growing job losses in activities that cater dominantly to the domestic market as well. In addition to quantity adjustment in the labour market, workers' incomes were also hit, with reports of falling real – and sometimes even nominal – wages of workers in industry and services as well as reduced incomes of self-employed workers, who constituted more than half the work force by 2005 (National Commission for Enterprises in the Unorganised Sector 2008). Agriculturalists, especially those producing export crops whose global prices had collapsed, faced growing difficulties on top of their existing financial problems, reflecting rising input costs and large burdens of debt. Meanwhile, liquidity trap conditions were evident as 'secure' borrowers were unwilling to invest because of greater uncertainty. Small-scale producers in all sectors were squeezed by the pincer movement of falling demand and credit crunch as even informal sources of credit dried up. Since these producers account for the bulk of employment in manufacturing and services and typically hire workers on informal casual contracts, their economic difficulties translate directly into reduced employment. Surveys of home-based workers reported rapidly declining orders and falling piece rate wages, even in nominal terms, for work that formed part of wider production chains for both domestic and export markets (All India Democratic Women's Association 2009).

Two other effects of the crisis on general living conditions deserve to be noted. First, the state governments – who in India's federal system are directly responsible for much of the public expenditure that directly affects citizens, such as on health, education, sanitation and infrastructure – have found their tax receipts falling below projections due to the downswing. Since they face hard budget constraints and many of them are subject to stringent fiscal responsibility conditions forced on them by the central government, this has constrained their expenditure and reduced essential spending on basic services, not to mention development. Second, while aggregate inflation rates have been near zero for the year April 2008–March 2009, the prices of food and essential medicines have continued to increase, even as unemployment has increased, wage incomes stagnated or fallen and cash crop producers faced falling prices.

Capital Inflows and the Financial Sector

Employment declines in the non-export sectors suggest that the routes by which the effects of the international crisis are being transmitted to India go beyond just external trade. One obvious alternative route is the effect of the crisis on cross-border capital flows, which showed a dramatic increase in the preceding boom. Foreign investment flows rose sharply from US$4.9 billion in 1995–96 to US$29.2 billion in 2006–07 and then more than doubled to US$61.8 billion in 2007–08 (Reserve Bank of India 2009b). In 2007–08, capital inflows into India amounted to over 9 per cent of GDP, even though the current account deficit in the balance of payments stood at just 1.5 per cent of GDP (Subbarao 2009). Thus, the accumulation of large foreign exchange reserves was the result of capital inflows that were far in excess of India's current account financing needs. The greater part of capital inflow was in the form of portfolio investment, which was stimulated by a continuous process of liberalization of the various rules governing such investment: its sources, its ambit, the caps it was subject to and the tax laws pertaining to it (Chandrasekhar 2008). The process of liberalization also kept alive expectations that the caps on foreign direct investment in different sectors would be relaxed over time, thereby providing the basis for eventual foreign control. Those who acquired shares could hope to sell them later at a profit to firms interested in acquisitions. One consequence was the rapid expansion of private equity in India and a private placement boom, which was not restrained by the extent of free-floating shares available for trading in stock markets.

However, liberalization was a necessary condition for such inflows, but not a sufficient one: while financial liberalization began early in the 1990s, the surge in foreign investment flows occurred much later. Until 2003, net inflows were relatively low, reaching a maximum of US$8.2 billion in 2001–02 even though rules regarding foreign portfolio investment in the Indian stock market and external commercial borrowing by Indian firms were liberalized in 1993. Net capital inflows rose to US$15.7 billion in 2003–04, partly encouraged by tax concessions offered to foreign investors in that year. Thereafter, for a variety of reasons, India was 'discovered' by foreign investors and effectively became the target of a capital investment surge. More recently, foreign investment flows to India more than doubled from US$29.2 billion in 2006–07 to US$61.8 billion in 2007–08. This occurred even as capital was fleeing other Asian emerging markets: net equity investment into Asian emerging markets (China, India, Indonesia, Malaysia, Philippines, South Korea and Thailand) fell from US$122.6 billion in 2006 to US$57.9 billion in 2008 (Institute for International Finance 2009). This suggests that India was serving as a hedge for financial investors when uncertainties were engulfing emerging markets elsewhere in Asia and the world.

Capital inflows rose also due to large increases in commercial borrowing by private sector firms. As constraints on external commercial borrowing by domestic companies were relaxed and because interest rates ruled higher in the domestic market, large Indian firms at the margin took the syndicated loan route to borrow money abroad at relatively lower interest rates. They engaged in a version of the carry trade, borrowing money in foreign exchange from the international markets where interest rates were lower and making investments in India (in addition to leveraging investments and acquisitions abroad). Net external borrowing by India rose from US$24.5 billion in 2006–07 to US$41.9 billion in 2007–08, with the bulk of the increase in the form of short-term borrowing. The stock of India's liabilities in the form of debt securities, trade credits and loans rose from US$105.1 billion at the end of June 2006 to US$175.6 billion at the end of September 2008 (Reserve Bank of India 2009d).

A surge of external equity and debt inflows of this kind, combined with a much smaller increase in the current account deficit and a liberalized exchange rate regime, is likely to exert upward pressure on the domestic currency. This would adversely affect the country's export competitiveness and encourage further speculative inflows of capital. To forestall such effects, the central bank typically seeks to manage the exchange rate by buying up foreign currency and building its reserves, and this was in fact the policy of the Reserve Bank of India. As a result, India's foreign exchange reserves increased from just US$76.1 billion at the end of March 2003 to US$309.7 billion at the end of March 2008, essentially due to increased inflows of short-term foreign capital (Reserve Bank of India 2009c). At more than 15 months' worth of imports, these reserves were clearly excessive and became a symptom of India's integration with the world system through the capital inflow route.

Dependence on portfolio equity and debt inflows of this magnitude meant that if any internal or external development was seen to warrant pulling out of India, the exit could be as strong as the earlier inflow of foreign capital. The outbreak of the global crisis therefore resulted in a sharp outflow of capital, especially portfolio capital brought into the stock market by foreign institutional investors (FIIs). Needing cash to meet commitments and cover losses at home, these FIIs sold out in Indian markets and repatriated capital abroad – as much as US$27 billion net outflow in the period April–December 2008 (Reserve Bank of India 2009g).

One consequence of the capital outflow was a collapse of India's stock markets, just as the earlier capital inflows had triggered a speculative bubble in both stock and real estate markets. They had caused an unprecedented rate of asset price inflation in India's stock markets and substantially increased volatility. FII investments were an important force, even if not always the only one, driving markets to unprecedented highs, with a high degree of correlation between cumulative FII investments and the level of the Bombay Stock Exchange (BSE)'s Sensitive Index (Sensex), as is evident from Figure 5.1.

Stock markets in developing countries like India are thin or shallow in at least three senses. First, stocks of only a few companies are actively traded in the market. Second, of these stocks there is only a small proportion that is routinely available for trading, with the rest being held by promoters, the financial institutions and others interested in corporate control or influence. Third, the number of players trading these stocks is also small. The net impact is that speculation and volatility are essential features of such markets. Because an increase in investment by FIIs triggers a sharp price increase, it provides additional incentives for FII investment and in the first instance encourages

Figure 5.1. Net foreign institutional investors' stock of equity investment and Bombay Stock Exchange Sensitive Index

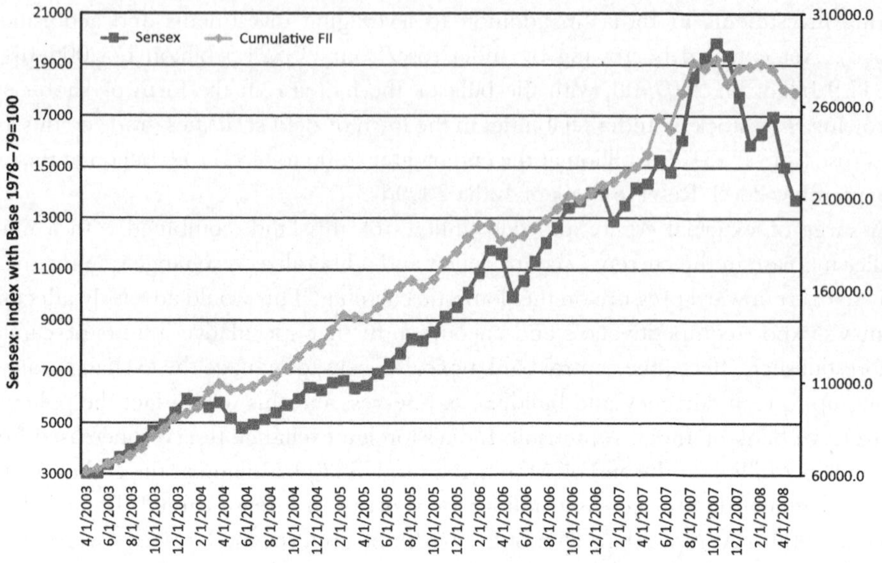

Source: Reserve Bank of India (2008).

further purchases, so that there is a tendency for any correction of price increases to be delayed. When the correction does begin, it typically has to be led by an FII pull-out and can then take the form of an extremely sharp decline in prices. In addition, the inflow of foreign capital can result in an appreciation of the rupee, which increases the return earned in foreign exchange. As a result, the investments turn even more attractive, triggering an investment spiral that implies an even sharper fall when any correction occurs. In turn, the growing realization by the FIIs of the power they wield in such shallow markets encourages speculative investment aimed at pushing the market up and choosing an appropriate moment to exit.

This implicit manipulation of the market, if resorted to often enough, obviously generates a substantial increase in volatility. And in such volatile markets, domestic speculators also attempt to manipulate markets in periods of unusually high prices. All that said, the four years ending in early 2008 were remarkable because of the prolonged bull run in the Indian stock market, which to some extent did help to finance the investment boom underlying India's growth acceleration. Between 2003–04 and 2006–07, which was a period when FII inflows rose significantly and stock markets were generally buoyant, equity capital mobilized by the Indian corporate sector nearly tripled in value, mostly through private placement. Such sales were encouraged by the high valuations generated by the boom and were, as in the case of stock markets, made substantially to foreign financial investors.

After such a speculation-induced bubble, the reverse tendency of collapse in stock markets was triggered by the exit of foreign investors, who then responded to the stock market decline in a cumulative process. This affected not just stock market valuations but also the external reserve position and the exchange rate. By October–December 2008 the entire capital account turned negative, with a deficit amounting to an estimated 1.3 per cent of GDP. While this was mainly due to net outflows under portfolio investment, banking capital and short-term trade credit, there were also falls in foreign direct investment and external commercial borrowing inflows. Even inflows under short-term trade credit declined. This led to an overall balance of payments deficit for that three-month period of as much as 6.2 per cent of GDP. In the circumstances it was not surprising that India's foreign exchange reserves, which stood at US$316 billion in June 2008, fell to US$248.6 billion by the end of January 2009. This was a significant fall, but the volume of reserves still remained high, amounting to around nine months' worth of imports (Reserve Bank of India 2009c).

Another consequence of the outflow of capital was a sharp depreciation of the rupee, by more than 30 per cent vis-à-vis the US dollar in the year to March 2009, taking the currency's value to more than 51 rupees to the dollar. The sharp depreciation of the rupee in the first quarter of 2009 obviously reflected the large overall balance of payments deficit, but it could generate its own momentum to cause further depreciation over time. One reason for this is the increase in India's external debt, which was associated with increased demand for foreign exchange to meet interest and amortization payment commitments. The resulting tightness in the foreign exchange market could create self-fulfilling expectations of future depreciation, as those with pending payment commitments buy up foreign exchange, exporters delay repatriation of revenues and speculators transfer foreign exchange out of the country.

One indicator of the last of these tendencies is the movement of foreign exchange out of the country in the form of outward remittances under the liberalized remittance scheme for resident individuals. These remittances totalled US$9.6 million, US$25 million and US$72.8 million in the three years ending 2006–07. But they shot up to US$440.5 million in 2007–08 (Reserve Bank of India 2009e). This is possibly indicative of the speculative trends pushing down the value of the rupee. In the face of determined speculation even reserves in excess of US$200 billion are no insurance against a crisis. Rupee depreciation and the stock market collapse thereby have increased the possibility of a currency crisis in future.

The Crisis and Credit-Financed Demand

A third way in which integration has influenced the way in which the global crisis has affected India is its impact on the role played by credit in financing private consumption and investment. Internal financial liberalization in India resulted in a process of institutional change in which the role played by state-owned financial institutions and banks was substantially altered. As regulatory structures for private banks were dismantled over the 1990s, and private banks cornered the most lucrative clients, even public sector banks had to alter their strategies to seek new sources of finance, new activities and new avenues for investments, so that they could shore up their interest incomes as well as revenues from various fee-based activities. So banks linked up with insurance companies and entered other 'sensitive' markets like the stock and real estate markets. This led to a relatively rapid transformation of banking in India, with growing exposure of commercial banks to the retail credit market with no or poor collateral, the associated accumulation of loans of doubtful quality in their portfolios, and a growing tendency to securitize personal loans.

Total bank credit grew at a scorching pace from 2005 onwards, at more than double the rate of increase of nominal GDP. As a result, the ratio of outstanding bank credit to GDP (which had declined in the initial post-liberalization years from 30.2 per cent at the end of March 1991 to 27.3 per cent at the end of March 1997) doubled over the next decade to reach about 60 per cent by the end of March 2008. Thus, one consequence of financial liberalization was an increase in credit dependence in the Indian economy, a characteristic imported from developed countries such as the USA. This increase in credit could be positive insofar as it reflected a greater willingness on the part of banks to lend: the growth in credit outperformed the growth in deposits, resulting in an increase in the overall credit–deposit ratio from 55.9 per cent at end March 2004 to 72.5 per cent at end March 2008. This increase was accompanied by a corresponding drop in the investment–deposit ratio, from 51.7 per cent to 36.2 per cent, which indicates that banks were shifting away from their earlier conservative preference to invest in safe government securities in excess of what was required under the statutory liquidity ratio norm. (Data in this and the subsequent four paragraphs are from the Committee on Financial Sector Assessment 2009.)

However, rapid credit growth meant that banks were relying on short-term funds to lend long. From 2001 there was a steady rise in the proportion of short-term deposits with the banks, with the ratio of short-term deposits (maturing up to one year) increasing from 33.2 per cent in March 2001 to 43.6 per cent in March 2008. On the other hand, the proportion of term loans maturing after five years increased from 9.3 per cent to 16.5 per cent. While this delivered increased profits, the rising asset–liability mismatch increased the liquidity risk faced by banks.

These changes do not appear to have been driven by the commercial banking sector's desire to provide more credit to the productive sectors of the economy. Instead, retail loans became the prime drivers of credit growth. The result was a sharp increase in the retail exposure of the banking system, with overall personal loans increasing from slightly more than 8 per cent of total non-food credit in 2004 to close to 25 per cent by 2008. Of the components of retail credit, the growth in housing loans was the highest in most years. As Table 5.2 indicates, the (new) private banks were the most enthusiastic adopters of such a strategy, followed by foreign banks.

This rapid increase in credit and retail exposure, with inadequate or poor collateral, would have brought more tenuous borrowers into the bank credit universe. A significant (but as yet unknown) proportion of this could be 'sub-prime' lending. According to one estimate, by November 2007 there was a little more than 400 billion rupees of credit that was of sub-prime quality, defaults on which could erode the capital base of the banks.[2] To attract such borrowers, the banks offered attractive interest rates below the benchmark prime lending rate. The share of such loans in total rose from 27.7 per cent in March 2002 to 76.0 per cent at the end of March 2008. This increase was especially marked for

Table 5.2. Personal loans as per cent of total outstanding credit of commercial banks

	1996	2000	2007
State Bank of India and Associates	9.5	10.7	22.0
Other Nationalized Banks	9.1	10.9	15.8
Foreign Banks	8.8	17.1	24.8
Regional Rural Banks	10.5	18.8	20.5
Private-sector Banks	9.7	7.9	37.3
All Scheduled Commercial Banks	9.3	11.2	22.3

Source: Reserve Bank of India, 1997–2008.

consumer credit and reflected a mispricing of risk that could affect banks adversely in the event of an economic downturn.

Additional evidence of mispricing of risk in the Indian financial system came from the exposure of the banking system to the so-called 'sensitive' sectors, like the capital, real estate and commodity markets. This increased to 20.4 per cent of aggregate bank loans and advances in March 2007, with real estate contributing 18.7 of that figure, the capital market 1.5 and commodities 0.1. Further, the off-balance sheet exposure of banks increased significantly from 57 per cent of total bank assets at the end of March 2002 to 363 per cent at the end of March 2008.

This increase was mainly on account of derivatives, whose share averaged around 80 per cent, and once again was led by private and foreign banks. Public sector banks followed, with their exposure rising subsequent to the amendment of regulations to permit over-the-counter transactions in interest rate derivatives. Since the current accounting standards in India do not clearly specify how to account for and disclose losses and profits arising out of derivatives transactions, the propensity of some players to use derivatives to assume excessive leverage made it difficult to gauge the actual market and credit risk exposure of commercial banks.

These changes in the financial sector point to two further ways in which the current global crisis can continue to affect India. First, the credit stringency generated by the exodus of capital from the country and the uncertainties generated by the threat of default of retail loans that now constitute a high proportion of total advances could freeze up retail credit and curtail demand, as is happening in the developed industrial countries. Second, individuals and households burdened with past debt and/or uncertain about their employment would prefer to postpone purchases and not to take on additional interest and amortization payment commitments. Thus, the off-take of credit can shrink even if credit is available, resulting in a fall in credit-financed consumption and investment demand. Since growth in a number of areas such as the housing sector, automobiles and consumer durables has been driven by credit-financed purchases encouraged by easy liquidity and low interest rates, this would immediately affect the demand for housing, automobiles and durables. This, in turn, would have second-order effects in terms of contracting demand for other sectors and economic activities. As a result, a wide range of industries, services and segments of the labour market are likely to be indirectly affected by the crisis.

A growth slowdown, if it is sharp and severe in terms of its employment effects, could lead to defaults on the accumulated legacy of retail credit. Combined with losses on investments triggered by the growing appetite for risky assets among scheduled commercial banks after liberalization, this poses a real danger of insolvencies because of an increase in the proportion of non-performing assets in the Indian banking sector.

The Indian Government's Response

When the crisis first broke internationally, within official circles in India there was a perception that the Indian economy would be less affected and the Indian financial sector would be relatively immune to the winds from the international financial implosion. The presence of a large nationalized banking sector and a somewhat more stringent regulatory regime for real estate lending by banks were seen to protect the Indian financial system from harmful contagion from abroad. However, as shown in previous sections, these expectations have been belied, with sharp changes not only in real economic indicators, particularly for export production and employment, but also in financial variables such as stock market behaviour, bank lending behaviour and currency market trends.

The initial responses of the government focused on the financial side of the current crisis, with three major components to the first stimulus package adopted in late 2008. These included measures by both the Reserve Bank of India and the government aimed at reducing interest rates and increasing the access to credit of large and small firms, state governments and individuals. At the same time, access to credit from foreign sources was sought to be enhanced through measures that lifted the remaining constraints on external commercial borrowing. The ceiling on FII investment in rupee-denominated corporate bonds was more than doubled. The slogan appeared to be, 'if domestic credit is unavailable or expensive, borrow from abroad'. There were also measures aimed at getting state governments and an infrastructure investment fund set up by the central government, the India Infrastructure Finance Company Limited (IIFCL), to borrow more to finance capital, especially infrastructure, expenditure. Finally, there were attempts to spur the demand for automobiles through various incentives to buyers and to banks to provide credit for such purchases. So banks and financial institutions were encouraged to lend, and different economic actors were invited to borrow and spend. This included borrowing in foreign exchange to finance expenditures in areas like real estate, which are unlikely to yield foreign currency revenues that can be used to meet future repayment commitments.

Even if they had worked, such policies would only have strengthened the very same economic tendencies that generated the crisis in the developed countries in the first place. In any case, and perhaps unsurprisingly, by April 2008 it was already evident that these monetary measures had all proved to be lacking and did not ease credit conditions in any meaningful way. This was partly because of the liquidity trap characteristics of the situation, as the most creditworthy potential borrowers were unwilling to borrow because of the prevailing uncertainties and expectations of slowdown, and partly because banks also suddenly became more risk-averse. This meant that all other enterprises, even those who desperately required working capital just to stay afloat, found it increasingly difficult to access bank credit even as they faced more stringent demand conditions.

In such a situation, reducing interest rates does not solve the basic problem of tightened credit provision, even though it may marginally reduce costs for those who are able to access bank credit. The real economy is unlikely to be revived through such measures in the absence of a strong fiscal stimulus. It is now increasingly accepted that there is no alternative to the standard Keynesian device of using an expansionary fiscal stance to create more economic activity and demand, and thereby lift the economy from slump. Even so, the Government of India took an inordinately long time to announce what turned out to be a relatively small fiscal package, involving less than 0.5 per cent of GDP in additional direct public spending. This was combined with various tax cut measures, with estimated revenue losses still less than 1 per cent of GDP.

While the overall fiscal deficit (of central and state governments together) in the fiscal year 2009–10 is likely to increase to around 12 per cent of GDP, a large part of it is likely to be the result of tax cuts and subsidies rather than direct spending. There are several problems with relying upon such price-based fiscal measures. To begin with, tax cuts have an impact in terms of supporting economic activity only if producers respond by cutting their own output prices, and such price cuts in turn generate demand responses, or if they enable firms that would otherwise have closed down to survive. But neither is inevitable, nor even very likely given prevailing market structures in India. Across the world, governments are finding that in times of economic uncertainty, tax cuts are much less effective in stimulating activity than direct government expenditure. Similarly, measures that try to provide additional export incentives (such as interest reductions for export credit) to exporting sectors such as textiles, garments and leather do not counteract the effect of large losses of export orders as the major markets start shrinking.

Therefore direct public spending would be a far more effective way of dealing with the current slowdown even in India. However, the fiscal stimulus provided thus far has been both too small to have much impact and also not directed towards forms of expenditure that are likely to have high multiplier effects. Some of the most critical areas of potential spending have been ignored or neglected, such as increased resources to state governments, direct investment to ensure mass and middle-class housing, interventions to improve the livelihood conditions of farmers, expansion of the public food distribution system, enlargement of employment schemes and provision of social security.

While monetary policies are not sufficient to address the current economic problems in India, obviously measures to control finance are required, especially to prevent excessive risk-taking that destabilizes the real economy. Yet the Indian government appeared to buck the recent global policy trend by moving towards more financial deregulation and privatization of existing public financial institutions. In particular, its strategy seemed to be to further inflate the embryonic credit bubble to prevent growth from slipping sharply, in other words generating another speculative bubble to drive the real economy recovery, regardless of the possibility that this could pave the way for a financial meltdown that would subvert such a recovery. But such a possibility must be acknowledged. Even if it is not as yet in a debt-driven crisis, the Indian economy is substantially dependent on rapid expansion of private credit to sustain growth.

In addition, the government strategy has pushed infrastructural investment financed not only with domestic debt, but also with external commercial borrowing. While infrastructure investment is clearly much needed, relying on external borrowing for such investment not merely adds to the debt spiral, but also involves a currency mismatch, since infrastructure projects do not directly yield foreign exchange revenues and the indirect impact on exports is likely to be positive but difficult to assess. On the other hand, with global interest rates much lower than domestic rates, firms may not adequately take account of exchange rate risks and opt for foreign borrowing whenever available. This could lead to solvency problems if the rupee depreciates sharply, and would strain India's foreign reserve position if the exodus of foreign capital continues.

One of the lessons of the global crisis is that if big financial firms are lightly regulated and permitted to discount risk when seeking profits, then it is likely that the government would eventually have to nationalize them, because letting them fail could have adverse systemic effects. So the neoliberal strategy of deregulation and a minimal role for the state by relying on debt-financed private consumption and investment leads eventually to a crisis-induced retreat from neoliberalism, in the form of nationalization and state-financed bailouts. As the Indian crisis unfolds, the reliance of the Indian state on encouraging more private debt-financed spending to trigger a recovery is likely to lead to a similar denouement.

An alternative strategy for more sustainable recovery would clearly have to rely on a different basis for future growth. Given that the recent economic expansion of the Indian economy did not provide improved living standards for the bulk of the population, such an alternative strategy seems to be fairly obvious: emphasize wage-led growth, based on fiscal and monetary policies that provide greater stimuli to production for mass consumption in the domestic market. Monetary policy would have to prioritize financial inclusion, in particular enlarging the access of farmers and small producers in the nonagricultural sector to institutional credit and other financial services. In terms of fiscal policy, significantly increased public spending on infrastructure (particularly in rural areas, such as ensuring universal access to electrification, sanitation and paved roads, for example) and health and education, would not only ease supply constraints significantly but also provide employment with very large multiplier effects. A special package for agriculturalists, to help them cope with the rising costs of cultivation and extremely volatile crop prices, would help stabilize the rural economy. Foodgrains and essential agricultural commodities procured at remunerative prices should be distributed through an extensive public distribution system at prices that help sustain the minimum required consumption by the poor, so as to ensure price stability without damaging incentives in production, suppressing non-food consumption and worsening poverty. Fiscal measures would also have to provide incentives to shift patterns of both consumption and production to more sustainable directions. Such increased expenditure need not lead to much larger fiscal deficits if the existing loopholes for tax evasion are effectively plugged.

Of course, all this is obviously only possible if the economy is not subject to destabilizing flows of capital and sharp fluctuations in imports and exports. A greater degree of management of both trade and capital accounts is therefore a precondition for the successful implementation of such a strategy.

Notes

1 Figures computed from data reported by Reserve Bank of India, available online at http://rbidocs.rbi.org.in/rdocs/Bulletin/PDFs/T%2042%20[Trade%20and%20Bal].pdf and Central Statistical Organisation at http://mospi.gov.in/qr_estimate_gdp_curr_prices_12march09.pdf (accessed 17 April 2009).

2 Ibid.

References

All India Democratic Women's Association (AIDWA). 2009. *Report on the Condition of Work of Home-Based Workers in Delhi.* New Delhi: AIDWA.

Bergsten, F. 2008. 'Trade Has Saved America from Recession'. *Financial Times* 30 June. Online: http://blogs.ft.com/economistsforum/2008/07/trade-has-saved-america-from-recession/ (accessed 21 April 2009).

Business Intelligence. 2009. 'Recession Hits TCS Too'. 1 March. Online: http://www.hispaset.org/2009/03/recession-hits-tcs-too.html (accessed 24 March 2009).

Business Line Bureau. 2007. 'Sub-prime Crisis Brewing Here, Warns Tarapore'. *Hindu Business Line* 17 October. Online: http://www.thehindubusinessline.com/2007/10/17/stories/2007101750750600.htm (accessed 15 September 2008).

Central Statistical Organisation. 2009. *Estimate of Gross Domestic Product for the Third Quarter (October–December) 2008–09.* Press Information, Government of India, 27 February. Online: http://mospi.nic.in/PRESS_NOTE-Q3_27feb09.pdf (accessed 24 March 2009).

Chandrasekhar, C. P. 2008. *Global Liquidity and Financial Flows to Developing Countries: New Trends in Emerging Markets and Their Implications.* G24 Working Paper, Geneva: UNCTAD.

Chandrasekhar, C. P. and Jayati Ghosh. 2004. *The Market That Failed: Neoliberal Economic Reforms in India.* 2nd edition. New Delhi: LeftWord.

______. 2006. *Tracking the Macroeconomy, Volume I: The Indian Economy.* Hyderabad: ICFAI University Press.

______. 2007. 'Recent Employment Trends in India and China: An Unfortunate Convergence?' *Indian Journal of Labour Economics* 50, no. 3: 383–406. Online: http://www.macroscan.org/anl/apr07/anl050407India_China.htm (accessed 26 May 2009).

Committee on Financial Sector Assessment (Government of India and Reserve Bank of India). 2009. *India's Financial Sector: An Assessment, Vols I–VI.* New Delhi: Foundation Books.

Cornia, G. A., ed. 2006. *Pro-poor Macroeconomics: Potential and Limitations.* Houndsmill, Basingstoke: Palgrave Macmillan and UNRISD.

Dasgupta, S. and A. Singh. 2006. *Manufacturing, Services and Premature De-industrialisation in Developing Countries: A Kaldorian Empirical Analysis.* Working Paper No. 327, Centre for Business Research: University of Cambridge.

Goldman Sachs. 2007. *BRICs and Beyond.* New York: Goldman Sachs Global Economics Department. Online: http://www2.goldmansachs.com/ideas/brics/BRICs-andBeyond.html (accessed 24 February 2009).

Indiatimes Infotech. 2009. 'TCS Q3: Story Beyond Numbers'. Online: http://infotech.indiatimes.com/quickiearticleshow/3988843.cms (accessed 24 March 2009).

Institute for International Finance. 2009. 'Capital Flows to Emerging Market Economies, Institute for International Finance'. 27 January. Online: http://www.iif.com/download.php?id51130eNm7tXk5 (accessed 22 March 2009).

Kohn, D. L. 2008. 'Global Economic Integration and Decoupling'. Speech at the International Research Forum on Monetary Policy, Frankfurt, Germany, 26 June. Retrieved from Board of Governors of the Federal Reserve System: http://www.federalreserve.gov/newsevents/speech/kohn20080626a.htm (accessed 27 March 2009).

Kose, M. A., C. Otrok and E. Prasad. 2008. *Global Business Cycles: Convergence or Decoupling?* Working Paper Series No 13, April, Social Science Research Network. Online: http://papers.ssrn.com/sol3/papers.cfm?abstract_id51116989 (accessed 11 March 2009).

Kregel, J. 1998. 'Instability, Volatility and the Process of Capital Accumulation'. In *Economic Theory and Social Justice* edited by G.Gandolfo and F. Marzano. London: Macmillan, 149–67.

______. 2008. *Using Minsky's Cushions of Safety to Analyse the Crisis in the U.S. Subprime Mortgage Market.* IDEAs Working Paper 04/2008. Online: http://www.networkideas.org/working/jun2008/04_2008.pdf (accessed 22 March 2009).

Labour Bureau. 2009. *Report on Effect of Economic Slowdown on Employment in India (October–December 2008).* Chandigarh: Ministry of Labour and Employment, Government of India.

Lakshman, N. 2009. 'Indian IT Commiserates at NASSCOM Show'. *Business Week*, 21 April. Online: http://www.businessweek.com/globalbiz/content/feb2009/gb20090212_376981.htm (accessed 21 April 2009).

National Commission for Enterprises in the Unorganised Sector (NCEUS). 2008. *The Global Economic Crisis and the Informal Economy in India: Need for Urgent Measures and Fiscal Stimulus.* New Delhi: Government of India. Online: http://nceus.gov.in/Global_Economic_crisis.pdf (accessed 11 March 2009).

National Science Board. 2008. *Science and Engineering Indicators 2008, Vols I and II.* Arlington, VA: National Science Foundation.

Patnaik, P. 2008. *The Value of Money.* New Delhi: Tulika and New York: Columbia University Press (2009).

Reserve Bank of India. 1997–2008. *Basic Statistical Returns of Scheduled Commercial Banks in India.* Various issues. Mumbai: Reserve Bank of India. Online: http://www.rbi.org.in/scripts/AnnualPublications.aspx?head5Basic%20Statistical%20Returns (accessed 11 March 2009).

______. 2008. *Handbook of Statistics on Indian Economy.* October. Online: http://www.rbi.org.in/scripts/AnnualPublications.aspx?head5Handbook%20of%20Statistics%20on%20Indian%20Economy (accessed 21 March 2009).

______. 2009a. *India's Overall Balance of Payments in Dollars.* March. Online: http://rbidocs.rbi.org.in/rdocs/Bulletin/DOCs/T43_TradeBal.xls (accessed 21 March 2009).

______. 2009b. *Foreign Investment Flows.* March. Online: http://rbidocs.rbi.org.in/rdocs/Bulletin/DOCs/T46_TradeBal.xls (accessed 21 March 2009).

______. 2009c. *Foreign Exchange Reserves.* March. Online: http://rbidocs.rbi.org.in/rdocs/Bulletin/DOCs/T44_TradeBal.xls (accessed 21 March 2009).

______. 2009d. *International Investment Position (IIP) of India as at the End of September 2008.* 19 March. Online: http://rbidocs.rbi.org.in/rbiadmin/scripts/BS_PressReleaseDisplay.aspx?prid520357 (accessed 21 March 2009).

______. 2009e. *Outward Remittances under the Liberalised Remittance Scheme.* March. Online: http://rbidocs.rbi.org.in/rdocs/Bulletin/DOCs/T46A_TradeBal.xls (accessed 21 March 2009).

______. 2009f. Invisibles in India's Balance of Payments: An Analysis of Trade in Services, Remittances and Income. *Reserve Bank of India Bulletin* March: 393–434.

______. 2009g. *International Investment Position (IIP) of India as at the End of December 2008.* 26 May. Online: http://www.rbi.org.in/scripts/BS_PressReleaseDisplay.aspx?prid520748 (accessed 30 May 2009).

Subbarao, D. 2009. 'Impact of Financial Crisis on India: Collateral Damage and Response'. *Reserve Bank of India Bulletin* March: 385–91.

Economic Times. 2009. 'IT Companies Find the Going Tough'. 26 April, 2.

World Bank. 2008. 'Remittances May Buoy Developing Countries Caught in Financial Crisis'. 24 November. Online: http://web.worldbank.org/WBSITE/EXTERNAL/NEWS/0,,contentMDK:21996712·pagePK:64257043·piPK:437376·theSitePK:4607,00.html (accessed 21 April 2009).

Chapter 6

THEORIZING FOOD SECURITY AND POVERTY IN THE ERA OF ECONOMIC REFORMS*

Utsa Patnaik

Introduction

The correct theorizing of the questions of food security and poverty has become particularly important at the present time, which is one of rapid changes in the economic environment in which small producers including farmers and workers are living. In a poor developing country, the incidence of poverty is very closely linked to the availability of food, in which the staple foodgrains still remain predominant, accounting for three-fifths of the daily energy intake of the population. The measurement of poverty in India has traditionally adopted a nutritional norm specified in terms of an average daily energy intake measured in calories. The National Nutrition Monitoring Bureau has informed us that,

> the NNMB has consistently confirmed in successive surveys that the main bottleneck in the dietaries of even the poorest Indians is energy and not protein as was hitherto believed [...] *the data also indicate that the measurement of consumption of cereals can be used as a proxy for total energy intake. This observation is of considerable significance as it helps to determine rapid, though approximate, estimates of energy intake at the household level.* (Krishnaswamy et al. 1997, emphasis added)

It is this strong link between the staple foodgrains intake and poverty based on a nutritional norm which enables us to put forward an analysis of the recent trends in food security and in poverty, in light of the impact of changing economic policies during the last 15 years.

The majority of academics and the Government of India today make two claims which I believe to be factually incorrect, claims which are underpinned by a wholly fallacious theoretical understanding of the current situation. They claim, first, that there is an 'oversupply' of foodgrains relative to demand (which they assume to be growing normally) and so infer that foodgrains production should be cut back in favour of 'diversification'; second, that poverty has been declining in India in the era of reforms, specifically in

* An earlier version of this chapter was published in *Social Scientist* 33, no. 7/8 (Jul–Aug, 2005).

the decade of the 1990s. My contention as regards both propositions is that they are incorrect, and that the correct position on theoretical and factual grounds is precisely the opposite. First, there is not oversupply of foodgrains but a decline in foodgrains supply and an even more drastic decline of effective demand for foodgrains especially in rural India owing to an abnormally fast loss of purchasing power during the last six years: so, far from cutting back foodgrains output, the correct policy is to raise purchasing power and restore effective demand as well as to restore access to affordable foodgrains through a combination of a universal, and not targeted, employment guarantee scheme and through reverting to a universal, not targeted, public distribution system.

Second, far from the percentage of population in poverty declining as claimed, the factually correct position on the basis of current data is that poverty is very high, affecting at least three-quarters of the rural and over two-fifths of the urban population. Moreover, the data show that the depth of poverty has increased considerably during the 15 years of reforms, with more people being pushed down into a poorer nutritional status than before in most of the Indian states and at the all-India level. The reason that many academics and the Planning Commission reach the conclusion that poverty is declining is that they use an estimation procedure which has no basis in logic and is indefensible on academic grounds. What that estimation procedure is and how it differs from the correct procedure is one of the main questions I will try to explain, for I believe that it is part of the 'right to information' that the intelligent citizen should be able to independently reach a judgement about the validity of the official procedure and not simply take the truth of certain statements for granted. My lecture today will focus on the correct theorizing of these two main questions: of the declining effective demand for foodgrains, and of the extent of poverty. This has become extremely important because the widely prevalent incorrect theorizing in academic and government circles is leading to policy formulations and measures which will only serve to worsen mass welfare and plunge even larger sections of the rural population in particular into higher unemployment and food deprivation.

The first and second sections will briefly discuss the fiscal contraction and other income-deflating macroeconomic policies combined with exposure to global price declines, which have led to massive loss of purchasing power in rural India in the last six years and are reflected in falling foodgrains absorption and falling energy intake. The third section will discuss the interpretation of the decline in foodgrains absorption, while the fourth and last section will take up the question of poverty estimation and how official and most academic estimates use a particular indirect method of estimation, which completely delinks poverty from nutrition norms by ignoring current data which show the ground reality of rising nutritional deprivation and increasing depth of poverty.

What Deflationary Policies and Trade Liberalization Have Meant for the Rural Economy in India

Deflationary macroeconomic policies are strongly favoured by international and domestic financial interest groups who are quite obsessive about controlling inflation and would prefer to see even an economy with a high rate of unemployment growing slowly and raising unemployment further rather than risk any possibility of prices rising owing to

Table 6.1. Policies followed by 78 countries under fund-guided reforms

	Percentage of Total Number of Countries Implementing Policy
1. Restraint on Central Government Expenditure	91
2. Limits on Credit Expansion	99
3. Reduction in Ratio of Budget Deficit to GDP	83
4. Wage Restraint	65
5. Exchange Rate Policy	54

Source: IMF study quoted in Cornia, Jolly and Stewart 1987.

Table 6.2. Reduction in rural development expenditures under economic reforms, selected years 1985–90 to 2000–01

	1985–90 Average	1993–94	1995–96	1997–98	2000–01
1. Rural Development Expenditure as Percentage of NNP	3.8	2.8	2.6	2.3	1.9
2. Above plus Infrastructure	10.5	8.4	6.9	6.4	5.8

Source: Government of India, Ministry of Finance, annual *Economic Survey*, for years 2001–02 to 2003–04, appendix table S-44. 'Rural development expenditures' here are the plan outlays of centre and states under the five heads of agriculture, rural development, irrigation and flood control, special areas programmes, and village and small-scale industry. Infrastructure includes all energy and transport including urban. Calculated from current values of expenditure and NNP at factor cost.

expansionary policies reducing unemployment. International creditors wish to maintain high real values of their financial assets and high real interest rates (inflation would erode both) and are happy with bouts of asset deflation in developing countries so that these assets can be snapped up at low prices by their corporations. Their insensate and obsessive fear of inflation can be seen in the policies advised uniformly by the International Monetary Fund to 78 developing countries in the 1980s and summarized in Table 6.1 from an IMF study. The first three policies – restraint on central government expenditure, limits on credit expansion, and reduction of budget deficit to GDP ratio, add up together to a strongly deflationary package, and all three were actually implemented at the same time by four-fifths of the concerned countries, while two-thirds capped wages and over half devalued their currency.

The results of the public expenditure–reducing, income-deflating policies of the decade up to the mid-1980s have been documented as a sharp decline in rates of investment in both capital formation and in the social sectors, leading to reduced or negative GDP growth and negative impact on the human development indicators (see in particular Cornia, Jolly and Stewart 1987). A number of studies since then have confirmed the adverse impact and have argued for expansionary policies (see Baker, Epstein and Pollin 1998; Halevy and Fontaine 1998; Patnaik 2000).[1]

India has been following exactly the same deflationary policy package since 1991. Its impact has been especially severe in India's agricultural sector, which saw

Table 6.3. Decelerating growth rates of agricultural output

Period	Foodgrains	Non-foodgrains	All Crops	Population
1980–81 to 1989–90	2.85	3.77	3.19	2.1
1990–91 to 2000–01	1.66	1.86	1.73	1.9

Source: Government of India, Ministry of Finance, *Economic Survey 2001–02*, 189. Note that slowing down of output growth is much steeper than slowing down of population growth implying falling per head output.

Table 6.4. Employment decline in rural India

	Year 1983	Year 1993–1994	Year 1999–2000	Growth per Annum	
				1983 to 1993–94 %	1993–94 to 1999–2000 %
RURAL					
1. Population, mn.	546.6	658.8	727.5	1.79	1.67
2. Labour Force, mn.	204.2	255.4	270.4	2.15	0.96
3. Workforce, mn.	187.9	241.0	250.9	2.40	0.67
4. Unemployed, mn. (2. – 3.)	16.3	14.4	19.5	–1.19	5.26

Source: Government of India, Ministry of Finance, *Economic Survey 2002–03*, 218.

sharp reduction in public planned development expenditures in rural areas, which has traditionally included agriculture, rural development, irrigation and flood control – all vital for maintaining output – to which we add also the outlays on special areas programmes, and village and small-scale industry to define overall 'Rural Development Expenditures' or RDE. The employment-generating programmes had assumed a special importance from the drought year 1987 onwards.

Over the 7th Plan period marking the pre-reforms phase, from 1985 to 1990; Rs. 51,000 crore was spent on rural development, amounting to 3.8 per cent of Net National Product (NNP), and Rs. 91,000 crore or nearly 7 per cent of NNP was spent on infrastructure.[2] By the mid-1990s, annual spending on rural development was down to 2.6 per cent of NNP, and after including infrastructure, less than 7 per cent was being spent compared to 11 per cent during the 7th Plan. Further declines took place so that by 2000–01 the share of spending under these heads was down to 5.8 per cent of NNP, the rural development part halving to only 1.9 per cent (see Table 6.2). I estimate that in constant 1993–94 prices, about Rs. 30,000 crore less was being spent by the end-decade year 1999–2000, compared to the beginning, 1990–91. A crude point-to-point comparison would suggest an annual income loss of between Rs. 120,000 and Rs. 150,000 crore assuming a multiplier value between 4 and 5. Actual income loss would have been greater taking the cumulative losses over successive years. The real per capita rural development expenditure, which was Rs. 150.9 in 1989–90, had declined to Rs. 136.6 by 1996–97 and reached its lowest point in 2000–01 at Rs. 124.4.[3] This harsh contractionary policy had nothing to do with any objective resource constraint but simply reflected the deflationary policies of the Bretton Woods institutions, which were internalized and sought to be justified by the Indian government.

There is no economic rationale for believing that 'public investment crowds out private investment', which is the common argument put forward for reducing the state's role in rural development. Precisely the contrary has been shown to hold for certain types of investment essential for an irrigation-dependent agriculture like India's, such as irrigation projects of all types. Private tube-well investment is profitable only where the water table remains high owing to seepage from state-built canal irrigation systems, and where community integrated watershed management (planting trees and using check-dams) is encouraged with state help. Private over-exploitation of ground water has now reached a crisis point in many states in India, with the water table falling rapidly and with even the richest farmers unable to reach water after investing heavily in deep bore-wells and submersible pumps. Other infrastructure investment such as rural power projects, roads, bridges, school buildings, clinics and so on, is never undertaken by private investors but is vital for stimulating development and providing livelihoods both directly to those employed in building them and through the important multiplier effects on employment and incomes of the increased wage incomes being spent on simple consumer goods and services within the villages. The market for machine-made textiles and other goods also thereby expands.

The net result of the unwise cut-back of public investment and in RDE has been a slowing of the rate of output growth – both foodgrains and non-foodgrains growth rates have almost halved in the '90s compared to the pre-reform '80s, and both have fallen below the population growth rate even though this too is slowing down (Table 6.3). This has led to declining per capita output during the '90s, for the first time since the mid-1960s agricultural crisis, which, however, had been short-lived, whereas per head agricultural output continues to fall today even after a decade; the agricultural universities earlier played a major role in developing and helping to disseminate new crop varieties, and the cut in funding for research in these universities by affecting the search for better rain-fed crop varieties has also contributed to the deceleration in the growth of yields. With increasing use of land for commercial and residential purposes, the gross sown area in India has remained static since 1991, so it is only through yield rise that output growth can be maintained, and it is here that the failure is evident.

The combination of the decline in state RDE and the near-halving of agricultural growth has produced a major crisis of rising unemployment. There is both fast growing open unemployment and a fall in the number of days employed of the workforce during the economic reforms period. Even with constant labour coefficients (labour days used per unit of crop output), a near halving of employment growth was to be expected given the decline in crop output growth, but the decline in jobs has been even more, as mechanization, especially of harvesting, and use of chemical weed-killers as opposed to manual weeding, has led to falling labour coefficients. Further, the rural non-farm employment growth, which was robust in the 1980s owing to reasonably high state RDE, declined in the 1990s. The ratio of labour force to population, or the participation rate, has declined (lower participation rate reflects difficulty of finding work), and the ratio of workforce to labour force has declined because open unemployment has been growing at over 5 per cent annually (Table 6.4). The elasticity of employment with respect to output was 0.7 during 1983 to 1993–94 but has declined to 0.01 or virtually zero, taking the reforms period 1993–94 to 1999–2000.

Let no one imagine that unemployed rural workers are migrating and finding employment in industry: there have also been massive job losses in manufacturing during the reform period, and the share of the secondary sector in GDP has fallen from 29 to around 22 per cent during the 1990s; in short, India has seen de-industrialization. The agricultural depression has reduced the share of agriculture in GDP from about a third at the beginning of the '90s to just over a fifth a decade later, but the labour force and population dependent on agriculture has hardly fallen, reflecting the decline in per head incomes. Thus both the material productive sectors have declined, and the only sector which has ballooned in an abnormal manner[4] is the tertiary or services sector, which now accounts for over half of GDP.

Only a small proportion of the services sector comprises IT-enabled high income services, business process outsourcing, domestic tourism services and the like. The major part in employment terms is still low-productivity activities in which the rural displaced workers stagnate at low income levels, servicing the requirements of the upper income elites who have been improving their real income position fast. Disposable incomes have risen even faster for this segment since a part of the neoliberal reforms include reduction in direct tax rates. Advanced countries usually have this upper-income 10 to 15 per cent minority of Indians in mind when they demand market access for their manufactures and agricultural products, and no doubt 100 to 150 million people is a large potential market. But the situation of the vast majority of the mainly rural population, who not merely stagnate at low income levels but whose position is considerably worse today than a decade earlier, cannot be ignored: a potentially highly destabilizing situation is in the making.

While income and employment reduction through deflationary policies is the first main reason for loss of purchasing power in rural India, the second main reason is the unwise opening to global markets through full trade liberalization at a time from the mid-1990s, when global markets went into recession and primary product prices started falling – a fall which continues to this day.

More Trade Leads to More Hunger in Developing Countries under Global and Local Deflationary Conditions

The land resources of India, more so than in most developing countries, have the potential for producing a highly diversified range of products – not only the crops and fruits grown in the summer season in temperate lands but also the typically tropical crops, which cannot be grown at all in advanced countries located in temperate regions. The crops of our lands have been demanded abroad in advanced countries for over three centuries for meeting their direct consumption and raw material needs. *But historically, the growth of exports from tropical agriculture under free trade regimes has always led to a fall in domestic foodgrains output and availability, plunging the mass of the population into deepening undernutrition and in extreme cases into famine.* In the half century before Indian independence, per capita foodgrains output fell by nearly 30 per cent while export crops grew ten times faster than foodgrains. I have earlier discussed some historical and current cases in developing countries of the inverse relation between primary sector exports and domestic foodgrains absorption (see Patnaik 1996, 2003a).

This is bound to happen since land is not a reproducible resource and heavy external demand made on our more botanically diverse lands by advanced countries to meet their ever-rising and diversifying needs leads to diversion of our land and resources away from locally consumed food staples to meet export demands. The position is worsened by exports out of more slowly growing food output itself. The Ricardian theory of comparative advantage, which says there is necessarily mutual gain from specialization and trade, contains a material and logical fallacy since the conclusion is based crucially on assuming that 'both countries produce both goods', which is factually untrue for agriculture. The advanced countries, mainly located in cold temperate regions, cannot produce tropical crops at all, so the cost of production of, say, coffee or rubber cannot even be defined in these countries, let alone relative cost and transformation frontiers (Patnaik 2005).[5]

In theory, more primary exports from developing countries can accompany more food production for domestic needs, but this can only happen when there is substantial rise in investment to raise productivity, for land is a non-producible resource whose 'supply' can only increase via investment permitting one hectare to produce what two hectares did earlier. It also requires that mass domestic demand grows and is not held in check by income deflating policies or excessive taxation, as was the case under colonial systems.

The deeply disturbing feature of the current thrust for liberalizing trade is that it has been taking place within an investment-reducing, deflationary regime. I predicted in 1992 that given the deflationary climate, food security would be undermined with trade liberalization in India, and that is precisely what has happened. As soon as trade was liberalized from 1991, within a few years, 8 million hectares of food-growing land were converted to exportable crops, leading to a fall in per head foodgrains output, but farmers did not benefit since their exposure to steeply falling global primary prices from mid-decade had plunged them into spiralling farm debt and insolvency. Nearly nine thousand recorded farmer suicides in India since 1998 are only the tip of the iceberg; there is a pervasive agrarian crisis, and foodgrains absorption in India is back to the level prevailing 50 years ago.

Trade liberalization and an export thrust make sense when local and global markets are expanding owing to expansionary developmental policies, which promote growth in the material productive sectors, rising employment and incomes. But when the opposite is the case, when both globally and in local economies the dominant policy sentiment is strongly deflationary, as at present, then trade liberalization spells lowered mass welfare in developing countries.[6] India's experience in the last 14 years provides a good illustration of this.

India, as a signatory to GATT 1994, removed all quantitative restrictions on trade and converted to tariffs by April 2001, lowering the average tariff rate at the same time to 35 per cent, or well below the bound rates, which were 100 per cent for crops and 150 per cent for agricultural processed products. India's thrust for trade liberalization could not have been worse timed, since advanced country markets were in recession and global primary product prices went into a steep tailspin with 40–50 per cent decline in unit dollar prices of all crops – cereals, cotton, jute, sugar, tea, coffee – and up to 80 per cent decline in some oil crops between 1995 and 2001 as Table 6.5 shows. With a brief spike in 2002, prices have continued to fall, and some prices are today lower than they were as far back as 1986. The price to growers is even lower than the world price as the activities of the state marketing boards have been replaced by private transnational companies for many crops.

As prices fell for Indian producers of export crops, their access to low-cost credit was reduced under financial sector reforms. Since the nationalization of banks in 1969 agriculture and small-scale industry had been treated as priority sectors offered bank credit at a lower-than-average interest rate, but that ended with financial reforms, thrusting farmers into dependence on private moneylenders and high-cost credit (interest rates are usurious, ranging from 36 to 60 per cent annually). Other crucial input prices including power tariff were raised as part of the neoliberal dicta on reducing subsidies (which were already meagre compared to developed countries'). Reduced tariff protection meant that producers of rice, fresh fruit and dairy products faced the undermining of their incomes from the inflow of usually heavily subsidized foreign goods.

More than six thousand indebted farmers, mainly cotton farmers, have committed suicide in Andhra Pradesh alone since 1998 as its government, which had entered into a state-level Structural Adjustment Program with the World Bank, raised the power tariff five times even as the cotton price fell by half (Table 6.6). Over one thousand farmer suicides have also taken place in Punjab, mainly in the cotton belt, new rounds of suicides are being recorded in Karnataka and Vidarbha, and in the four years between 2001 and 2005, over 1250 suicides have been recorded in Wayanad in Kerala as prices for the local growers of coffee, tea and spices have nosedived even more steeply than global prices once large companies took over purchase and marketing. Thus by 2003 the price of coffee to the grower was only one quarter and that of tea and pepper only one third of the prices prevailing in 1999.

The agrarian crisis was the main reason for the decisive mass rejection of neoliberal policies and the May 2004 electoral defeat of the NDA coalition at the centre as well as the TDP government in Andhra Pradesh. In recognition of the employment crisis, the new United Progressive Alliance (UPA) promised to implement a National Rural Employment Guarantee Act, which has been recently formulated and passed by Parliament, but which has been diluted by taking the household as the unit, where only one member is entitled to work, and by providing the option of setting the wage below the statutory minimum wage.

India has exported record volumes of wheat and rice during the last six years, and its share in global exports of rice and wheat has risen quite noticeably. Despite the drastic slowing down of output growth noted in Table 6.3, India exported 22 million tonnes of foodgrains during the two years 2002 and 2003 (Bhalla 2005), and the share of grain exports in total exports has risen from under one-fifth to almost a quarter. There is higher global trade integration reflected in the rising trade–GDP ratio. During the severe drought year starting from monsoon 2002, despite grain output being 30 million tonnes lower than in the previous year, from June 2002 to November 2003 a total of 17 million

Table 6.5. Prices of some important traded primary products, in US dollars

	1988	1995	1997	2000	2001 (Jan.)	Per Cent Change 2001 over 1995
Wheat (US HW)	167	216	142	130	133	– 38.2
Wheat (US RSW)	160	198	129	102	106	– 46.5
Wheat (Argentine)	145	218	129	112	118	– 45.9
Maize (Argentine)	116	160	133	88	80	– 50.0
Maize (US)	118	159	112	97	92	– 22.0
Rice (US)	265.7	—	439.0	271	291	– 33.7
Rice (Thai)	284	336	316	207	179	– 46.7
Cotton	63.5	98.2	77.5	66	49.1	– 50.0
Groundnut Oil	590	991	1010	788*	—	– 20.5†
Palm Oil	437	626	93.5	74.7*	—	– 88.1†
Soyabean Oil	464	479	625	71.4*	—	– 85.1†
Soyabean Seed	297	273	262	199	178	– 34.8
Sorghum Seed	110	156	111	102	99	– 36.5
Sugar	10.2	13.3	11.4	10.2	9.2	– 30.8
Jute	370	366	302	276*	—	– 24.6†

* Numbers relate to 1999.
†Per cent change is 1999 compared to 1995. The 2004 price data show that sugar, cotton and jute prices continue to remain flat around 2001 levels while the cereals show some rise.
Source: *Food Outlook*, various issues from 1986 to 2001; available from Global Information and Early Warning System on Agriculture, UN Food and Agriculture Organization; and *Monthly Commodity Price Bulletin*, UNCTAD 2001. For the cereals, edible oils and seeds the unit is US$ per ton; for cotton and sugar, US cents per pound; and for jute, US$ per metric ton.

tonnes of foodgrains were exported by the former NDA government. Superficially it looks as though policies of trade liberalization have 'worked'.

However, the crucial fact which is suppressed in official publications and in the writings of pro-reform economists, and this is true even after the elections and the change in government, is that the vastly increased grain exports have been coming out of more and more empty stomachs as millions of rural labourers and farmers have suffered job loss and income decline. Foodgrains absorption in India today has reached a historic low as a result of the massive decline in purchasing power, especially in villages, owing to the combination of rising unemployment, rising input and credit costs for farmers and exposure to global price declines. Loss of purchasing power is pervasive, affecting both the 158 million wage-dependent workers as well as the 120 million cultivating workers and their families. Targeting the food subsidy from 1997–98 by restricting supply of cheaper grain to only those officially identified as 'below the poverty line' has also added to the institutional denial of affordable foodgrains to the poor, not merely owing to mistakes of wrong exclusion from the set of the officially poor, but also owing to the gross official underestimation of the numbers in poverty, discussed at the end of the chapter.

Table 6.6. Suicides of farmers in Andhra Pradesh by district

	District	1998	1999	2000	2001	2002	Total
1.	Warangal	77	7	7	28	903	1022
2.	Ananthapur	1	1	50	50	10	112
3.	Mahaboobnagar	14	2	25	10	—	51
4.	Karimnagar	31	10	6	30	1220	1297
5.	Guntur	32	10	1	6	—	49
6.	Khammam	20	5	3	6	2	36
7.	Medak	15	3	2	8	—	28
8.	Adilabad	9	8	5	13	—	35
9.	Nalgonda	5	1	10	11	8	35
10.	Nizamabad	9	1	—	11	457	478
11.	Rangareddy	5	—	3	6	—	14
12.	Kurnool	4	4	2	4	—	14
13.	Chittoor	3	—	—	2	—	5
14.	Krishna	4	1	1	3	1	10
15.	Prakasam	1	3	—	2	—	6
16.	West Godavari	1	—	—	5	—	6
17.	East Godavari	—	—	1	2	—	3
18.	Srikakulam	—	1	—	—	—	1
19.	Cuddapah	—	—	—	4	—	4
20.	Visakhapatnam	—	—	—	1	—	1
	Unknown	2	1	—	—	—	3
	Total	233	58	116	202	2601	3210

Note: The total number of suicides up to 2004 is over 5000. Data is from police records up to January 27, 2002, presented by Kisan Sabha at a symposium on farmer suicides held at Hyderabad (Andhra Pradesh), 3 February 2002. The table has been partially updated by incorporating information for the entire year 2002, so far available for the three districts only (Warangal, Karimnagar and Nizamabad) as reported in *The Hindu*, Hyderabad edition, January 6, 2003. For the other districts the figures given in the last column continue to refer to a single month, January 2002. Additional suicides numbering 1,700 have taken place since then, for which the district break-up is not yet available.

Large Decline in Foodgrains Absorption per Head Is Owing to Falling Purchasing Power, Not 'Voluntary Choice'

The per capita availability or absorption of foodgrains in India has declined alarmingly during the decade of deflationary neoliberal economic reforms, to only 155 kg annually, taking the 3-year average ending in 2002–03. This current level is the same as 50 years ago during the 1st Plan period, and it is also the level seen during 1937–41 under colonialism. This means that the food security gains of the four decades of protectionism up to 1991 have been totally reversed.

After independence, from the early 1950s to four decades later, taking the three years ending 1991, the per capita foodgrains availability climbed slowly from 155 kg to 177 kg – the achievement not only of the 'Green Revolution' but of expansionary policies slowly raising mass incomes and demand, without too much rise in already high inequality. While the Green Revolution had many problems, its positive achievement in raising grain availability and absorption should not be underestimated. All this was reversed from the early 1990s. As the new regime of deflationary economic reform policies from 1991 eroded mass employment and incomes, we find a decline of per capita absorption to 174 kg by the triennium ending in 1998 and a very steep fall after that to the current abysmally low 155 kg level. Forty years of successful effort to raise availability has been wiped out in a single decade, with over four-fifths of the decline coming in the last six years.[7]

Availability or absorption is calculated from the hardest data we have, on annual net output[8] adjusted only for change in public stocks and in trade, so by definition it has to cover all final uses: direct use for consumption as grain and its products, use as feed for converting to animal products (a part of this is exported), and industrial use. Per head availability/absorption (the two are used as synonyms) is now one of the lowest in the world, with only sub-Saharan Africa and some of the least developed countries registering lower absorption than India. Since urban India has been increasing average absorption and average calorie intake, it is rural India where the fall has been very steep. For comparison, China absorbed 325 kg grains per capita (excluding tubers) in the mid-1990s, compared to India's less than 200 kg at that time. Mexico absorbed 375 kg, Western European countries absorbed 600 kg or more, and the USA absorbed 850 kg. Except under abnormal conditions of war or famine, grain absorption is always observed to rise as a country's average income rises. This is why the fall in India is so unusual, and it is not being correctly theorized.

Although grain output per head fell by about 12 kg over the five years ending in 2002–03, as may be seen in Table 6.7, the per head absorption has fallen much more, by 21 kg over the same period. The average Indian family of five members is absorbing 100 kg less of foodgrains annually than a mere five years ago, and since in urban India absorption has risen (calorie intake has also risen), it is the rural family which is absorbing even less than the average fall indicates. This abnormal fall is because of the loss of purchasing power for reasons already discussed, and it has been reflected in a massive build-up of unsold public food stocks, reaching 63 million tonnes by July 2002, some 40 million tonnes in excess of the normal stocks for that time of year. Rather than starting large-scale food-for-work schemes to restore lost work and incomes, between June 2002 and October 2003, over 17 million tonnes of foodgrains were got rid of by the NDA government by exporting out of stocks with subsidy, and it went mainly to feed European cattle and Japanese pigs.

There can be two very different ways that such huge food stocks can build up: demand growth is normal but output increases much faster, or alternatively output increase is normal, but demand reduces very fast owing to loss of incomes, and the demand curve shifts downwards. In both cases supply exceeds demand, but for very different reasons. As already shown, output growth has not been normal but has actually gone down, so the first reason does not hold. It is mass effective demand, hence absorption, which has declined to a much greater extent, so it is the second reason and not the first which accounts for the present paradox of increasing rural hunger and record grain exports. If rural demand had been maintained even at the 1991 level, the absorption of foodgrains today would be 26 million tonnes higher than it is, and there would be no crisis in the agriculture of Punjab and Haryana, which have lost an internal market to that extent in the last six years alone. Instead of rural per capita calorie intake declining to below the urban average, as has been the case in the 1990s, energy intake would have been maintained.

Since all-India per capita income has been rising during the reform period, such a drastic fall in foodgrains absorption is clearly only compatible with a drastic rise in the inequality of income distribution as we earlier pointed out (Patnaik 2003b). But rising inequality can also occur when all incomes are rising. Rising inequality per se is neither necessary nor sufficient for the observed drastic *absolute* decline in grain absorption.[9] The only scenario which is compatible with it is a particular type of rise in inequality, namely absolute decline in real incomes and rise in absolute poverty, concentrated mainly in the rural areas, combined with a large rise in real incomes for the top fractiles of the population, concentrated mainly in urban areas. The data are partly reflecting this: one indicator is the decline in the per capita real expenditure on consumption by the lowest four-fifths of the rural population during the end-1990s and a very sharp rise by the top one-fifth of urban population, which has been noted by Sen and Himanshu (2005). But even these findings with *expenditure* are likely to understate the true extent of *income* decline for the mass of the rural population (we have no direct data on incomes). This is because this mass has been obliged to lose assets to maintain consumption and stay alive, while the well-to-do have been saving much more over and above their greatly enhanced real expenditure and have entered real estate and financial markets. In short, there are, in addition to the changes in observed flow variables like expenditure, also stock adjustments going on, namely changes in the distribution of assets which are adverse for the poor and which the data we have do not capture adequately as yet.

The official position is one of wholesale denial of these obvious facts and the creation of what can only be called a fairy-tale, fit only for intellectual infants. It is argued that there is voluntary reduction in foodgrains intake and thus there is 'overproduction' requiring a cut-back in cereals output – a position not supported by the facts. The full fairy-tale set out in official publications goes like this: every segment of the population is reducing demand for cereals because average income is rising. (Here, the increased income is assumed to be distributed in the same way as earlier, with no increase in inequality.) People of all expenditure classes are voluntarily diversifying their diets away from cereals. The only reason that farmers continue to produce more cereals than demanded, and hence big stocks build up, is because too much output has been encouraged by 'too high' administered, minimum support prices (MSP) of cereals. So MSP should be cut, cereals output in excess of what is demanded at present should be discouraged, and the output pattern in agriculture should be diversified to more commercial export crops under the aegis of agro-businesses.

This analysis is completely incorrect and is inconsistent with the hard facts of rising unemployment, falling output growth, immiserization of farmers in debt and land loss, and the resulting deep agrarian distress. It is dangerous in reaching policy conclusions which are the opposite of those required and which if implemented will reduce food security further and pauperize even more farmers.

To give an analogy, albeit an imperfect one, suppose that a patient has been wrongly diagnosed by a doctor and loses weight rapidly to the extent of 30 kg. The doctor then blames the tailor for making the clothes of the patient too big and advises that the old clothes should be thrown away and new ones sewn to fit his wasted body. Such advice will certainly alarm the patient, for it shows that an abnormal situation is being rationalized as normal and no treatment to restore the patient to health will be followed. The official position on foodgrains output and food security, regrettably shared by many academics who seem not to have applied their minds to the matter, is indicative of such illogical reasoning and is alarming indeed for farmers and labourers in distress. The official prescription of reducing MSP, ending open-ended procurement and cutting back on output will worsen food deprivation and deepen poverty for the millions of farmers and labourers already in deep distress. The idea that price fall benefits 'the consumer' ignores the fact that three-fifths of consumers in a poor country are themselves rural producers or dependent for jobs on producers and that deflation harms their incomes.

It is an alarming scenario too for the farmers of northern India who over the last four decades have been asked to specialize in foodgrains production, and have performed magnificently, selling their rising surpluses uncomplainingly to the Food Corporation of India even when the domestic procurement price was far below the world price in the 1970s and again in the decade up to the late 1990s. They have ensured cheap food to urban areas and food deficit regions by not seeking to maximize their own incomes. Today, as a result of the official embracing and putting into practice of mindless deflationary policies which have reduced mass purchasing power, they have lost internal grain markets to the tune of 26 million tonnes and are being given the irresponsible advice to 'diversify' and export to world markets even though these continue to be in recession, and even though all international organizations predict continuing fall in agricultural terms of trade up to 2009–10. Calculations by the Food and Agriculture Organization (FAO) show that the terms of trade for agriculture globally, with 1990–91 as base year equal to 100, were about 50 by 2001, compared to over 200 in the 1970s.

The question that is neither raised nor answered in official publications like the *Economic Survey* and the Reserve Bank of India's *Report on Currency and Finance,* which articulate the fairy tale of voluntary diversification, is this: how can people suffering employment loss and facing unprecedented crop price declines be inferred to be better off and be voluntarily reducing cereals demand, and how is it that the current reduced level of total absorption of foodgrains per head of 155 kg per annum is not seen in any country except the least developed and sub-Saharan African countries? The observed falling share of food expenditure in total expenditure for almost every expenditure group is officially cited as proof of every income segment including the poorest diversifying diets and becoming better off, and seems to have persuaded some academics. No attention is paid to steadily falling average calorie intake in rural India as 'diversification' proceeds. The argument is quite fallacious and is based on a simple confusion between the necessary and sufficient conditions for improvement.

A falling share of food expenditure in total expenditure, as a well as a falling share of grain expenditure in food expenditure, are necessary, but not sufficient indices of the consumer becoming better off, particularly when we are considering not an advanced country's rich population but a population already at a low standard of life. The food spending share of total spending can fall and is actually observed to fall, when people are getting worse off because their real income is constant or falling, since owing to greater monetization of the economy and higher cost of utilities, they are forced to spend more on the bare minimum of nonfood essentials. Thus even when price-index adjusted income is unchanged over time, some food expenditure has to be sacrificed at the later date to buy fuel (which is jointly demanded with foodgrains and is no longer available from common property resources), incur higher transport costs in search of work, incur higher health costs and so on. Since the overwhelmingly large part of food expenditure itself is on staple grains, it is this which falls when food expenditure is cut. Data for sub-Saharan African countries show dietary 'diversification' as per capita income declines. We observe a falling share of calories from cereals and a rising share from animal products, even as, with the large decline in cereal intake, absolute calorie intake is seen to decline quite steeply (see Patnaik 2003b for a discussion). In effect, a sub-Saharan Africa already exists in rural India today.

The official solution is inhumane in rationalizing increasing hunger as a voluntary choice, basing its prescriptions on bad theory and fallacious reasoning. The only solution which is both humane and based on sound economic theory is to restore lost internal purchasing power through a *universal* Employment Guarantee and to revert to a universal Public Distribution System. The Finance Minister unwisely cut rural development expenditures drastically to only Rs. 13,500 crore last year – the same absolute sum as was spent 15 years earlier in 1989–90. This is an all-time low of only 0.6 per cent of NNP, and this gratuitous act of deflation in the face of farm crisis has worsened the problems of unemployment and hunger. It may be compared to the Rs. 51,000 crore spent by the NDA in 2003–04 in the aftermath of drought, which sum itself was inadequate at 2.5 per cent of NNP, substantially lower than the pre-reform 7th Plan outlays of nearly 4 per cent of NNP.

To meet the 10th Plan budget estimates of outlays on rural development, the government now needs to spend at least Rs. 100,000 crore during fiscal 2005–06 and 2006–07, of which up to Rs. 30,000 crore should be on the national rural employment guarantee, and the remainder on the urgent and neglected needs of agriculture, rural development, irrigation, and village and small-scale industry. Although Rs. 100,000 crore may sound a large sum, it is still less than 4 per cent of anticipated NNP in the next two years and inadequate for the needs of 700 million people, three-fifths of the nation, whose fate depends on the government's policy.

The bizarre official efforts to reinvent increasing hunger as free choice are buttressed by spurious estimates of the population in poverty, discussed in the last section.

Table 6.7. Summary of annual per capita foodgrains output and availability in India in the 1990s (3-year average)

Three-Year Period Ending in	Average Population (millions)	Net Output per Head		Net Availability per Head			
		Cereals (kg)	Foodgrains (kg)	Cereals (kg)	Pulses (kg)	Foodgrains (kg/year)	(g/day)
1991–92	850.70	163.43	178.77	162.8	14.2	177.0	–
1994–95	901.02	166.74	181.59	160.8	13.5	174.3	478
1997–98	953.07	162.98	176.81	161.6	12.6	174.2	477
2000–01	1008.14	164.84	177.71	151.7	11.5	163.2	447
2002–03	1050.67	153.85	164.09	142.9	10.12	153.0	419
Individual Year							
*2003–04**	*1087.6*	*158.33*	*170.83*	*n.a.*	*n.a.*	*n.a.*	*n.a.*
*2004–05**	*1107.0*	*151.21*	*162.35*	*n.a.*	*n.a.*	*n.a.*	*n.a.*

Change in Per Capita Availability of Foodgrains	**%**
Triennium Ending 1991–92 to Triennium Ending 1997–98	–1.6
Triennium Ending 1997–98 to Triennium Ending 2002–03	–12.2
Total Change, 1991–92 to 2002–03	–13.6

Source: For output, trade and stocks, Reserve Bank of India, *Report on Currency and Finance*, various years; and Government of India, Ministry of Finance, *Economic Survey*, various years. For population, the annual compound growth rate of 1.89 per cent has been derived from the census population totals for 1991 and 2001 and used to interpolate for inter-censal years. Before 1991 and from 2001 onwards, the population figures given in the *Economic Survey* have been used. The asterisk (*) indicates provisional.

Alternative Measures of Head-Count Poverty: Or, How to Count the Poor Correctly versus Illogical Official Procedures

Poverty studies in India since the early 1970s have been based on the use of a 'poverty line' expenditure level, defined as that level of expenditure per capita per month on all goods and services, whose food expenditure component provided an energy intake of 2400 kcal per capita in rural areas and 2100 kcal per capita in urban areas. All persons spending below the poverty line expenditure are considered to be poor. The recommended dietary allowance (RDA) of energy was specified by the Indian Council for Medical Research and recommended by the Nutrition Expert Group to the Planning Commission in 1969. This is obviously a very minimalist definition of poverty, since no norms are set for essential nonfood items of spending such as fuel for cooking and lighting, clothing, shelter, transport, medical care or education.

The database for estimating poverty has been the National Sample Survey Rounds on Consumption Expenditure, which takes the household as the sampling unit. These surveys present the distribution of persons by monthly per capita expenditure groups, and since the quantities of foods consumed and their calorie equivalents are available, they also present the calorie intake per capita per diem by the same expenditure groups. That particular expenditure group whose food expenditure met the calorie requirement in 1973–74 was identified and the relevant expenditure was defined as the poverty-line expenditure (often this is mislabelled as poverty-line *income*, but we have no information on income). Large sample surveys are carried out at 5-yearly intervals, the latest available data being from the 55th Round relating to 1999–2000, from which the relevant data for all India is reproduced in Table 6.8 using two published reports of the NSS.

A good idea of the current magnitude of head-count poverty can be obtained by the non-expert without doing any calculations, simply by inspecting the data in Table 6.8. Looking at the first, third and fifth columns, 69.7 per cent or say seven-tenths of the rural population of India, spending less than Rs. 525 per month per person, was below the average calorie level of 2403 (nearly the same as the 2400 norm), which was obtained only by the next higher spending group of Rs. 525–615. Since persons in the lower part of this group also obtained below 2400 calories, the poverty percentage is a bit higher than seven-tenths, and on plotting the data on a graph we obtain the more exact figure of 74.5 per cent below Rs. 565, the expenditure required to access the energy norm.[10] But the official Planning Commission figure of rural head-count poverty from the same data is only 27.4 per cent! The difference between the estimate obtained by direct inspection of the latest data and the figure as given by the Planning Commission is 47 per cent, so nearly half of the actually poor rural population, about 350 million persons, are excluded from the set of the officially poor.

Again, from direct inspection we see that about two-fifths of the urban population spending below Rs. 575 per capita per month obtained less than 2091 calories (very close to the 2100 urban norm), which was the average for the next higher spending group. The exact percentage in urban poverty, on plotting the graph, is 44 per cent. The Planning Commission figure for urban poverty for the same year is only 23.5 per cent. What explains this big difference?

The Planning Commission has never officially given up the nutritional norm of 2400 calories. The majority of economists in India believe that this norm is still being followed. The reality is that the actual estimation procedure followed by the Planning Commission has delinked its poverty estimates completely from the nutrition norm. The poverty line was obtained following the norm only in the year 1973–74 using the 28th Round NSS data, a date three decades in the past. For that year at prices then prevailing, the rural and urban poverty lines were Rs. 49.09 and Rs. 56.64 per capita per month, since at these expenditures the 2400 rural and 2100 urban calorie intake norms were satisfied. It was found that 56.4 per cent of the rural and 49 per cent of the urban population were below these poverty lines.[11]

For later years, strange though it may seem, no use was made of a single iota of the actual consumption data and calorie equivalents, thrown up by as many as five successive large-sample surveys (in 1977–78, 1983, 1988–89, 1993–94 and 1999–2000). There was no official attempt to update the poverty lines on the basis of the available current information on what expenditure was actually required to meet the nutrition norm. Rather, the 3-decade-old poverty lines (Rs. 49.1 and Rs. 56.6, rural and urban), were simply adjusted upwards by using a price index, while assuming an invariant 1973–74 consumption basket. The adjusted poverty line was then applied to the cumulative distribution of persons by expenditure groups in current NSS data to obtain the 'poverty percentage'. Thus the current data were and are being used selectively, with only the distribution of persons by expenditure classes being used and the associated energy intake part being ignored completely. The declining energy intake corresponding to official poverty estimates is never mentioned, nor do academics following the same method ever mention the lowered calorie intake corresponding to their estimates (vide the papers in *Economic and Political Weekly*, 2003, special number tendentiously titled 'Poverty Reduction in the 1990s'). The credibility of official and similar academic poverty estimates would certainly come into question if the educated public at large was informed how far below RDA the consumption standard has been continuously pushed by the official method.

For example, the official price index adjusted poverty line for 1999–2000 was Rs. 328 only (about 6.7 times Rs. 49), and this has been applied to the first and last columns of Table 6.8 to read the population below this line which came to 27 per cent. *No attention was paid to the fact that at this expenditure a person could access at most only 1890 calories, over 500 calories per day below the RDA, and nor is this fact ever mentioned to the public when poverty estimates are quoted by the Planning Commission.* This amounts to suppression of information and is not an academically acceptable procedure. The same applies to the academics who follow the official method and who never allude to the lower and lower calorie intake inherent in their price index adjusted poverty lines over time.

Academics writing earlier (Nayyar 1991), however, estimated poverty both by direct inspection of current data and by the official price index adjustment to a base year method. Nayyar explicitly noted that the poverty figures estimated by the official method diverged more and more over time from the much higher poverty percentages yielded by directly using current data. As the base year of the official method gets further back in time, the divergence has assumed absurd proportions. For 1993–94 the official price index adjustment method gave a rural poverty line of only Rs. 205, and 37.3 per cent were below it in the 50th Round distribution of persons by expenditure groups, and so deemed to be 'in poverty', but the fact that at this poverty line only 1970 calories per diem could be accessed (over 400 calories below the RDA) was never mentioned to the public. Inspecting the same current 50th Round data showed that 74.5 per cent of persons, or double the official estimate, had an intake below the RDA of 2400 calories, because their monthly expenditure was below Rs. 325, the realistic poverty line at which the nutrition RDA could be accessed.

Mehta and Venkataraman (2000), in a short but significant paper, later also pointed out for the 50th Round data this large divergence between the results of applying the official definition and following the official price-adjustment procedure. They do not refer to the earlier discussion by Nayyar (1991) who had already pointed out the divergence for earlier Rounds and who also analysed state-wise divergence.

In 1999–2000, as we have already noted, the official estimate gives only 27.4 per cent in poverty because these are the persons spending below the price index adjusted official poverty line of Rs. 328, but again the further lowering of the associated energy intake standard to 1890 calories, over 500 calories per day below RDA, is never mentioned. The same current 55th Round data shown in Table 6.8 continue to give 74.5 per cent

Table 6.8. Percentage distribution of persons by monthly per capita expenditure (MPCE) groups and average calorie intake per diem, 1999–2000, all-India

RURAL				URBAN			
Monthly per Capita Expenditure in Rupees	Calorie Intake per Diem per Capita	% of Persons	Cumulative % of Persons	Monthly per Capita Expenditure in Rupees	Calorie Intake per Diem per Capita	% of Persons	Cumulative % of Persons
Below 225	1383	5.1	5.1	Below 300	1398	5.0	5.0
225–255	1609	5.0	10.1	300–350	1654	5.1	10.1
255–300	1733	10.1	20.2	350–425	1729	9.6	19.7
300–340	1868	10.0	30.2	425–500	1912	10.1	29.8
340–380	1957	10.3	40.5	500–575	1968	9.9	39.7
380–420	2054	9.7	50.2	575–665	2091	10.0	49.7
420–470	2173	10.2	60.4	665–775	2187	10.1	59.8
470–525	2289	9.3	69.7	775–915	2297	10.0	69.8
525–615	2403	10.3	80.0	915–1120	2467	10.0	79.8
615–775	2581	9.9	89.9	1120–1500	2536	10.1	89.9
775–900	2735	5.0	94.9	1500–1925	2736	5.0	94.9
900 or more	3178	5.0	100	1925 or more	2938	5.0	100
ALL	2149	99.9		ALL	2156	99.9	
SUMMARY				SUMMARY			
470–525 and less	2289 and less	69.7		500–575 and less	1968 and less	39.7	
525–615	2403	10.3		575–665	2091	10.0	
615–775 and more	2581 and more	19.9		665–775 and more	2187 and more	50.2	

Source: National Sample Survey Organization (55th Round, 1999–2000) Report No. 471, *Nutritional Intake in India* for calorie intake data by expenditure groups and Report No. 454, *Household Consumer Expenditure in India – Key Results* for the distribution of persons. The calorie intake data refers to the 30-day recall so the distribution of persons by the same recall period is taken above.

of persons actually in poverty, namely with intake below 2400 calories because their expenditure was below the Rs. 565 actually required to access the RDA. (However, greater poverty depth is seen by 1999–2000, with more of the population moving below 1800 calories as compared to 1993–94). Thus in 1993–94 the official method had left out 37.2 per cent of the total rural population who were actually poor, while by 1999–2000 the official method was leaving out 47.1 of the total rural population, or around 350 million persons, who were actually poor. Table 6.9 summarizes the official poverty lines, the poverty percentages and the falling calorie intakes at poverty lines, and it gives the true poverty lines required to access the RDA, along with the true poverty percentages.

There is no theoretically acceptable basis to the official claims of poverty reduction in the 1990s. *The basic point is that the method of comparison over time is not logically valid when the consumption standard is being altered, as is being done in the indirect estimates.* The consumption standard in 1973–74 was 2400 calories at which 56 per cent was in poverty; by 1983 the official estimate of 45.7 per cent in poverty corresponded to 2060 calories intake; by 1993–94 the standard implicit in the official estimate (37 per cent in poverty) was down further to 1970 calories; and in 1999–2000 for the official estimate (27.4 per cent) it was even lower at 1890 calories. By the 60th Round, 2004–05, it is likely to be below 1800 calories and correspond to less than one-fifth of the rural population. We will once more hear spurious claims of further 'poverty reduction' without any mention of the lowering of the energy intake. All this has been happening because the price adjustment to a base-year poverty line does not capture the actual current cost of accessing the minimum nutrition norm, and this failure becomes more acute as the base year recedes further into the past.

How can anyone say how 'poverty' has changed over time using the above method? To give an analogy, when a set of runners are lined up in a row on a circular racetrack for a long-distance race, if the person in the innermost circle crosses the finishing rope first, it cannot be validly inferred that he has won the race: for the distance run by him is much less than that run by others. For a valid comparison of the runners' performance, the distance run has to be the same standardized distance for all the runners, and this is done by staggering the runners. Similarly, in the official method the per cent of persons below the same standardized consumption level or levels needs to be compared, but this is not the case in the indirect method. Rather, the method used implies that the percentages below un-standardized and changing consumption levels are sought to be compared over time (see Table 6.9).[12] This is not legitimate, and any statement about decline (or change generally) is not valid. Present-day heated debates between the estimators about whether poverty has 'declined' by ten points or seven points, when poverty has not declined at all, can be likened to debates over whether the inner-circle runner has 'won' by one metre or two metres, when the fact of the matter is that he has not 'won' at all, because the premise for valid comparison is violated.

The official rural monthly poverty line expenditure for the year 2004 (obtained by updating the 1999–2000 poverty line of Rs. 328, using the CPIAL), is Rs. 354 or Rs. 11.8 daily, equivalent to 26 US cents at the prevailing exchange rate. This paltry amount will actually buy at most one bottle of water, but it is supposed to cover all expenditure on food, fuel, clothing, shelter, transport, health and education – in short all daily spending

Table 6.9. The rural poor as percentage of rural population in India

	1973–1974 (%)	1993–1994 (%)	1999–2000 (%)	MPCE (Poverty Line) Rs. 1973–1974	1993–1994	1999–2000
Applying Official Definition (those below MPCE giving 2400 calories)	56.4	74.5	74.5	49	325	570
Official Estimates	56.4	37.3	27.1	49	206	328
Corresponding Calorie 'Norm'	2400	1970	1890			

Source: Calculated from NSS Reports on Consumer Expenditure, 50th Round, 1993–94, and 55th Round, 1999–2000. MPCE is monthly per capita expenditure. Note that base year 1973–74 is the only year the official definition was correctly applied. In all later years the nutrition norm is continuously diluted. The same exercise can be carried out for urban India.

on goods and services for one person! Estimates of Indian poverty for 1999–2000, 55th Round, by some individual academics like Deaton (2003b, 367) and Bhalla (2003) are even lower and imply a poverty line of 20 US cents or less expenditure per day, one-fifth of the World Bank's dollar-a-day measure. There is no logic in arguing that purchasing power parity should be considered and instead of one dollar therefore around one-third of that should be taken as the local poverty line, for the comparison is not between advanced and developing countries at all but between developing and other developing countries. A quarter US dollar in India purchases exactly as much as Rs. 11 does, at the prevailing exchange rate, and a quarter US dollar purchases exactly as much as 2 yuan does in China (whose current rural poverty line is also far too low, at 2.2 yuan per day). Poverty level incomes in the USA are not set three times higher than the Chinese or Indian ones but are at least thirty times higher.

Obviously, it is not difficult for either the Planning Commission or the individual academics to 'adjust' Indian poverty figures downwards when the consumption level embodied in the rural poverty line is depressed to such subhuman levels as Rs. 11 or less per day. Few people can actually survive long below these levels: those who are there today are on their way to early death. The poverty estimators should try a test on themselves. Let them be handed the weekly equivalent of their own estimated monthly poverty line – they need not even exert themselves to earn it as the poor are obliged to do – and let them spend only one week in a village living on that amount, which would range from Rs. 60 to Rs. 80. Since they will not be confident of drinking the local water all they would be able to buy would be a bottle of water a day and no food, let alone other necessities. What they would undoubtedly gain from their one-week stay would be weight loss. Urban poverty lines are almost equally unrealistic.

Sometimes, to justify the indirect method it is argued that the original rural consumption norm of 2400 was 'too high'. First, it is not 'too high' because the average intake of those below it works out to about 1950 calories, which is lower than in any other country in the world except the least developed countries. Second, even if it is accepted for the sake of argument that it was 'too high' it does not justify comparing 1999–2000 'poverty' figures, which are all those persons below an intake of 1890 calories, to those persons below an intake of 1970 calories in 1993–94 and those persons below an intake of 2400 calories in 1973–74.

By all means, let us consider lower norms, in fact take several alternative norms including 2400, but when comparing over time, compare the proportion of population under the same norm at the two or more points of time – for only then will the comparison be valid. The indirect estimates fail on this simple but essential criterion of comparability over time and those who nevertheless undertake such comparison are committing a logical fallacy – *the fallacy of equivocation.* This a well-known type of verbal fallacy, in which the same term is used with two completely different meanings in the course of the argument, so the inference is not true. In this case, 'poverty line' was defined and initially calculated with respect to a nutrition norm, while 'poverty line' as actually calculated is delinked from the norm, so the inference regarding change (whether rise, fall or constancy) is not true.[13]

Not only is the official comparison of poverty percentages, and claims of poverty reduction over time, quite spurious; the comparison of the poverty levels of states at a given point of time is equally invalid. As Table 6.10 shows, we have a bizarre picture when we calculate the maximum calorie intake levels below which people are designated as 'poor' by the official method in the different states of India. The calorie intake corresponding to the official state-wise poverty lines, from which the state poverty percentages have been officially derived for the year 1999–2000, varies from only 1440 in Kerala, nearly 1000 calories below RDA, to 2120 in Orissa, less than 300 calories below RDA.

The fact is that the official method in India today adheres to no nutrition norm at all. Nutrition has dropped out of the picture completely in the indirect method, nor is there any lower bound set, to the extent of decline in the calorie intake corresponding to whatever the price-adjusted poverty line happens to be. That is why we find states with 1500 calories or less intake corresponding to their official poverty lines in 1999–2000. In as many as nine states, the calorie intake associated with the official poverty lines was below 1800 calories in the 55th Round, while in four states it was 1600 calories or less (see Table 6.10). None of this is mentioned when poverty estimates are quoted by those making them. Not even the late P. V. Sukhatme, who was a consistent critic of the 2400 calorie RDA being too high, would have accepted 1800 calories as a reasonable norm for estimating who the poor are, let alone 1600 calories or less. He had used a norm of 2200 calories in one of his own estimates (Sukhatme 1977). By 2004–05 the all-India official poverty line itself will correspond to an intake of 1800 calories or less, and at least eight states will have a 1600 or less calorie intake corresponding to the state-specific official poverty lines. The fact that comparability conditions are blatantly violated is obvious. Officially it is inferred that poverty is much higher, for example, in Orissa at 48 per cent, than in neighbouring Andhra Pradesh at only 11 per cent. But how can we possibly infer that Orissa is 'poorer' than Andhra, when the 'officially poor' are those persons with below 2120 calories intake in Orissa but the 'officially poor' are those persons with below 1600 calories intake in Andhra? (As a matter of fact, the below 2400 and below 2100 calories poverty percentages are both higher in Andhra than in Orissa, as the same table shows in the last two columns.) Similarly, how can it be inferred that rural Gujarat, with only 13 per cent officially in poverty, is much better off than West Bengal, with 33 per cent officially poor, when the associated calorie 'norm' in Gujarat has been pushed down to only 1680 compared to 1900 in West Bengal? As a matter of fact, the below 2400 calories poverty percentage is marginally lower for West Bengal, compared to Gujarat, and the below 2100 calories percentage is substantially lower for West Bengal. And so the anomalies can be multiplied. Furthermore, how can, for each state, the official estimate in 1999–2000 be compared with that in 1993–94 and inference about 'decline' be drawn, when the associated calorie intake has been lowered in each state? (Except one, Gujarat.)

As a teacher, if I were to follow the illogical procedure of saying that student A who has 53 per cent marks is 'better' than student B who has 59 per cent marks, because I apply a 50 out of 100 marks standard to student A and apply a different, 60 marks out of 100 standard to student B, I would rightly face a court case. Yet our Planning Commission and individual academics have been allowed to get away with making patently illogical and untrue statements on poverty. The Deputy Chairman of the Planning Commission recently congratulated the Andhra Pradesh government on its success in reducing poverty. This 'reduction' was solely the effect of applying an extraordinarily low price-adjusted poverty line of Rs. 262 per month in 1999–2000, or less than Rs. 9 per day, at which less than 1600 calories could be accessed (see Table 6.10). Looking directly at nutrition poverty, on the other hand, we find that the proportion of persons below an intake of 1800 calories in that state has doubled to 40 per cent by 1999–2000 compared to 1983 (Table 6.11). To complete the story, the proportion below 2100 calories has risen to 62 per cent at the later date, compared to 56 per cent only five years earlier in 1993–94, and 44 per cent in 1983.

What is the reason, the reader might ask, for the official method producing consistently lower estimates than the direct method, and why has the divergence been growing until now? The indirect estimate gives only 27 per cent compared to nearly 75 per cent by the direct estimate. It is not primarily a matter of the price index used: different price indices (different in terms of the extent of price rise, but all with the same base year quantity weights) do give different results, but this accounts for difference of at most 10 per cent or so of population in poverty, not the difference of over 47 per cent of population which is actually observed. The basic reason for the large and increasing difference *is the assumption of an invariant consumption basket in the indirect method, held unchanged for three decades.* In effect the official estimators are saying – if a person in a village consumed the same quantities of foods and other goods and services as 32 years ago, then Rs. 328 per month is enough to access these quantities in 1999–2000 and Rs. 354 per month is enough in 2004. If you do not get the calorie standard, it is the result of your free choice that has led you to consume in a different pattern.

This is not however a reasonable position to adopt. It is as unreasonable as telling a 32-year-old man that the one metre of cloth which was enough to clothe him when he was one month old, and which cost say Rs. 10 at that time, can be bought after price index adjustment for Rs. 70 today, and if this expenditure leaves him semi-naked today, then it is his problem of free choice to be in that state. Such a position ignores the irreversible structural changes the person has undergone which means his set of choices has altered over time. Of course, this is only an analogy – we are not arguing that the proportion of adults in the population has risen! We wish, through the analogy, to drive home the point that over the last three decades certain irreversible structural changes have taken place in the economy. There has been increasing monetization of the economy and disappearance of common property resources, along with higher cost of utilities and health care. With a given real income people have to spend relatively more on essential nonfood requirements, overcoming illness and earning a living. The actual current rural consumption basket which satisfies the nutrition norm, and to which the total monthly expenditure on all goods and services corresponds, costs almost double the price-adjusted poverty line (from Table 6.8 summarized in Table 6.9, at least Rs. 570 is required compare to the official Rs. 328). The official poverty lines are simply far too low and are getting further lowered as the base year becomes more remote.

Rohini Nayyar (1991), in her careful doctoral study, estimated poverty using both methods and noted the widening divergence in the results between 1961–62 and 1977–78. She took some solace from the fact that though poverty levels estimated by the two different methods were drawing apart quite fast, at least they did seem to *move in the same direction* over time. The ranking of the states of India according to their poverty levels estimated using the two methods was highly correlated: Nayyar found that Spearman's rank correlation coefficient worked out to 0.89 and 0.84 (using the official estimate on the one hand, and two different direct estimate norms of 2200 and 2000 calories) and was significant at the 1 per cent level.

But in the 1990s this conclusion no longer holds. The poverty levels calculated by the two methods are moving fast in opposite directions, and the rank correlation may soon become negative. Spearman's rank correlation, taking the poverty ranks of the states by the official indirect method, and by the direct method for 1999–2000, 55th Round data, works out to only 0.236 and 0.075 (using the same two direct estimate norms), and neither is statistically significant at the 1 per cent level (Ram 2004). Inspection of Table 6.10 will tell the reader why this is the case: some of the states with the lowest official poverty, such as Andhra Pradesh, a byword for agrarian distress, have some of the highest actual poverty. In general, the official method produces the largest divergence from the direct method in the case of the southern and eastern states.

The rot in poverty studies discussions seems to have set in with neoliberal reforms in India, particularly in the late 1990s. The Indian Government was eager to claim success for the economic reforms, and the pro-reform economists were eager to see poverty reduction in the data. In such a milieu, the inconvenient direct estimates showing high and, in some states, increasing levels of poverty were swept under the carpet. Discussion of direct estimation of poverty virtually disappeared from the literature. The dominant trend of discussion focused on the official indirect method, which, to the great satisfaction of the pro-reform academics and the World Bank estimators, not only showed very low 'poverty' levels but actual decline in these levels. Not one of the authors using the official indirect method alluded to the nutritional implications of their own estimates. This meant that they were using and presenting the NSS data selectively, taking only the distribution of persons by expenditure classes to read off the poverty proportion corresponding to their indirect poverty line, while ignoring the associated energy intake figures completely. Such lack of transparency and selective use of data is not acceptable academic procedure. Owing to this lack of transparency, to this day most economists in India not directly working with the data, and including even those examining research theses on poverty, are not aware that drastically lowered consumption levels over time and arbitrary variation of consumption levels across states are the necessary implications of following the indirect method and arriving at low poverty estimates. They assume that the original norms are being followed when this is not true.

There is a debate among the academics following the official, indirect method, that owing to change in the recall period during the 55th Round, 1999–2000, compared to earlier rounds, actual expenditure is slightly overstated in every expenditure class, and hence the distribution of persons by expenditure classes has been affected. Making the required adjustment for comparability alters this distribution slightly and raises the 27 per cent below the Rs. 328 official price-adjusted poverty line by another 2 to 3 per cent (Sundaram and Tendulkar 2003, Deaton 2003a, Sen and Himanshu 2005). If these adjustments are correct, quite obviously, the percentage of persons below the directly observed poverty line of Rs. 570 would rise to an even greater extent than 2 to 3, since a higher proportion of people than before would also come into the expenditure interval Rs. 328 to Rs. 570, and thus the difference between the official estimate and the direct estimate would increase further. Thus all those with less than 2400 calories intake per diem in 1999–2000 would be more than 74.5 + 3 = 77.5 per cent of the rural population, which is a rise compared to 74.5 per cent in the 50th Round, 1993–94. Similarly, those below 2100 calories would rise from 49.5 per cent to more than 52.5 per cent.[14]

However, we have chosen to give the direct estimate for 1999–2000 unadjusted for the recall period in all our tables, since the main point being made in this section is the type of mistake involved in the indirect method itself, which is leaving out nearly half the rural poor, *and this basic problem with all indirect estimates not only remains but gets further aggravated whenever adjustments are made by the estimators on account of altered recall period.* It may be noted that with the adjustment for the recall period, they are leaving out more than 47 per cent of the actually poor rural population from their set of 'the poor' while without the adjustment, they are leaving out exactly 47 per cent of the population.

Some economists who are critical of the official price-adjustment method which delinks the estimates from nutrition have correctly put nutrition back at the centre of their own analysis, but they have followed another direct poverty estimation route, as compared to inspecting current NSS data – the method we have followed. They have estimated the minimum cost of accessing the calorie RDA on the basis of *current* nutrient prices, and thus have obtained a normative food expenditure. By comparing with the actual expenditure on food in the NSS, they arrive at the percentage of persons failing to reach the RDA, and this is 66 per cent at the all-India level for the 55th Round (see Coondoo, Majumdar, Lancaster and Ray 2004; Ray and Lancaster 2005). Subramanian (2005) has used an indirect method with base years closer to the present, as well as the direct method we use, to see how the trends in poverty behave under alternative scenarios.

Many critical voices (Suryanarayana 1996; Mehta and Venkataraman 2000; Swaminathan 1999 and 2002) which continued to draw attention to the high prevalence of undernutrition and malnutrition, to the secular decline in average rural calorie intake,

Table 6.10. Official poverty percentage by states and associated calorie 'norm'

STATE	1993–94		1999–2000		1999–2000
	Official Poverty Percentage	Implied Calorie 'Norm'	Official Poverty Percentage	Implied Calorie 'Norm'	<2400 cal. Poverty Percentage
Andhra Pradesh	15.92	1700	11.05	1590	84.0
Assam	45.01	1960	40.04	1790	91.9
Bihar	58.21	2275	44.30	2010	77.0
Gujarat	22.18	1650	13.17	1680	83.0
Haryana	18.02	1970	8.27	1720	47.5
Karnataka	29.88	1800	17.30	1600	82.0
Kerala	25.76	1630	9.38	1440	82.5
Madhya Pradesh	40.64	1970	37.06	1850	78.5
Maharashtra	37.93	1780	23.72	1760	92.0
Orissa	49.72	2150	48.01	2120	79.0
Punjab	11.95	1810	6.35	1710	47.5
Rajasthan	26.46	2130	13.74	1925	53.5
Tamil Nadu	32.48	1650	20.55	1510	94.5
Uttar Pradesh	48.28	2220	31.22	2040	61.0
West Bengal	40.80	2080	31.85	1900	81.0
ALL INDIA	37.27	1970	27.09	1890	74.5

Source: As Table 6.8. From the basic data by states, the ogive or cumulative frequency distribution of persons below specified per capita expenditure levels was plotted, and on the same graph the relation of per capita expenditure and per capita calorie intake was plotted. Calorie intake corresponding to the official estimates was then obtained from the graphs. For 1993–94 the midpoint value of each spending class has been used in the absence of the arithmetic average in the published tables, while for 1999–2000 the average has been used. We find that for several expenditure classes the midpoint value coincided with the arithmetic mean, and for the others the difference of midpoint value from mean was very small, suggesting that the same would be true for 1993–94.

to high direct poverty estimates using reasonable calorie norms, and which criticized the indirect estimates, have been sought to be silenced by the pro-reform economists, by the simple expedient of ignoring them altogether. Not one critical author is referred to in the articles by those presenting their indirect estimates at a conference and later collecting them in a special issue of the *Economic and Political Weekly* tendentiously titled 'Poverty Reduction in the 1990s' (Deaton 2003a and 2003b; Tendulkar and Sundaram 2003; etc.). The only article on energy intake while juxtaposing the official and direct estimate does so somewhat uncritically.[15]

The critical writers on the other hand have given cogent arguments to suggest why per capita calorie intake should be involuntarily declining in the lower-expenditure classes over time. (It is also declining in higher-expenditure classes but the problems of the initially over-fed who may be reducing intake do not concern us at present.) They have pointed out that there has been substantial monetization of the economy over the last three decades. Wages which used to be paid in kind as grain or meals, valued at low farm-gate prices in earlier NSS rounds, are now paid in cash which the labourer has to exchange for food at higher retail prices, and so can buy less of it for a given real income. Common property resources have disappeared over the last three decades: fuel wood and

Table 6.11. States with one-third or more of rural population with less than 1800 calories daily energy intake

	Latest NSS Data, 2004	Position in 55th Round, 1999–2000
Tamil Nadu	55.4	43.0
Kerala	42.8	4.0
Gujarat	41.0	30.0
Karnataka	41.8	35.0
Maharashtra	39.2	27.5
Madhya Pradesh	38.5	32.2
Andhra Pradesh	36.9	28.5
West Bengal	34.1	22.5

Source: Abstracted from estimates for all states, using NSS Reports No. 471 and 454 for the 55th Round, and Reports No. 387 and 353 for the 38th Round. Estimation method as in note to Table 6.10. Note that in 1983 only 3 states – Kerala, Tamil Nadu and West Bengal – had more than one-third of rural population below 1800 calories intake. By 1999–2000 all three states had improved, West Bengal substantially, while Andhra Pradesh, Assam, Karnataka, Madhya Pradesh and Maharashtra saw worsening. Thus by 1999–2000, five states had more than one-third of population below 1800 calories intake (six if we include the borderline Madhya Pradesh).

fodder, earlier gleaned and gathered (and not fully valued in the NSS data) now have to be purchased, restricting the ability of the poorer population to satisfy basic food needs out of a given real income and leading to the observed energy intake decline. Staple grains and fuel wood or other fuels are obviously jointly demanded since no one can eat raw grain, and with a given real income a part of expenditure on grain has to be enforcedly reduced to purchase fuel. To this we have to add higher medical, transport and education costs as state funding is reduced and some services are privatized. The correct thrust of these arguments is that undernutrition and poverty is very high, affecting three-quarters of the rural population by now, and observed calorie intake decline for the lower fractiles is involuntary. By 1999–2000, for the first time, average calorie intake in rural India has fallen below average urban calorie intake.

Concluding Remarks

This chapter has embarked on a brief but sharp critique of the prevalent analysis and prescriptions regarding food security and poverty because of two reasons. First, the agrarian crisis is serious and widespread, and it has been created by public policies which have been deflationary, combined with trade liberalization when world primary prices have been declining. It is manifesting itself in slowing output growth, rising unemployment, unprecedented income deflation for the majority of cultivators and labourers, enmeshing of cultivators in unrepayable debt, and loss of assets including land to creditors. Kidney sales and 9000 recorded farmer suicides are only the tip of the iceberg of increasing deprivation, a crucial index of which is an unprecedented fall in foodgrain absorption to levels prevalent 50 years ago and a decline in average calorie intake in rural India.

Second, the prevalent analysis by policymakers, the Planning Commission and the government, however, can be summed up as an obdurate refusal to face the facts, and an attempt to construct a counter-factual fairy story which is illogical and in patent contradiction of the trends in the economy. 'We must learn truth from facts' (Mao Zedong) 'or the facts will punish us' (added by Deng Hsiao Ping) is a dictum that our policymakers would do well to bear in mind. Their theorization interprets severe loss of purchasing power and enforced decline in effective demand for foodgrains, as its very opposite, as 'over-production' in relation to an allegedly voluntary reduction of foodgrains intake by all segments of the population, and reaches the dangerous inference that foodgrains output should be cut back. It refuses to recognize that, while in developed societies consumers can be separated from a minority who are agricultural producers, in a poor country like India the majority of consumers are themselves rural and directly involved in production as cultivators and labourers, so deflationary policies hit them hard in both these roles of producers and consumers. Price deflation does not benefit even landless labourers since it is part of a process of income deflation, which raises unemployment faster than prices fall. Our economists estimating poverty by the indirect method are still caught in the old conceptual trap of equating relative food price decline with declining poverty, without understanding that the adverse unemployment effects of deflation can stamp out any benefit of food price fall: they should study the economics of the Great Depression for some insights into how deflationary processes actually operate.

As Table 6.11 shows, by 1999–2000 as many as five states had one-third or more of the rural population with less than 1800 calories intake, and in another three states the percentage of persons with below 1800 calories intake had risen between 1983 and 1999–2000, though not exceeding one-third at the latter date. (Note that Meenakshi and Viswanathan (2003) obtain a larger number than we do, eight states with more than one-third of population below 1800 calories in the 55th Round – but their use of kernel density functions to obtain the calorie distribution ogive is perhaps overestimating the nutrition poverty figures, since their method includes all high-income but calorie-deficient people as well).

Despite this worsening situation at the ground level being reflected in the nutrition data, it would be very sad indeed if the present Planning Commission were tempted to make further spurious claims of 'poverty reduction', as the previous ones have done, the moment the next large-sample NSS data on consumption becomes available. Their indirect method – which selectively uses the data by ignoring the nutrition part of it – is bound to show a further steep and spurious 'decline' in rural poverty by 2005–06, to around 18–19 per cent of rural population from 27.4 per cent in 1999–2000. This is because, owing to the unprecedented income deflationary situation itself, the rise in prices has been at a historic low from 2000 to date. The CPIAL actually declined in 2000–01 compared to the previous year, and rose only 1 per cent the next year. With low inflation, the CPIAL-adjusted official poverty line for 2004 works out to only Rs. 354, a mere Rs. 26 or 8 per cent more than the Rs. 328 of 1999–2000. (By contrast the CPIAL rose 46 per cent between 1993–94 and 1999–2000.)

It comes as no surprise that the recently released 60th Round NSS data relating to January–June 2004 shows that only 22 per cent of all-India rural population is below Rs. 354, the official price-adjusted poverty line, if Schedule 1 is used, and only 17.5 per cent is below it if Schedule 2 is used.[16] This is a share which is falling every year, solely because few persons can survive below such low spending levels – indeed it is amazing that there are people surviving at all on less than Rs. 12 per day. One can imagine how adverse their height, weight, morbidity rates and life expectancy would be relative to the average.

Of course, this alleged 'decline in poverty' will be necessarily associated with a further fall in the calorie intake level corresponding to the official poverty line, from 1890 calories to somewhere around or below 1800 calories, in short at least 600 calories below RDA. This information on declining nutrition standard associated with the official estimate is likely to be quietly suppressed as it has been in the past. The government should bear in mind, however, that any claims of 'poverty reduction' it might be misguided enough to make will no longer carry credibility since the arbitrary and illogical nature of its method of calculation is today much better understood, and the contrast of any such claims with all other adverse trends in the rural economy is too glaring to be ignored.

Since such a large fraction of the population is already at very low energy intake levels, they have been trying to maintain consumption by liquidating assets against debt. Thus there are not only adverse flow adjustments (lowered nutrition levels) but also stock adjustments going on, reflected in the emerging recent data on rising landlessness. We may expect to see a rise in the already high concentration of assets in rural areas. In such a scenario labour bondedness against debt is also likely to be increasing.

The official refusal to recognize the seriousness of the crisis at the theoretical level, the consequent refusal to restore lost purchasing power through an immediately implemented universal employment guarantee and the refusal to extend effective support to producers through continuing open-ended procurement at reasonable prices all bode ill for the agrarian crisis, which is not being addressed. In fact, the deflationary hammer has been applied once more on the rural population by the finance minister in the very first budget of the UPA government. The 10th Plan, 1992–1997, sets out that Rs. 300,000 crore are to be spent by the Centre on Rural Development Expenditures (adding up as before five items).[17] Three years of the Plan or two-thirds of the period is over: Rs. 100,000 crore or only one-third of the planned outlays have been spent, of which Rs. 85,000 crore spending was during the last two years of NDA rule, mid-2002 to mid-2004, while there was a sharp cut-back to Rs. 15,000 crore only in 2004–05. As in 1991 the first years after a general election are being used by the neoliberal lobby in the new government which controls finance to apply mindless deflation, although unlike in 1991 there is a deep agrarian crisis today. This cynical move to cut rural development expenditures in the face of rising unemployment and agrarian distress can only be in order to please international financial institutions and meet the arbitrary provisions of the FRBM Act.

To achieve the 10th Plan target now, at least Rs. 100,000 crore must be spent both in 2005–06 and 2006–07, of which about Rs. 25,000 to Rs. 30,000 crore should be on universal employment guarantee and Rs. 70,000 to Rs. 75,000 crore on rural development expenditures. This level of planned spending would total only about 2.5 per cent of NNP, and it needs to be stepped up steadily in later years to reach the 4 per cent of NNP which prevailed in the late 1980s during the 7th Plan before economic reforms began.

The entire false analysis which reinvents increasing hunger as voluntary choice is today sought to be reinforced by bogus poverty estimates and invalid claims of decline in poverty. In such a situation it is the duty of all academics and activists who have not lost their sanity to critique the official analysis and prescriptions, which if carried through will worsen immeasurably the already pitiable condition of the majority of the rural population.

Notes

1 See Baker, Epstein and Pollin 1998, Halevy and Fontaine 1998, Patnaik 2000.

2 In infrastructure we are including the expenditures on energy and transport.

3 Rural development expenditure per capita is deflated by the all-India consumer price index. Using instead the implicit deflator from NAS for public consumption expenditure (base 1993–94 = 100) gives similarly a decline from Rs. 228.8 in 1993–94 to Rs. 191.9 in 2000–01.

4 A rising contribution of services to GDP from an initial situation of a high share of industry to GDP has been typical for advanced economies. India however is seeing a fast shift to services from a relatively low initial share. See my discussion in Patnaik 1996, 2003c of manufacturing and mining output, less than 30 per cent of GDP, which is now down to about one-fifth. This shift to services reflects de-industrialization and worsening income distribution.

5 A shorter version is also available in Patnaik 2003a.

6 See my discussion in Patnaik 1996, 2003c.

7 I have discussed this in more detail in Patnaik 2003b and 2004.

8 The official practice for 50 years, which I have followed in Table 6.7, is to deduct 12.5 per cent from gross output, in tonnes, of foodgrains (cereals plus pulses) on account of seed, feed and wastage, and to the net output so obtained add net imports and deduct net addition to public stocks.

9 Rising inequality is not necessary because we can have a fall in grain absorption when all incomes are falling and inequality is unchanged. It is not sufficient because if with increasing inequality all incomes are rising, grain absorption will not fall.

10 The required graphs are 1) the ogive of cumulative percentage of persons below specified expenditure levels and 2) the relation between per capita expenditure in each expenditure group and the per capita calorie intake for each expenditure group. With two relations and three variables – calorie intake, percentage of persons and per capita expenditure – knowing the value of any one variable determines the other two.

11 It is a curious matter of chance that poverty lines were Rs. 49.1 and Rs. 56.6 while the corresponding poverty percentages were 56.4 and 49.

12 The analogy can be carried a little further. If the race is a short one over a straight segment of the course, lining the runners up in a straight line at the starting point is okay. Similarly if the base year of the price index is very close, say two to three years, then comparison over time can be made using the official method – which ignores every non-base year actual calorie intake – without leading to too much inaccuracy. But for a long race (a base year further back in time) absence of standardization will arise and make comparison invalid.

13 I have discussed the fallacy of equivocation involved in the indirect estimates in Patnaik 2005b.

14 We could easily find out how much higher the direct estimate would be than 74.5 per cent if those making the adjustment to the distribution of persons by expenditure class had bothered to present the associated average calorie intake by expenditure class. As usual, however, they ignore the nutrition part completely in their papers.

15 Meenakshi and Viswanathan (2003) present 'calorie deprivation' as though it is an independent topic, not essentially related to official poverty estimates, and although they usefully juxtapose their estimates of population below differing calorie norms, and the official estimates, they do not refer to the falling energy equivalent of the official or individual poverty lines over time, which affects comparability. Their method of estimating the calorie distribution ogives using

kernel density functions gives higher estimates of population below various calorie norms than our estimates using the grouped data and the simple method described in the note to Table 6.10. This is probably because their estimate includes all well-to-do persons who have lower calorie intake than RDA. There is no reason, however, to consider rich race jockeys, super models or anorexic people as part of the poor.

16 Two schedules were canvassed for the first time for different sets of households in the 60th Round. Schedule 2 departs from Schedule 1 because it uses a recall period of 7 days and not 30 days for a range of consumer items.

17 Namely, agriculture, rural development, irrigation and flood control, special areas programmes, and village and small-scale industry.

References

Baker, D., G. Epstein and R. Pollin, eds. 1998. *Globalization and Progressive Economic Policy.* Cambridge: Cambridge University Press.

Coondoo, D., A. Majumdar, G. Lancaster and R. Ray. 2004. 'Alternative Approaches to Measuring Temporal Changes in Poverty with Application to India'. Working Paper, December.

Cornia, G. A., R. Jolly and F. Stewart, eds. 1987. *Adjustment with a Human Face,* vol. 1. Oxford: Clarendon Press.

Deaton, A. 2003a. 'Adjusted Indian Poverty Estimates for 1999–2000'. *Economic and Political Weekly* 38, no. 4: 322–6.

______. 2003b. 'Prices and Poverty 1987–2000'. *Economic and Political Weekly* 38, no. 4: 362–8.

Halevy, J., and J.-M. Fontaine, eds. 1998. *Restoring Demand in the World Economy.* Cheltenham: Edward Elgar.

Kindleberger, C. P. 1986. *The World in Depression, 1929–1939.* Pelican History of World Economics in 20th Century Series. London: Penguin.

Krishnaswamy, Kamala et al. 1997. '25 Years of National Nutrition Monitoring Bureau'. Hyderabad: National Institute of Nutrition.

Meenakshi, J. V. and B. Viswanathan. 2003. 'Calorie Deprivation in Rural India'. *Economic and Political Weekly* 38, no. 4: 369–75.

Mehta, J., and S. Venkataraman. 2000. 'Poverty Statistics: Bermicide's Feast'. *Economic and Political Weekly* 35, no. 27: 2377–9, 2381–2.

Nayyar, R. 1991. *Rural Poverty in India: An Analysis of Interstate Differences.* New Delhi: Oxford University Press.

Patnaik, P. 1999. 'Capitalism in Asia at the End of the Millennium'. *Monthly Review* 51, no. 3: 53–70.

______. 2000. 'The Humbug of Finance'. Chintan Memorial Lecture, delivered on 8 January 2000 at Chennai, India. Available online (www.macroscan.org), also included in *The Retreat to Unreason* by P. Patnaik. Delhi: Tulika (2003).

Patnaik, P. and C. P. Chandrasekhar. 1995. 'The Indian Economy Under Structural Adjustment'. *Economic and Political Weekly* 30, no. 47: 3003–13.

Patnaik, U. 1996. 'Export-Oriented Agriculture and Food Security in Developing Countries and India'. *Economic and Political Weekly* 31 nos. 35–7: 2429–31, 2433–7, 2439, 2441–9. Reprinted in *The Long Transition: Essays on Political Economy.* Delhi: Tulika (1999).

______. 2002. 'Deflation and Deja-Vu'. In *Agrarian Studies: Essays on Agrarian Relations in Less Developed Countries* edited by Madhura Swaminathan and V. K. Ramachandran. Delhi: Tulika.

______. 2003a. 'On the Inverse Relation between Primary Exports and Domestic Food Absorption under Liberalized Trade Regimes'. In *Work and Welfare in the Age of Finance* edited by J. Ghosh and C. P. Chandrasekhar. Delhi: Tulika.

______. 2003b. 'Food Stocks and Hunger: Causes of Agrarian Distress'. *Social Scientist* 37, nos. 7–8.

______. 2003c. 'Global Capitalism, Deflation and Agrarian Crisis in Developing Countries'. Social Policy and Development Programme Paper Number 13, United Nations Research Institute for Social Development (UNRISD). October.

______. 2004a. 'The Republic of Hunger'. *Social Scientist* 32, nos. 9–10: 9–35.

______. 2004b. 'Alternative Ways of Measuring Poverty and Implications for Policy: A Critical Appraisal from the Indian Experience'. Draft paper presented at Conference on *The Agrarian Constraint and Poverty Reduction: Macroeconomic Lessons for Africa*, Addis Ababa December 17–19, organized by the Ethiopian Economic Association and International Development Economics Associates (www.networkideas.org).

______. 2005a. 'Ricardo's Fallacy'. In *Pioneers of Development Economics* edited by K. S. Jomo. Delhi: Tulika and London and New York: Zed.

______. 2005b. 'The Nature of Fallacies in Economic Theory'. Satyendranath Sen Memorial Lecture delivered at the Asiatic Society, Kolkata, 10 August 2004, forthcoming in the *Journal of the Asiatic Society*.

Ram, R. 2004. 'Poverty Estimates in India: A Critical Appraisal'. MPhil Dissertation submitted to Jawaharlal Nehru University, July.

Ray, R. and G. Lancaster. 2005. 'On Setting the Poverty Line Based on Estimated Nutrient Prices: Condition of Socially Disadvantaged Groups During the Reform Period'. *Economic and Political Weekly* 40, no.1: 46–56.

Sen, A. and Himanshu. 2005. 'Poverty and Inequality in India: Getting Closer to the Truth'. In *Data and Dogma: The Great Indian Poverty Debate* edited by A. Deaton and V. Kozel. New Delhi: Macmillan.

Subramanian, S. 2005. 'Unravelling a Conceptual Muddle: India's Poverty Statistics in the Light of Basic Demand Theory'. *Economic and Political Weekly* 40 no. 1:57–66.

Sukhatme, P. V. 1977. 'Incidence of Undernutrition'. *Indian Journal of Agricultural Economics* 32, no. 3: 1–7.

Sundaram, K. and S. D. Tendulkar. 2003. 'Poverty *Has* Declined in the 1990s: A Resolution of Comparability Problems in NSS Consumer Expenditure Data'. *Economic and Political Weekly* 38, no. 4: 328–37.

Swaminathan, M. 1999. *Weakening Welfare: The Public Distribution of Food in India.* New Delhi: LeftWord.

______. 2002. 'Excluding the Needy: The Public Provisioning of Food in India'. *Social Scientist* 30, nos. 3–4: 34–58.

Chapter 7

GLOBALIZATION, THE MIDDLE CLASS AND THE TRANSFORMATION OF THE INDIAN STATE IN THE NEW ECONOMY

Anthony P. D'Costa

Introduction

It is clear that states in the developing world have been overextended. Not only did they inherit the ill-fitting economic and social structures of colonial rule, but they were also expected to guarantee political democracy and foster economic development. However, the full logic of the market was not accepted by most late developers until recently (D'Costa 1995). Postcolonial governments, in their quest to meet a wide array of social and economic demands for diverse constituencies, intervened in national economic management without necessarily having the institutional foundations to do so. The intensification of global economic interconnectedness since the 1970s has been another source of pressure on developing states (Held, McGrew, Goldblatt and Perraton 1999; Stallings 2003). Transnational corporations extracting a variety of state subsidies, multilateral financial institutions imposing structural adjustment programmes, rapid technological change and the hyper-mobility of finance capital have all eroded the ability of states to regulate and coordinate national economic activities (Castells 2002). In this way, national economies have been incorporated 'into overarching structures of power', and by extension, the national autonomy of states has been eroded (Howard and King 1989, 19). This also applies to China and India, today's rising stars, which continue to face internal institutional weakness and external constraints in meeting their national and social obligations (Bagchi and D'Costa 2012; Bardhan 2010).

The onslaught faced by states can be conceptualized in terms of the changing role of the state, or more precisely, a switch from society-centric development aspirations to more economic and business-led goals (see D'Costa 2009). In the past, national development efforts focused not just on the economy but also tried to address social issues such as poverty and inequality directly. This move away from such social goals to more narrow economic growth and business expansion characterizes the transformation of the state with the perception that the state is now irrelevant. For analytical convenience, state transformation can take one of two forms: 1) state failure or an internal collapse in the context of neocolonial economic structures, such as that experienced by a number of sub-Saharan African countries (Hoogvelt 2001; Castells 2003), or 2) a reinvention of relatively 'strong' interventionist states toward narrow economic goals (D'Costa 2009).

Naturally, why the state changes its course is a seminal question. In this chapter I offer one explanation for this transformation by theoretically linking the Indian middle class to the general process of globalization and empirically investigating the relationship between a globalized 'new economy' sector – the Indian information technology (IT) industry – and the transformation of the state. There are many factors that impinge on the workings of the state. However, the novelty of this case study is that it broadly links the selective rise of the middle class to the internalization of neoliberal policies, an outcome that the state was engaged in pre-empting in an earlier period (D'Costa 1995). It also places significant agency on the Indian middle class and by extension India's IT professionals (among other new economy workers) in an international setting.[1] India is an apt case to study because the Indian state has been society-centred in its development aspirations since independence, but now embraces global capitalism for economic growth. This chapter offers some insights into how this transformation of the state came about.

The rise of the middle class resulting from government policies can be called the embourgeoisment process. I explore the relationship between embourgeoisment, an endogenous process of middle-class expansion, and the transnationalization of this class.[2] I argue that the dialectical interaction between the Indian middle class and its subsequent transnationalization results in state transformation in a neoliberal direction (D'Costa 2005). I hypothesize that the state is transformed by two constituencies – the Indian middle class (an internal constituency), and transnational forces (external constituencies). However, the internal constituency is a creature of the state's attempt to bring about national economic development (D'Costa 2005). I argue that in a cumulative, path-dependent manner, the Indian middle class has altered the working of the state ideologically by establishing extensive links with the global economy. This development is both an acknowledgement of the selective *success* of the state in creating a globally linked Indian capitalist class (Mazumdar 2012) and its relative weakness in managing economic and social transformation in an increasingly integrated global economy.

It is beyond the scope of this chapter (though methodologically germane to the study) to provide evidence of what the state is *not* doing for various social sectors. Suffice it to say, the adoption of neoliberal-type policies in favour of global economic integration does not demonstrate a strong impetus for a social development agenda. This is principally because the main beneficiaries of globalization are capital and workers in the new global economy, specifically those with structurally relevant skills and education, which is the middle class. This is evident from increasing income and wealth disparities, heightened social polarization and growing regional inequality (D'Costa 2003 and 2011).

In section 2, I present some of the mechanisms by which the role of the state is reduced in the social sphere. First, I discuss the relationship between embourgeoisment and internationalization, that is, how the growth of the middle class in India extends itself outward through policy changes in favour of greater international economic participation, to highlight the social forces behind state transformation. Second, I develop a framework that shows the interrelationships between embourgeoisment and state transformation, mediated by transnationalization and internalization of neoliberal policies. In section 3, the specific case of new economy workers and how they contribute to the internalization of transnational influences is presented. In addition to providing the empirical data on the growth of the Indian IT industry, I analyse the different ways by which Indian IT workers are not only globally present but are actively engaged in transforming the Indian economy, and thus reinventing the state. The final section concludes with a brief discussion of the implications of a transnationalized new economy workforce for the social obligations of the state.

Embourgeoisment and State Transformation

Embourgeoisment is synonymous with the rise of the middle class, a heterogeneous group with increasing education levels and rising incomes (D'Costa 2005; Stern 2003; Frankel 1988). It also proceeds from increasing proletarianization, coterminously contributing to an upwardly mobile middle class and relatively stagnant marginalized populations. Embourgeoisment reflects gradual but increasing economic and social mobility, with an elite segment assimilating foreign (specifically Western) lifestyles and consumption patterns (Robison and Goodman 1996; Shurmer-Smith 2000; Dubey 1992; D'Costa 2010).[3] The purchase of consumer durables increasingly takes centre stage in the economy from both the buyers' and sellers' points of view. Social differentiation is accentuated by the consumption of such goods. With globalization, wealth and education drive social mobility. The state, in its nation-building efforts, supports capital accumulation, in part by educating and training its citizens. The incipient middle class is the primary beneficiary of the government's education policies (Carnoy 1984). Ultimately, embourgeoisment is synonymous with class differentiation and expanding markets (see Yadav 1999). The beneficiaries of global economic integration are typically export-oriented firms and the highly mobile, educated technical and business professionals.

Ideologically, open economies and international competitiveness are integral consequences of embourgeoisment, facilitating the internalization of external economic forces (Cerny 2000, 22; Grimes 2000; Pieterse 2000, 8–13). The confluence of secular expansion of (exogenous) global markets with nationally-derived embourgeoisment generates a local demand that is out of sync with local production capability in a closed economy. Thus, the 'triumph' of the neoliberal model of capitalism also creates global abundance relative to effective demand, compelling deregulation and economic openness (Biersteker 1992). Both forms of external influences – tangible global markets and the ideology of neoliberalism – condition national markets (see Bardhan 2002, 131). There are demonstration effects on local consumption and diffusion of best industry practices on local production (Sklair 1995 and 2001). In the end, national market development is a self-reinforcing, cumulative process, contingent on embourgeoisment at home and capital accumulation at the global level.

While much theorizing on the role of the state has been carried out over the last two decades (Chang 2002; Evans 1995; Wade 1990; Amsden 1989), there has not been an explicit treatment of how the state itself might be undermining its own social relevance in the long haul. Two interrelated mechanisms that influence the changing role are the systemic aspect of capitalist dynamics and the specific forms by which individual states reduce their engagement with their national economies. Both require that liberal markets be adopted, even in traditionally strong states such as Japan and South Korea. There are also cases whereby traditionally interventionist but relatively less effective states have tried to reinvent themselves through selective neoliberal policies (D'Costa 2009).[4] India is one such case. The emergence of a viable domestic bourgeoisie under state tutelage has also emboldened the capitalist class and the state in the wider international political economy. The business classes are likely to favour neoliberal policies that offer access to new opportunities from the world economy.[5] Globally, this translates into the diffusion of consumerism (Scholte 2000, 113–16), the convergence of economic thinking among academics, policymakers, business executives and financiers, and the pursuit of economic growth and exports by nearly all states (see Amsden 1992).

There are several mechanisms by which global forces of economic integration are internalized. In India, for example, the regulatory state, which has not been able to achieve wider development due to patronage politics and corruption (Bardhan 1998), is considered a fetter on growth and consumption. Beginning in the late 1970s, vociferous demands have been made by various social segments, especially the bourgeoisie, to diminish the role of the state in economic management. This was followed in the mid-1980s with external pressures from multilateral organizations such as the World Bank and the IMF in compelling states to reduce budget deficits and thus the withdrawal of the state from social sectors. The process of embourgeoisment indicates the growth of new markets, and in the context of global excess capacity (a typical problem of capitalism), transnational capital finds such markets highly attractive. By strongly articulating the Indian economy with the global one through liberal economic reforms in the 1980s and 1990s, the national ideological basis for state intervention was eroded. Instead, a new mantra of a liberal economic order was echoed internally (see Scholte 2000, 34–5; Marchak 1993).

The turn toward neoliberalism was also related to macroeconomic instability: for example, growing balance of payments deficits due to increasing middle-class demands. Transfer payments in the form of government subsidies to a variety of urban, rural, industrial and agricultural constituencies (all part of the broader Indian middle class) have contributed to unsustainable budget deficits and a corresponding slowdown in public investments (Bardhan 1998; Nayar 1992). The government of Rajiv Gandhi began a major overhaul of economic policies in the mid-1980s. This led to macroeconomic imbalances, such as international debt and trade deficits and a run on foreign exchange reserves, ultimately culminating in the economic crisis of 1990–91. The crisis itself led to the 1991 market reforms, whereby the Indian economy was thrown open to the international economy. Such structural preconditions as well as post-reform growth reinforced middle-class sentiments toward market-friendly reforms (see Sen 2010). But capitalism is global in scope; hence, increasing domestic demand and creating greater economic space through reforms are likely to attract global capital as well. Therefore, it should come as no surprise that trade, foreign direct investment, technology transfers and the broader financial movements such as portfolio investments have intensified in the Indian economy since the late 1990s.

Figure 7.1. The process of internalization

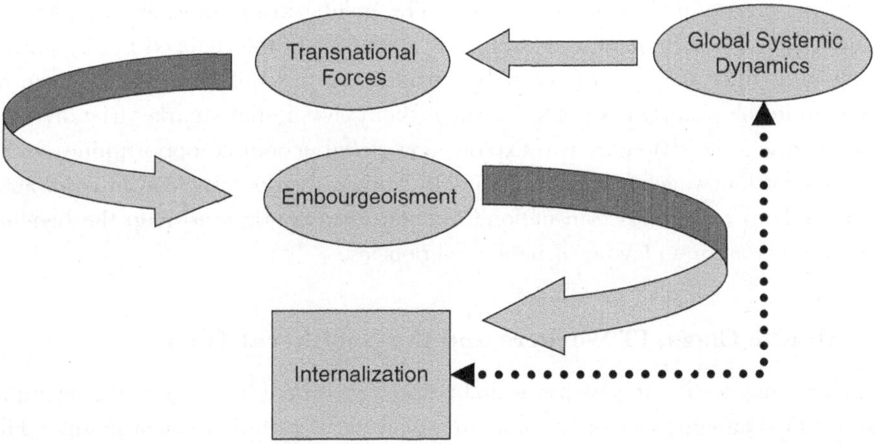

Embourgeoisment has created a vested interest in keeping the economy open. For example, the rise of Indian capitalists at home and abroad has created significant industrial interests. Some of the better known examples of recent India-related capitalist success stories include the textile and petrochemical giant, Reliance Corporation, owned by the Ambani family, the Mittal family in steel, the metals-based Caparo Group, and software magnate Premji of Wipro (D'Costa 2000; Damodaran 2008). Even the government of India played the capitalist market game with its joint venture with Suzuki Motors, cornering more than 70 per cent of the rapidly expanding passenger car market (D'Costa 2005). These capitalist successes require open economies, which nicely complement the many Indian professionals who go through a rigorous screening process in universities in India and abroad and now work for global firms. Many of them, like their US counterparts, have begun their own firms in the US. This repeated success, in terms of economic mobility and entrepreneurial achievement, dampens collective, publicly supported solutions for Indian development.

Embourgeoisment also provides the ideological ammunition to sustain market reforms and engineer international economic integration. While embourgeoisment redirects the state toward the interests of capitalists, the global economy also imposes market discipline that few states can effectively avoid (Mittelman 2000, see also Gore 2000). For example, the strong South Korean state was pressured to introduce transparent banking laws because of the growing indebtedness of the corporate sector, which could be interpreted as the Korean government facilitating the sale of national assets to foreign multinationals (Gills and Gills 2000) and introducing 'coercive liberalism' in general (Wade in Woods 2000, 11; see also Gao 2001; Blomström, Gangnes and La Croix 2001; Itoh 2000; Kosai 1996). The implication of this is that the systemic logic of global capitalism, including downsizing, diversification and relentless innovation-based competition (Ugarteche 2000; D'Costa 1999; Brenner 1998; Boyer 1997) can make even strong states move toward irrelevance or compel their reinvention.

The process of state transformation is summarized in Figure 7.1. There are two levels from which the transformative forces operate: global and national. The former represents the increasing integration of national economies, giving rise to systemic disequilibria and crises, prompting deeper integration. The pulling in of transnational forces such as foreign direct investment and exports is ideologically internalized by the emerging middle class since they are the clear beneficiaries of this shift in direction, even more now than in the past (D'Costa 2011). States themselves initiate market-friendly policies as the bourgeoisie is prepared to exploit new global economic opportunities with the advantage of low wages and expanding skills. Hence, the domestic constituency actively accommodates exogenous transnational influences to continue to reap the benefits of state transformation in favour of neoliberal policies.

The Middle Class, IT Workers and the Neoliberal Turn

In the previous section it was shown that embourgeoisment has created the institutional basis for the changing role of the state in a dialectical, path-dependent manner. Here I extend the process of embourgeoisment to the international sphere to demonstrate how global forces are internalized by the Indian middle class. The empirical evidence is drawn from the IT industry, which occupies a hegemonic position in India's industrial milieu. Briefly, there are three key implications of a transnationalized neoliberal economy, driven by the needs of the IT workforce. The first is the de facto neglect by the state of other lower-value sectors. This indifference is reflected in most of India's social indicators at the national and regional levels. The second implication is the importance of India's education system and the limited and unequal access to education by different social sectors. Globally induced employment and high wage growth tend to minimize the state's obligation to address the inegalitarian social basis of the industry and the subsequent reproduction of income inequality. Third, given the enormity of the social demands on the state and the conspicuous visibility of India's globally oriented industries, it is incumbent on both the state and successful sectors to work together to address India's social problems. Failure to do so is likely to hamper future development by way of dampened demand and social strife.

Indian companies and professionals have come a long way in learning the technical, commercial and organizational aspects of the global economy while amassing considerable wealth for themselves. The Indian state and middle classes have a responsibility to the neglected social sectors to spread the benefits of embourgeoisment and transnationalization. Narrowly, this would include fostering domestic market development for both production and consumption of IT-related goods and services (D'Costa 2004). More broadly, it would call for a wide array of social policies to increase access to higher education and employment for the historically underprivileged groups and low-income households through massive investments in basic and higher education. It would also call for supporting the traditional sectors in agriculture and industry, including massive investments in rural infrastructure, access to credit, adequate compensation to producers, and long-term employment for farmers who part with their agricultural land for large-scale industrial use. I conclude this section suggesting that the neoliberal turn has focused the state on the middle classes to the detriment of those who are socially and economically excluded from the new economy.

Figure 7.2. Globalization and expansion of India's IT industry

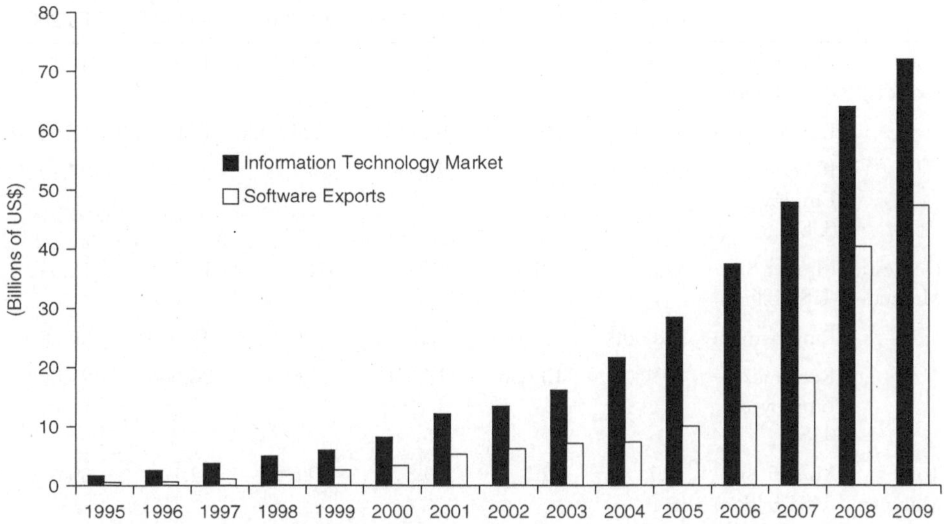

Source: NASSCOM 2002, 2003, 2010.
Note: IT = hardware, peripherals, networking, domestic and export market for software and services, and IT-enabled services.

Growth of the Indian software industry

The Indian information technology industry as a whole is now estimated to be worth over US$70 billion annually (Figure 7.2). India's export of software services was US$47 billion in 2008–09, which represented 65.7 per cent of India's software services; and software and IT-enabled services exports represented 16 per cent of all of India's exports in 2008. The share of the IT sector to GDP has consistently increased since the mid-1990s (see D'Costa 2004), from 1 per cent in 1999 to 5.8 per cent in 2009 (NASSCOM 2010). India's overall exports quadrupled between 1995 and 2006 to US$103 billion and crossed US$250 billion in 2010–11 (Ministry of Finance, various years). Of the top 20 software and IT-service exporters from India in 2009–10, the vast majority were Indian and the rest were foreign subsidiaries operating out of India. The top 20 exporters were responsible for 71 per cent of the industry's total exports.

New economy labour and state transformation

The expansion of the Indian IT industry is predicated on the growth of human capital; more specifically, of technical talent. While this development could be seen as a purely endogenous matter, the highly internationalized IT sector suggests otherwise. Both domestic and foreign forces are at play in the expansion of the Indian IT industry. The critical domestic factor is India's tertiary education system, which the government has actively developed over the decades since independence, initially to meet the needs of the earlier import substitution industrialization strategy. The state was able to establish an elite educational infrastructure, which in the 1980s became a good fit with the needs

Table 7.1. Employment in the Indian IT and ITES industry

		FY2004	FY2005	FY2006	FY2007	FY2008	FY2009
Total Exports	Market Size (US$ billion)	12.9	17.7	23.6	31.3	40.4	47.1
	Employment	512,000	706,000	928,000	1,243,000	1,560,000	1,736,615
	Revenue/ Employee (US$)	25,195	25,071	25,431	25,181	25,897	27,122
Domestic Market	Market Size (US$ billion)	3.8	4.8	6.7	8.2	11.7	12.5
	Employment	318,000	352,000	365,000	378,000	450,000	500,000
	Revenue/ Employee (US$)	11,950	13,636	18,356	21,693	26,000	25,000
Total Market	Market Size (US$ billion)	16.7	22.5	30.3	39.5	52.1	59.6
	Employment	830,000	1,058,000	1,293,000	1,621,000	2,010,000	2,236,615
	Revenue/ Employee (US$)	20,120	21,267	23,434	24,368	25,920	26,647

Source: National Skill Development Corporation (15).

of the global IT industry. As the integration of the Indian industry proceeded, the private sector also became engaged with human capital development directly related to the industry. The southern Indian states of Andhra Pradesh, Karnataka and Tamil Nadu, already ahead of other states in private education, responded flexibly to the growing demand for technical talent (see Okada 2004, 299). Subsequently, India had available a large technical talent pool to meet the demand for IT professionals, as is evident from the growth in employment in the IT and IT-enabled services (ITES) (Table 7.1). Total employment more than doubled between 2004 and 2009. Although the Indian government's National Skill Development Initiative is highly optimistic, with an anticipated 500 million skilled workforce by 2022, the size of the technical talent pool is bound to increase.

A large share of the global talent pool is found in India and China (D'Costa and Parayil 2009). In 1980, together they accounted for about 10 per cent (7 million) of the global population with tertiary education and in 2000 they accounted for 18 per cent (35 million). India's undergraduate enrolment stood at 10 million in 2004, of which 11 per cent was in engineering (National Council of Applied Economic Research 2005, in Bound 2007, 11). India's stock of young talent was roughly 14 million, which is roughly one-and-a-half times that of China's talent pool and double that of the US (Bound 2007, 11). More recent estimates for 2010 show that India had 11 per cent of the 129 million 25- to 34-year-olds with a tertiary degree compared to the US's 14 per cent and China's 18 per cent (OECD 2012, 2). In science and engineering doctoral level studies, the top ten sending countries to the US represented 67 per cent of the total between 1989 and 2009 (US National Science Foundation 2012, 2–129). During this period, India was in the second spot after China, with nearly 25,000 students or 11.1 per cent of the total.

Technical talent circulates internationally in three ways: students move abroad for technical education and subsequently return; professionals emigrate permanently; or talent moves overseas temporarily via special visa schemes (see Glanz 2001; Table 7.2). All three types, but especially the first and the third, contribute to a political economy in which economic integration becomes practically possible and ideologically justified. The benefits of the industry's links to the global economy in the form of rising revenues, employee earnings, international travel (and thus exposure to various types of markets), and growing global visibility reinforce the importance of a 'hands-off' state.

While the ideological shift of the state is driven by the middle class, state transformation is reinforced by students seeking a foreign education, professionals working abroad and entrepreneurs capturing global opportunities. Their English-language ability gives them an advantage in Anglophone societies over other Asian students. However, as can be seen from Table 7.2, India's share of US F1 (student) visas is smaller than China's and smaller by a wide margin than South Korea's share. This anomaly can be explained by the high cost of undergraduate education in the US and India's much lower per capita income compared to other Asian countries. Also, India has some high-quality educational institutions, hence overseas study at the undergraduate level is less attractive. However, India's share of F1 visas since 1997 has more than doubled, to nearly 10 per cent, suggesting not only that the US is becoming more attractive for Indian students (a classic form of social networks in action), but that Indian households are becoming relatively more affluent, consistent with the embourgeoisment process. Although the US continues to lead globally in the number of doctoral degrees in science and engineering (S&E), with nearly 41,000 PhDs earned in 2009, a large share of this is earned by foreign students, with many from India and China. For example, 30 per cent of S&E doctorates earned by foreigners in the US between 1983 and 2003 were earned by students of Chinese and Indian origin (US National Science Board 2006, Figure O-32).

Since a significant percentage of these students can be expected to return to India after completing their studies due to family obligations and increasingly better employment prospects at home, the implication of this on the changing role of the state toward globalization is apparent. First, the expatriate population is generally wealthy and thus creates an external constituency for a more global orientation of the home economy. Second, their ties to India remain strong both economically (through remittance income) and socially (through family links). Third, many of them return home and establish commercial links between the domestic and export markets, either based on their own entrepreneurial investments or working on behalf of multinational firms (Saxenian 2004). All of these cumulatively contribute to the business model of exports through outsourcing arrangements, which further entails the temporary international movement of technical talent from India, creating fluid constituencies for state transformation, both internally and externally.

Table 7.2. Indian students and technical professionals in the US by nonimmigrant visa category (percentage share)

	Fiscal 1997			Fiscal 2006			Fiscal 2011		
	F1 Visa	H1B Visa	L1 Visa	F1 Visa	H1B Visa	L1 Visa	F1 Visa	H Visa	L Visa
Africa	4.2	3.1	1.6	4.5	2.2	1.6	3.8	1.8	1.6
Asia	55.8	59.2	40.7	64.7	70.7	60.7	71.5	51.6	58.6
China	4.5	4.0	8.3	10.3	7.0	2.6	32.7	4.6	4.0
Taiwan	5.6	1.8	0.8	6.1	1.9	..	2.4	0.7	0.4
India	4.0	39.3	4.4	9.6	47.9	43.8	5.6	38.5	38.5
Japan	13.2	3.6	19.5	8.6	2.8	7.0	3.7	1.1	7.1
S. Korea	13.6	1.1	3.0	15.6	2.4	1.6	11.0	1.9	2.6
Europe	23.5	25.9	41.1	18.4	16.4	25.5	13.9	8.9	23.4
S. America	9.7	4.6	5.7	5.7	6.2	5.5	6.6	3.2	6.4
Total (Nos.)	266,483	80,547	36,589	273,870	135,421	72,613	476,072	312,082	147,677

Source: US Department of State 2012, online: http://www.travel.state.gov/pdf/FY11AnnualReport-Table%20XVII.pdf (accessed 10 July 2012); US Department of State 2007, online: http://travel.state.gov/pdf/FY1997_NIV_Detail_Table.pdf (accessed 13 June 2007).
Note: .. = negligible share, H1 and L1 visas are subsets of H and L visas.

India enjoys a pre-eminent position in the distribution of US-based employment-sponsored visas for different countries. Between 1997 and 2006, India's share of US H1B visas (a five-year employment-sponsored work visa) increased from 39 per cent to 48 per cent. Interestingly, some of the leading sponsors (or visa petitioners) in 2006 were Indian firms with offices in the US such as Satyam (1st with 3268 petitions), Patni (4th with 1776) Infosys (5th with 1726), Larsen and Toubro (11th with 878), Polaris (15th with 678) and TCS (17th with 552).[6] Transnationalization of Indian IT firms entails not only the exports of professionals and software from India but also the export of capital, that is foreign investments, which in turn hire back talent from India. As Indian companies open offices in the US for marketing as well as R&D purposes, they staff them with Indian professionals. This movement of people is a form of intra-company transfer made possible by the US L1 visa program (temporary visas for employees transferred from one branch of a company in one country to the US branch or head office). Here, too, the share of LI visas granted to Indians is the highest, at 44 per cent, having increased ten-fold since 1997.[7]

The movement of Indian workers to the largest IT market via these US state-sponsored programs suggests a continuing reinforcement of a market-oriented dynamic at home. In this global engagement, the government of India is very much in the foreground. In addition to massive investments in technical education, it is now playing a critical role in providing information technology infrastructure. The government has established several successful software technology parks, which support firms that produce solely for export with infrastructural benefits such as state-of-the-art satellite communication systems. These export units have been exempt from income taxes for over a decade. The industry lobby NASSCOM works very hard to ensure that the IT sector continues to get state help even as it publicly claims the industry's success has come 'in spite of the government'. Observing the significant role the Indian diaspora has been playing in their adopted countries such as the US, the Indian government now enthusiastically recognizes Persons of Indian Origin (PIO) and Overseas Citizens of India (OCI) and grants 15-year and lifelong visas respectively to these non-citizens. These goodwill steps not only extend the Indian state's reach beyond its borders but are also expected to facilitate the return of expatriate professionals to India (see D'Costa 2009).

The effects of these transnational linkages on the reinvention of the state are two-fold. First, the process of embourgeoisment, where there is mobility for some social groups and exclusion for others, is reinforced. Second, the intellectual and pragmatic preference of globally linked Indian middle-class groups justifies the appropriateness of the neoliberal order for India. This conviction arises due to a particular class position as the Indian middle class has been the primary beneficiary of globalization. Hence, the internalization of neoliberal ideas is no longer driven exogenously; rather there is a strong domestic constituency promoting these ideas and demanding that the government meet their needs. The power of neoliberalism as enshrined in intellectual property rights is particularly relevant in the Indian software industry. The private industry association NASSCOM is a significant piracy watchdog in India. NASSCOM recognizes that once the Indian industry matures there will be considerable economic gains from the strict implementation of copyright rules. The language of the 'level playing field' is being echoed by the would-be gainers of neoliberalism as Indian businesses find liberalized trade and investment, along with overseas acquisitions, to their advantage. Perhaps the strongest evidence for the transformation of the state due to embourgeoisment and transnationalization is in the Indian state of West Bengal. The pro-labour Communist Party of India (Marxists) of West Bengal governed the state for over three decades based on a platform of social transformation generated by rural development and worker rights. However, in the last few years before it was voted out of power, it made a rapid ideological about-face by trying to attract foreign capital, tame its militant trade unions, and work with industrial capitalists to promote investments in the state.

Implications of a transnationalized new economy workforce

The Indian state has distanced itself from its societal role by working closely with capital, which is increasingly tied to the global economy. This fundamental transformation of the state is consistent with a simple instrumentalist view of the state but in reality is a more complicated product of the dialectical capitalist development process set in motion at India's independence. The social and class differentiation underlying embourgeoisment is linked to the creation of an external constituency by way of emigration of middle-class professionals, which provides both the ideological and material ammunition for global integration and subsequently also the forces of advanced capitalist imperatives of growth, efficiency and reduced role of the state. What then are the implications for distributive justice on tertiary education, currently monopolized by the Indian middle class as a prerequisite to enter the highly internationalized IT industry?[8]

Elsewhere it has been shown that there are severe distortions in the Indian social system with this particular form of development since the state is stepping away from its social development role due to greater demands placed on it by both the domestic bourgeoisie and global capitalist structures (D'Costa 2011). India's education policy since independence has been biased in favour of the upper classes (and upper castes), and thus the IT industry has absorbed mostly the better-off social groups. While literacy rates have vastly improved since Indian independence – from 18 per cent in 1951 to 74 per cent in 2011 – they remain woefully inadequate. Education is a public good and serves middle-class aspirations well. However, the persistence of social inequality bars most from a quality education and thus acts as a major barrier to upward mobility for minorities such as scheduled castes and tribes.

India's embrace of globalization has resulted in very uneven development. About 70 per cent of India's population lives in rural areas, with the majority eking out a living. Nearly 300 million people live below the official poverty line. More importantly, as the rise of the Indian IT industry has been accompanied by the dismantling of social safety nets, those most in need of government investment have been neglected. The internationalized IT sector employs less than 1 per cent of India's employed, while the agricultural sector, which is seeing large cutbacks in funding, employs over 50 per cent, and the informal sector as a whole employs 85 per cent of the working population (National Commission for Enterprises in the Unorganised Sector (NCEUS) 2009; also Drèze and Sen 1998).

The Indian IT industry has created massive wage inequality within the country, which rests on access to higher education. The faster growth of the software services sector relative to other sectors implies a widening income gap and income polarization, if embourgeoisment remains a selective process. With local wages chasing foreign rates (D'Costa 2006), in the context of an education policy biased toward upper classes/castes (Agarwal 2006; Mohanty 2006; Hasan and Mehta 2006), inequality is further accentuated. Although social mobility of some members of underprivileged groups has been made possible through the reservations system, one could argue that current high economic growth rests on structural inequality.[9] This implies that without the class/caste bias it would not have been possible to generate enough English-speaking technically educated graduates to drive post-independent India's industrialization and subsequently India's IT growth.

Conclusion

This chapter has examined the transformation of the Indian state, as mediated by the rise of the Indian middle class, drawing on the experience of the internationalized IT industry. I have argued that the change in the role of the state in favour of neoliberal policies rests on the dialectical relationship between the processes of embourgeoisment and the subsequent internalization of neoliberalism by the Indian state. The ideological shift away from society-centred goals such as greater equality and access to education to more business-led goals was framed in terms of internal and external constituencies. Thus the analysis relied on the interaction and articulation of endogenous and exogenous factors to explain some of the institutional reasons for state transformation.

By grounding the analysis on the systemic and integrative aspects of global capitalism, this study departs from the simplistic argument that credits exogenous forces. Theoretically and empirically, the chapter has demonstrated how transnational influences have been internalized by the Indian bourgeoisie. Middle-class students, professionals, entrepreneurs and the state (peopled by white-collar bureaucrats) have ideologically absorbed globalization. India's internationalization has been no doubt evolutionary, and when all the details are sifted through, the trajectory is remarkably predictable – embourgeoisment, transnationalization and internalization. The role of Indian middle-class IT professionals in this process cannot be underestimated.

The rapid growth of the IT industry and the high status of the industry in the world economy reflect one mechanism by which global forces are absorbed by Indian middle-class professionals and the state. The internationalization of India's workforce can be seen in the mobility of students for advanced education, the high demand for Indian professionals in the global IT market, and multinational investments in India and the overseas expansion of Indian business. Consequently, the focus of the state on largely economic matters dealing with integration and competitiveness rather than social distribution is evidence of a new direction for the role of the state.

The about-face of states such as India that traditionally have been strong, interventionist, developmental, mercantilist and inward-looking leads us to believe that there are internal constituencies of exogenous forces. This interpretation avoids the pitfalls associated with a binary understanding of internal versus external factors. More importantly, it allows us to situate the notion of changing states in the larger context of capitalist dynamics, highlighting the relationship between embourgeoisment and transnationalization. It also reveals the contradiction between progressive elements of the middle class, made possible partly by access to tertiary education, clashing with the socially regressive policies that have emanated from the broader development of the middle class and its embrace of the market system. The question as to why states would shoot themselves in the proverbial foot becomes less puzzling when we consider that the alternative of not following the logic of capitalism inflicts far greater perceived costs on the domestic economy and the globally oriented bourgeoisie than the marginalized and the dispossessed.

Neoliberal reforms in the context of transnationalization of economic production do not imply the irrelevance of states. On the contrary, states such as India are reinventing themselves. The Indian state is using its economic and administrative clout to exploit contemporary global market opportunities (D'Costa 2009). The real test is whether the Indian state, along with the Indian bourgeoisie, is willing to share the benefits of growth with the wider society. If not, it is unlikely that there will be an easy way out of this social and economic impasse without major political negotiations and upheavals in the future.

Notes

1 The US has the largest IT market in the world and continues to be a bastion of neoliberal ideology despite periodic and systemic crisis in major capitalist markets. India is heavily reliant on the US IT market, and there is an influential Indian diaspora present there.
2 Defining the middle class is problematic. It is also distinct from the traditional understanding of the bourgeoisie. The middle class in late industrializing countries is rooted in state-led capitalist development and generally does not originate from the landed gentry (Frankel 1988). Typically, white-collar employees and petty bourgeoisie are the main segments (see Shurmer-Smith 2000, 29–38; Dubey 1992). The process of embourgeoisment has been treated more fully elsewhere (D'Costa 2005; Stern 2003).
3 By global consumption norms there is no intent to imply that people uncritically accept international goods (see Jackson 2004). Rather, as incomes rise consumers everywhere have access to high-value, foreign goods. There is some convergence of consumption since global strategies of multinationals tend to homogenize markets despite some of the outward appearances of product differentiation.
4 This shift is a result of global capitalist market logic, which India had tried to resist earlier (D'Costa 1995; Encarnation 1989).
5 This interpretation of the transformation of states is consistent with Pedersen's society-centred explanation of economic liberalization in India (Pedersen 2000). However, his trying to link the 1991 reforms to the emergence of a new crop of entrepreneurs (the 'quiet revolution'), underplays the larger context of state-sponsored embourgeoisment over several decades.
6 See My Visa Jobs website (www.myvisajobs.com).
7 So high is the visibility of Indian professionals in the US IT industry that visa fees have been increased, which is expected to impact Indians and Indian firms in the US disproportionately. The Indian industry and government are not happy about it.
8 Of course the formation of an Indian middle class predates India's participation in the global IT industry. But prior advantage has placed this class in an ever more advantageous position.
9 A total of 22.5 per cent of central government jobs and admissions to government professional colleges are reserved for scheduled castes and tribes. Additional slots are reserved for 'other backward castes'.

References

Agarwal, P. 2006. 'Higher Education Policy: Many Contradictions'. *Economic and Political Weekly* 41, no. 45: 4645–8.

Amsden, A. H. 1989. *Asia's Next Giant: South Korea and Late Industrialization*, New York: Oxford University Press.

______. 1992. 'The South Korean Economy: Is Business-Led Growth Working?' In *Korea Briefing, 1992* edited by D. N. Clark. Boulder, CO: Westview Press, 71–95.

Bagchi, A. K. and A. P. D'Costa, eds. 2012. *Transformation and Development: The Political Economy of Transition in India and China*. New Delhi: Oxford University Press.

Bardhan, P. 1998. *The Political Economy of Development in India*. Expanded edition. New Delhi: Oxford University Press.

______. 2002. 'The Political Economy of Reform in India'. In *Facets of the Indian Economy: The NCAER Golden Jubilee Lectures* edited by R. Mohan. New Delhi: Oxford University Press, 123–35.

______. 2010. *Awakening Giants, Feet of Clay: Assessing the Economic Rise of China and India*. Princeton: Princeton University Press.

Biersteker, T. J. 1992. 'The "Triumph" of Neoclassical Economics in the Developing World: Policy Convergence and Bases of Governance in the International Economic Order'. In *Governance*

Without Government: Order and Change in World Politics edited by J. N. Rosenau and E.-O. Czempiel. Cambridge: Cambridge University Press, 102–31.

Blomström, M., B. Gangnes and S. La Croix. 2001. *Japan's New Economy: Continuity and Change in the Twenty-First Century*. New York: Oxford University Press.

Bound, K. 2007. *India: The Uneven Innovator*. London: Demos.

Boyer, R. 1997. 'State and Market: A New Engagement for the Twenty-First Century?' In *States Against Markets: The Limits to Globalization* edited by R. Boyer and D. Drache. London: Routledge, 84–114.

Brenner, R. 1998. 'The Economics of Global Turbulence: A Special Report on the World Economy, 1950–98'. *New Left Review*, no. 229: 1–265.

Carnoy, M. 1984. *The State and Political Theory*. Princeton: Princeton University Press.

Castells, M. 2002. *The Rise of the Network Society* (The Information Age: Economy, Society and Culture, Vol. I). Malden, MA: Blackwell Publishers.

______. 2003. *End of Millennium* (The Information Age: Economy, Society and Culture, Vol. III). Malden, MA: Blackwell Publishers.

Cerny, P. G. 2000. 'Structuring the Political Arena: Public Goods, States and Governance in a Globalizing World'. In *Global Political Economy: Contemporary Theories* edited by R. Palan. London: Routledge, 21–35.

Chang, H. J. 2002. *Kicking Away the Ladder: Development Strategy in Historical Perspective*. London: Anthem Press.

D'Costa, A. P. 1995. 'The Long March to Capitalism: India's Resistance to and Reintegration with the World Economy'. *Contemporary South Asia* 4, no. 3: 257–87.

______. 1999. *The Global Restructuring of the Steel Industry: Innovations, Institutions, and Industrial Change*. London: Routledge.

______. 2000. 'Capitalist Maturity and Corporate Responses to Liberalization: The Steel, Auto, and Software Sectors in India'. *Contemporary South Asia* 9, no. 2: 141–63.

______. 2003. 'Uneven and Combined Development: Understanding India's Software Exports'. *World Development* 13, no. 1: 211–26.

______. 2004. 'The Indian Software Industry in the Global Division of Labor'. In *India in the Global Software Industry: Innovation, Firm Strategies and Development* edited by A. P. D'Costa and E. Sridharan. Basingstoke: Palgrave Macmillan, 1–26.

______. 2005. *The Long March to Capitalism: Embourgeoisment, Internationalization, and Industrial Transformation in India*. Basingstoke: Palgrave Macmillan.

______. 2006. 'ICTs and Decoupled Development: Theories, Trajectories and Transitions' In *Political Economy & Information Capitalism in India: Digital Divide, Development Divide and Equity* edited by G. Parayil. Basingstoke: Palgrave Macmillan, 11–34.

______. 2009. 'Economic Nationalism in Motion: Steel, Auto, and Software Industries in India'. *Review of International Political Economy* 16, no. 4: 618–46.

______. (ed.) 2010. *A New India? Critical Reflections in the Long Twentieth Century*. London: Anthem Press.

______. 2011. 'Geography, Uneven Development and Distributive Justice: The Political Economy of IT Growth in India'. *Cambridge Journal of Regions, Economy and Society* 4, no. 2: 237–51.

D'Costa, A. P. and G. Parayil. 2009. 'China, India, and the New Asian Innovation Dynamics'. In *The New Asian Innovation Dynamics: China and India in Perspective* edited by G. Parayil and A. P. D'Costa. Basingstoke: Palgrave Macmillan, 1–26.

Damodaran, H. 2008. *India's New Capitalists: Caste, Business, and Industry in a Modern Nation*. Basingstoke: Palgrave Macmillan.

Drèze, J. and A. Sen. 1998. *India: Economic Development and Social Opportunity*. Oxford: Clarendon Press.

Dubey, S. 1992. 'The Middle Class'. In *India Briefing, 1992* edited by L. A. Gordon and P. Oldenburg. Boulder, CO: Westview Press, 137–64.

Encarnation, D. J. 1989. *Dislodging Multinationals: India's Strategy in Comparative Perspective*. Ithaca: Cornell University Press.

Evans, P. 1995. *Embedded Autonomy: States and Industrial Transformation*. Princeton: Princeton University Press.

Frankel, F. R. 1988. 'Middle Classes and Castes in India's Politics: Prospects for Political Accommodation'. In *India's Democracy: An Analysis of Changing State-Society Relations* edited by A. Kohli. Princeton: Princeton University Press, 225–61.

Gao, B. 2001. *Japan's Economic Dilemma: The Institutional Origins of Prosperity and Stagnation*. Cambridge: Cambridge University Press.

Gills, B. K. and D. S. Gills. 2000. 'South Korea and Globalization: The Rise to Globalism'. In *East Asia and Globalization* edited by S. S. Kim. Lanham, MD: Rowman and Littlefield, 81–103.

Glanz, J. 2001. 'Trolling for Brains in International Waters', *New York Times* (April 1).

Gore, C. 2000. 'The Rise and Fall of the Washington Consensus as a Paradigm for Developing Countries'. *World Development* 28, no. 5: 789–804.

Grimes, W. W. 2000. 'Japan and Globalization: From Opportunity to Restraint,' In *East Asia and Globalization* edited by S. S. Kim. Lanham, MD: Rowman and Littlefield, 55–79.

Hasan, R. and A. Mehta. 2006. 'Under-representation of Disadvantaged Classes in Colleges: What Do the Data Tell Us?' *Economic and Political Weekly* 41, no. 35: 3791–6.

Held, D., A. McGrew, D. Goldblatt and J. Perraton. 1999. *Global Transformations: Politics, Economics and Culture*. Stanford: Stanford University Press.

Hoogvelt, A. 2001. *Globalization and the Postcolonial World: The New Political Economy of Development*. Baltimore: Johns Hopkins University Press.

Howard, M. C. and J. E. King. 1989. *A History of Marxian Economics: Volume I, 1883–1929*. Princeton: Princeton University Press.

Itoh, M. 2000. *Globalization of Japan: Japanese Sakoku Mentality and U.S. Efforts to Open Japan*. New York: St. Martin's Press.

Jackson, P. 2004. 'Local Consumption Cultures in a Globalizing World'. *Transactions* (Institute of British Geographers) 29, no. 2: 165–78.

Kosai, Y. 1996. 'Competition and Competition Policy in Japan: Foreign Pressures and Domestic Institutions'. In *National Diversity and Global Capitalism* edited by S. Berger and R. Dore. Ithaca: Cornell University Press, 197–215.

Marchak, M.P. 1993. *The Integrated Circus: The New Right and the Restructuring of Global Markets*. Montreal: McGill-Queen's University Press.

Mazumdar, S. 2012. 'Big Business and Economic Nationalism in India'. In *Globalization and Economic Nationalism in Asia* edited by A. P. D'Costa. Oxford: Oxford University Press, 59–83.

Ministry of Finance, Government of India, various years. *Economic Survey*. Online: http://finmin.nic.in/the_ministry/dept_eco_affairs/economic_div/eco_survey/index.htm

Mittelman, J. H. 2000. *The Globalization Syndrome: Transformation and Resistance*. Princeton: Princeton University Press.

Mohanty, M. 2006. 'Social Inequality, Labour Market Dynamics and Reservation'. *Economic and Political Weekly* 41, no. 35: 3777–89.

Myvisajobs.com. 2006. 'Top 500 H1B Visa Sponsors'. September 2006. www.myvisajobs.com (accessed 6 October 2007).

NASSCOM. 2010. 'Executive Summary' of Strategic Review 2009, www.nasscom.in/upload/60452Executive_summary.pdf (accessed 26 October 2010).

NASSCOM. Various years. Online: www.nasscom.org.

NASSCOM Press Information Note. Online: www.nasscom.org (accessed 16 May 2007).

National Commission for Enterprises in the Unorganised Sector (NCEUS). 2009. *The Challenge of Employment in India: An Informal Economy Perspective, Volume I, Main Report*. New Delhi: National Commission for Enterprises in the Unorganised Sector, Government of India.

National Skill Development Corporation. n.d. *Human Resource and Skill Requirements in the IT and ITES Industry Sector (2022): A Report*. New Delhi: National Skill Development Corporation, http://www.nsdcindia.org/pdf/IT-ITES-Industry.pdf (accessed 10 October 2012).

Nayar, B. R. 1992. 'The Public Sector'. In *India Briefing, 1992* edited by L. A. Gordon and P. Oldenburg. Boulder, CO: Westview Press, 71–101.

OECD. 2012. *Education Indicators in Focus*. 2012/05 (May). http://www.oecd.org/edu/50495363.pdf (accessed 10 September 2012).

Okada, A. 2004. 'Bangalore's Software Cluster: Building Competitiveness through the Local Labor Market Dynamics'. In *Industrial Clusters in Asia: Analyses of their Competition and Cooperation* edited by A. Kuchiki and M. Tsuji. Tokyo: Institute of Developing Economies and Japan External Trade Organization, 276–314.

Pedersen, J. D. 2000. 'Explaining Economic Liberalization in India: State and Society Perspectives'. *World Development* 28, no. 2: 265–82.

Pieterse, J. N. 2000. 'Shaping Globalization'. In *Global Futures: Shaping Globalization* edited by J. N. Pieterse. London: Zed Books, 1–19.

Robison, R. and D. S. G. Goodman. 1996. 'The New Rich in Asia: Economic Development, Social Status and Political Consciousness'. In *The New Rich in Asia: Mobile Phones, McDonald's and Middle-Class Revolution* edited by R. Robison and D. S. G. Goodman. London: Routledge, 1–18.

Saxenian, A. 2004. 'The Silicon Valley Connection: Transnational Networks and Regional Development in Taiwan, China and India'. In *India in the Global Software Industry: Innovation, Firm Strategies and Development* edited by A. P. D'Costa and E. Sridharan. Basingstoke: Palgrave Macmillan, 164–92.

Scholte, J. A. 2000. *Globalization: A Critical Introduction*. New York: St. Martin's Press.

Sen, K. 2010. 'New Interpretations of India's Economic Growth in the Twentieth Century'. In *A New India? Critical Reflections in the Long Twentieth Century* edited by A. P. D'Costa, London: Anthem Press, 23–42.

Shurmer-Smith, P. 2000. *India: Globalization and Change*. London: Arnold.

Sklair, L. 1995. *Sociology of the Global System*. Baltimore: Johns Hopkins University Press.

_______. 2001. *The Transnational Capitalist Class*. Oxford: Blackwell.

Stallings, B. 2003. 'Globalization and Liberalization: The Impact on Developing Countries'. In *States, Markets, and Just Growth: Development in the Twenty-First Century* edited by A. Kohli, C.-I. Moon and G. Sørensen. Tokyo: United Nations University Press, 9–38.

Stern, R. W. 2003. *Changing India: Bourgeois Revolution on the Subcontinent*. Cambridge: Cambridge University Press.

Ugarteche, O. 2000. *The False Dilemma, Globalization: Opportunity or Threat*. London: Zed Books.

US Department of State. 2007. http://travel.state.gov/pdf/FY1997_NIV_Detail_Table.pdf (accessed 13 June 2007).

US National Science Board. 2006. *Science and Engineering Indicators 2006*, Vol. I. Washington, DC: US National Science Foundation.

US National Science Foundation. 2012. 'Chapter 2: Higher Education in Science and Engineering' In *Science and Engineering Indicators, 2010*. http://www.nsf.gov/statistics/seind12/pdf/c02.pdf (accessed 10 September 2012).

Wade, R. 1990. *Governing the Market: Economic Theory and the Role of Government in East Asian Industrialization*. Princeton: Princeton University Press.

Woods, N. 2000. 'The Political Economy of Globalization'. In *The Political Economy of Globalization* edited by N. Woods. New York: St. Martin's Press, 1–19.

Yadav, Y. 1999. 'Politics'. In *India Briefing: A Transformative Fifty Years* edited by M. Bouton and P. Oldenburg. Armonk, NY: M. E. Sharpe.

Chapter 8

THE WORLD TRADE ORGANIZATION AND ITS IMPACT ON INDIA

Parthapratim Pal

GATT to WTO: High Expectations from the Organization

The last two decades have witnessed a number of important changes in economic policies adopted in most developing countries. Many of these measures fall under the common definition of globalization. Trade liberalization is considered one of the main components of globalization. Widespread trade liberalization adopted during the last two decades has resulted in a sharp increase in the volume of trade among nations. To supervise and monitor this growing volume of trade, a trade regulatory body was formed in 1994. This organization is called the World Trade Organization (WTO). The formation of this organization is having an important bearing on the growth of international trade.

The WTO is the successor of the original GATT (General Agreement on Tariff and Trade), which supervised international trade from 1947 until the inception of the WTO. However, the WTO is a much bigger organization than GATT – in terms of both membership and coverage of rules. WTO rules are not only a revised, enhanced and updated version of the original GATT, but they also include additional agreements on key areas where clarifications or amplifications were felt necessary. Also, unlike GATT, the WTO covers trade in services (under General Agreement on Trade in Services – GATS) and Trade Related Intellectual Property Rights (TRIPS). Another big advantage of the WTO is that as an organization, it is allowed to take legal action if a country violates its trade rules. The WTO also contains provisions to legally settle trade-related disputes among countries. There were no such legal provisions in GATT.

The WTO was established in 1994 amidst great expectations that it would lead to a more open and fair world trading system. During that time, the predominant view among policymakers was that the WTO would usher in a new regime of global trade governance which would bring significant welfare benefits to developing countries. The underlying hypothesis was that a free and fair system of international trade and more effective integration of developing countries with the global market would allow developing countries to pursue export-led growth.

Also, from the perspective of developing countries, the establishment of the WTO was seen as a positive step because the WTO introduced new rules to open up trade in agriculture, textiles and the services sector. As a very high percentage of exports from developing countries belongs to these three sectors, it was felt that developing countries would benefit from the WTO. But there was also a worry that stricter intellectual property rules and removal of import restrictions might harm domestic industries of developing countries. However, most experts were of the opinion that, overall, the WTO system of trading would help developing countries increase their share in the international market. It was also assumed that trade would lead to higher growth and would contribute significantly to the overall economic development of these countries.[1]

Unfulfilled Promises and New Challenges

More than fifteen years after the WTO was established, if one looks back at its performance, a mixed picture emerges. While there has been growth in world trade and some countries have benefited from it, many expectations of least-developed and developing countries from the WTO remain unfulfilled. These countries feel that, in spite of its initial promise, the WTO did not bring fundamental changes in the international trade regime and the disadvantages faced by developing countries have not been adequately taken care of. It was also felt that poorer countries were increasingly being marginalized in global trade. Among developing countries, there is also a growing resentment towards the institutional make-up of the WTO. It is felt that the procedural requirements of the WTO are costly and require a level of expertise which sometimes is beyond developing countries.

Moreover, negotiations at the Doha Development Round are not progressing well. For a number of reasons the Doha Round of trade talks has hit repeated roadblocks. Consequently, uncertainty has crept in about the multilateral trading system. Also, due to a number of economic and strategic reasons, many countries are exploring the formation of regional trading blocks.[2] As trading among these blocks is outside the purview of the WTO, the proliferation of Regional Trading Agreements (RTAs) in recent years can be perceived as a decline in the importance of the WTO as the supervisor of international trade.

The WTO is also facing three big new challenges which resulted from some recent economic events. The first is related to the increased protectionist tendencies among major countries of the world. During the financial crisis, which originated in the US real estate market, global trade shrank significantly, and to prevent leakage of domestic demand, some countries started imposing protectionist measures in different guises. There was an apprehension that retaliatory steps could be adopted by other countries, which would have led to a collapse of world trade as it happened during the Great Depression of the 1930s. But countries and multilateral organizations including the WTO managed to prevent such an occurrence. World trade has recovered after the crisis, and the WTO and other multilateral organizations deserve a certain amount of credit for this. However, protectionist tendencies in some big countries like the US are still quite strong, and it remains to be seen how the WTO deals with this new challenge.[3] The financial crisis has also led to an understanding that too much export orientation can be problematic for countries. There is an interest shift in mainstream thinking about the role of domestic demand in economy. For example, Prasad (2009) says: 'With the increasing importance of Asian emerging markets in the world economy, rebalancing growth in developing Asia toward more reliance on domestic demand and less on exports is an important component of the global effort to stabilize world financial and economic systems' (Prasad 2009, 19). Increased emphasis on domestic demand and domestic markets may also imply that the motivation for faster completion of WTO trade talks will be less for developing countries.

The second big issue that has emerged in recent times is that countries are increasingly resorting to exchange rate management to help their exports. WTO rules impose a number of conditions and restrictions on trade-promoting measures such as subsidies and export incentives. In a period of slowing demand, countries are therefore using alternative export-promoting measures such as artificial depreciation of exchange rates. There is growing apprehension that such exchange rate management may lead to currency wars among some countries.[4] It is also possible that uncooperative behaviour in the currency market may spill over and may affect the Doha Round of trade talks. It is not yet clear whether the WTO is the organization responsible for dealing with this issue. It is possible that it is more in the ambit of the International Monetary Fund (IMF). This is another challenge that is facing the multilateral system right now.

The third big challenge to the WTO stems from the crisis in the eurozone. The financial crisis did not start in Europe; however, since 2010 Europe has been affected by the crisis and is suffering the maximum damage from it. The eurozone is a big trading block and a slowdown in this region will not only put a downward pressure on export growth of other countries but will also affect a large number of countries through a general decline in business sentiment. How world trade recovers from these major setbacks is something to watch for.

The WTO and India

India was a founder member of GATT and for India, the establishment of the WTO coincided with a period when it started moving towards a more open trade regime. Until the 1980s, India followed import-substituting industrialization strategies, and not much emphasis was put on exports. However, since the mid-1980s, India has moved away from inward-looking economic policies and gradually started opening up. To make the economy more globally integrated, policymakers initiated trade liberalization, started moving away from a regime of quantitative restrictions to a tariff-based regime and started reducing their average level of protection. The establishment of the WTO in 1994 also expedited trade liberalization in this country.

As mentioned before, the establishment of the WTO has led to the belief that the sectors in which the developing countries enjoy a comparative advantage will be opened up and increased market access will allow developing countries to pursue export-led growth. India expected to gain in three areas, namely agriculture, textiles and clothing, and services. Given India's comparative advantage in these sectors, it was expected that India would manage a strong export growth rate in the post-WTO period.

India's foreign trade data show that in nominal terms, both exports and imports have grown in tandem during the post-WTO period, with imports growing at a slightly higher rate (16.8 per cent on an average annual basis) than exports (14.3 per cent on an average

Table 8.1. India's foreign trade (in millions of US$)

Year	Exports			Imports			Trade Balance		
	Oil	Non-oil	Total	Oil	Non-oil	Total	Oil	Non-oil	Total
1994–95	416.9	25913.6	26330.5	5927.8	22726.5	28654.4	–5510.9	3187.1	–2323.8
1995–96	453.7	31341.2	31794.9	7525.8	29149.5	36675.3	–7072.0	2191.7	–4880.4
1996–97	481.8	32987.9	33469.7	10036.2	29096.2	39132.4	–9554.4	3891.7	–5662.7
1997–98	352.8	34653.7	35006.4	8164.0	33320.5	41484.5	–7811.2	1333.1	–6478.1
1998–99	89.4	33129.3	33218.7	6398.6	35990.1	42388.7	–6309.2	–2860.8	–9170.0
1999–2000	38.9	36783.5	36822.4	12611.4	37059.3	49670.7	–12572.5	–275.8	–12848.3
2000–01	1869.7	42690.6	44560.3	15650.1	34886.4	50536.5	–13780.4	7804.2	–5976.2
2001–02	2119.1	41707.6	43826.7	14000.3	37413.0	51413.3	–11881.2	4294.6	–7586.6
2002–03	2576.5	50142.9	52719.4	17639.5	43772.6	61412.1	–15063.0	6370.3	–8692.7
2003–04	3568.4	60274.1	63842.6	20569.5	57579.6	78149.1	–17001.1	2694.5	–14306.5
2004–05	6989.3	76546.6	83535.9	29844.1	81673.3	111517.4	–22854.8	–5126.7	–27981.5
2005–06	11639.6	91450.9	103090.5	43963.1	105202.6	149165.7	–32323.5	–13751.7	–46075.2
2006–07	18634.6	107779.5	126414.1	56945.3	128790.0	185735.2	–38310.7	–21010.5	–59321.2
2007–08	28363.1	134541.1	162904.2	79644.5	171794.6	251439.2	–51281.5	–37253.5	–88535.0
2008–09	27547.0	155252.5	182799.5	93671.7	205162.2	298833.9	–66124.8	–49909.6	–116034.4
2009–10	28192.0	150559.5	178751.4	87135.9	201237.0	288372.9	–58943.9	–50677.5	–109621.4
2010–11	41918.0	212484.1	254402.1	106068.2	246506.7	352575.0	–64150.3	–34022.6	–98172.9

Source: *RBI Handbook of Statistics*, data for 2010–11 are provisional.

annual basis). As a result, net exports have always been negative during this period. India's total exports grew from US$44.5 billion in 2000–01 to almost US$163 billion in 2007–08, registering an average annual growth of about 22 per cent. In 2008–09, growth in total exports slowed down considerably to 13 per cent over the preceding year. There has been a recovery since.

The composition of India's exports (in nominal terms) shows that exports of primary products (essentially comprising agricultural and allied products, and ores and minerals) have increased from US$7 billion in 2000–01 to US$25 billion in 2008–09, whereas those of manufactured products have increased from US$34 billion to US$123 billion over the same period. Due to establishment of some big petroleum refining facilities, export of refined petroleum products has become a major item in India's export basket. Consequently, petroleum products, whose exports have increased from almost US$2 billion to US$27 billion over the stated period, have registered the maximum growth.

Exports of India's agricultural products have been rising steadily from US$6.0 billion in 2000–01 to US$17.5 billion in 2008–09, though their share in India's export basket still remains low (around 9 per cent). The share of primary products in total exports has declined from 16 per cent to 13.7 per cent between 2000–01 and 2008–09. The share of manufacturing products has also come down from 77 to 66 per cent, and that of petroleum products has increased from 4 per cent to about 15 per cent over the same period. Interestingly, the share of textiles, which was the predominant sector in the export basket in 2000–01 (25 per cent), has been declining continuously and reached 11 per cent in 2008–09. Engineering goods, representing a very broad category, continues to be the sector with the highest share in India's export basket, currently accounting for about 25 per cent. The share of chemical and chemical products has remained stable over time (12 to 14 per cent), while the share of gems and jewellery has declined from 17 per cent in 2000–01 to around 15 per cent in 2008.

In spite of the growth of exports, India's balance of merchandise trade has declined because of the higher growth rate of imports. The non-oil trade balance showed some sign of improvements until the year 2003–04. This can be grossly attributed to the increase in exports of manufactured goods. But the non-oil trade balance has become negative from 2004–05 onwards due to a major surge in imports. The total trade balance also continues to be negative, and it has worsened over the years.

One area where India has done remarkably well in the past few years is in the exports of services. According to data from the Ministry of Commerce, India's services exports in 2008–09 crossed US$100 billion.[5] Indian services exports reached US$131.97 billion in 2010–11.

Services trade liberalization holds significant promise for India. As GATS cover a broad range of services like tourism, education, consultancy services and manpower exports, India, which has an abundant supply of skilled and unskilled labour, is expected to benefit from such an agreement. India has achieved a high level of services exports through back office processing, call centres and medical transcription industries. In a higher-value segment, services exports through software development and business process outsourcing is another potential growth area for the economies of this region.

Figure 8.1. Composition of India's export basket (in millions of US$)

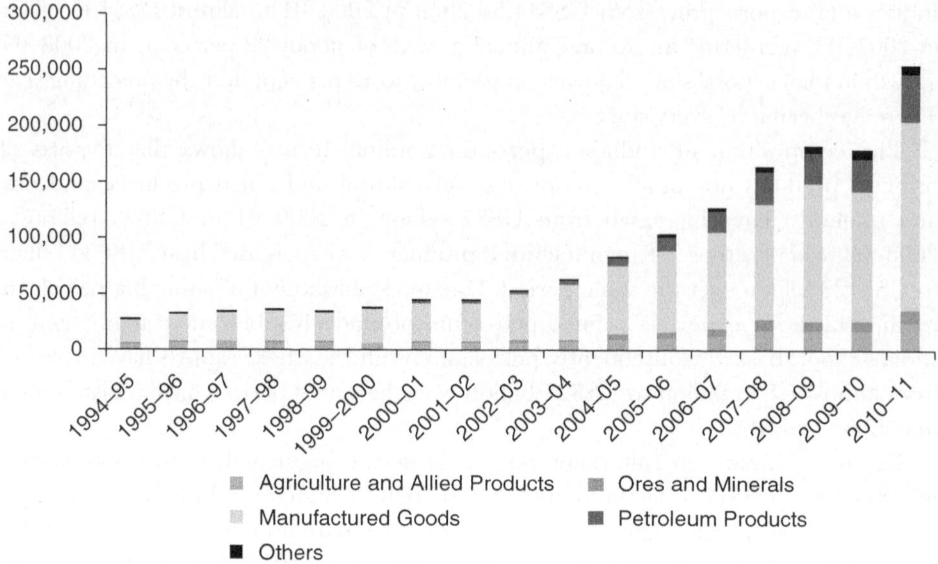

Source: *RBI Handbook of Statistics.*

The Indian software industry has already gained substantially, in both revenue and employment terms, from these services.

On the flip side, the potential to gain from services trade liberalization has been somewhat offset by the fact that so far services have been liberalized dominantly in sectors of primary interest to developed countries, like telecommunications and banks and insurance sectors. And in these sectors, the entry of foreign firms is threatening to push many domestic firms out of the market. Also, there have been some serious concerns about the future growth potential of India's services trade. The developed world is still recovering from the recession that has hit the world economy around 2008–09, and there are increasing restrictions on services trade in some major developed countries.[6]

For India, however, the biggest area of concern has been agriculture. This is one area where it will be extremely difficult to align domestic concerns with the international pressure for further trade liberalization. During the Uruguay Round, India agreed to liberalize its agriculture sector as part of a single undertaking in the WTO. The Agreement on Agriculture (AoA) was one of the most promising agreements for developing countries as it proposed to eliminate the distortions in world agricultural trade and promised significant improvement in market access for developing countries. But the implementation and effectiveness of AoA have been one of the biggest disappointments of the WTO. After the implementation of the Uruguay Round, it was found that between 1995 and 2003, developing countries had only secured a marginal increase in their market share in agriculture. A regional breakdown of developing countries further reveals that the increase in market share was due to the good performance of the Latin American countries (Table 8.2). As the table shows, the share of developing Asia has remained stagnant at 16.5 per cent during the period 1995 to 2003.

Table 8.2. Share of developing countries in world agricultural exports by region, 1990–2003 (in percentage terms)

	1990	1995	1996	1997	1998	1999	2000	2001	2002	2003
All Developing Countries	39	39½	39½	40	41½	42	40	40	41	41½
of which:										
Africa	6	5½	5½	5	5½	5½	4½	4½	5	5
Developing Asia	15	16½	16	15½	16	16½	16	15½	16½	16½
Latin America and the Caribbean	16	15½	16	17½	18	17½	17	17½	17½	17½
Middle East	2	2	2	2	2	2½	2½	2½	2½	2½

Source: WTO (2005).

Das (2003) also highlights that during the course of the implementation of the AoA, agriculture exports from the developed countries to the developing countries increased while the exports from the developing countries did not. Quoting a study of 14 developing countries by the Food and Agriculture Organization (FAO) for the first four years (1995–98) of the implementation period of AoA,[7] Das points out that with very few exceptions, the growth of food imports far exceeded the growth of agriculture exports in the countries under study. The ratio of food imports to agriculture exports for 11 countries under study was found to be higher in 1995–98 than in 1990–94. The increase in this ratio was particularly high in some cases: for example, 86, 80 and 49 per cent in Senegal, Bangladesh and India respectively. The study finds that there were immediate surges in food imports, but agriculture exports could not be raised due to weak supply, market barriers and competition from subsidized exports. The FAO study cites instances of the severe problems faced by domestic production on account of the adverse impact of imports on a sizeable population engaged in agricultural production and trade. Chand (2005) also analyses the impact of WTO trade liberalization on South Asian countries. Using data for the period 1991–2002, Chand shows that the impact of the WTO on these countries has largely been negative.

A recent paper by Aksoy and Ng (2010) examines the growth and structure of agricultural trade between 1990 and 2007. They find that,

> [...] despite tremendous change in the past 20 years in global specialization and trade in manufacturing, remarkably little structural change has occurred in global agricultural trade flows. The developing country share in world agricultural exports increased from 32 percent in 1990/91 to only 42 percent in 2006/07. Most of this gain came from expansion of exports to other developing countries (about 12 percentage points). However, only 47 percent of their agricultural exports are to other developing countries, showing the continuing importance of industrial country markets for their exports. For low-income countries, other developing countries

> accounted for 51 percent of their exports and 69 percent of imports in 2006/07; up from 27 percent and 57 percent respectively in 1990/91. Thus, other developing countries are now a bigger market for the exports of low income countries than the industrial ones. (Aksoy and Ng 2010, 26)

It is not unexpected that there has not been any major structural change in agriculture after WTO disciplines were introduced. It is now quite apparent that though AoA has succeeded in reducing the widespread use of quantitative restrictions in agriculture trade, agriculture still remains a distorted sector. Some countries have devised ways to comply with the rules of the AoA and still maintain a fairly high level of import restrictions. Moreover, some large developed countries have managed to comply with the WTO rules and yet maintain high agricultural subsidies. Using some loopholes in the Agreement, these countries have retained, and in some cases increased, the overall level of subsidy given to their farm sector. As a result, the gains of developing countries from agricultural trade liberalization have been less than expected. Moreover, for South Asian countries, the structural constraints of their agriculture sector and certain domestic factors also played a role in their poor export performance.

But on the other hand, opening up their agriculture sector to international trade has made the farming community of the developing countries vulnerable as they are now facing unfair competition and problems of protecting their domestic markets from cheap and subsidized exports from developed countries. Farm subsidies artificially depress the international prices of agricultural goods and consequently lower the incomes of farmers in developing countries. Subsidized and artificially cheap exports from developed countries can also displace domestic production in developing countries and hence can have a negative impact on the farming community in these countries. For example, commodities like wheat, coarse grains, sugar, dairy products and cotton attract high levels of subsidies in developed countries. These commodities are of great significance for livelihood and food security in developing countries, and exposing farmers to unfair competition in these subsectors can threaten the livelihood of millions of farmers in these countries.

Until the Uruguay Round, India maintained Quantitative Restrictions (QRs) as it faced Balance of Payment problems. Article XVIIIB of the GATT 1994 provided a legal basis for such a measure. As QRs are non-price based instruments and are physical restrictions on the volume of imports, they essentially insulate domestic markets from the price signals of international commodity markets. These also helped domestic production by protecting it from international competition. However, the BOP provisions have been tightened in the WTO agreements, and it has become very difficult to maintain or initiate QRs. Member countries have little option but to dismantle the QRs and move to a tariff-only regime. Unlike QRs, tariff is a price-based mechanism, and therefore, under this regime, the instability of international commodity prices is likely to be transmitted directly to domestic markets (see Pal and Wadhwa 2007). This threat of volatility increases the risk perception of the farmers and creates further uncertainty for these people.

The Doha Round of negotiations aims to liberalize agriculture trade further by bringing down agricultural tariffs quite significantly. However, it is uncertain whether this will result in better market access for agricultural exports from India. It is recognized that the market access improvement will depend, to a large extent, on whether India is able to compete with other efficient agricultural exporters. However, India is currently going through a period of major stagnation in its agriculture sector. This sector also suffers from poor infrastructure and lacks adequate logistical support for its exports. Given these domestic constraints, it is uncertain whether India will be able to compete with the more efficient agricultural exporters from Latin America and other parts of Asia. Therefore, even if tariff liberalization opens up some market access at the margin, it is uncertain whether India will be in a position to benefit from this (Pal 2007).

As far as the defensive interests of the developing countries are concerned, the impact of the WTO tariff reduction formula will depend, to a very large extent, on the exact formula adopted for agricultural tariff reduction. For India, the Doha Round of tariff reduction commitments will greatly reduce the overhang between bound and applied tariff rates, which in turn will reduce the policy flexibility available to these countries. Given the international volatility of commodity prices, this lack of flexibility is likely to increase the vulnerability of the agriculture sector. In this context, it will be paramount to have access to defensive instruments like Special Safeguard Measures (SSM) and Special Products (SP). India should remain cautious about opening up its agriculture sector. For most farmers of this country, agriculture is not a commercial proposition but a means to secure subsistence and livelihood. India should make no commitments which may threaten the livelihood and food security of the millions of small farmers of this region. It will be up to the policymakers not to get into any deal which can threaten the food and livelihood security of more than 600 million people of this region.

WTO and Policy Space Available to Developing Countries

Our discussion shows that India has managed to increase its merchandise and services exports in the post-WTO period but, the increase in imports has also been very high. On the other hand, the opening up of agricultural trade has also increased the vulnerability of poor Indian farmers. There is also a debate over whether the WTO rules and commitments are restricting the policy space for industrialization for developing countries. The crux of the debate revolves around the concepts of static and dynamic comparative advantage. The WTO implicitly works on the principle of static comparative advantage and assumes that countries will specialize in their respective areas of comparative advantage as dictated by their resource endowments or technology. Given this premise, WTO rules try to promote free trade by gradual reduction of tariff rates and they also include a number of provisions to ensure that countries do not indulge in unfair trade practices. These include rules like anti-dumping measures and countervailing duties to prevent predatory pricing, 'technical barriers to trade' to ensure that standards are met, Trade Related Intellectual Property Rights (TRIPs) to ensure that copyrights and patents are not violated, etc. However, there are enough reasons to question the basic premise of the WTO that countries should focus on present factor endowment and technology to develop their export sectors. A number of authors (Eric Reinert, Yilmaz Akyuz, Ha-Joon Chang and Mehdi Shafaeddin to name a few) have questioned the basic premise of trade specialization based on static comparative advantage. They argue that the universal and across-the-board policies of the WTO may lead to premature trade liberalization, which would seriously affect the industrialization process of developing countries. These authors cite actual experience of successful early industrializers to show that the role of state and interventionist trade and industrial policy is crucial to promote dynamic comparative advantage in countries. Two famous examples are given of South Korea and Finland. During the 1960s, South Korea's traditional exports consisted of resource-intensive low-end products like fish, cheap apparel, wigs and plywood. In the late 1960s, the South Korean government set up the Pohang Iron and Steel Company (POSCO). South Korea had no 'comparative advantage' in steel at that time as it possessed neither iron ore nor coal. However, the government actively protected and nurtured POSCO through a mix of protection and incentives, and today, POSCO has become one of the most efficient steel makers in the world. This is an example of how interventionist policies can lead to dynamic comparative advantage for an economy. The second example is of Nokia, which started as a timber company and gradually moved to footwear, to manufacturing for Philips, a manufacturer of own-brand household electronics and finally became a mobile-phone giant. While Nokia was going through such interesting technological transformation, the electronics subsidiary of Nokia was cross-subsidized by its sister companies for 17 years before it became viable (see Lin and Chang 2009). Therefore, there are numerous examples across the world that show that countries have progressed by developing comparative advantage in high-technology areas rather than getting stuck in exports of low-value-added goods which were dictated by the principles of static comparative advantage.

It is notable from India's export composition that light manufacturing goods, agriculture and primary commodities taken together still dominate India's export basket. It is important that India tries to move up the value chain in its exports. This is becoming more important because the adverse terms of trade problems that were highlighted by the Prebisch–Singer hypothesis about primary goods gradually seem to be catching up with light manufacturing goods as well. The only escape from this problem is through higher-value addition and moving up the value chain. This also reduces the risks of volatile demand that come from exchange rate fluctuations (as higher-value products tend to be less price sensitive). But the present WTO regime will not allow full flexibility to developing countries to pursue the development models used by successful industrializers of the past. Table 8.3 shows the WTO restrictions on the policies followed by some early industrializers. It is up to the policymakers to ensure that the WTO recognizes the different economic and developmental needs of countries and allows them to pursue appropriate trade and industrial policies. Otherwise, if developing countries are forced to specialize based on their static comparative advantage, then they will be pegged at the lower end of the value chain, which will hurt their long-term economic objective.

Some of these concerns were raised during the Doha Round of trade talks, and the Doha Ministerial Declaration promised to address the major problems facing developing countries. However, the Doha Round of trade talks is not progressing well. The negotiations have been repeatedly stuck on issues related mainly to agriculture subsidies and market access. It has been nine years since the Doha declaration, and still the negotiations show no sign of completion. It is not very surprising that that the Doha

Table 8.3. Policies followed by now-industrialized countries during their phase of development and current WTO rules which prohibit them

Country	Policy	Economic Rationale	WTO Restriction
USA	High tariff and non-tariff barriers	Infant industry protection	Tariff liberalization, removal of non-tariff measures
UK	High tariff and non-tariff barriers Colonial exploitation	Infant industry protection Extraction of resources	Tariff liberalization, removal of non-tariff measures
Japan	State supported investment in R&D Adaptation of designs of products developed by other countries Learning curve pricing	Improve competitiveness Taking advantage of economies of scale	Countervailing duties Trade Related Intellectual Property Rights Anti-dumping laws
South Korea	State supported export growth Directed credit Export subsidies Learning curve pricing Interventionist industrial policy	Strategic and innovationist trade policy Economies of scale	Countervailing duties Outright ban of export subsidies Anti-dumping duties Privatization as pushed by the World Bank

Source: Compiled by the author from Chang (2002).

Round is taking so long to conclude. In the earlier rounds of multilateral trade talks, negotiations were essentially done by a few developed countries, and most developing countries had little or no role in these negotiations. In the Doha Round, the number of active players in negotiations has increased significantly (Table 8.1). Dani Rodrik (2008), professor of international political economy at the John F. Kennedy School of Government, Harvard University, points out that in the Doha round there are 153 countries, of which Rodrik reckons probably 60 or 70 are actively involved in the negotiations. And as the WTO works on a 'consensus' based approach, every member has a potential veto power.[8] Therefore, it is not completely unexpected that this round of trade negotiation is dragging on for so long.

Moreover, the present economic recession has complicated the scenario even more. Countries are now more focused on restoring their domestic economy and preventing job losses. Right now, turning the attention back to further trade liberalization may not be the first priority for many countries. As discussed above, the rise of protectionist sentiments across the world makes it difficult for the WTO to push forward the agenda of further trade liberalization. The next ministerial of the WTO at Bali may give an indication of whether and how the round is likely to be concluded. The immediate focus of the WTO should be to ensure that the global trade revives and countries do not impose retaliatory protectionist measures to block each other out. A revival of global trade will be the best catalyst for the successful conclusion of the Doha Round.

Are There Alternatives?

As the multilateral trade talks are not progressing, most countries are opting to increase trade through bilateral channels. However, RTAs are not also free from problems. As discussed before, North–South RTAs exacerbate the power imbalance between the trade partners. This is evident from the fact that many North–South RTAs are now pushing WTO-plus clauses. Second, as Ghosh (2004) and Bhagwati (2008) argue, by pushing aggressive trade treaties on a bilateral basis, developed countries are weakening the power of developing countries in multilateral trade negotiations. Third, in North–South RTAs, developing countries are accepting long-term commitments in exchange for uncertain and often transient market access promises. As mentioned before, in such RTAs, developed countries manage to push through a number of conditions like stricter TRIPS regulations, highly unfavourable Bilateral Investment Treaties (BITs), and a wide range of market access openings and extraneous clauses like labour and environmental rules. These can have serious long-term repercussions on a developing country. Whereas stricter TRIPS laws can lead to serious issues like availability of life-saving drugs and medicines at an affordable price, BITs can restrain the options of developing countries to use FDI as a policy instrument to improve the sectoral/regional balance of their economy. BITs are particularly troublesome because not only are the BITs used to introduce harsh labour and environmental commitments on developing countries but the clauses of the BITs also try to align a developing country's financial and legal systems to a market-oriented system which favours such enterprises. This can have serious implications for developing countries.

In this context, South–South trade blocks may emerge as a viable alternative for developing countries to expand their market. With growing income in many parts of the developing world, this may provide many countries from the South with significant market access. There might be some concerns about lack of trade complementarities among the developing world. But it can be pointed out here that developing countries are currently a diverse lot and have enough variety in their export basket to generate sufficient trade among themselves. Also, with increased industrialization, it will be possible for some developing countries to engage in intra-industry trade and allow their firms to exploit the economies of scale.

This policy option should be studied carefully by the trade policymakers from India. In spite of being one of the most populous countries of the world, India does not trade much with the South Asian countries. So far India has tried to improve intra-SA trade by reducing tariff barriers. But this has not given much boost to trade within SA. Recent studies tend to indicate that the real problem which is preventing increase of trade among the South Asian countries may have to do more with high logistics and transaction costs, which are an outcome of procedural and regulatory inefficiencies of this region. Along with reducing trade barriers, the governments of this region should focus more to improve trade-related infrastructure such as land customs stations, approach roads, railway links, and banking and communication facilities, and to facilitate construction of warehouses and containerization. Development of production networks can only happen if the logistics chain is developed.

However, one should be more careful about North–South trade blocks. Most North–South RTAs tend to cover much more than liberalization of tariffs and quotas. Most of these RTAs have provisions on enforcement of labour laws, environmental laws, services, intellectual property rights issues, competition policy, government procurement and investment. It is notable that many of these provisions, especially issues like labour and environment, investment and competition policy are no longer on the mandate of WTO negotiations. These issues have been dropped from the Doha Development Agenda mostly because of strong opposition from developing countries. However, most North–South RTAs contain these issues, and because of the asymmetry in negotiating power in such RTAs, developed countries not only manage to include these new issues but also impose stricter rules on issues like TRIPS and opening up of services on developing countries. In fact, RTAs are also being used by some developed countries to remove controls on capital flows.[9]

Inclusion of these clauses in the trade agreement leads to a number of problems for developing countries. First, inclusion of these clauses reinforces the problems mentioned above and further reduces the policy space available to developing countries. It is important to note that the provisions of most North–South RTAs go well beyond the WTO rules and are likely to impose many more restrictions on the developing countries. They will also force countries to adopt more 'market-friendly' measures in areas like investment and IPR issues. As the UNCTAD Trade and Development Report 2007 points out, these new RTAs have increasingly included provisions for deeper integration among countries and include policies which require a much higher degree of harmonizing national policies with 'a reform agenda that favours greater freedom for market forces'. For a developing country, where the level of industrialization is not high, such measures can have a serious negative impact on its industrialization and growth of the economy.

Notes

1 The preamble establishing the WTO says:

> [...] trade and economic endeavour should be conducted with a view to raising standards of living, ensuring full employment and a large and steadily growing volume of real income and effective demand, and expanding the production of and trade in goods and services, while allowing for the optimal use of the world's resources in accordance with the objective of sustainable development, seeking both to protect and preserve the environment and to enhance the means for doing so in a manner consistent with their respective needs and concerns at different levels of economic development. ('Agreement Establishing the World Trade Organization', available online at http://www.wto.org/english/docs_e/04-wto.pdf)

2 This has been discussed in detail in Pal 2009.

3 In an 8 June 2012 speech, WTO director general Pascal Lamy noted: The implementation of new measures restricting or potentially restricting trade has remained unabated over the past seven months, which is aggravated by the slow pace of rollback of existing measures. The accumulation of these trade restrictions is now a matter of serious concern. Trade coverage of the restrictive measures put in place since October 2008, excluding those that were terminated, is estimated to be almost 3 per cent of world merchandise trade, and almost 4 per cent of G-20 trade. The discrepancy between the commitments taken and the actions on the ground add to credibility concerns. This situation is adding to the downside risks to the global economy and what is now a volatile global context. (Available online at the WTO website: http://www.wto.org/english/news_e/sppl_e/sppl234_e.htm)

4 'Currency Turmoil Could Jeopardise Fecovery: WTO Chief', *Economic Times*, 19 October, 2010.
5 Government of India Ministry of Commerce and Industry, Department of Commerce Press Release. Online: http://commerce.nic.in/pressrelease/pressrelease_detail.asp?id=2632
6 'India Conveys "Serious Concern" to US on Outsourcing Ban', *Economic Times*, 10 September, 2010.
7 See FAO 2001.
8 Though the WTO has the provision of a 'one country one vote' system in its constitution, so far voting has not been used.
9 Williamson (2006, 1848) points out that in the post-Asian crisis period trade agreements are used by the US treasury to impose free movement of capital on developing countries. Williamson says: Since then the main pressure for liberalizing capital flows has come from the US treasury. When countries wanted to negotiate bilateral free trade agreements with the US, they found the treasury insisted that US negotiators demand that the partner country commit itself to never re-imposing effective capital controls for any length of time. Several of the partner countries that had made effective use of such controls in the past, like Chile and Singapore, found themselves forced to choose between abandoning their aim of securing a free trade agreement with the US and abandoning their ability to control capital movements with the object of avoiding or at least attenuating crises. Given that governments, like markets, typically take a rather short-term view of costs and benefits, and that the countries could not see the prospect of a crisis on the horizon at the time the negotiations were taking place, the US treasury got its way.

References

Aksoy, M. Ataman and Francis Ng. 2010. 'The Evolution of Agricultural Trade Flows'. Policy Research Working Paper 5308, Washington, DC: World Bank.

Bacchetta, M. and B. Bora. 2003. 'Industrial Tariff Liberalization and Doha Development Agenda'. Geneva: WTO (paper available at the WTO website).

Barton, J. H. 2001. 'Differentiated Pricing of Patented Products'. Mimeo, WHO Commission on Macroeconomics and Health. Online: http://cmhealth.org/cmh_papers and reports.htm.

Bhagwati, J. 2008. *Termites in the Trading System: How Preferential Agreements Undermine Free Trade.* New Delhi: Oxford University Press.

Chand, R. 2005. 'India's Agriculture Trade During Post WTO Decade: Lessons for Negotiations'. Paper presented at a seminar titled *Off the Blocks to Hong Kong: Concerns and Negotiating Options on Agriculture and NAMA* organized by CENTAD, 22 July, New Delhi.

Chanda, R. 1999. 'Movement of Natural Persons and Trade in Services: Liberalising Temporary Movement of Labour under the GATS'. New Delhi: ICRIER.

_______. 2002. 'Movement of Natural Persons and the GATS Major Trade Policy Impediments'. In *Development, Trade and WTO: A Handbook* edited by B. Hoekman, A. Mattoo and P. English. Washington, DC: World Bank.

Chang, H.-J. 2002. *Kicking Away the Ladder? Policies and Institutions for Economic Development in Historical Perspective.* London: Anthem Press.

Debroy, B. 2005. 'The SPS and TBT Agreements: Implications for Indian Policy'. ICRIER. Working Paper no. 163. Online: http://www.icrier.org/wp163.pdf.

FAO. 2001. 'The Role of Agriculture in the Development of LDCs and their Integration into the World Economy'. Paper prepared for the Third United Nations Conference on the Least Developed Countries (Brussels, 14–20 May). Online: http://www.fao.org/docrep/003/Y0491e/y0491e00.htm.

Fink, C. 2000. 'How Stronger Patent Protection in India Might Affect the Behavior or Transnational Pharmaceutical Industries'. World Bank Policy Research Working Paper no. 2352. Washington, DC: World Bank.

Ghosh, J. 2004. 'Regionalism, Foreign Investment and Control: The New Rules of the Game outside the WTO'. Paper presented at a seminar on 'The Economics of New Imperialism', Jawaharlal Nehru University, New Delhi.

Gulati, A. 1998. 'Indian Agriculture in an Open Economy'. In *India's Economic Reforms and Development: Essays for Manmohan Singh* edited by I. J. Ahluwalia and I. M. D. Little. New Delhi: Oxford University Press.

Hoekman, B. 1996. 'Assessing the General Agreement on Trade in Services'. In *The Uruguay Round and the Developing Economies* edited by W. Martin and L. A. Winters. Cambridge: Cambridge University Press.

ILO. 2005. 'Promoting Fair Globalization Textiles and Clothing in a Post-MFA Environment'. Report for discussion at the Tripartite Meeting on Promoting Fair Globalization Textiles and Clothing in a Post-MFA Environment. Geneva: ILO.

Kathuria, S., W. Martin and A. Bharadwaj. 2000. Implications for South Asian Countries of Abolishing the Multifibre Arrangement'. World Bank Working Paper Series no. 2721. Washington, DC: World Bank.

Laird, S. 2002. 'Market Access Issues and the WTO: An Overview' in *Development, Trade and WTO: A Handbook* edited by B. Hoekman, A. Mattoo and P. English. Washington, DC: World Bank.

Lin, J and H.-J. Chang. 2009. 'Should Industrial Policy in Developing Countries Conform to Comparative Advantage or Defy it? A Debate Between Justin Lin and Ha-Joon Chang'. Development Policy Review 27, no. 5: 483–502.

Mehta, R. 2005. 'Non-tariff Barriers Affecting India's Exports'. Background note for distribution at *Off the Starting Block to Hong Kong: Concerns and Negotiating Options on Agriculture and NAMA for India*. Organized by CENTAD. New Delhi.

Nambiar, R. G., B. L. Mungekar and G. A. Tadas. 1999. 'Is Import Liberalisation Hurting Domestic Industry and Employment?' *Economic and Political Weekly* 34, no. 7: 417–24.

Nayyar, D. and A. Sen. 1994. 'International Trade and the Agricultural Sector in India' in Economic Liberalization and Indian Agriculture'. In *Economic Liberalisation and Indian Agriculture* edited by G. S. Bhalla. New Delhi: Institute for Studies in Industrial Development.

Nordas, H. K. 2004. 'The Global Textile and Clothing Industry post the Agreement on Textiles and Clothing'. Discussion Paper no. 5, WTO Secretariat. Geneva.

Pal, P. 2002. 'Implementation Issues of the Agreement on Agriculture and Its Implications for Developing Countries'. Online: www.networkideas.org and www.kisanwatch.org.

_______. 2004. 'The WTO Agreement on Agriculture and Its Impact on Employment and Gender in India'. Paper prepared for a conference on Gender and Macroeconomics, University of Utah, June.

_______. 2005. 'Current WTO Negotiations on Domestic Subsidies in Agriculture: Implications for India'. ICRIER Working Paper no. 177. New Delhi: ICRIER.

Pal, P. and S. Prakash. 2005. 'WTO Ministerial Meet: Doomed to Failure?' *Economic and Political Weekly* 40, no. 39: 4212–3.

Pal, P. and D. Wadhwa. 'Commodity Price Volatility and Special Safeguard Mechanisms'. *Economic and Political Weekly* 42, no. 5: 417–27.

Prasad, E. 2009. 'Rebalancing Growth in Asia'. *Finance and Development* 46, no. 4. Washington, DC: International Monetary Fund.

Rodrik, Dani. 2008. 'Don't Cry for Doha'. Online entry on *Dani Rodrik's Weblog*. Online: http://rodrik.typepad.com/dani_rodriks_weblog/2008/07/dont-cry-for-doha.html.

Rubin, H. A. 1999. *Global Software Economics*. Unpublished. New York: Hunter College, Department of Computer Science.

Scherer, F. M. and J. Wattal. 2001. 'Post-TRIPS Options for Access to Patented Medicines in Developing Countries'. ICRIER, Working Paper no. 62. New Delhi: ICRIER.

Shafaeddin, S. M. 2002. 'The Impact of China's Accession to WTO on the Exports of Developing Countries'. UNCTAD Discussion Paper no. 160. Geneva: UNCTAD.

Tewari, M. 2005a. 'Post MFA Adjustments in India's Apparel and Textiles Industry: Emerging Issues and Trends'. ICRIER Working Paper Number no. 167. New Delhi: ICRIER.

______. 2005b. 'The Role of Price and Cost Competitiveness in Apparel Exports, Post MFA: A Review'. ICRIER Working Paper Number no. 173. New Delhi: ICRIER.

UNCTAD. 1998. 'Market Access: Development since Uruguay Round, Implications, Opportunities and Challenges'. Report prepared by the secretariat of UNCTAD and WTO. Geneva: UNCTAD.

______. 2000a. *World Investment Report 2000: Cross Border Mergers and Acquisitions and Development.* New York and Geneva: United Nations.

______. 2000b. 'Subsidies, Countervailing Measures and Developing Countries: With a Focus on the Agreement on Subsidies and Countervailing Measures'. UNCTAD Paper no. UNCTAD/DITC/COM/23. Online: http://www.unctad.org/en/docs/poditccomd23.en.pdf.

Williamson, J. 2006. 'Why Capital Account Convertibility in India Is Premature'. *Economic and Political Weekly* 42. No. 19, 1848–50.

Whalley, J. 1999. 'Notes on Textiles and Apparel in the Next Trade Round'. Paper presented at a conference on Developing Countries in the Next WTO Trade Round, held at Harvard University, November 5–6.

World Bank. 2002. *Global Economic Prospects 2002.* Washington, DC: World Bank.

______. 2005. *World Development Indicators 2005.* Washington, DC: World Bank.

______. 2006. *Global Economic Prospects 2006.* Washington, DC: World Bank.

WTO. 2002. *Trade Policy Review of India.* Geneva: World Trade Organization Secretariat.

Chapter 9

THE CHANGING EMPLOYMENT SCENARIO DURING MARKET REFORM AND THE FEMINIZATION OF DISTRESS IN INDIA

Sudipta Bhattacharyya and Uma Basak

Introduction

The Indian economy remained by and large interventionist in nature from the time of its independence in 1947 until the late '80s. The central government in India has since 1991 adopted a policy of market economic reform under the Structural Adjustment Program of the IMF and the World Bank. This study has addressed some interesting developments that occurred since 1991, particularly in the labour market. The empirical data sources for employment and unemployment of the workforce are mainly the various rounds of surveys conducted by the National Sample Survey Office (NSSO). This study is based on NSSO surveys of various rounds from the 43rd Round (pre-reform period, 1987–88) to the latest 66th Round (2009–10). We have subdivided the reform period into three parts: 1993–94 to 1999–2000 (55th Round of NSSO), 1999–2000 to 2004–05 (61st Round of NSSO) and 2004–05 to 2009–10 (66th round of NSSO). Henceforth we will refer to these three periods as the 'first reform period' or '1990s', the 'second reform period' or 'early 2000s' and the 'third reform period' or 'late 2000s'.

The summary of the NSSO trends of data is that casualization increased and diversification shrank in the first reform period and the process opposite to that happened in the second period.[1] Nevertheless, there is an increasing trend of casualization for all categories during the third reform period, that is, between 2004–05 and 2009–10. The labour force participation rate (LFPR) during the reform period, similarly, showed a downfall in the first part (1990s), a recovery in the second part (early 2000s) and again a decline in the third part (late 2000s). During the second part of the reform the recovery level is not the same for males and females.[2] Some proponents of reforms looked at the fall in the age-specific LFPR for the young and old age groups during a phase of reform that they term as a 'withdrawal symptom', which is indeed a welcome tendency.[3]

The basic objective of the chapter is to analyse changes in the level of living of urban and rural workforces against the backdrop of the market economic reforms introduced in the '90s. The basic questions are (1) whether the 'withdrawal hypothesis' sustains at all during the reform period and (2) whether there was any substantial shift in the process of casualization and diversification during the period of economic reform. In this chapter we will explain the observed changes in the labour market, females in particular following an industrial stagnation, and a decline in agricultural growth and wage rate. We propose some important research questions as follows: (i) In the context of recovery and decline in labour force participation in the second reform period, what is the implication of gender-wise discrimination; (ii) In the case of an apparent positive shift, it is based on quality or remunerative employment; (iii) What changes actually occurred during the third reform period?

General Trend

The changing pattern of employment is observed from household type categorized on the basis of the major economic activity from which the household derives its major incomes. NSSO data on household type shows rural households are increasingly diversifying from agriculture to nonagriculture. While a shift from wage employment to self-employment was observed over the period 1987–88 to 2004–05, just the opposite happened in the subsequent period (Table 9.1). In the urban areas there is a shift from pre-reform levels of regular wage and salaried households to casual labour households and self-employed households. The proportion of regular wage and salaried households declined from 43.4 per cent in 1993–94 to 41.7 per cent in 1999–2000, 41.3 per cent in 2004–05 and ultimately 39.7 per cent in 2009–10, showing a lower proportion than in 1993–94. The proportion of urban casual labour households, in contrast, increased from 13.2 per cent in 1993–94 to 14 per cent in 1999–2000 and declined in 2004–05 to 11.8 per cent. It increased again to 13.4 per cent in 2009–10. The urban self-employed households increased from 33.7 per cent in 1993–94 to 34.4 per cent in 1999–2000, to 37.5 per cent in 2004–05, and declined to 34.7 per cent in 2009–10 (Table 9.1).

Agricultural and nonagricultural labour households together constitute rural households dependent on wage labour. Agricultural labour households showed a marginal increase during the 1990s from 30.3 per cent in 1993–94 to 32.2 per cent in 1999–2000. After that they declined drastically to 25.8 per cent in 2004–05 and remained stagnant almost at that level (25.6 per cent) in 2009–10. We have already noted that the 2000s are marked by a prolonged agrarian crisis where agricultural investment was not at all viable. As a result there was a drastic decline of demand for agricultural labour. Wage labourers who found no jobs in agriculture were absorbed in other nonagricultural jobs in the informal sector. From a stagnant 8 per cent, the level of nonagricultural labour households increased to 10.9 per cent in 2004–05 and 14.8 per cent in 2009–10 (Table 9.1).

We found that during the period from 2004–05 to 2009–10, while the self-employed households in nonagriculture remained stagnant at 15.5 per cent, the self-employed households in agriculture declined from 35.9 per cent to 31.9 per cent. Therefore, the third reform period experienced a decline in self-employment as well as wage employment.

The drastic fall in agricultural labour households should imply a welcome tendency as it ideally leads to diversification of the workforce. In the present phase of economic reform, the decline in agricultural labour households does not indicate a process of mechanization as an integral part of labour saving capitalist development in agriculture.

Table 9.1. Percentage distribution of households by household type (rural and urban)

	1987–88	1993–94	1999–2000	2004–05	2009–10
RURAL					
Self-Employed in Agriculture	37.7	37.8	32.7	35.9	31.9
Self-Employed in Nonagriculture	12.3	12.7	13.4	15.8	15.5
Total Self-Employed	50	50.5	46.1	51.7	47.4
Agricultural Labour	30.7	30.3	32.2	25.8	25.6
Nonagricultural Labour	9	8	8	10.9	14.8
Total Labour	39.7	38.3	40.2	36.7	40.4
Others	10.1	11.2	13.7	11.6	12.2
Total	100	100	100	100	100
URBAN					
Self-Employed	33.5	33.7	34.4	37.5	34.7
Regular Wage/Salaried	44.2	43.4	41.7	41.3	39.7
Casual Labour	12.7	13.2	14.0	11.8	13.4
Others	9.3	9.7	9.7	9.4	12.1
Total	100	100	100	100	100

Source: NSSO, Report No. 537: 'Employment and Unemployment Situation in India', Statement 3.4, p. 32; NSSO, Sarvekshana Special No. Sept 1990, Statement 6, p. 24.

Rather, this is the reflection of lack of demand for agricultural labour as agriculture has not been sustainable anymore precisely because the cost of production increased substantially because of the policy of withdrawal of subsidies. On the other hand, because of the withdrawal of the universal Public Distribution System (PDS) and collapse of the government's effective intervention in agricultural marketing, the farmers were compelled to sell their product at lower prices in distress. As a result, private investment in agriculture declined. On the other hand, fixed capital formation by the public sector in agriculture declined in both absolute terms and in relation to GDP. The growth of institutional credit to agriculture declined from 6.64 per cent achieved in 1981–91 to 2.6 per cent during the post-reform period (1991–99) (Narayanamoorthy 2007). The cut in expenditures on rural development and infrastructure, including irrigation, along with withdrawal of food, fertilizer and credit subsidies, is the major reasons behind the decline in the productivity of agriculture. The increasing self-employment in nonagriculture does not indicate agriculture-led development,[4] as agriculture itself grew slowly during the market reform period due to a massive cut in public investment in agriculture along with cuts in fertilizer subsidy and credit. The fact is that growth of wage employment in agriculture fell by 3.18 per cent during the period from 1999–2000 to 2004–05. The displaced labourers from crisis-ridden agriculture fell back on nonagriculture and became 'self-employed' or recognized as others. We observe a 5.8 percentage point decline in self-employed agricultural households over the entire period corresponding to a 3.2 percentage point increase in self-employed nonagricultural households. As a result there is an inflated magnitude of shifting of households depending on agricultural works to nonagricultural activity. This transition of occupational scenario does not justify the process of capitalist development in the present context.

The declining proportion of self-employment in agriculture actually reflects that agriculture is not at all a profitable occupation for a number of reasons. The data on distribution of operational holdings as available from the 48th Round and 59th Round (Jan–Dec 2003) indicates a sharp decline in the total number of operational holdings between 1992 and 2003 and increasing landlessness. Thus we are in a critical situation when a large number of petty farmers mostly dependent on tenanted land are quitting agriculture. In fact, the Situation Assessment Survey of farmers conducted by the NSSO in 2003 (GOI 2005) laid bare the fact that about 27 per cent of farmers did not like their ancestral profession as it becomes unprofitable and 40 per cent of farmers were willing to quit this profession.

Employment and Gender Divide

Gender inequality: Participation

The labour force participation rate (LFPR) is the key concept we used first to explain the changing employment status. The LFPR is the percentage of working population and unemployed people (seeking work) and can be an indicator of well-being as it provides an idea of the economically active population. Table 9.2 shows that the rural labour force participation rate (RLFPR) (based on usual plus subsidiary status) for males increased from 54.9 per cent in the pre-reform period (1987–88) to 56.1 per cent in 1993–94 (reform period) but the rate for females remains almost constant in rural areas. In the first part of the reform period, the RLFPR for both males and females declined from 56.1 per cent to 54 per cent for males and from 33 per cent to 30.2 per cent for females. In 2009–10 the RLFPR for males remained more or less stagnant at 55.6 per cent, while the RLFPR for females substantially declined from 33.3 per cent to 26.5 per cent. In the next five-year period 1999–2000 to 2004–05 there was an obvious recovery in RLFPR from 54 per cent to 55.5 per cent for males and from 30.2 per cent to 33.3 per cent for females. But the RLFPR at 2004–05 for males remained below the 1993–94 level and almost remained stagnant for females for the same period. The story remains similar for urban areas as well. The urban labour force participation rate (ULFPR) increased marginally for both the male and female populations between 1987–88 and 1993–94. For the first reform period it was almost unaltered for the male population while for the female population the decline was substantial, from 16.5 per cent to 14.7 per cent. In the second reform period the ULFPR increased substantially from 54.2 per cent to 57 per cent for males and from 14.7 per cent to 17.8 per cent for females. During the period from 2004–05 to 2009–10 the ULFPR declined about 1 per cent for males, from 57 per cent to 55.9 per cent, and 3 per cent for females, from 17.8 per cent to 14.6 per cent. The LFPR for both rural and urban areas is less than the level attained in 1993–94. In particular there was an indication of worsening of participation of the female, with some exceptions in the second reform period.

Table 9.2. Labour force participation rate (LFPR) in India

	1987–88	1993–94	1999–2000	2004–05	2009–10
Rural Male	54.9	56.1	54	55.5	55.6
Rural Female	33.1	33	30.2	33.3	26.5
Urban Male	53.4	54.3	54.2	57	55.9
Urban Female	16.2	16.5	14.7	17.8	14.6

Source: NSSO, Report No. 537: 'Employment and Unemployment Situation in India', Statement 4.1, p. 63; NSSO, Sarvekshana Special No. Sept 1990, Statement 43, p. 119 (for 43rd Round).
Note: We have considered usual (principal plus subsidiary) status.

Table 9.3. Age-specific worker participation rate (WPR) principal and subsidiary status

Period/Age Group	5–14	15–29	30–59	60 and Above	All
		Rural Males			
1987–88	10.16	79.2	97.31	66.8	53.9
1993–94	7.5	77.5	97.93	69.9	55.3
1999–2000	4.71	74.1	97.3	63.9	53.1
2004–05	3.56	74.2	97.6	64.4	54.6
2009–10	2.08	64.84	98.06	64.6	53.7
		Rural Females			
1987–88	9.64	46.1	56.81	21.8	32.3
1993–94	7.23	44.7	57.7	24.1	32.8
1999–2000	4.93	40	55.2	21.8	29.9
2004–05	3.74	41	59.82	25.3	32.7
2009–10	1.99	28.8	47.07	22.6	26.1
		Urban Males			
1987–88	4.45	62.7	96.02	48	50.6
1993–94	3.59	61.8	96.08	44.2	52.1
1999–2000	2.67	59.3	95.22	40.2	51.8
2004–05	2.6	62.3	95.56	36.6	54.9
2009–10	1.53	56.4	96.35	34.1	54.3
		Urban Females			
1987–88	3.4	18.3	28.71	13.8	15.1
1993–94	2.53	17.3	29.07	11.3	15.5
1999–2000	1.94	14.9	26.05	9.4	13.9
2004–05	1.9	18.4	28.87	10	16.6
2009–10	0.67	14.4	23.98	7	13.8

Source: NSSO, Report No. 537: 'Employment and Unemployment Situation in India', Statement 5.2, p. 79; NSSO, Sarvekshana Special No. Sept 1990, Statement 24, p. 64.

Based on 1999–2000 NSSO data in comparison with that of 1993–94, the proponents of economic reforms argued that the decline in LFPR is an otherwise welcome tendency as age-specific LFPR indicates a decline in labour force participation for younger (school-going) and old age group people. These scholars explained this trend by the withdrawal hypothesis (Chadha and Sahu 2002), which states that with the higher level of development, the population belonging to the school-going age group and the old age group withdraw their participation from the labour force. The claim has been substantiated by a decline in the age-specific worker participation rate or WPR (principal status plus subsidiary status) for all categories of younger age and old age groups in 1999–2000 in comparison to 1993–94. This was no doubt an indication of great achievement. There was continuous decline in child work participation for 5–14 age groups during the period from 1987–88 to 2009–10 both for males and females in rural and urban areas. Yet the withdrawal hypothesis is not sustained in the true sense considering other age groups and at least where female workers are concerned. This point will be clear by analysing the secondary data on worker participation over the entire period (pre-reform to post-reform) we have taken in this study.

Considering WPR for all age groups (Table 9.3, Figure 9.1) the most crucial observations are: (1) There was a decline in work participation for females in both rural and urban areas, while the same for males increased in urban areas and remains constant in rural areas during the period from 1987–88 to 1999–2000. (2) There was an increase in WPR for both males and females during the period from 1999–2000 to 2004–05 in rural and urban areas. (3) There was a decline in WPR for both males and females in rural and urban areas between 2004–05 and 2009–10. The decline was sharp for females, and the percentage figures of WPR, 26.1 per cent for urban areas and 13.8 per cent in rural areas, were the lowest level since 1987–88. This was a clear case of gender discrimination in the employment structure.

Considering WPR for the potential working age group 30–59 years (Table 9.3, Figure 9.2) the observations are: (1) A decline in WPR for rural females, urban males and urban females during the '90s. WPR remained constant for rural males during the same period. (2) In the next period (1999–2000 to 2004–05) WPR showed an increase for rural and urban females but remained stagnant for males. (3) Participation increased for males both rural and urban in the next period between 2004–05 and 2009–10 but there was a massive decline in work participation by females in both rural and urban areas. For rural males the WPR level (98.06 per cent) in 2009–10 is higher than the 1993–94 level (97.93 per cent) but for urban males WPR remains constant (around 96 per cent) at the 1993–94 level. For rural females the decline was from 59.82 per cent to 47.07 per cent during the period from 2004–05 to 2009–10 and for urban females the decline was from 29 per cent to 24 per cent for the same period. The WPR levels at 2009–10 for rural and urban females of the working age group were indeed lower than in 1993–94 and the pre-reform level in 1987–88. Therefore it cannot be established that participation increased particularly for females in India during the neoliberal regime. There is clear gender discrimination in opportunities for work.

We have already welcomed the fact that WPR for older people has declined during the '90s. However, the 61st Round data show that there is a sudden increase in participation

Figure 9.1. Age-wise WPR, all ages: India (rural and urban)

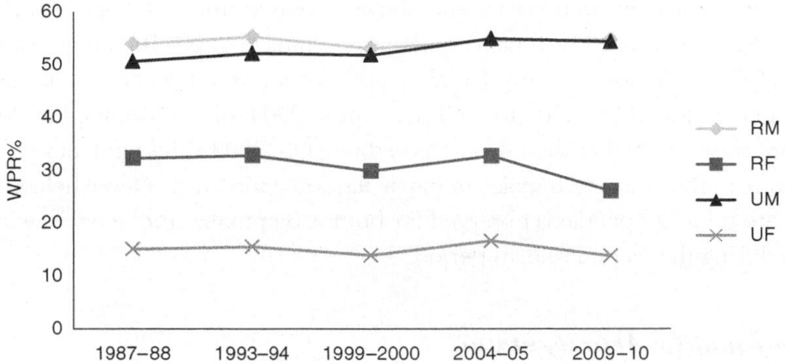

Figure 9.2. Age-wise WPR, 30–59: India (rural and urban)

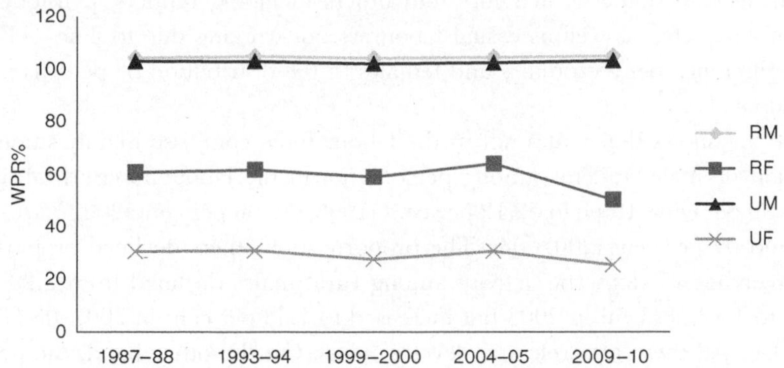

Figure 9.3. Age-wise WPR, 60 and above: India (rural and urban)

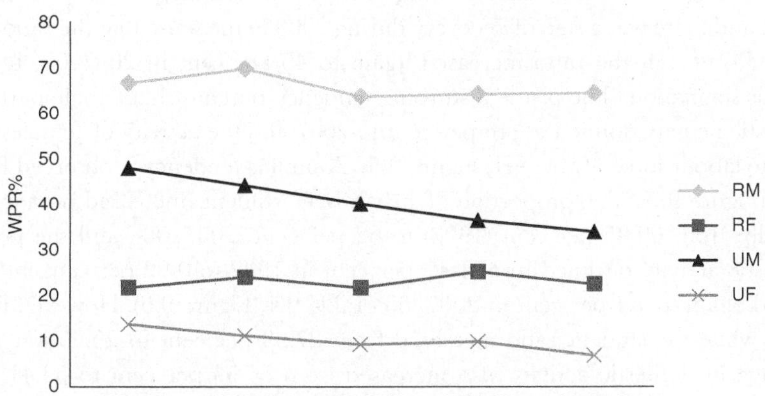

in the old age group (60 and above) for all categories (Table 9.3, Figure 9.3). WPR for rural males in the age group 60 years and above increased from 63.9 per cent in 1999–2000 to 64.4 per cent in 2004–05 and remains constant in 2009–10. The most striking point is that the WPR for the rural female workforce above 60 years increased sharply from 21.8 per cent in 1999–2000 to 25.3 per cent in 2004–05 but declined in 2009–10, yet the latter was even higher than that achieved in 1999–2000. This tendency refutes the withdrawal hypothesis where females in particular are concerned. Nevertheless, decline in participation for old people is observed for both urban males and females, with some oscillation during the second reform period.

Gender inequality: Activity status

The gender aspects will be clear if we consider the percentage of persons not in the labour force as in Table 9.4. NSSO annual series data on household consumer expenditure and employment provide distribution of persons not in the labour force. These are persons neither working nor seeking or available for work. Persons in this category are students, those engaged in domestic activities and others including rentiers, pensioners, those living on alms, etc., as well as casual labourers not working due to illness. There is a distinct difference between males and females in the distribution of persons not in the labour force.

Table 9.4 shows that males not in the labour force comprise mainly students. The proportion of male students among persons not in the labour force (rural) increased from 47.99 per cent (1993) to 52.12 per cent (1998), 57.08 per cent (2002), 57.3 per cent (2003) and 61 per cent (2007–08). The proportion of others declined proportionately. The percentage of domestic activity among rural males declined from 2.23 per cent in 1993 to 1.12 per cent in 2003 but increased to 1.58 per cent in 2007–08 (Table 9.4, Figure 9.4). All these are welcome developments. On the other hand, the percentage of students among female persons not in the labour force increased from 20.73 per cent to 28.97 per cent in 2003 and further increased to 31.45 in 2007–08. This positive tendency has however been negated by the fact that the female percentage of domestic activity among persons not in the labour force increased from 44.54 per cent to 47.20 per cent during 1993–98. In the following year the unwelcome tendency was somehow checked, and there was a sign of recovery during 2003 in the sense that the ratio declined to 43 per cent, but the ratio increased again to 46 per cent in 2007–08. It is better termed as stagnation. The prime disturbing tendency remains that female participation in domestic activity dominates (46 per cent in 2007–08) the activity of females who are not in the labour force (Table 9.4, Figure 9.5). A similar tendency is observed for urban females (Figure 9.7). The proportion of urban male students increased broadly, though marginally, from 60.85 per cent (1993) to 62 per cent (2007–08), and the percentage in domestic activity declined from 1.49 per cent in 1992 to 0.92 per cent in 2003 but increased again to 1.4 per cent in 2007–08 (Table 9.4, Figure 9.6). However, for urban females, while the student ratio increased from 27.93 per cent to 29.56 per cent, the percentage in domestic activity also increased from 50.53 per cent to 53.47 per cent during 1992–2003. The student ratio declined and domestic activity increased further in

Table 9.4. Percentage distribution of persons not in labour force

	Students	Domestic Activity	Others
1	2	3	4
RURAL MALES			
Jan–Dec 1992	49.20	2.29	48.51
Jan–June 1993	47.99	2.23	49.78
Jan–June 1998	52.12	2.45	45.43
July–Dec 2002	57.08	1.57	41.35
Jan–Dec 2003	57.30	1.12	41.35
July 07–June 08	61.0	1.58	37.33
RURAL FEMALES			
Jan–Dec 1992	20.73	44.53	34.74
Jan–June 1993	20.67	44.54	34.79
Jan–June 1998	24.01	47.20	28.92
July–Dec 2002	28.03	46.03	25.80
Jan–Dec 2003	28.97	43.09	27.80
July 07–June 08	31.45	46.26	22.28
URBAN MALES			
Jan–Dec 1992	60.85	1.49	37.66
Jan–June 1993	58.05	1.91	40.04
Jan–June 1998	59.91	2.59	37.50
July–Dec 2002	61.68	1.13	37.41
Jan–Dec 2003	61.70	0.92	37.30
July 07–June 08	62.0	1.40	36.51
URBAN FEMALES			
Jan–Dec 1992	27.93	50.53	21.54
Jan–June 1993	27.75	51.10	21.16
Jan–June 1998	27.90	53.30	18.79
July–Dec 2002	29.19	53.69	17.35
Jan–Dec 2003	29.56	53.47	16.96
July 07–June 08	28.53	56.25	15.21

Note: Cols 2+3+4 = 100
Sources: NSSO, Reports No. 397 (Jan–Dec 1992); 400 (Jan–June 1993); 448 (Jan–June 1998); 484 (July–Dec 2002); 490 (Jan–Dec 2003); 531(July 2007–June 2008).

2007–08 for urban females (Table 9.4, Figure 9.7). Therefore, the domination of female participation in domestic activity in urban areas is far greater than in rural areas. The gender inequality is still pertinent for both rural and urban areas. The present authors emphasized the point earlier in their observation of NSSO data on West Bengal (Basak

Figure 9.4. Outside the labour force: Rural males

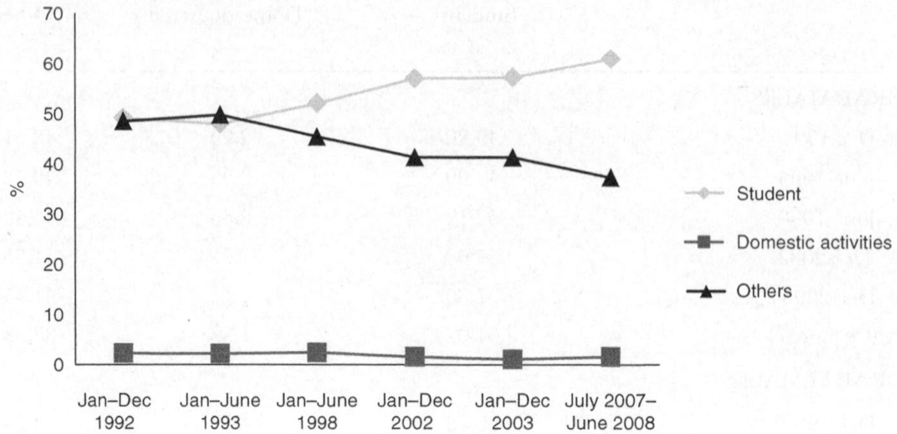

Figure 9.5. Outside the labour force: Rural females

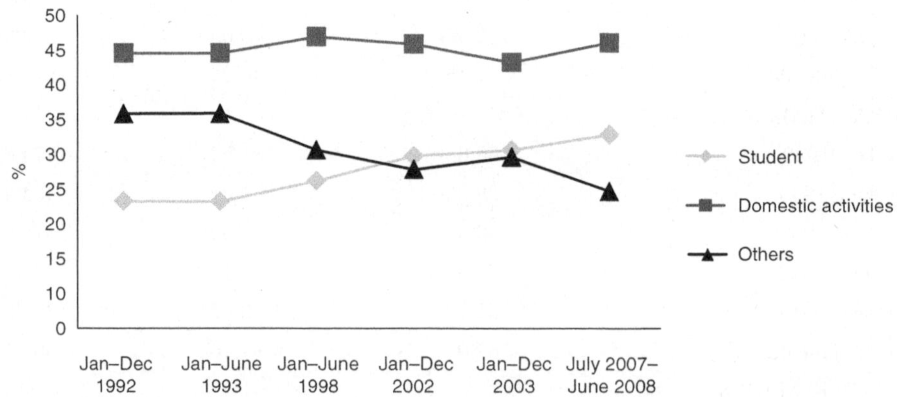

Figure 9.6. Outside the labour force: Urban males

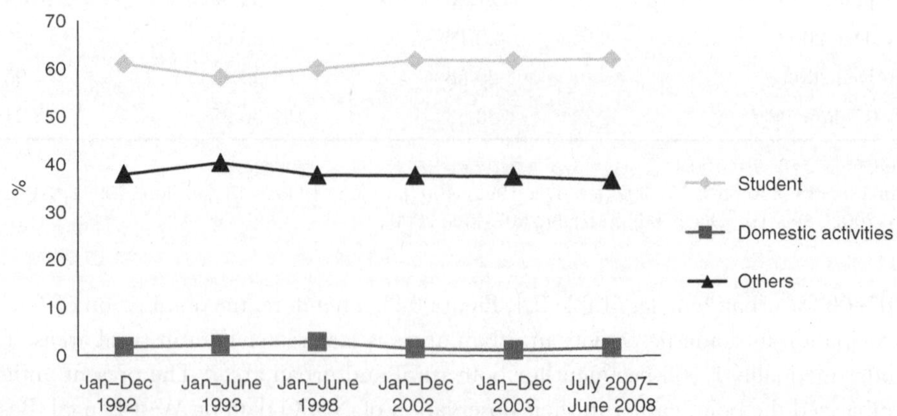

Figure 9.7. Outside the labour force: Urban females

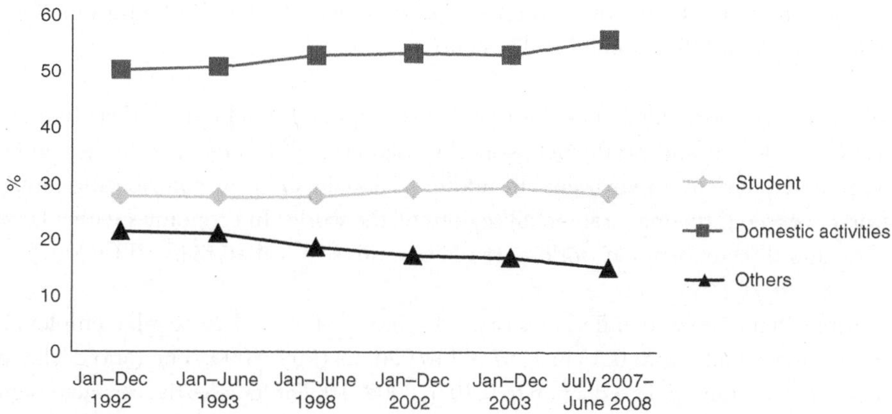

and Bhattacharyya 2005). There is a welcome development that the proportion of students not in the labour force increased both for males and females during the period from 1993 to 2003. However, the domination of domestic activity for females not in the labour force has overshadowed the above process of development.

Gender inequality: Feminized casualization

One of the important hypotheses of our study is that the casualization of both urban and rural labour forces increased during the 1990s owing to the economic reforms. The distribution of employed persons by status of employment is shown in Table 9.4. The prime observations are: (1) casualization increased mainly in rural areas and (2) the index of casualization as measured by casual to regular employment is particularly adverse for rural females.

It is revealed from Table 9.4 that the casually employed rural males increased from 31.40 per cent in 1987–88 to 36.2 per cent in 1999–2000 and then declined to 32.9 in 2004–05, but increased sharply again to 38 per cent during 2009–10. The proportion of rural regular employment (RE) for males decreased from 10.0 per cent in 1987–88 to 8.5 per cent in 1993–94, increased in the subsequent period (9.0 per cent in 2004–05) and returned to 8.5 per cent in 2009–10. In fact, the proportion of regular employment during reform could not touch the pre-reform rate. The ratio of casual to regular employment (CTR) for rural males increased from 3.14 in 1987 to 4.11 during 1999–2000, declined to 3.66 in 2004–05 but increased further to 4.47 in 2009–10. For rural females the same ratio showed an initial increase during the period from 1987–88 (9.59) to 1993–94 (14.33) and then declined to 12.77 in 1999–2000 and further to 8.81 in 2004–05. But the ratio increased again to 9.06 in 2009–10. Clearly enough, the magnitude of the casual to regular employment ratio for rural females was far greater than for males in all the years. Further scrutiny shows that the number of regular jobs for females is much lower than those for the males, though casual employment is marginally higher for females in comparison to males (Table 9.4). This is the prime reason behind the varying magnitude of CTR between males and females. In fact, data on employment reflect that female workers are always few in regular paid jobs in India and over the periods. The ILO report on 'Global Employment Trends for Women 2007' mentions that:

> Women have more difficulties not only in participating in labour markets but also in finding decent and productive work. Women are still less likely to be in regular wage and salaried employment. In addition, female share in contributing family workers exceeds the male rate in all regions of the world. In economies with a large agricultural sector, women work more often in this sector than men. (ILO 2007)

The urban data shows a different story. The index of casual to regular employment increased marginally from 0.33 in 1987–88 to 0.40 in 1999–2000. The ratio declined to 0.36 in 2004–05 but increased again to 0.40 in 2009–10. For females the casual to regular ratio declined monotonically from 0.92 in 1987–88 to 0.64 in 1999–2000 and further to 0.47 in 2004–05 but increased marginally to 0.50 in 2009–10 (Table 9.5). There is a trend of low casualization in urban areas. The difference in magnitude of the index between males and females narrowed over time because there is a tendency of increasing proportion of regular employment for urban females.

Table 9.5 clearly indicates that in rural areas more than 50 per cent of male and female workers are self-employed. The proportion of self-employment for rural males declined from 58.6 per cent to 55 per cent between 1987–88 and 1999–2000 and then increased to 58.1 per cent in 2004–05 but declined drastically to 53.5 in 2009–10. Similarly, for rural females, the proportion self-employed, after declining from 61.9 per cent to 57.3 per cent between 1987–88 and 1999–2000, increased massively to 63.7 per cent in 2004–05, but ultimately declined to its lowest ever level of 55.7 per cent. As a whole, urban and rural India experienced a rapid change of employment status from casual employment to self-employment from the first to the second reform period and again changed drastically to casual in the third reform period for males and females, but largely for females. In urban areas, the magnitude of self-employment is greater for females in comparison to males in almost all periods. The other side of the coin is that the regular and casual employment ratios for almost all years are far higher for males in comparison to females in the urban areas. The 66th Round NSSO data indicate that 41 per cent of male urban workers are self-employed, and the same ratio for urban females is 47 per cent in many years. However, considering the remuneration, self-employment does not indicate any rosy picture of employment. In fact, the sharp increase in female self-employment indicates nothing but compulsion to take any non-remunerative work as they do not find paid jobs. A large part of employment growth is in subsidiary status of employment (Unni and Raveendran 2007). The 61st Round of NSSO data (2004–05) indicated that just under half of all self-employed workers thought of their work as remunerative. The 66th Round of NSS data (2009–10) revealed that about 49 per cent of self-employed in the rural areas and 58 per cent in urban areas considered their current earnings as remunerative. Among them, 45 per cent in rural areas and 21 per cent in urban areas regarded Rs. 3000 or less as remunerative, which is below the poverty line income. ILO (2007) also mentioned that, 'The poorer the regions, greater the likelihood that women work as unpaid contributing

Table 9.5. Status of rural and urban employment from 1987–88 to 2009–10

		SE	RE	CE	CE/RE
	1	2	3	4	5
Rural	1987–88	58.6	10	31.4	3.14
Male	1993–94	57.7	8.5	33.8	3.98
	1999–2000	55	8.8	36.2	4.11
	2004–05	58.1	9	32.9	3.66
	2009–10	53.5	8.5	38	4.47
Rural	1987–88	60.8	3.7	35.5	9.59
Female	1993–94	58.6	2.7	38.7	14.33
	1999–2000	57.3	3.1	39.6	12.77
	2004–05	63.7	3.7	32.6	8.81
	2009–10	55.7	4.4	39.9	9.06
Urban	1987–88	41.7	43.7	14.6	0.33
Male	1993–94	41.7	42	16.3	0.39
	1999–2000	41.5	41.7	16.8	0.4
	2004–05	44.8	40.6	14.6	0.36
	2009–10	41.1	41.9	17	0.4
Urban	1987–88	47.1	27.5	25.4	0.92
Female	1993–94	45.8	28.4	25.8	0.91
	1999–2000	45.3	33.3	21.4	0.64
	2004–05	47.7	35.6	16.7	0.47
	2009–10	41.1	39.3	19.6	0.5

Source: NSSO, Report No. 537: 'Employment and Unemployment Situation in India', Statement 5.7, p. 85; NSSO, Sarvekshana Special No. Sept 1990, Statement 34, pp. 94–5.
Note: Cols 2 + 3 +4 = 100
SE: self-employed
RE: regular employed
CE: casually employed

family members or low-income own-account workers.' The growth of low-paid jobs, therefore, raises doubt on the rosy picture of de-casualization. This point will be discussed later in the question of diversification of employment scenario.

Gender inequality: Feminization of non-diversification

The most important aspect of rural employment is the question of diversification of economic activities. Extensive literatures are available on this subject. Here we observe only that the distribution of rural households according to the main sources of income

Table 9.6. Structural change in workforce: Rural males and females in agriculture

	1987–88	1993–94	1999–2000	2004–05	2009–10
Rural Males	74.5	74.1	71.4	66.5	62.8
Rural Females	84.7	86.2	85.4	83.3	79.4

Source: NSSO, Report No. 537: 'Employment and Unemployment Situation in India', Statement 5.9, p. 89.

and workforce diversification is limited by agricultural employment and non-agricultural employment. The structure of employment generation within non-agricultural employment is not considered.

Table 9.6, based on NSSO data, shows that the proportion of rural males dependent on agriculture (considering principal and subsidiary status) declined by 0.4 per cent during the pre-reform period (1987–88 to 1993–94) and further declined by 11.3 per cent during the reform period (1993–94 to 2009–10). The shifting of the workforce is obviously significant in the period from 1999–2000 to 2009–10 (–8.6) in comparison to 1993–94 to 1999–2000 (–2.7). Apparently a dramatic change is observed after economic reform. The proponents of economic reform have argued that India has experienced a positive restructuring of the workforce in favour of nonagricultural activities during the late '90s onwards for the first time since independence (Sundaram 2001). As we shall discuss later, the apparent diversification was due to a steady decline in the demand for agricultural labour following the dismal performance of agriculture during the reform period. This phenomenon was aggravated in the 2000s with the prolonged agrarian crisis and farmers' suicides. A large proportion of the workforce had to leave agriculture for this push factor and was compelled to adopt non-remunerative self-employment. The rise of self-employment in the 2000s indicated this phenomenon. This tendency can be better termed as 'disguised proletarianization' rather than 'diversification'. As a matter of fact, the share of the rural male workforce in agriculture, 62.8 per cent in 2009–10, is itself an alarmingly high percentage and not a relief at all for a developing economy. In fact, rural female workers continued to engage in agriculture, as high as 79.4 per cent in 2009–10 in comparison to 62.8 per cent for males. This was in spite of a 6.8 per cent decline in the female workforce dependent on agriculture by 16 years of economic reform (1993–94 to 2009–10) (Table 9.6). Thus the structural transformation of employment during reform as claimed by the reformists was weakly assigned to the rural male workforce only. We therefore observe a phenomenon which we can better call *feminization of non-diversification.*

Conclusion

During the first phase of economic reform, 1993–94 to 1999–2000, a process of casualization of the workforce and an occupational shift towards decline in diversification took place. During the second reform period (1999–2000 to 2004–05) we have observed an apparent phenomenon of de-casualization, a steep increase in self-employment and re-diversification in terms of increase in nonagricultural employment. Both the LFPR and the WPR increased in this phase. Again in the third phase of reform (2004–05 to 2009–10) we have witnessed the reappearance of casualization and a decline in self-employment. The period of economic reform was accompanied by a process of decline in agricultural growth even below the population growth rate, a decline in agricultural investment and a decline in agricultural and nonagricultural wages (Jha 2007, Himanshu 2005). All these factors are responsible for the decline in agricultural wage employment and self-employment. Even the industrial growth stagnated since the mid-'90s. There was no scope for Lewisian transformation as the pull factor did not operate in the industrial sector, as the latter is characterized by labour-saving technology and the growth trajectory was not satisfactory and subject to fluctuation (Mazumdar, Chapter 12 in this volume). The cheap exports from other countries, particularly China, following trade liberalization and a policy of de-reservation have adversely affected the small-scale sector (Mahalingam 2007). Only high-skilled salaried classes drew the benefits of liberalization, and this manifested in the service-led high growth rate of the economy (D'Costa, Chapter 7 and U. Patnaik, Chapter 6 in this volume). All these factors contributed to the process of 'jobless growth' for the economy as a whole during the period of liberalization (Bhattacharya and Sakthivel 2003, Ghosh 2006a).

Only the second reform period (1999–2000 to 2004–05) showed some 'welcome tendencies' where casualization shrunk and self-employment increased. However, the so-called welcome tendencies in this particular period have not been substantiated by any development of remunerative or productive employment. The countrywide deep agrarian crisis, the decline in agricultural investment and the decline in the small-scale sector led to a push back of labourers who had no option but to take low-paid/non-remunerative employment as compulsion. This is helplessness and desperation on the part of the population who after having no employment in the agricultural and nonagricultural sectors had no other option but to declare themselves as self-employed (and 'became [their] own boss') in a hand-to-mouth situation (Ghosh 2006b). After a temporary phase of the apparent welcome development, the third phase of economic reform (2004–05 to 2009–10) was characterized by the usual process of casualization and decline in self-employment. Particularly when there was a decline in the wage employment programme (say IRDP, NREP), how was it possible that the nonagricultural employment would rise?

The distress of the workforce was by and large feminized, as we have seen that the female participation increased, but the increase was more for the old age group. Occupation-wise distribution reveals that the proportion of 'domestic activity' in female participation rate, not in the labour force, dominates and overshadows the relative increase in 'students' for the same. For all the years, the proportion of female casual employment was considerably greater than that of males. This can be described as 'feminized casualization'.

Market economic reform in the Indian economy was expected to unfold a process of capitalist development that was supposed to expand investment and raise wage employment. Instead we have seen an economy with agrarian crisis, industrial slowdown/fluctuation and jobless growth. Such a phenomenon can be termed as 'arrested capitalist development' as used by Patnaik (2007). There is also a rise in the rural unemployment rate between the 55th and 61st Rounds of NSSO irrespective of definition by usual status, current weekly status and current daily status. The rise in unemployment is sharper for females than males, indicating more gender inequality (Mukhopadhyay and Rajaraman 2007). The 66th Round data (2009–10) revealed a decline in the unemployment rate nevertheless, the rate being higher than the 1993–94 level.

Notes

1 Though the picture is not very clear for urban data regarding diversification. The Labour Force Participation Rate (LFPR) is a percentage of working population and unemployed people (seeking work). Labour force in terms of usual status includes persons who have for a relatively longer part of the year either worked or looked for work and also those who have worked for at least for some time among the rest. Thus under usual status we obtain two estimates: 1) principal status, and 2) principal and subsidiary status.

2 There was a sharp decline in the rural female workforce for the group 30–44 years from 59.8 per cent to 57.2 per cent during 1993–94 to 1999–2000 and then a recovery in 2004–05 at 61.43 per cent. This group constitutes more than one-third of female workers. Obviously, change in the rate of participation of this group has a large impact on the development aspect. In the subsequent period (2004–05 to 2009–10) there is a massive decline in the rural female workforce (47.3 per cent) in the same age group. The WPR for urban females for the same age group declined from 29.5 per cent to 26.6 per cent during the period from 1993–94 to 1999–2000 and then increased sharply to 31 per cent in 2004–05. WPR declined sharply to 25.2 per cent. In other words, there is no further increase in the rate of work participation of the rural male workforce during the era of economic reform. Rather, there was a decline in WPR for the working age group.

3 See Chadha and Sahu (2002). The authors observed a decline in age-group specific labour force participation during the 1990s along with an increase in the proportion of school-going rural children in the age group 10–14 from 65.3 per cent in 1993–94 to 71.1 per cent in 1999–2000. They suggested that this was due to rising rural incomes or decline in poverty during the period. Thus, withdrawal of children/adolescents from the labour market due to rising income is the convincing explanation for the increase in the proportion of school-going children.

4 The concept of agriculture-led development has gained a concrete theoretical shape in the hands of Kalecki. In Kalecki's formulation, in an underdeveloped mixed economy, the rate of supply of necessities (food) may be limited by institutional factors, such as feudal land ownership and domination of peasants by merchants and moneylenders. As a result, 'the average rate of increase in the supply of necessities over the planning period is kept down to a rather low level' (Kalecki 1970, 153). According to Kalecki's formulation, the rate of increase of supply of necessities as fixed by institutional barriers to the development of agriculture determines the rate of growth of national income (152). Therefore, according to Kalecki, '[…] the main "financial" problem of development is that of adequate agricultural production. The key to "financing" a more rapid growth is the removal of obstacles to the expansion of agriculture, such as feudal landownership and domination of peasants by moneylenders and merchants' (ibid.).

References

Basak, U. and S. Bhattacharyya. 2003. 'Rural Employment, Market Reforms and Gender Inequality in West Bengal'. *Indian Journal of Labour Economics* 48, no. 3: 553–61.

Bhattacharya, B. B. and S. Sakthivel. 2003. 'Economic Reforms and Jobless Growth in India in the 1990s'. *Indian Journal of Labour Economics* 46, no. 4: 845–65.

Chadha, G. K. and P. P. Sahu. 2002. 'Post-reform Setbacks in Rural Employment: Issues That Need Further Scrutiny'. *Economic and Political Weekly* 37, no. 21: 1998–2026.

Ghosh, J. 2006a. 'The Jobless Young'. Online: www.macroscan.org (accessed 10 October 2010).

_______. 2006b. 'Being Your Own Boss'. Online: www.macroscan.org (accessed on 10 October 2010).

Government of India. 2005. 'Income, Expenditure and Productive Assets of Farmer Households, 2003'. *Situation Assessment Survey of Farmers*, Report no. 497. New Delhi: National Sample Survey Organization.

Himanshu. 2005. 'Wages in Rural India, Sources, Trends and Comparability'. *Indian Journal of Labour Economics* 48, no. 2: 375–406.

International Labour Organization. 2007. *Global Employment Trends for Women Brief, March.* http://www.cinterfor.org.uy/public/english/region/ampro/cinterfor/temas/gender/news/getw07.pdf (accessed 20 November 2009).

Jha, P. 2007. 'Some Aspects of Well Being of Agricultural Labour in the Context of Contemporary Agrarian Crisis'. www.macroscan.org. (accessed 10 October 2010).

Mahalingam, T. V. 2007. 'The China Effect'. *Business Today*, March 25, 87–95.

Mukhopadhyay, A. and I. Rajaraman. 2007. 'Rural Unemployment 1999–2005: Who Gained, Who Lost?' *Economic and Political Weekly* 42, no. 30: 3116–20.

Narayanamoorthy, A. 2007. 'Deceleration in Agricultural Growth: Technology Fatigue or Policy Fatigue?' *Economic and Political Weekly* 42, no. 25: 2375–9.

Patnaik, U. 2007. 'New Data on the Arrested Development of Capitalism in Indian Agriculture'. *Social Scientist* 35, nos. 7–8: 4–23.

Sundaram, K. 2001. 'Employment and Poverty in 1990s: Further Results from NSS 55th Round Employment and Unemployment Survey, 1999–2000'. *Economic and Political Weekly* 36, no. 32: 3039–49.

Unni, J. and G. Raveendran. 2007. 'Growth of Employment (1993–94 to 2004–05): Illusion of Inclusiveness?' *Economic and Political Weekly* 42, no. 3: 196–9.

Chapter 10

PRIVATIZATION AND DEREGULATION*

Ashok Rudra

In a mature academic community, differences of opinion can be debated without any ill feelings or injuries. It is regrettable that often debates degenerate into quarrels. That is one reason why one sometimes hesitates to enter into a debate. I have also hesitated to take up the challenge thrown by T. N. Srinivasan at all economists in India who might be opposed to the World Bank–IMF policy line that has been adopted by the government of India. It would be sad indeed if my opposing Srinivasan in public should lead to any deterioration of the excellent relations we have maintained with each other over more than 35 years. Of course, I have always thought that on policy questions Srinivasan is quite mad, mad as a March hare; I am sure Srinivasan on his part has never taken me seriously on these questions. But these differences have never affected our personal relations, and I hope it will continue to be so in future. If despite this anxiety I feel called upon to make some comments on two of his recent writings in the *EPW* (Srinivasan 1991a; 1991b), that is because in these pieces he has made a large number of assertions and sweeping generalizations on matters of the utmost gravity for the country. Srinivasan is a serious scholar and his writings are usually analytically rich. But unfortunately, in the two recent pieces that I am talking about, there is hardly any trace of any analytics; only a number of diktats. He must be exceedingly happy to see the government of India adopt lock, stock and barrel the policy measures he, along with some others, has advocated for nearly 30 years. In his joy he seems to have allowed his writing to read like a victory speech. A victory speech does not contain any analysis or arguments.

Some more caution. While I do think that the policies long advocated by Srinivasan and his fellow thinkers and now adopted by the government of India would immensely harm the poor of the country, I do not have the slightest doubt that his concern for the poor of the country is not any less than that of myself or anybody else. If he is supporting policies which I would oppose, that is mainly because of the difference between us about what is good for the country. This difference arises because of our different ideologies, a matter that I shall take up in a later section.

---

* A previous version of this chapter appeared in *Economic and Political Weekly* 26, no. 51 (21 December 1991).

Privatization

One of Srinivasan's diktats is directed against the public sector and it runs as follows:

> There are many enterprises in the public sector which have no logic, rhyme or reason. They ought to be privatized right away. (Srinivasan 1991b, 2145)

The sentence reads as if there is in the economic science (?) any logic as to what kind of enterprise should be in which sector, public or private. Elsewhere, Srinivasan talks about the comparative advantages of the public and the private sectors. Surely, there cannot be any a priori comparative advantage, as in the case of trade, in which natural resource endowments or geographical location may contribute to such advantage. Srinivasan gives some idea about the kind of 'logic' he has in mind. He writes: 'Hotels, airlines, various manufacturing enterprises which generate no externality or public goods should have no place in the public sector. A whole bunch of such money-losing public enterprises should be and can be gotten rid of overnight.' He ends up with the 'hope that the arena for the public sector would be narrowly circumscribed' (Srinivasan 1991b, 2145).

It would seem that according to Srinivasan, enterprises which generate externality or supply public goods may have some place in the public sector. So far, so good; this agrees with not my logic, but my values. By implication Srinivasan would obviously like to see in the private sector all non–money losing enterprises producing goods for private consumption. I would like Srinivasan to explain why profit-making consumer goods industries, including hotels and airlines, should not be in the public sector. If such enterprises make a lot of profit and that profit is reinvested for the expansion of the economy, what is wrong about that? Srinivasan would probably say that the 'if' in my question is a very big 'if'. That brings us to the crux of the matter. One is assuming, *axiomatically*, that public sector enterprises are inefficient and private sector ones are efficient. This has become such a habit of thought among many economists that one may raise one's eyebrows that I should question it.

Now, if one were discussing the performance of the public sector in India, there would be not much difference of opinion. It is, indeed, true that the record of most public enterprises in India, in *absolute* terms, is very poor. The litany of the innumerable weaknesses and vices of these enterprises, repeated ad infinitum and ad nauseam by advocates of privatization, is really quite unnecessary. But the question is, are public enterprises in any way destined to be poor performers? What is at issue is a comparison of public enterprises with private enterprises – not just in the India of today but in all generality in the world as a whole, not only as they actually are but also as they might potentially be.

Talking about logic, surely the fact that public enterprises in India are bad in performance *does not* imply that private enterprises in India are necessarily better? Surely, by all logic, they could even be worse? It is not a problem of logic at all but of empirical analysis. Just as one can cite any number of instances of the vices of existing public sector enterprises in India, the record of private enterprises in India is also not particularly glorious, and not all their faults are due to wrongheaded intervention by the government.

To compare the merits of the two sectors in abstraction is absurd. A comparison between the losses caused by bureaucratic ham-handedness and profligacy on one side and the myopia and rapacity of the private sector owners and managers on the other cannot be carried out in general terms. The exercise has to be carried out empirically, with rigour and in painstaking detail. Has anybody carried out such an exercise for India (or for any other countries or for the world as a whole)? What criteria have been used for judging performance? Actually, one goes by mere superficial observations, for which even 'casual empiricism' is a high sounding phase. The usual line of berating the public sector is to point at the indisputable fact that many public enterprises run at a loss or at very low rates of profit. For many, this fact by itself clinches the issue. It is surprising that the gross fallacies in this comparison should not be noticed. By the nature of things, a private enterprise, when ceasing to make profits, goes out of business. As such, a valid comparison should not be between the average profitability of private enterprises *that continue in business* and that of all public enterprises. It is like comparing the health standards of two populations in one of which people are left to die whenever they are sick and the other with a health service that tries to keep the sick alive for as long as possible. In such a comparison the barbaric society that lets all the sick die will necessarily show a better average health standard. For comparison to be valid the sick should be given low ratings and the dead should be given zero ratings. Similarly, a valid comparison would put on one side the private enterprises that go out of business or are kept going by subsidies and keep on the other side the public enterprises that run at a loss; it would weigh against each other not only the balance in the profit–loss account but also the losses in the form of assets that have to be written off. A second elementary error lies in overlooking the fact that in most economies the public sector is given the charge of running the public utilities on a non-profit basis. Whether the policy is right or wrong is a different matter. What concerns us here is that a non-profit making public utility is not to be judged as inefficient for not making profit. An aggregate over the public sector that includes many such units may not be compared validly with an aggregate over the private sector.

A third error is to assume that enterprises cannot possibly engage in competition if they happen to be publicly owned. That perfect competition is more possible among non-private enterprises than among private enterprises was theoretically demonstrated by Lange and others more than fifty years back. In actual practice different kinds and degrees of competition and coalition are observable in both the public and the private sectors. Nationalized banks in France compete with each other and function more efficiently than private banks in Britain and America. (This, of course, is a casual observation.) Even in India, different nationalized banks compete with each other and different units of the LIC work with different efficiencies.

One should not glibly talk about the public sector and the private sector, as if they are universal homogeneous categories. As a matter of fact, there is a large variety in the organization, structure, practices, traditions, and ethos of the private sector in different time–place contexts – Padmini Swaminathan's article (1991) makes many sensible observations. Likewise, there is no reason to think that the possibilities of structure, organization, working rules, etc., of public enterprises are exhausted by the models exhibited by India or the USSR.

No serious comparison is possible if one does not take into account these variations within the two sectors even in the same country. To make any generalization one has to take account of the variety that one would encounter if one would not restrict oneself to a single country but think of all countries in the world.

As a matter of fact, it is not known that anybody has ever carried out any serious comparative analysis like the above. What one actually does is to go by stray examples and anecdotes. For example, Srinivasan cites the example of electricity distribution in Tamil Nadu being some time in the past so very efficient 'in the hands of municipalities as well as private enterprises' (Srinivasan 1991b, 2144). Example of this kind one can produce as many as one wants for defending whatever one wants to defend. Thus, Calcutta has perhaps the worst electricity supply in India, but Calcutta Electric Supply Corporation is a British private enterprise. On the other hand, the Calcutta Metro, a central government public enterprise, has been ranked first for its performance among all the undergrounds of the world. (The ranking was done by an international team of experts.) Pan Am is a private American airline, and it is kept going artificially by all kinds of American state support, including an obligation imposed on invitees by American agencies to suffer the discomforts of that airline notorious for its poor service. (This is a good example of the theme 'Physician, heal thyself' that I shall take up a little later.) Swiss Air, Air France and most other international airlines are state monopoly enterprises, and many of them render superb service and make good profit. Such selective comparisons establish nothing.

Import Competition?

Privatization is only one item in Srinivasan's proposed reforms package; another important part is the liberalization of the trade regime, which includes removal of quantitative restrictions and free inflow of foreign capital. It is strange that this reform is urged to be carried out in a short space of time, and the strangeness is not reduced by the fact that the government of India has accepted the same advice coming from the IMF. I suppose one will agree that the best example in history of benefits being reaped from the freeing of movements of commodities and capital is offered by the European Common Market. Over how many years has the process of merging the markets been spread? The process is still not complete even after 25 years and even with the 1992 deadline for a common currency. None of the countries that joined the EEC agreed to remove any restriction overnight and at a single stroke. There have been, over the last quarter of a century, innumerable meetings for negotiating the process of relaxations; plenty of protective clauses for particular partners and particular commodities being retained or made afresh at every stage. This is all very understandable. No country ever wanted to give up any particular piece of protection before ensuring that competition would not ruin any of its existing industries. The idea with which the ECM began was to create conditions in which industries that would be set up anew would all be competitive, whereas the existing industries would get enough time and receive all kinds of appropriate assistance to adjust themselves to the competition. It is precisely the gradualness that holds the key to the success of the ECM. Let us not forget here that the ECM began with the target of a customs union. A customs union surely does not mean allowing free flow of commodities and capital from all the world over? The countries joining a customs union are all protected from the rest of the world by a common barrier. Customs union theory argues that unionization ensures good results for all the joining countries, provided that each country is initially competitive with the others at least in many of its industries.

Let us now turn to history. It is good that Srinivasan himself states that 'there are no *laissez-faire* economies in the world' (Srinivasan 1991a, 1850). However, all through his writings Srinivasan is uncompromisingly against any kind of protectionism. But is not the history of development of each of the now-developed capitalist countries a history of protectionism? It is not only France and Germany that used all kinds of measures to protect their industries against competition by the British. Britain itself practised protectionism from the first half of the 14th century, when Edward II prohibited the import of foreign cloth. The British wool industry would never have survived but for export promotion and import restrictions practised from the 15th century. And would Manchester have thrived if not initially protected from Indian textiles and given all other kinds of state support?

Students of history know that *laissez-faire* was indeed practised during a certain period in history (prohibition of cotton import in 1774, curtailment of monopoly privileges of the East India Company in 1807, repeal of the Corn Law in 1846, repeal of the Navigation Acts in 1849, etc.). But this was a relatively short period when Britain had attained superiority over its nearest trade rivals. This period ended soon. Phyllis Deane, the noted historian, no Marxist and no leftist, has this to say about British trade policy in the heydays of the country's economic expansion: '[...] far from being triumphant by the 1850s, the *laissez-faire* movement had been finally routed by new techniques of government control of the economy which had their own built-in tendency to develop, grow and multiply!' (Deane 1979, 237). She goes further and admits that in the sphere of foreign trade the government was ready to take decisive action. The Foreign Office, for example, accepted responsibility for 'the political control of trade' (235). She illustrates her point with the example of the naval action to protect the British opium smugglers of Canton. I am not thinking for a moment that I am giving any lessons to anybody – the few examples that I have given are all too well known. But precisely because these are so well known that the question is interesting and urgent: how can one possibly argue for the unconditional abolition of protection in the name of the virtues of competition? One knows all the different ways in which protectionism in India has been counterproductive and has been abused. There is no need to defend the policy of across-the-board import substitution that was followed in India for too long a time. There is no need to hammer the elementary points about comparative advantage and the benefits of trade. All these points may be conceded and yet without any inconsistency one may recognize the case for infant industry protection or for discrimination in the national interest. One should of course not set up in the first instance industries that stand no chance of facing up to international competition. That does not mean that one should not give all help to existing industries so that they can stand up to that competition. This is the policy that has been followed by every single country that is developed today, Britain to Japan. It is important to emphasize this obvious point as it has become fashionable to talk of 'globalizing' the economy, meaning that the best course of action to follow is to throw the doors and windows wide open so as to permit free inflow of foreign commodities and foreign capital. The idea is that the

Indian industries, subjected to the sudden blast of competition, would either become competitive or would be wiped out. The point that we are labouring is that no country in the world ever practised such a draconian policy and came out stronger.

'Physician, Heal Thyself!'

We would like to raise in this section some questions. If Srinivasan should comment on them that may help me to appreciate some of his views which appear to me to lack consistency.

If the public sector is necessarily and intrinsically inefficient, how is it that the IMF–World Bank and the government of India or Srinivasan do not find any fault with public sector financial institutions? The New Industrial Policy does not recommend the privatization of banks, and it happens that on the very day these lines are being written (November 22, 1991) newspapers report the vice president of the World Bank to have declared that it is not necessary for India to privatize its banks; it is enough if industries are privatized. Surely, this cannot but mean that the public sector financial organizations have been performing with 'efficiency' the tasks given to them? And what is that task? It is well known that all private sector enterprises depend heavily for long-term capital loans as well as equity participation on the various public sector industrial development banks. If private sector enterprises would raise capital and finance their expansion, one may understand, if not accept, the case for giving them total freedom of action. But in India it is public sector institutions that mobilize the voluntary as well as the forced savings of the public by floating loans and utilizing other fiscal measures, and then they hand over the major part of that capital to the private sector. Are we to understand that the public sector can only be good at mobilizing resources but not at utilizing them? And that the private sector does not know how to earn but knows only how to spend?

The IMF imposes some of what are called peculiar English 'conditionalities' on the loan recipient countries. Those who do not find anything wrong with these conditionalities argue that it is only legitimate that a banking institution should ensure the creditworthiness of its clients. Fair enough, the argument is eminently reasonable. But then, why should the argument not apply to private sector enterprises taking loans from the state? Insofar as the state is the principal source of capital for the private sector, is it not only natural that the state should have a say in how the private sector should utilize that capital? What are licences but a kind of 'conditionalities'? Regulation by the IMF–World Bank is good, but regulation by the government of India is bad – is that the argument?

If competition is good, why are India and other Third-World countries deprived of the benefits of competition between loan-giving countries and international agencies? Why is it that India has to deal with a consortium and not with individual countries? So, once again, competition is good for enterprises in India but not to be followed by bigger economic powers?

If protectionism is bad, why has Srinivasan (or the IMF–World Bank) nothing to say about the protectionism and trade discrimination that is practised by America and other leading capitalist countries in the world? We have already mentioned the small but conspicuous example of Pan Am being made to survive by federal patronage. Examples of such measures by the developed countries are so very plentiful that it is neither necessary nor possible to give any detailed account of that. Let us give only one instance, and let us take it from no leftist source but from a highly reputable bourgeois source, namely the Organisation for Economic Co-operation and Development (OECD). In a study about the world fertilizer economics sponsored by the OECD, Kahnert (1971) made, among others, the following points:

1 Much of the fertilizer imports by the Third-World are financed by tied aid.
2 Very often the condition is imposed that the import has not only to be made from the US but also that a good share of it has to be transported by US flagships.
3 The free market transport cost from the US is four times higher than from the Gulf countries.
4 For the same route US flagships cost more than the free market.
5 As a result of the above, India had to pay twice as much for importing fertilizers from the United States as what it would have paid if the import was made from the Gulf countries.

Will Deregulation Eliminate Corruption?

Srinivasan in one place talks of the 'unleashing of rapacious rent-seeking and political corruption' (Srinivasan 1991b, 2143). Until Bofors I would have let this comment pass. But not any more. Until Bofors we in India were all agreed that public life in our country was honeycombed with corruption as a typical product of the country's state of underdevelopment. We assumed that the developed capitalist countries were free of such corruption. Those who have been against the regulatory system that prevailed in the economy ascribed to that regime a large part of the responsibility for that corruption. However, we now know better; we know that the difference is only in the scale of corruption. In India clerks may take bribes of ten or twenty rupees or at most a few hundred rupees; officers may take bribes to the tune of thousands and lakhs. But we never could conceive of bribes running up to several hundreds of crores. But that is the dimension of the bribes that have been associated with the Bofors guns and the German submarines. They, of course, do not call it a bribe in those countries. They call it 'commission' and treat it as a perfectly normal part of ordinary transactions. There is no corruption in Western countries as they do not regard the giving or taking of commission as corruption. That corruption is not a moral issue in the developed capitalist countries as it is in India is clear from the fact that, while in India a government fell because of suspicions of its connivance in a particular case of corruption, in Sweden the government has been providing all possible protection to Bofors, which was accused of being a party to that very corruption.

I am not digressing. The all too easily accepted idea that controls and regulations breed corruption and, therefore, deregulation and delicensing would eliminate corruption requires to be re-examined. The existence of corruption on the billion-dollar scale in the G-7 countries indicates that free market economies are by no means corruption-free economies.

While discussing the evils of the regulatory system in India, Srinivasan grants that 'there are a few price and distribution controls, particularly with respect to a limited and well-defined set of subsidies relating to food and other essential needs of vulnerable groups in the population that one might conceivably argue should possibly continue' (Srinivasan 1991b, 2144). Would he not include a few other items in his accommodation for 'arguable propositions'? What about location of industries? Left to market forces the location in each case would be in regions already furnished with adequate infrastructural facilities. How can one possibly correct regional imbalance and protect environment if there is no control over industrial location? Similarly, left to market forces, the choice of techniques would be necessarily far from appropriate. They would not only not maximize employment, they would also not maximize even profit. Industrialists in India in both the private and the public sectors do not go in for any economic calculations while importing technology. They simply go in for the latest models and brands in the Western world. There is, therefore, a very good case for regulating these choices. That in actual fact regulation has not yielded the best choices of locations and techniques does not mean that deregulation would give any better results.

Capitalism Stinks!

'Given the hang-ups and inhibitions involving multinationals [...]', Srinivasan writes in one place (1991b, 2145). It is with this kind of a snigger that Srinivasan right through his two pieces gives out his ideological bias. Economic policy can hardly be free of ideology, and it is as well to state it explicitly rather than keep it obscure behind mockeries and taunts. For the sake of honest discussion, I put my ideological cards on the table. I hate capitalism. People like myself are much less concerned about the efficiency of a social system in the matter of production of commodities than about the kind of social values the system encourages and the cultural atmosphere it engenders. Capitalism stinks. It stinks of lust. Lust for money and lust for commodities. Neoclassical economic theory has it that 'social welfare' is maximized when everybody is goaded by this lust to compete with each other for maximizing profits and maximizing utility. Of course, social welfare in this theory is equated to nothing more than Pareto-optimality which hardly approximates any of the properties of a good society as have been envisioned through the ages by social philosophers. Such thinkers have not mostly been economists, and economics occupies very little space in their thinking. I am thinking of thought leaders like Christ and Buddha, Voltaire and Rousseau, Gandhi and Tagore, and of course Marx. What is common among all these very different great men who lived and died for improving the lot of mankind is their concern for spiritual and moral values. What distinguishes Marx from his predecessors is his realization that spiritual values can flourish only on some material foundations, that human society till his days had never had enough of material goods for the spiritual fulfilment of all men, that hungry people cannot afford to be either moral or spiritual. Marx realized that to achieve a good society it is necessary to have an economic order that can produce much more than what was possible anywhere in the world during his time. His good society is one in which every person can live in reasonable comfort and has plenty of leisure for the pursuit of intellectual, spiritual and cultural activities. His vision of a good society is far from one in which one is condemned, as in capitalism, to produce more and more and consume more and more. What is called 'consumerism' today was named by him commodity fetishism and condemned as a vice typical of capitalism. The ideologues of capitalism make a virtue of competition. In Marx's good society people do not compete with each other, they cooperate. They would regard competition as a law of the jungle. Capitalism is barbaric – in the words of Oscar Wilde, a capitalist is one who knows the price of everything but the value of none. In a capitalist society everything is commodified – there is a price for everything. In Marx's good society all important things are priceless, that is, beyond the reach of money.

Given these values, we do not accept GDP growth rate alone as constituting a satisfactory yardstick for choosing between alternatives. Even within the domain of economics there are various other measures like life expectancy, literacy, measures relating to health and educational services, etc., which have to be taken into account for judging the quality of development as opposed to mere growth. Among social scientists more and more are dissatisfied with growth maximization alone. India is a country with a legacy not only of Gandhi but also of Tagore, and the Gandhian legacy cannot be dismissed as having caused only waste of national resources.

Given this understanding of ours it is quite clear that the collapse of the Soviet kind of regimes is no cause for us to change our views about what is a good society. One has not thrown away the Bible because no community on earth ever lived fully up to the ideals of the Bible.

Conclusion

By way of conclusion I would put forward the following hypotheses to be refuted. The first is that the performance of an industry depends on various factors which do not all get determined by private or public ownership of the means of production. The second is that abrupt removal of protections is likely to spell disaster for the economy; some amount of protection and regulation is absolutely essential for making industries competitive.

Until these hypotheses are definitively refuted, what one would like to see is experimentation with various institutional frameworks and operational rules for industries within the confines of the means of production being in public hands. One would also like to see experiments with different measures for making our industries more and more internationally competitive without the draconian measure of removing overnight all restrictions on imports of commodities and capital. I would also welcome the reconstitution of regulatory mechanisms for ensuring that choice of industries conforms to the genuine needs of the people, choice of locations of industries conforms to the requirements of regional balance and choice of techniques conforms to what is appropriate, given the resource endowments of the country.

References

Deane, Phyllis. 1979. *The First Industrial Revolution*. Cambridge: Cambridge University Press.

Kahnert, Friedrich. 1971. 'Aid Tying and Export of Nitrogenous Fertilisers from the Persian Gulf'. Technical Paper Series. Paris: Organisation for Economic Co-operation and Development.

Srinivasan, T. N. 1991a. 'Indian Development Strategy – An Exchange of Views'. *Economic and Political Weekly* 26, nos. 31–2: 1850– 52.

______. 1991b. 'Reform of Industrial and Trade Policies'. *Economic and Political Weekly* 26, no. 37: 2143–5.

Swaminathan, Padmini. 1991. 'Industrial Policy Statement – Missing Dimensions'. *Economic and Political Weekly* 26, no. 39: 2237–9.

Chapter 11

MACROECONOMIC IMPACT OF PUBLIC SECTOR ENTERPRISES: SOME FURTHER EVIDENCE*

R. Nagaraj

Public sector enterprises (PSEs) have been getting a bad press these days. They are widely perceived as an important reason for the increasing fiscal imbalance in recent years and for the widespread, and allegedly growing, inefficiencies in the non-farm sectors of the economy. A gradual reduction in the role of the public sector, especially in the sphere of production, is, therefore, widely perceived to be an integral element in the policy reform to restore sustainable – if lower, but consistent with the economy's real resources – economic growth.

In the context of the recent stabilization efforts and structural adjustment in India, the Statement of Industrial Policy (24 July 1991) stated: 'Public enterprises have shown a very low rate of return on capital invested. This has inhibited their ability to regenerate themselves in terms of new investment as well as in technology. The result is that *many of the public enterprises have become a burden rather than being an asset to the Government*' (emphasis added).

The 'Programme for Structural Reform' submitted to the IMF on 11 November 1991 to secure its financial assistance for the ongoing reform process stated:

> India's severely constrained budgetary circumstances create both the need and opportunity for rationalising the scope of public sector activity, and *for placing greater reliance on the private sector for resource mobilisation and investment.* Public enterprises have absorbed large amounts of budgetary support for their expansion or operations, but in many cases they have failed to generate adequate returns on the investment of public money and *contributed significantly to the public sector saving gap and fiscal deficit.* (Reproduced in *Reserve Bank of India Bulletin*, April 1992, p. 789, emphasis added.)

* Along with the usual disclaimers, I would like to thank Kirit S. Parikh, V. K. Ramachandran, Bernard D'Mello, Madhura Swaminathan and Rajeev Gupta for their comments and for their help in writing this chapter. A previous version of this chapter appeared in *Economic and Political Weekly* 28, nos. 3–4 (16–23 January 1993): 105–9.

Such views seem to be shared by many policy advisors as well. In his introduction to a recently published set of essays on the Indian economy, Bimal Jalan (1992) opined that 'the public sector has *become a big drain on the exchequer*' (emphasis added).

Considering the significance of these pronouncements for the policy reforms in India, the underlying premises of the aforementioned views warrant a close empirical scrutiny. A preliminary attempt has been made in Nagaraj (1991) at discerning the long-term trends in the performance of PSEs in general and in their resource mobilization in the '80s in particular, mainly using *National Accounts Statistics* and *Transactions of Public Sector* (CSO 1983) as together they provide a comprehensive and consistent time series since 1960–61, disaggregated by type of institution. The institutional categories used are: administrative departments (ADs), departmental enterprises (DEs) and non-departmental enterprises (NDEs); NDEs are further subdivided into non-departmental financial enterprises (NDFEs) and non-departmental non-financial enterprises (NDNFEs).[1] Our study concerned itself with NDNFEs as they include all the non-financial PSEs in the economy. Although DEs should be strictly included to fully capture the production activities of the government, we have ignored them as they form a relatively small and declining proportion of the total public sector. Moreover, aggregating them with NDNFEs posed some operational difficulties. NDNFEs, nevertheless, form a substantially comprehensive category as they include not only the PSEs owned and managed by the central government but also those of other (administrative) levels of the Indian union which are quantitatively significant, such as the state electricity boards and road transport corporations. Our study showed, among other things, that:

(1) While the share of the public sector in financing the sector's expenditure and investment declined since the mid-1970s (and there was hence an increasingly greater recourse to debt), the contribution of NDEs to public saving has steadily increased. The problem of growing fiscal imbalance, therefore, appears to be on account of the growing expenditure and subsidies of the ADs and not on account of the publicly owned enterprises, ignoring the DEs.
(2) Reversing the trend of about a decade, ending in the late '70s, operating surplus as a proportion of value added in NDEs and the share of NDNFEs in gross domestic saving and their internal resource as a proportion of their gross domestic capital formation have increased steadily in the '80s, although from a very low level.
(3) The observed improvements in resource generation and profitability appear to hold even after excluding the contributions of NDFEs and the petroleum sector.

Admittedly, our earlier exercise has some limitations. It could not reject the hypothesis that the growing fiscal imbalance could be due to the increasing deficit of the public enterprise sector,[2] or trace its financial burden on the budget. Moreover, the study did not isolate the contributions of (i) increases in administered prices and (ii) improvements, if any, in resource utilization to the observed upturn in NDNFEs' resource mobilization in the '80s.

Continuing our enquiry, this note attempts to address the following questions, using more or less the same data sources:

(1) Has the deficit of the public enterprise sector increased over the years? If yes, does it account solely or predominantly for the growing gross fiscal deficit?
(2) Has the financial burden of the NDNFEs on the budget increased over the years?
(3) Is the internal resource generation of NDNFEs lower than that of the private corporate sector in recent years? Has the trend for the former declined while that of the latter increased?
(4) Is the observed improvement in resource generation in the '80s entirely on account of increases in administered prices?

I

Although concern over the PSEs' alleged poor financial performance has been growing, not many serious efforts seem to have been made to quantify and assess the PSEs' contribution to the deteriorating macroeconomic and fiscal imbalances. The International Monetary Fund's attempt (Short 1984) to grapple with the problem is, to our knowledge, a major effort to fill the analytical and empirical gap. In this study, Short estimated the broad dimensions of the size, role and impact of PSEs for selected years to arrive at a significant conclusion that their growing deficit forms an important reason for the stabilization problems of a large number of countries.[3] While the generalization, based on estimates for selected years, could be questioned for lack of required empirical rigour, Short's methodology appears useful for a more careful enquiry. Therefore, using some of his measures, this study traces the macroeconomic impact of PSEs in India. Besides providing evidence on the Indian experience, this attempt could also enable assessment of the validity of Short's generalization with time-series data, albeit limited to one country.

Overall deficits of PSE

These are defined as 'the difference between (1) current plus capital expenditure; and (2) revenue plus receipts of current transfers and of non-governmental capital transfers. Government capital transfers are also conventionally included in receipts in defining the overall deficit' (Short 1984: 144).[4] Figure 11.1 shows the trends in (i) the combined gross fiscal deficit of central and state governments in India and (ii) the overall deficit of the public enterprise sector as a proportion of the gross domestic product at current market prices for the period 1960–61 to 1989–90.[5] The figure suggests, ignoring the observation for 1973–74, a secular deterioration in the fiscal deficit, with some fluctuation from (–)4.3 per cent in 1969–70 to over (–)10 per cent in the latter half of the '80s. Although the overall deficit of PSEs has also deteriorated from (–)1.4 per cent in 1972–73 to (–)3.7 per cent in 1986–87, the trend in it is significantly less sharp than that of the fiscal deficit, as reflected in the sharply widening gap between the two curves. Moreover, a distinct reduction in the PSEs' overall deficit is discernible since 1987–88, taking its level back to

Figure 11.1. Public enterprise sector deficit and fiscal deficit as percentage of GDPmp

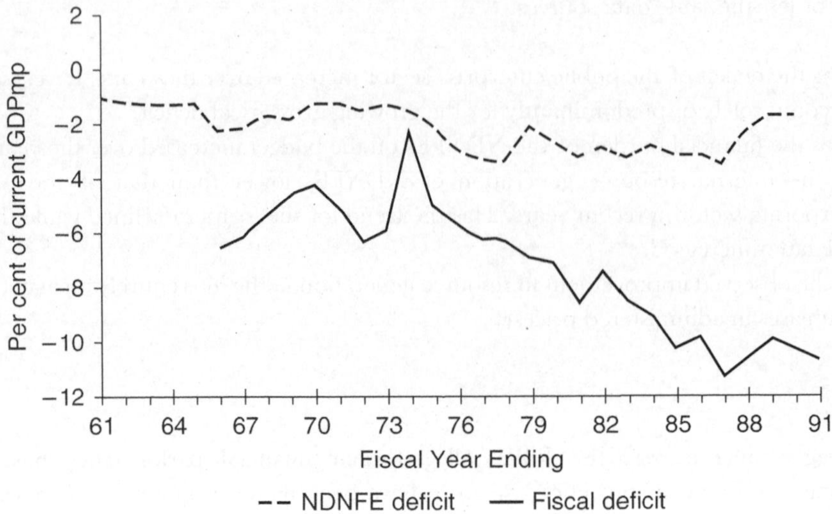

Source: CSO (1983), NAS (various issues), Public Finance (various issues).

Figure 11.2. Budgetary burden of PSEs as percentage of GDPmp

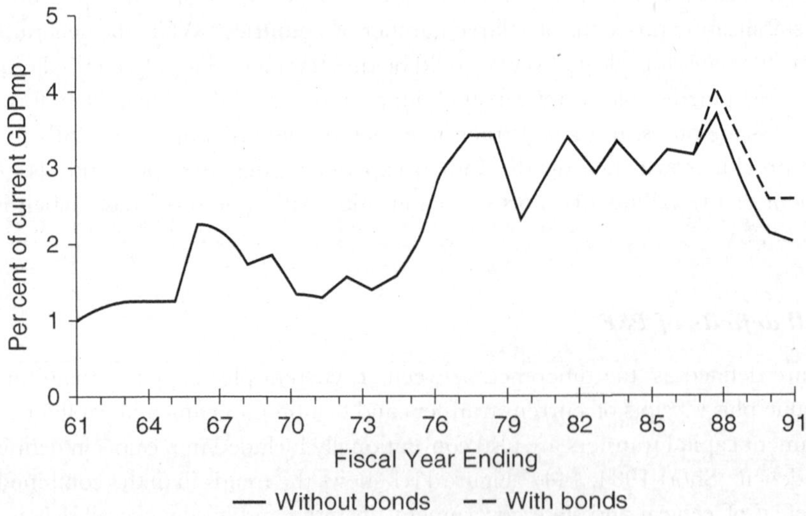

Source: CSO (1983), NAS (various issues).

that during the early '70s. The visibly divergent trends in the two series would seem to indicate that the growing fiscal deficit is perhaps not attributable to the overall deficit of the public enterprise sector.[6]

Admittedly, the foregoing finding does not take into account revenue from the oil account. To the extent it represents a macroeconomic measure of taxation, PSEs' deficits

Figure 11.3. Budgetary burden on PSEs as percentage of PSEs gross expenditure

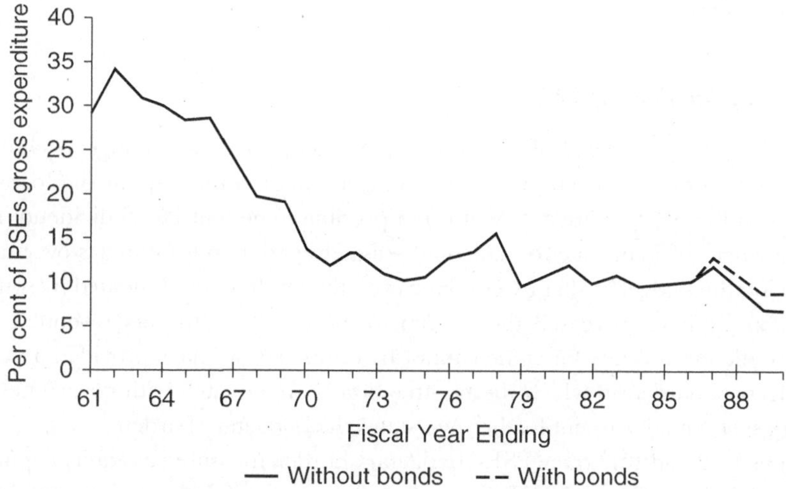

Source: CSO (1983), NAS (various issues).

Figure 11.4. Share of internal resources in public and private corporate sectors

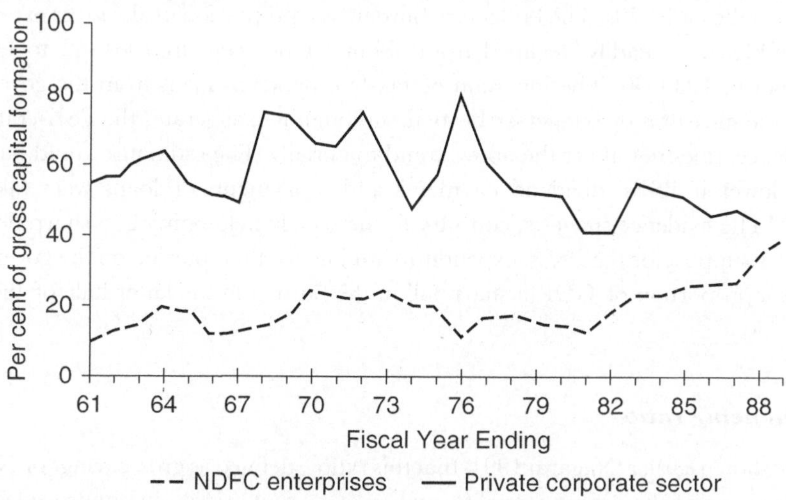

Source: CSO (1983), NAS (various issues), RBI bulletin (various issues).

are understated. However, as shown in our earlier exercise (Nagaraj 1991), profitability of PSEs, even excluding the oil sector, showed a distinct improvement in the '80s. Hence, there is a reasonable basis to argue that the overall deficit of the public enterprise sector is not a reason for the observed deterioration of the fiscal deficit of the economy. This seems to be consistent with our earlier finding (Nagaraj 1991) that the deteriorating fiscal deficit is mainly on account of Ads' declining saving, which has turned negative since the mid-'80s, rather than on account of the alleged decline in surplus generation of the enterprise sector.

'Budgetary burden' of PSEs

Another indicator to assess PSEs' macroeconomic impact is their 'budgetary burden', as defined by Short to be the government's contribution of equity capital and loans, net of dividend and interest payment.[7] As it is not possible to net out PSEs' dividend payment and repayment of loans due to inadequate disaggregation, our estimates overstate their 'burden' on the budget to that extent. However, the tax-free bonds floated by some PSEs since 1986–87 have increased the burden to the extent of the tax revenue foregone. But since the tax revenue foregone cannot be estimated, we have provided a variant of the budgetary burden in which the tax-free bonds are equated with government loans, although such an adjustment further overstates the budgetary burden.

Figures 11.2 and 11.3 trace PSEs' budgetary burden measured as equity capital, loans and net capital transfers to NDNFEs as a proportion of (i) GDP at current market prices and (ii) gross expenditure[8] of NDNFEs, for the period 1960–61 to 1989–90. Budgetary burden as a proportion of GDP increased from 1.4 per cent in 1972–73 to 3.5 per cent in 1977–78 and fluctuated around that level for about a decade. However, a sharp fall in it is discernible since 1986–87 after reaching 3.7 per cent, bringing it back to the level attained in the early '70s. The budgetary burden as a proportion of the gross expenditure of NDNFEs has steadily declined from about 34 per cent in 1961–62 to less than 7 per cent in 1989–90. The inclusion of tax-free bonds as loans from the government in both the measures of budgetary burden, although it exaggerates the PSEs' budgetary dependence, does not affect the above trend materially. The estimates would have been further lower if PSEs' dividend payments and repayments of loans were taken into account. The evidence suggests, contrary to the widely held opinion, a sharp decline in budgetary support for the PSEs' expenditure and hence their burden on the government. Even as a proportion of GDP, a sharp fall in the burden in the latter half of the '80s is undeniable.

Self-financing ratio

We have shown earlier (Nagaraj 1991) that this ratio – defined as gross savings of NDNFEs as a proportion of their gross capital formation at current prices – has improved distinctly in the '80s, thus reducing NDNFEs' dependence on the government for financing their growth. Figure 11.4 compares self-financing ratios for NDNFEs and the private corporate sector[9] for the period 1960–61 to 1988–89. While the ratio for the public enterprise sector shows generally an upward trend, especially in the '80s, almost the obverse seems discernible for the private corporate sector, with the two ratios converging to more or less similar levels of around 40 per cent towards the end of the decade.[10] This finding seems to question the basis for the commitment given to the IMF for placing greater reliance on the private corporate sector for mobilizing resources for industrial growth, as evident from the official memorandum quoted earlier.[11]

Figure 11.5. Index of capacity utilization (weighted by capital employed)

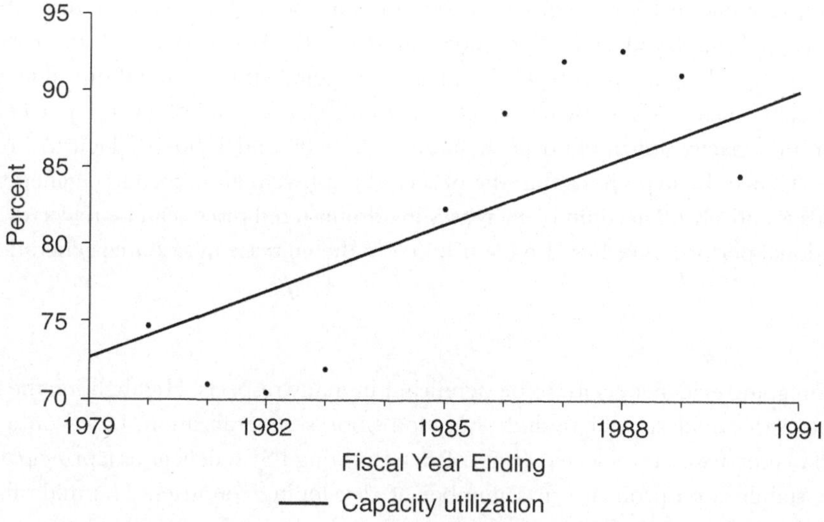

Source: Public Enterprise Surveys.

Figure 11.6. Index of capacity utilization (weighted by value added)

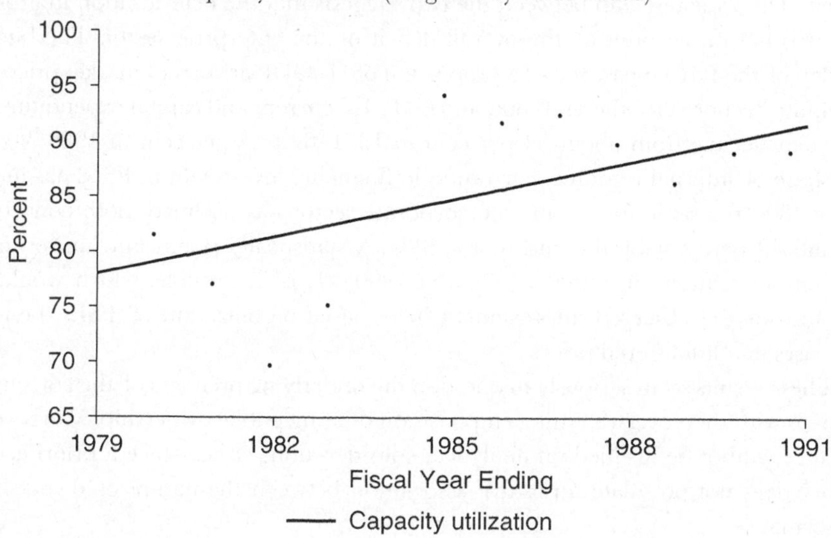

Source: Public Enterprise Surveys.

Trends in capacity utilization in PSEs

Highlighting the significant improvement in surplus generation in the '80s, our earlier study (Nagaraj 1991) admitted its inability, due to the limitations of the data, to ascertain if any part of it was attributable to improvement in resource use. As is widely known, capital or total factor productivity measurements have numerous conceptual, methodological and empirical problems (Griliches 1987). As a measure of operational performance, we have computed a weighted average index of capacity utilization of 14 central public sector enterprises, accounting for about 55 per cent of this subset of PSEs' capital employed and value added in 1990–91. Two variants of the index are computed by taking as weights their shares in (i) capital employed and (ii) value added. The results suggest a statistically significant trend growth rate of over 1 per cent per annum in capacity utilization over the period 1979–80 and 1990–91 (Figures 11.5 and 11.6).[12] Hence the hypothesis that the observed improvement in resource generation in the '80s is entirely on account of increases in administered prices can be rejected. Better operational performance has also contributed to the increase in resource generation.

II

The foregoing evidence seems to be significant in many respects. Highlighting the merits of time-series analysis, our findings question Short's generalization, based on a cross-country comparison for selected years, of deteriorating PSEs' deficits as a principal cause of the stabilization problems in a number of developing countries. The main findings of this study, in terms of the questions posed at the beginning, can be summarized as follows: Although the overall deficit of PSEs has increased marginally over two decades, the increase seems insignificant compared to the sharp deterioration in the gross fiscal deficit. The widening gap between the two suggests that the deterioration in gross fiscal deficit is not on account of the overall deficit of the enterprise sector. The budgetary burden of the PSEs measured as a proportion of (1) GDP at current market prices shows a definite decline since the mid-'80s, and (2) PSEs' current and capital expenditure shows a secular decline from about 34 per cent in 1961–62 to 7 per cent in 1989–90. While the share of internal resource generation in financing investment in PSEs has increased in the '80s, the same for the private corporate sector has declined, both converging to around 40 per cent by the end of the '80s. A statistically significant improvement in capacity utilization, during 1978–79 and 1990–91, is discernible, which would partly account for the observed improvement in resource mobilization of PSEs, besides the increases in administered prices.

These results seem seriously to question the underlying premises of the current policy reforms with their overwhelming emphasis on diluting public ownership. Moreover, such a stance cannot be justified on analytical considerations either, since a priori economic theory does not postulate a positive association between the nature of ownership and performance.[13]

Notes

1 For the definitions of these categories see CSO (1989) and Nagaraj (1990).
2 In this study, the terms PSEs, NDNFEs, public enterprise sector and publicly owned enterprises are used synonymously.
3 To quote Short 1984 (180–81): 'It is clear that the overall deficits of public enterprises are extremely large in many countries. As a result, public enterprises make sizeable demands on governments, bank credit and foreign borrowing. The precise effects of these demands will vary from country to country depending on economic circumstances. However, their large

size strongly suggests that, in many developing countries, public enterprises have been a major cause of stabilisation problems and, as a result, have contributed significantly to inflation and balance of payments difficulties. [...] As a consequence, measures to reduce the overall deficits of public enterprises may often be particularly appropriate for countries facing stabilisation problems.'

4 This measure is arrived at, using the *NAS*, in the following manner: Overall deficit = (total revenue – total expenditure)/GDPmp at current prices. Total revenue is gross output – (net current transfers + net property income + all loans excluding those from government + net capital transfer); and total expenditure is intermediate consumption + compensation to employees + (indirect taxes – subsidies) + direct taxes + gross investment + net acquisition of financial assets.

5 Gross fiscal deficit *is* defined as excess of total government expenditure over revenue receipts and grants as a proportion of GDP at current market prices. As a relatively comprehensive measure we have used consolidated accounts of the centre and the states and union territories rather than that of merely the central government, as is widely done. For justification, see Blejer and Cheasty (1991).

6 The documentation of the overall deficit of PSEs should not be construed as its justification, even if it has not increased significantly over the long period. Such a justification, if any, should be based on the impact of the deficit on the economy's efficiency of resource use and social well-being.

7 However, as Short admits, this is incomplete since it ignores the tax revenue collected from PSEs on the one hand and subsidized credit provided by government financial institutions and purchase preference given to PSEs. As these are difficult to quantify, Short restricts his estimate to the measurable aspects of the budgetary burden.

8 Gross expenditure is defined as the sum of intermediate consumption, compensation to employees and gross investments of NDNFEs.

9 The internal resources of the private corporate sector are defined as retained earning plus depreciation.

10 This result, based on a long time-series analysis, questions the World Bank's (1988) findings of a higher internal resource generation by the private corporate sector based on the average for the first five-year period of the '80s. To quote the report: 'The saving performance of CPEs, which financed only 26 per cent of their investments from internal resources during 1980–85, has been substantially lower than that of the private corporate sector, where internal resources financed 55 per cent of investments on the average during the same period' (World Bank 1988, 2).

11 Perhaps the declining self-financing ratio in the private corporate sector is related to the increasing share of dividends as a proportion of profit before tax, which has gone up from 19.4 per cent in 1980–81 to 27.5 per cent in 1987–88 (RBI 1990). This observation is tentative, subject to closer scrutiny.

12 The estimated trend equations are as follows:

$$\text{Log } Y_1 = 1.89 + 0.007t \qquad R^2 = 0.41,\ N = 13$$
$$(0.0025) \qquad t = 2.77$$
$$\text{Log } Y_2 = 1.88 + 0.006t \qquad R^2 = 0.34,\ N = 13$$
$$(0.0026) \qquad t = 2.38$$

where Y_1 is the weighted average capacity utilization of 14 central government PSEs accounting for 55 per cent of capital employed; and Y_2 is the same with weights being value added. The estimated coefficients of 't' in both the equations are statistically significant at a 95 per cent confidence level.

13 A growing analytical literature questions the widely posited positive relationship between ownership and performance. See Vickers and Yarrow (1991) and Estrin and Perotin (1991). Arguing against premature obituaries of market socialism, Bardhan and Roetner (1992, 101–2) say: 'Our claim is that competitive markets are necessary to achieve an efficient and vigorous economy, but that full-scale private ownership is not necessary for the successful operation of

competition and markets. Contrary to popular impression, this claim has not yet been disproved by either history or economic theory!' Even in management literature one does not find any analytical support for the alleged superior efficiency of private ownership. Reviewing the studies on privatization, Goodman and Loveman (1991, 38) conclude: 'Ownership of a good or service is far less important than the dynamics of the market or institutions that produce it [...] Accountability and consonance with the public's interest should be the guiding lights. They will be found where competition and organizational mechanism ensure that managers do what, we, the owners, want them to do.'

References

Bardhan, P. and J. E. Roemer. 1992. 'Market Socialism: A Case for Rejuvenation'. *Journal of Economic Perspectives* 6, no. 3: 101–16.

Blejer, M. I. and A. Cheasty. 1991. 'The Measurement of Fiscal Deficits: Analytical and Methodological Issues'. *Journal of Economic Literature* 29, no. 4: 1644–78.

Central Statistical Organisation. 1983. *Transactions of Public Sector: 1960 to 1979–80*. New Delhi: Government of India.

_______. 1989. *National Accounts Statistics: Sources and Methods*. New Delhi: Government of India.

Estrin, S. and V. Perotin. 1991. 'Does Ownership Always Matter?' *International Journal of Industrial Organisation* 9, no. 1: 55–72.

Goodman, J. and G. W. Love. 1991. 'Does Privatization Serve the Public Interest?' *Harvard Business Review* 69, no. 6: 26–8, 32, 34–6.

Griliches, Z. 1987. 'Productivity: Measurement Problems'. The New Palgrave Dictionary of Economics, vol. 3, edited by J. Eatwell, M. Milgate and P. Newman. New York: Stockson Press.

Jalan, B., ed. 1992. *The Indian Economy: Problems and Prospects*. New Delhi: Viking Penguin India.

Nagaraj, R. 1991. 'Public Sector Performance in the Eighties: Some Tentative Findings'. *Economic and Political Weekly* 26, no. 50: 2877–83.

Reserve Bank of India. 1990. *Selected Financial and Other Ratios in Public Limited Companies, 1980–81 to 1987–88: All-India*. Vol. 1. New Delhi: Reserve Bank of India.

Short, R. P. 1984. 'The Role of Public Enterprises: An International Comparison', in *Public Enterprise in Mixed Economies: Some Macroeconomic Aspects*, edited by R. H. Floyd, C. S. Gray and R. P. Short. Washington, DC: International Monetary Fund.

Vickers, J. and G. Yarrow. 1991. 'Economic Perspectives on Privatization'. *Journal of Economic Perspectives* 5, no. 2: 111–32.

World Bank. 1988. *India: Review of Public Enterprises—Propositions for Greater Efficiency in the Central Government Public Enterprises* II—Main Text, Report No 7294-IN, October 12. Washington, DC: World Bank.

Chapter 12

LIBERALIZATION, DEMAND AND INDIAN INDUSTRIALIZATION

Surajit Mazumdar

Introduction

While assessing the impact of liberalization measures initiated since 1991 on Indian industry, some historical background is worth keeping in mind. Every major capitalist nation in history has succeeded in attaining that position only on the back of a successful industrialization process. Following the British Industrial Revolution in the latter part of the eighteenth century, the nineteenth and twentieth centuries witnessed a number of industrialization-driven transformations of countries in the developed world, and in the second half of the twentieth century even in parts of the Third World. In the two-and-a-half century world history of modern industrialization, however, the Indian story stands out as a rather distinct one. It has been a long history of industrial development, but one that has failed to eliminate a persistent industrial backwardness.

India was one of the great manufacturing regions of the world of the pre-industrial revolution era, but its initial interaction with modern industry was a negative and destructive one.[1] Colonialism and the forced integration of India into the international economy as an imperial appendage provided the context for its de-industrialization in the nineteenth century. Even before that process was completed, a modern factory sector came into being in the mid-nineteenth century. At that time much of what subsequently came to be called the industrialized world, with a few exceptions such as Britain, was still primarily agrarian. In the 150 years since, India's industrial sector has grown and its structure constantly evolved. Yet India has remained one of the most stunted cases of industrialization, understood as a process of rapid growth of per capita output and an increase in the share of the industrial sector in output and employment at the expense of agriculture.

India's industrialization of course was never a priority for the colonial government. The initial development of modern factory industry for nearly a century therefore lacked the crucial backing of the state. There is therefore nothing particularly surprising in the fact that industrial development in colonial India remained extremely limited. Between 1900–01 and 1946–47, the secondary sector's output grew at barely 1.5 per cent per annum (Sivasubramonian 2000). At independence India remained primarily an agrarian economy, with the agricultural sector accounting for over half the output and three-quarters of total employment. The modern industrial sector, even after nearly a century of development, accounted for less than 7 per cent of total output. It also co-existed with a surviving traditional manufacturing sector (or its modified version) that was as large in terms of its contribution to national output and accounted for a larger share in employment.

The situation did change with independence in 1947, and the pace of industrial growth in the six decades since then has been considerably greater than in the previous half century. The industrial structure, which was initially dominated by light industries like textiles, has over time also become significantly more diversified in nature. However, industrial growth has exhibited persistent instability. The share of industry in output and employment in India has also remained substantially below the levels attained by other countries.

If we were to compare India with the six largest developed countries and the other five amongst the six largest developing ones, apart from itself,[2] then the following emerges. India's per capita gross domestic product (GDP) is the lowest amongst these twelve countries. It is the only one amongst them with more than half its labour force still in agriculture. The share of agriculture in total employment in India is 53 per cent, the next largest share being China's at below 40 per cent. While the share of industry in output in India has not ever crossed 30 per cent, the peak levels of this share for all the other 11 countries has at least touched 35 per cent. In most of them, including the late industrializers, it has exceeded 40 per cent and crossed 48 per cent in China's case. As regards the industrialization of employment, its maximum extent has for most developing countries tended to be lower than what the developed economies had earlier attained. But with just 21.5 per cent of its workforce in the industrial sector, the bulk of it in the unorganized or informal component of industry and a large part in construction, India stands behind even other developing countries on this count.

Industrial Development since 1991: An Assessment

Amongst those with a neoliberal persuasion, India's industrial backwardness is mainly the legacy of the interventionist and protectionist economic policies adopted by the Indian state after independence, and persisted with until the liberalization of the 1990s (Bhagwati 1993, Lal 2008). Strangely, many who argue thus do not similarly relate the limited industrialization of the colonial period to the pursuit of policies such as free trade. Nor do they find any of the roots of India's stunted industrialization in its colonial past. Instead, it is argued, if post-independence planners had not been victims of flawed thinking and had not taken more than four decades to realize their mistake, India would have moved much further on the road to industrialization. In this view, the 'economic reforms' introduced since 1991 liberated the Indian economy from the shackles which prevented it from realizing its industrialization potential. Had this been a correct understanding, the industrialization momentum should have been greatest and most sustained after 1991. However, that has far from been the case.

In the pre-liberalization period two spells of relatively rapid industrial growth – from independence until the mid-1950s and then in the 1980s – were separated by a decade or decade and a half of relative stagnation. As Table 12.1 indicates, the period between 1991 and 2007–08 is also similarly divisible into a sequence of three phases, though of

Table 12.1. Annual average rates of growth industrial real GDP in India at 2004–05 prices (per cent per annum)

Sector	1990–91 to 1996–97	1997–98 to 2002–03	2003–04 to 2007–08	2008–09 to 2011–12
Mining and Quarrying	3.87	4.15	4.73	3.33
Manufacturing	8.10	4.40	9.90	6.79
Electricity, Gas and Water Supply	7.68	4.53	7.60	5.34
Construction	3.37	6.94	12.68	6.53
Industry	6.40	4.97	9.94	6.33

Source: Central Statistical Organization (CSO), National Accounts Statistics (NAS).

shorter durations. The relatively higher growth trend of the 1980s appeared to have initially received a further impetus from liberalization. However, in the second half of the 1990s, industrial growth again slackened for a period of about six years before rebounding from 2003–04 onwards. This growth was, however, again halted in the aftermath of the global economic crisis. The industrial growth rate in 2008–09 was reduced to just 3.8 per cent and manufacturing growth to a mere 2.4 per cent. The recovery that took place subsequently has also proved to be a short-lived one. Industrial growth again remained depressed in 2011–12, being below 4 per cent. Thus, the evidence clearly points to the conclusion that the unstable nature of Indian industrial growth has survived the transition to a liberalized economy.

It can be also seen from Table 12.1 that the movements in the manufacturing sector's growth mirror those of overall industrial growth, as was also the case in the past. Significant changes between industrial growth before and after liberalization have been the following two. There has been a clear deceleration in the growth of the electricity sector after 1991, even more so since the mid-1990s. In contrast, construction activities have experienced accelerated growth since the mid-1990s with this growth being exceptionally high in the period between 2003–04 and 2007–08.

The fluctuating nature of manufacturing growth has meant that despite it touching very high levels in some years, seen over longer time periods its performance appears less spectacular. Indeed, even after close to two decades of liberalization the industrialization performance of the first decade and a half of planning has not been surpassed. This is demonstrated in Figure 12.1 which shows the average rates of growth attained by India's industrial and manufacturing sectors over *all* 15-year periods between 1950–51 and 2010–11 (that is, 15-year periods ending in 1964–65, 1965–66, 1966–67 and so on until 2010–11). The best 15-year periods were clearly right at the beginning, the Nehruvian period or at the end; the latter, however, not better than the former. Moreover, with industrial growth having collapsed thereafter, the curve will be pushed downwards again.

If we look at not merely industrial growth but also the movements in the sector's share in output, the post-liberalization industrial performance appears in an even poorer light. The greatest degree of industrialization of the Indian economy's output again took place in the early years after independence (Figure 12.2). Measured at constant 2004–05

Figure 12.1. Average 15-year rates of growth of industrial and manufacturing GDP at 2004–05 prices (per cent per annum over previous 15 years), 1964–65 to 2010–11

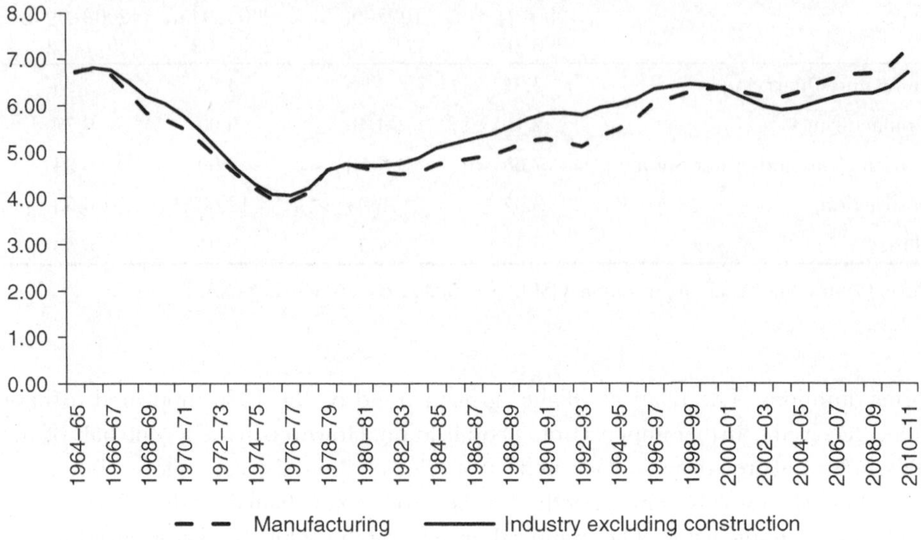

Source: CSO, NAS.

prices, the share of industry in output increased from 16.19 per cent in 1950–51 to 25.01 per cent by 1966–67, an increase of just a little less than 9 percentage points. After that, however, the share went up only very slowly, *and even this has ceased after liberalization*. The 1995–96 share of 28.44 per cent was surpassed only in two years after that, 2006–07 and 2007–08, and that, too, barely. The share of the manufacturing sector in total GDP, as that of industry excluding construction, also peaked in the mid-1990s. The story is more or less the same if data at current prices is used – excluding construction, the peak value of the industrial share in output, as of manufacturing, remains in the mid-1990s.

It may of course be argued that the share of the industrial sector in aggregate GDP has stagnated after liberalization because the overall growth rate has been pushed up by the rapid growth of the services sector, which was not a feature of the early years of planning. What this however amounts to saying is that while the industrial sector was the *leading* growth sector of the economy in the initial years after independence, after liberalization the services sector has decisively displaced it from that position. Why this has happened in an economy not yet fully industrialized is a bigger question that cannot be addressed here. What is noteworthy, however, is the fact that it makes the failure to achieve rapid and sustained industrial growth after liberalization an even more intriguing phenomenon.

The industrial growth performance after liberalization could not surpass that of the Nehru years despite the former period enjoying several advantages over the latter. The rapid pace of industrial expansion in the early years of planning was achieved in a context where a slow-growing and unstable agricultural sector was the largest sector of the economy. It was also twice the size of the industrial sector even in the mid-1960s. At the beginning of the 1990s, however, the size of the agricultural sector relative to industry was much smaller. By the later part of that decade in output terms the size of

Figure 12.2. Share of industrial sector in GDP at 2004–05 prices (percentage), 1950–51 to 2010–11

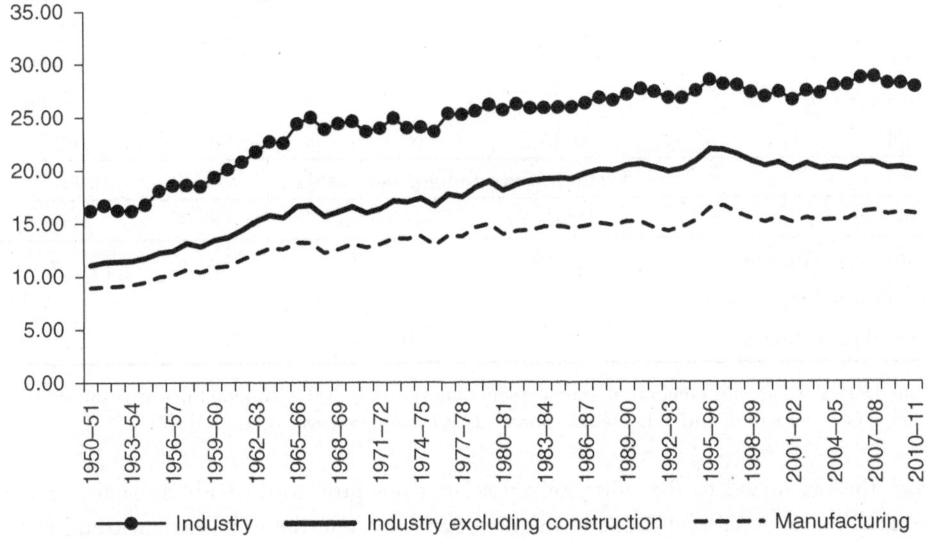

Source: CSO, NAS.

the industrial sector exceeded that of agriculture. In the meantime services had replaced agriculture as the largest sector. With the 1990s the services sector also entered a phase of rapid and sustained growth. This decisive replacement of a slow-growing and highly unstable agriculture by the rapidly and steadily growing services sector, however, neither improved industrial growth levels nor removed their instability. One might also add to this the fact that unlike in the 1950s and 1960s, when India's savings rate averaged around 10 per cent, in the most recent 15-year period savings have remained in excess of 25 per cent of GDP and risen to nearly 37 per cent in 2007–08. More generally, the initial conditions for industrialization at independence, which were a legacy of the colonial era, and the effects of partition were certainly more adverse than those existing after four decades of post-independence industrialization. Seen in the light of all of these, the industrial growth performance of the Indian economy after liberalization must be considered disappointing, far short of what was promised.

The story is even worse when it comes to industrial employment. More than 61 per cent of the industrial sector output and nearly 70 per cent of manufacturing output is produced within the organized segment of industry. Moreover, these shares have been rising. Yet, employment in organized industry has hardly shown any significant long-term increase (Table 12.2). The levels have tended to fluctuate with industrial growth. After some marginal increase in the first half of the 1990s, organized industrial employment actually started *falling* in absolute terms in the second half. Employment growth did revive after 2003–04 but barely compensated for the earlier decline, and this was truer for regular employment (DGET). In other words, over the last two decades, the major part of the incremental industrial employment in India has been provided by the unorganized sector or by casual employment in the organized sector. This shift of industrial employment

Table 12.2. Organized manufacturing sector employment (in lakhs)

Organized Manufacturing Sector Employment (DGET)				
Sector	1991	1997	2004	2010
Public Sector	18.52	16.61	11.89	10.66
Private Sector	44.81	52.39	44.89	51.84
Total	63.33	69	56.78	62.5
Factory Sector Employment (ASI)				
Category	1990–91	1997–98	2003–04	2009–10
Number of Workers	63.07	76.52	60.87	91.58
Number of Employees	81.63	99.98	78.03	117.23
Total Persons Engaged	82.79	100.73	78.70	117.92

Note: DGET = Director General of Employment and Training; ASI = Annual Survey of Industries.
Source: Government of India, Economic Survey; CSO, Annual Survey of Industries.

from the organized to the unorganized sectors has little to do with restrictive labour regulations, as neoliberal thinking might suggest. Rather, the employment trend in the organized sector is almost entirely related to the patterns of technological modernization and structural change in manufacturing activities (Papola 2008, Guha 2008). Moreover, a large part of the growth of employment in the unorganized nonagricultural activities, including in manufacturing, is distress driven (Roy 2008). Even within the organized industrial sector, wage levels have been kept down and the functional distribution of income has moved decisively in favour of profits (Kannan and Raveendran 2009).

Liberalization and the Problem of Industrial Demand

The discussions on Indian industrialization in the past have highlighted a number of mutually related factors acting as long-term constraints on industrial development in India from the demand side. These, rather than state intervention per se, were the true failures of the pre-liberalization economic policy regime. The liberalization measures since 1991 have not redressed these past shortcomings; in many ways they have in fact aggravated the attendant problems. The demand constraint has become consequently the paramount constraint on industrial development after liberalization.

A key structural feature of the Indian economy emphasized in earlier literature was the persistent narrowness of its domestic market (Bagchi 1970; Patnaik 1979, 1984; Nayyar 1977). Apart from its direct effect, this narrowness had a number of additional implications reinforcing the market constraint on industrial growth. It weakened the inducement to invest and had a limited capacity to provide the base on which exports of manufactured products could be developed over time. Dependence of the industrial sector on the demand generated by the relatively well-to-do also made the industrial structure more biased towards relatively capital- and import-intensive production than it need have been.

To a large extent the roots of India's domestic market narrowness lay in the failure to bring about appropriate institutional reform in the agrarian sector. Completing such

Figure 12.3. Share of different expenditure groups in non-food private final consumption expenditure in the domestic market at current prices, 1990–91 to 2009–10 (percentages)

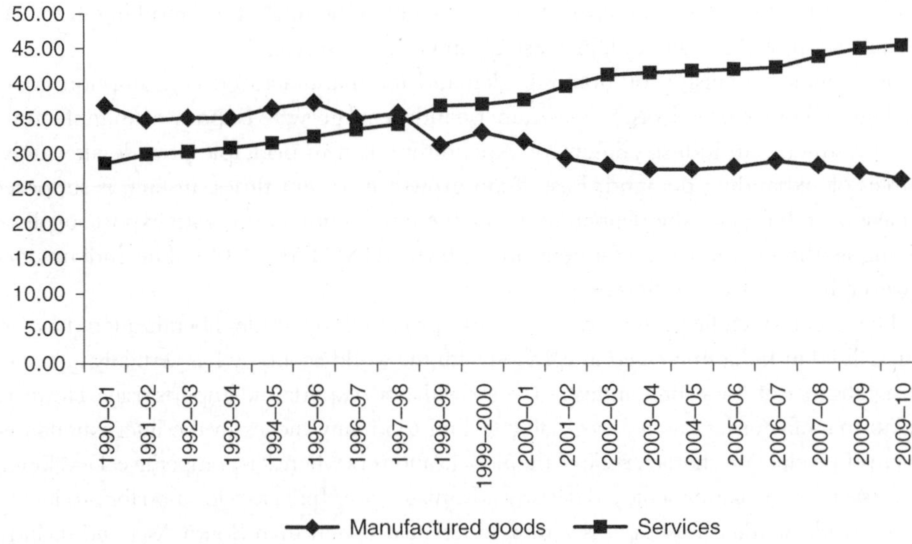

Note: Manufactured goods excludes fuels.
Source: CSO, NAS.

reforms were of course never part of the liberalization programme. Instead, fiscal compression and other measures associated with neoliberal economic policies contributed to the emergence of a deep-rooted agrarian crisis in India since the 1990s (Patnaik 2003, 2007, Reddy and Mishra 2008). Despite the decline in the relative size of the agricultural sector, a large part of the workforce still depends on it for its livelihood. A backward agriculture also holds down the reservation wage in nonagricultural activities. The grim agrarian situation has consequently underlain the stark reality that a large part of the Indian population remains condemned to extremely low levels of income and therefore excluded from the market for industrial products (Sengupta, Kannan and Raveendran 2008, Vakulabharanam 2010). Indeed in India, even food consumption levels have fallen for large segments of the population in comparison to pre-liberalization days.

Liberalization in India, like elsewhere, has thus not only aggravated income inequalities but done so in ways that have particularly reinforced the narrowness of the domestic market. The almost exclusive dependence on upper-income groups for providing an expanding consumption demand has imparted an extremely distorted pattern to this expansion. In a country where penetration levels of manufactured consumption goods are exceptionally low, the consumption demand pattern has been tending towards the post-industrialization pattern, shifting in favour of services. In non-food private final consumption expenditure in the domestic market (excluding that on gross rental and water charges), the share of manufactured commodities has been consistently declining. Only the share of expenditure on manufactured fuels has to an extent been moderating this decline. Since the early 1990s, expenditures on services have increasingly displaced those on manufactured consumer goods (Figure 12.3). In other words, there is a double squeeze on industrial demand related to income distribution trends under liberalization. At one end the holding down of incomes of a large majority of the population keeps them out of the market for manufactured goods. At the other, rising incomes of those already in the market are resulting in further diversification of their demand, increasingly in favour of services.

Inadequate expansion of domestic demand for manufactured consumption goods need not of course be a decisive constraint on industrial growth. Exports of manufactures and investment, an industry-intensive expenditure, can in principle provide alternative sources of expanding demand. East Asian growth in recent times, in fact, is supposed to have been based on the deliberate use of these in combination, with export surpluses serving as the engine for investment and growth (UNCTAD 2008). The Indian story, however, has been very different.

The great manufacturing export success promised by trade liberalization has not materialized in India. Increased integration with the world economy has certainly increased the significance of trade for its industrial sector, with both exports and imports rising. However, Indian manufacturing has not been able to find too many niches in the internationalized system of production characteristic of the globalization era where it is competitive. Developing East Asia in particular has enjoyed decisive advantages over India as a location for production for the world market. East Asia is a more integrated region than South Asia and includes countries with extremely diverse economic conditions. It has a larger population with higher average incomes and therefore a larger regional market. Its industrial base has been more developed and considerably larger and its infrastructure far superior to that of India. India does not even have the advantage that some developing countries in Latin America, North Africa, Eastern Europe and even East Asia have, namely that of geographically proximity to any of the three major developed regions. Indian industry has therefore remained mainly domestic market oriented; been at best a supplementary producer for the world market; and lived under constant threat of competitive imports from East Asia.

India's manufactured exports did experience somewhat rapid growth between the beginning of the current century and the breaking out of the global crisis. This export surge was also not primarily driven by items like textiles and garments, leather products, and gems and jewellery which had traditionally dominated Indian manufactured exports. Instead, relatively more capital-intensive chemicals, engineering products (iron and steel, transport equipment, machinery and instruments), and petroleum products played a major role. The consequent shift in the composition of Indian exports of course runs contrary to the neoliberal predictions, based on the comparative advantage principle, of labour-intensive exports leading Indian exports. In addition, in many of the products leading the export expansion, India was a relatively marginal exporter amongst many developing countries experiencing similar growth of their exports. Finally, India's imports eventually outpaced exports even in the case of these very same categories of products.

The export surge after 2000–01 and the changes in the composition of manufactured exports, while important for the growth of this period, were not therefore indications of India achieving any significant export breakthrough. The most spectacular feature of India's merchandise trade account in recent times, in fact, has been the burgeoning of the trade deficit to unprecedented levels (Figure 12.4). It touched 7.4 per cent of GDP in 2007–08 and then nearly 10 per cent in 2008–09 before moderating a little in

Figure 12.4. India's trade deficit as a ratio of GDP (per cent), 1990–91 to 2010–11

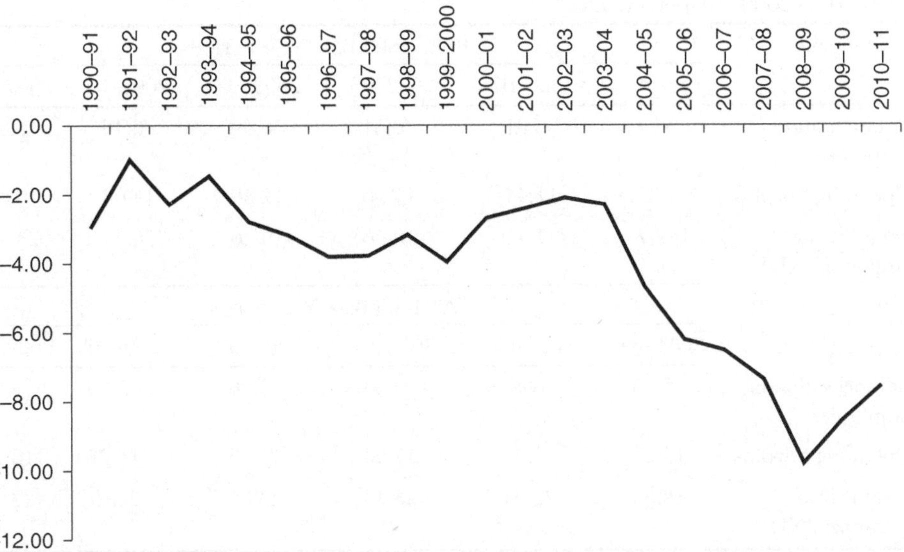

Source: Reserve Bank of India, Handbook of Statistics on the Indian Economy, 2011.

Figure 12.5. India's imports as a percentage of GDP, 1990–91 to 2010–11

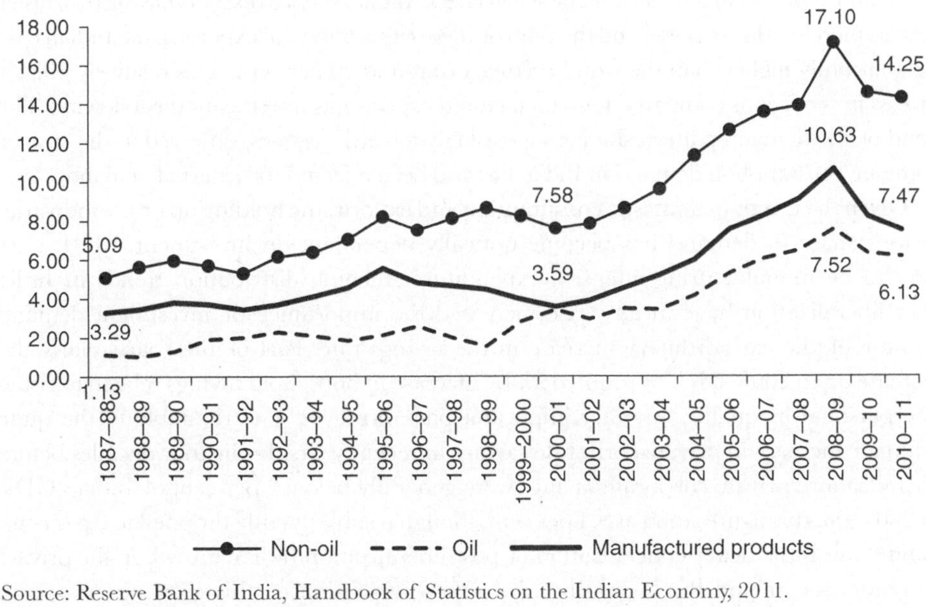

Source: Reserve Bank of India, Handbook of Statistics on the Indian Economy, 2011.

the background of an economic slowdown. Rather than the traditional deficit in India's oil trade, non-oil imports and particularly those of manufactured goods played the most important role in the widening of the trade deficit (Figure 12.5).

Compared to the performance in manufactured exports, India has, however, done relatively better in services exports. These exports and large flows of remittances have

Table 12.3. Shares of private organized sector NDP and its components in aggregate NDP, 1990–91 to 2009–10 (percentages)

Component	1999–2000 Base Year Series					
	1990–91	1996–97	2002–03	2003–04	2004–05	2007–08
Compensation of Employees	7.72	6.01	6.61	6.69	6.46	6.82
Operating Surplus	6.35	11.44	11.96	12.56	14.08	16.62
Total Private Organized NDP	14.07	17.45	18.56	19.26	20.54	23.44
	2004–05 Base Year Series					
	2004–05	2005–06	2006–07	2007–08	2008–09	2009–10
Compensation of Employees	6.35	6.48	5.93	5.80	5.70	5.55
Operating Surplus	13.21	15.55	17.24	17.85	17.27	16.78
Total Private Organized NDP	19.55	22.04	23.16	23.65	22.97	22.32

Source: CSO, NAS.

primarily generated an invisible surplus that has partially counteracted the growing trade deficit and kept the current account deficit in check. India's services exports have grown faster than its merchandise exports, and the ratio of these exports to total exports in the Indian case is significantly higher than the world average of around 20 per cent. This relatively greater success in services as compared to manufactured exports has thus meant the following. The trend of the demand pattern shifting increasingly towards services, observed in the case of domestic consumption demand in India, has also been a feature of external demand.

Given the trends in domestic consumption and exports, the holding up of the industrial sector's share in demand has become critically dependent on investment, which does tend to be manufacturing-intensive expenditure. Income distribution trends in India after liberalization have in any case increased the importance of investment demand because of the extraordinary increase in the savings rate. Part of this, particularly the increase up to 2003–04, is accounted for by increase in household savings related to rising interpersonal inequality. Another important part, however, is attributable to the quite dramatic increase in private corporate savings in recent years. In the four decades before liberalization, private corporate savings were generally below 2 per cent of India's GDP. In 2007–08, this figure stood at 9.4 per cent, though it subsequently dropped to 8 per cent. Behind this is the heavy concentration of post-liberalization Indian growth in the private corporate sector and the increasing tilt in the distribution of this growing income in favour of profits. These are indicated in Table 12.3, which shows the trends in the share of the private organized sector and its components in aggregate NDP. The first of these went up from a little over 14 per cent in 1990–91 to over 23 per cent by 2007–08. Moreover, this entire increase went into surplus incomes, with the share of operating surplus in private organized NDP increasing from just above 45 per cent in 1990–91 to over 75 per cent in 2009–10.

Table 12.4. Annual rates of growth of real private corporate and registered manufacturing gross fixed capital formation (per cent per annum)

At 1993–94 Prices			At 1999–2000 Prices		
Period	Registered Manufacturing	Private Corporate Sector	Period	Registered Manufacturing	Private Corporate Sector
1990–91 to 1996–97	19.5	21.94	1999–2000 to 2002–03	–4.91	–2.02
1996–97 to 2002–03	–6.06	–3.75	2002–03 to 2007–08	28.51	31.39

Source: CSO, NAS.

Figure 12.6. Private corporate and registered manufacturing GFCF at 2004–05 prices, 2007–08 to 2010–11 (rupees crore)

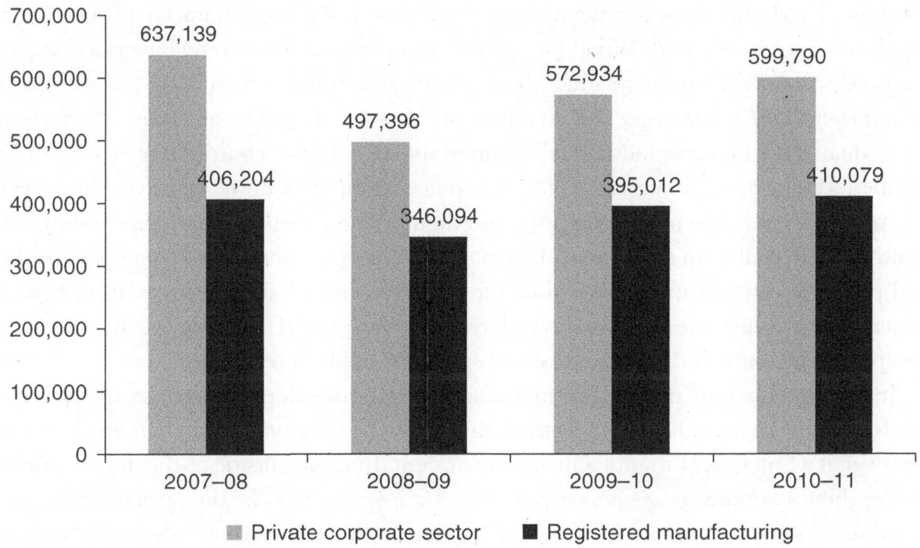

Source: CSO, NAS.

Along with the rise in the savings rate, the investment rate has also gone up. Indeed, in the most recent phase of very high growth in India, investment was the single most important driver of domestic demand growth. From a little under 24 per cent in 2002–03, the gross fixed capital formation to GDP ratio climbed to nearly 33 per cent by 2007–08 before declining a little thereafter. The main agency for this rapid growth of investment was the private corporate sector. Private corporate investment, however, has exhibited extreme instability in the post-liberalization period, producing instability also in aggregate investment. After increasing rapidly in the initial half-decade following liberalization, real private corporate fixed capital formation levels collapsed after 1996–97. They then revived only after 2002–03 to grow at an even faster pace than in the previous boom.

Two notable correlations with the sharp fluctuations in corporate investment have been of capital formation in the organized manufacturing sector (Table 12.4) and of industrial growth. The former reflects the facts that a significant part of corporate investment tends to go into the manufacturing sector, and that the bulk of the investment in organized manufacturing is undertaken by private corporate firms. The second correlation highlights the importance of investment for industrial demand. It indicates that investment fluctuations and that too within the manufacturing sector have been important in producing the fluctuations in demand causing instability of industrial growth. These two correlations have also been exhibited in the period after the global crisis erupted – both corporate and manufacturing investment growth collapsed a second time around (Figure 12.6) even as industrial growth slipped.

An important strand in the literature on Indian industrialization has always emphasized the importance of public investment for 'crowding-in' private investment and industrial growth. The failure to sustain the growth of public investment after the mid-1960s was seen as an important factor behind the subsequent industrial stagnation. Public investment growth was considered important for two reasons flowing from the dual character of investment. It was necessary to expand demand for private industry and for eliminating critical gaps in the production structure in spheres where private investment left to itself was unlikely to be sufficient. One could argue that in a liberalized economy, public investment performing these dual roles becomes additionally important as a factor contributing to enhancing competitiveness of the industrial sector. In the neoliberal view, however, private investment can play the same role more efficiently, and high public investment and expenditure only crowds out such efficient investment. This view, of course, has dominated after liberalization, and public investment has been one of the major victims of fiscal conservatism. Both its pattern and the fluctuations it has shown have, however, proved the fallacy of the contention that private investment can be a proper substitute for public investment.

Investment creating demand for manufactured products does not necessarily have to be investment in the manufacturing sector. The extent of capacity creation in manufacturing, however, is a function of manufacturing investment. In India outside of the manufacturing sector, there certainly exists a vast potential for investment – in the agricultural sector, in infrastructure, as well as in the social sector. A public investment driven investment process could channel investment in these directions. But liberalization has privileged the private sector over the state as the agency for channelling investible resources to productive investments, and within the private sector too it has similarly privileged the private corporate sector over other private units in the household sector. The private corporate sector is not an equally effective agency for investments in different sectors and of different kinds. In comparison to others, however, manufacturing represents one of the most natural outlets for private corporate investment. In addition, relative to industry and manufacturing, the services that have been growing rapidly have very limited capacity to absorb investment given their relatively low capital requirement per unit of output.

Thus ascendancy of the private corporate sector in the Indian economy's investment process has tended to bias that process towards the manufacturing sector. On the other hand, every other component of demand is becoming increasingly biased towards services. This has resulted in an investment–growth asymmetry, a tendency towards a mismatch between the investment pattern and the growth pattern (Mazumdar 2008). In the 1980s, the organized manufacturing sector accounted for less than 19 per cent of the increase in the Indian economy's fixed capital stock[3] and contributed nearly 13 per cent of the growth in total output. Between 1990–91 and 2007–08, on the other hand, its share in the increase in fixed capital stock *increased* to nearly 30 per cent while its contribution to increase in output *fell* below 9 per cent. Capital–output ratios in Indian industry have increased significantly after liberalization, reversing the trend of decline in the 1980s. The contribution of services to aggregate growth, on the other hand, increased from 46 per cent in the 1980s to over 60 per cent in the period after 1991 without any sharp increase in its share in the increase in fixed capital. The private corporate sector itself has been at the very centre of this asymmetry, and its enlarged share in the economy's production has virtually entirely been contributed by services, and of late also construction, but not manufacturing.

The presence of the investment–growth asymmetry makes any process of rapid growth of private corporate investment in India inherently unsustainable. Rapid capital accumulation by the corporate sector when it happens would mean rapid expansion of manufacturing capacity. This would tend to outstrip demand expansion because in the aggregate demand for manufactured products, private corporate capital formation is only one part and has to counter the demand bias in favour of services from all other sources. On the capacity creation side, however, it is the most important determinant of the pace. No matter what 'favourable' climate may exist or be created for inducing private corporate investment in the economy, as long as the investment–growth asymmetry remains a structural feature of the Indian economy, sustained growth of investment and industrial growth based on that would be impossible.

The investment–growth asymmetry has already generated one episode of collapse of investment in the 1990s. A set of favourable conditions, many external, may have revived corporate investment from 2003–04. However, even without the global crisis the sustenance of the positive investment climate was unlikely. This is because the pace of investment in the manufacturing sector again was again outstripping demand growth. The sharp rise in the manufacturing investment to GDP ratio was not matched by a corresponding increase in the importance of the manufacturing sector's share in total output. It has in fact been pointed out that both investment and industrial growth started slowing down even before the global crisis erupted in full force (Rakshit 2009; Ghosh and Chandrasekhar 2009). In other words, the investment collapse that coincided with the crisis was something that was in any case inevitable.

Conclusion

Contrary to the claims made by its proponents, industrial deregulation and trade liberalization have failed to resolve the fundamental problems underlying India's stunted industrialization. Liberalization of the Indian economy has not been accompanied by a virtuous circle of sustained growth of industrial output, investment and employment. On the contrary, liberalization has reinforced the market constraint that has plagued its industrial sector throughout the period after independence. This has resulted in an industrial development pattern characterized by instability in growth, increasing capital intensity but with declining capital productivity, and absence of employment generation. India under liberalization may have therefore experienced growth, primarily through its services sector, but it has ceased to industrialize in the usual sense of the term. Unless special conditions keep stimulating private investment from time to time, unstable industrial growth could potentially even give way to long-term industrial stagnation and de-industrialization. If such eventualities are to be avoided and industrial development is to be put on a stable footing, then a paradigm shift in state industrial policy has to happen because the measures necessary are incompatible with the designated role of the state in a liberal policy regime. Income distribution patterns have to be altered so that the market for manufactured products is widened. Investment in agriculture and other sectors like infrastructure that could both absorb capital as well as expand the market for manufactured products has to be promoted. A lot of this restructuring of the investment pattern depends on there being appropriate growth of public investment. Sustained public investment in any case would generate stability in investment and growth. Public investment in economic and social infrastructure could also contribute to increasing the international competitiveness of Indian manufactured products and generate increases in their exports. But, each of these sets of measures involves a more 'activist' state of a kind that is anathema to neoliberalism.

Notes

1 Even if these are considered only very broadly indicative of what really happened, Paul Bairoch's estimates (cited in Simmons 1985) bring out India's industrial regression during this period. According to these estimates, India's share in world manufacturing production fell from just under 20 per cent at the beginning of the century (it was nearly 25 per cent in 1750) to under 2 per cent by the end. During this period, India's per capita industrialization level fell to a sixth of its original level.

2 These 11 countries are: The United States, Japan, the United Kingdom, Germany, Italy and France (developed); and China, Brazil, Mexico, South Korea and Indonesia (developing).

3 This is excluding the capital stock in real estate and dwellings.

References

Ahluwalia, I. J. 1985. *Industrial Growth in India: Stagnation Since the Mid-Sixties*, Delhi: Oxford University Press.

Babu, M. S. 2005. 'India's Recent Economic Growth: Some Limits and Limitations'. *Economic and Political Weekly* 40, no. 30: 3249–52.

Bagchi, A. K. 1970. 'Long-Term Constraints on India's Industrial Growth'. In *Economic Development in South Asia* edited by E. A. G. Robinson and M. Kidron. London and Basingstoke: Macmillan, St. Martin's Press.

Balakrishnan, P. and M. S. Babu. 2003. 'Growth and Distribution in Indian Industry in the Nineties'. *Economic and Political Weekly* 38, no. 38: 3997–9, 4001–5.

Bhagwati, J. 1993. *India in Transition: Freeing the Economy*. Oxford: Clarendon Press.

Byres, T. J., ed. 1999. *The Indian Economy, Major Debates since Independence*. New Delhi: Oxford University Press.

Chandrasekhar, C. P. 2003. 'Neo-Liberal Reform and Industrial Growth: Towards Revival or Recession?' *Social Scientist* 32, nos. 11–12: 3–22.

Chandrasekhar, C. P. and J. Ghosh. 2002. *The Market That Failed: Neoliberal Economic Reforms in India.* 2nd ed. New Delhi: LeftWord Books.

Ghosh, J. and C. P. Chandrasekhar. 2009. 'The Costs of 'Coupling': The Global Crisis and the Indian Economy'. *Cambridge Journal of Economics* 33, no. 4: 725–39.

Guha, A. 2008. 'Evolution of Indian Organised Manufacturing Industrial Structure: A Comparison between Liberalised and Pre-Liberalised Regimes'. In *Industrial Development and Globalisation: Essays in Honour of Professor S. K. Goyal* edited by S. R. Hashim, K. S. Chalapati Rao, K. V. K. Ranganathan and M. R. Murthy. New Delhi: Academic Foundation, 63–88.

Kannan, K. P. and G. Raveendran. 2009. 'Growth Sans Employment: A Quarter Century of Jobless Growth in India's Organised Manufacturing'. *Economic and Political Weekly* 44, no. 10: 80–91.

Lal, D. 2008. 'An Indian Economic Miracle?' *Cato Journal* 28 (Winter), 11–33.

Mazumdar, S. 2008. 'Investment and Growth in India under Liberalization: Asymmetries and Instabilities'. *Economic and Political Weekly* 43, no. 49: 68–77.

Nagaraj, R. 2003. 'Industrial Policy and Performance since 1980: Which Way Now?' *Economic and Political Weekly* 38, no. 35: 3707–15.

Nayyar, D. 1978. 'Industrial Development in India: Some Reflections on Growth or Stagnation'. *Economic and Political Weekly* 13, no. 31–3: 1265–7, 1269, 1271, 1273, 1275–8. Reprinted in Nayyar (1994), 219–43.

Nayyar, D., ed. 1994. *Industrial Growth and Stagnation: The Debate in India.* Bombay: Oxford University Press for Sameeksha Trust.

Papola, T. S. 2008. 'Industry and Employment: Dissecting Recent Indian Experience'. In *Industrial Development and Globalisation: Essays in Honour of Professor S. K. Goyal* edited by S. R. Hashim, K. S. Chalapati Rao, K. V. K. Ranganathan and M. R. Murthy. New Delhi: Academic Foundation, 111–32.

Patnaik, P. 1979. 'Industrial Development in India since Independence'. *Social Scientist* 7, no. 11: 3–19.

_______. 1984. 'The Market Question and Capitalist Development in India'. *Economic and Political Weekly* 19, 31: 1251–60.

Patnaik, U. 2003. 'Food Stocks and Hunger: The Causes of Agrarian Distress'. *Social Scientist* 31, nos. 7–8: 15–41.

_______. 2007. 'Neoliberalism and Rural Poverty in India'. *Economic and Political Weekly* 42, no. 30: 3132–50.

Rakshit, M. 2009. 'India amidst the Global Crisis'. *Economic and Political Weekly* 44, no. 13: 94–106.

Reddy, D. N. and S. Mishra. 2008. 'Crisis in Agriculture and Rural Distress in Post-Reform India'. In *India Development Report 2008* edited by R. Radhakrishna. New Delhi: Oxford University Press, 40–53.

Roy, S. 2008. 'Structural Change in Employment in India since 1980: How Lewisian Is It?' *Social Scientist* 36, nos. 11–12: 47–68.

Sengupta, A., K. P. Kannan and G. Raveendran. 2008. 'India's Common People: Who Are They, How Many Are They and How Do They Live? *Economic and Political Weekly* 43, no. 11: 49–63.

Simmons, C. 1985. '"De-Industrialization", Industrialization and the Indian Economy, c. 1850–1947'. *Modern Asian Studies* 19, no. 3: 593–622.

Sivasubramonian, S. 2000. *The National Income of India in the Twentieth Century.* New Delhi: Oxford University Press.

UNCTAD. 2008. *Trade and Development Report: Commodity Prices, Capital Flows and the Financing of Investment.* New York and Geneva: United Nations.

Vakulabharanam, V. 2010. 'Does Class Matter? Class Structure and Worsening Inequality in India'. *Economic and Political Weekly* 45, no. 29: 67–76.

Chapter 13

ON FISCAL DEFICIT, INTEREST RATE AND CROWDING-OUT*

Surajit Das

Introduction

Today's world economy is characterized by a demand-constrained situation in general. Not only the developing world but also the developed world is facing the problem of lack of aggregate demand, which is being manifested in the form of coexistence of large-scale involuntary unemployment and underemployment along with unutilized capacity all over the globe. The level of actual output that is being produced is well below the level of potential output. This is so not because of a shortage of labourers but because of the fact that there is not enough demand in the market for that output to be sold and profit to be realized. In short, present day capitalism is suffering from an acute demand problem. Keynes (1936, 129) argued that a policy of 'digging holes and filling them up' can be beneficial for a demand-constrained economy characterized by large involuntary unemployment. The fiscal deficit always finances itself in the sense that it always generates an equal amount of extra net import plus private savings in excess of private investment in the ex post situation. But the expansionary government policy even under a demand-constrained situation is argued to be detrimental because the higher fiscal deficit would necessarily crowd out private investment by increasing the real rate of interest in the economy.

The objective of this particular work is to discuss, both theoretically and with support of empirical evidence, whether or not there is any necessary danger of crowding-out of private investment through increase in interest rate as an inevitable consequence of expansionary fiscal policy by deficit financing in an economy operating well below the full-employment level. The plan of this chapter is as follows. We shall examine the chronological and sequential development of the theory and the problematic aspects of it in the second section. Throughout this section, we assume that the price level is constant so that the nominal and the real rates of interest are the same if not specified otherwise. In the third section, we will analyse the available empirical evidence from the Indian economy on the relationship between the fiscal deficit to GDP ratio and real

---

* Parts of this chapter appeared in an earlier version in the MPhil dissertation submitted at Jawaharlal Nehru University, New Delhi, 2002.

Figure 13.1. Savings–investment identity and rate of interest

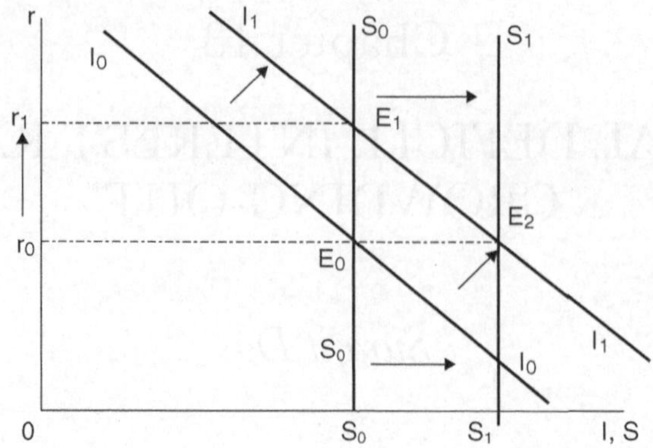

interest rate for the period from 1980–81 to 2006–07 considering various interest rates such as deposit rates of different maturity period, lending rates, yields on government bonds, etc. deflated by the GDP deflator of respective years. The fourth section deals with a similar kind of data analysis for 82 countries around the world and considering five kinds of interest rates, namely real government bond yields, treasury bill rates, deposit rates, lending rates and the money market rate of interest, for the period 1981 to 2005. This work ends with some concluding remarks.

Theoretical Overview

The debate regarding the influence of fiscal deficit on interest rates is not a new debate at all – it started from the days of Great Depression of the 1930s when people started talking about raising the level of output and employment by expansionary fiscal policy or demand management policies in general. To discuss different versions of the widely believed theory of crowding-out and also the contrary arguments, let us first consider the treasury view (Kahn 1972) or the fixed-pool-of-savings view. In pre-Keynesian literature, the rate of interest was believed to be determined by the savings–investment equality. First, we consider the simple case where the savings do not depend upon the rate of interest. If the investment demand increases due to increased government investment expenditure (by, say, deficit financing) then the rate of interest will adjust in such a way that full crowding-out takes place and ex post savings–investment identity is maintained. In other words, if savings cannot increase with an increase in investment demand, the increased investment demand will be curtailed through an increase in the rate of interest to maintain the ex post identity between savings and investment.

In Figure 13.1, the initial rate of interest r_0 is determined by the equality (at point E_0) between savings (S_0S_0) and investment (I_0I_0). Now, if the government investment increases by deficit financing, the negatively sloped investment curve shifts rightward (from I_0I_0 to I_1I_1), and the new intersection point (E_1) of the investment and savings schedules is at a higher level of rate of interest (r_1). However, at any given nominal interest rate the savings curve can also shift rightward from its initial position (i.e. from S_0S_0 to S_1S_1) through income adjustment. If the income adjustment takes the form exclusively of output adjustment, with no change in price in terms of the 'wage unit', then the real interest rate need not be affected at all. Even if price adjustment takes place instead of output adjustment, investment generates an equal amount of savings at any given interest rate (say r_0) through forced savings. The equilibrium point, that is, the intersection of investment and savings curves, can shift from E_0 to E_2 and both ex post investment and savings can come to equality at a higher level as compared to the initial situation at any given r_0.

The dependence of savings on income was never recognized by the 'treasury view'. If we restate this view taking into account the dependence of the level of savings on the level of income, it would be as follows: for any given level of real income (y) there would be an amount of real savings (s = private savings + government savings), which is a function of income, for any given distribution of income and rate of taxation. If, according to this doctrine, government investment increases, the private investment is bound to fall by the real rate of interest adjustment to maintain the ex post savings–investment identity because the savings out of the given income cannot increase any more. Let the given level of output be y* and the private savings and government savings (i.e. tax revenue net of government consumption) generated from that level of income be s_p^* and s_g^* respectively. Now, if private investment is denoted by I_P and government investment by I_g then in a simple closed economy framework the ex post identity $s_p^* + s_g^* \equiv I_p + I_g$ must hold. Since, according to the treasury view, the left-hand side of the equation is constant, on the right-hand side if I_g component rises, then I_p has to be lower by an exactly equal amount because the sum of these two has to remain constant. (It is a different matter that even under full employment savings could rise through forced savings as a result of price adjustment relative to money wages due to increased investment demand.) From the above argument it follows that if the fiscal deficit for financing government investment rises, the rate of interest in the economy would necessarily rise to crowd out private investment (exactly the same conclusion would follow if the fiscal deficit rises for financing government consumption as well, with private savings remaining unchanged).

However, in reality the aggregate level of private (household + corporate) savings, that is, GDS less the government savings in an economy, increases with increase in the aggregate level of activity. If we look at the empirical evidence from India, for example, for 1950–51 to 2006–07 we see that (with $R^2 = 0.73$ and the residual stationary),

$$\ln(\text{FD of Pvt GDS}) = -13.22 + 1.99 \ln(\text{FD of real GDP}) + 0.11 \text{ inflation}$$
$$(-6.91) \qquad (10.86) \qquad (2.58)$$

FD ⇒ First Difference, ln ⇒ logarithm and Real GDP is GDP at constant prices.

But then, why is the theory propounded as if the level of income is given? This is because there is an underlying assumption that the economy is at full employment, which determines the fixed pool of savings. Even the possibility of forced savings under a full-employment situation through price adjustment is also ruled out. That is precisely why the savings schedule is vertical and any rise in investment demand does not lead to

Figure 13.2. Partial crowding-out and rate of interest determination

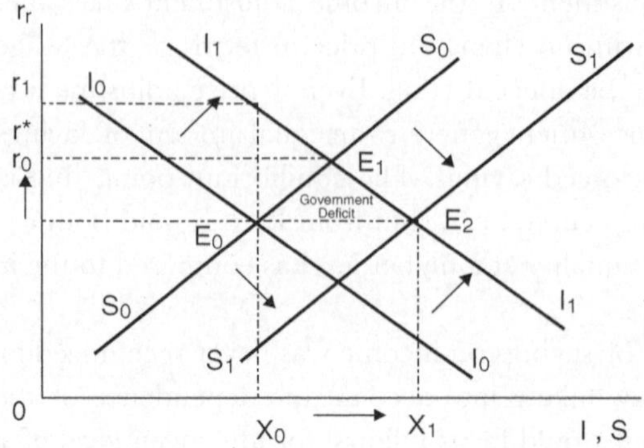

increased ex post investment and savings but raises the rate of interest (from r_0 to r_1). In today's world, existence of large-scale involuntary unemployment is an undeniable fact. Therefore, it is inappropriate to use theories assuming full employment (directly or indirectly) to draw policy conclusions. If there is an increase in the autonomous investment demand, output adjustment is perfectly possible through the Keynes–Kahn multiplier in the context of a demand-constrained economy. Even in a full-employment situation, aggregate investment would always generate its equal amount of savings in an ex-post situation through price adjustment and forced savings as opposed to the fixed-pool-of-savings view.

There is in fact no reason to believe that if the government raises demand by deficit financing, then there won't be any output adjustment. With the rise in demand, both income and savings increase through various rounds of the multiplier. In fact, in a demand-constrained economy which is operating well below full employment, if the aggregate demand rises, the aggregate supply would also increase until the two (measured in 'wage units') would be exactly equal. To put it differently, the process of increase in income and employment due to increase in demand would continue until an amount of savings is generated which is exactly equal to the increase in home and foreign investment. That means, in fact, 'investment determines savings', which is diametrically opposite to the position taken by the treasury view that 'savings determine investment'. Hence a fiscal deficit always finances itself in the sense that it generates an equal amount of 'excess private savings'; that is, savings in private hands in excess of private investment at any given level of the interest rate. Therefore, there is no valid reason to believe that increased government investment financed by borrowing would necessarily increase the real rate of interest and cause crowding-out of private investors to maintain ex post savings–investment identity.

Another, slightly more sophisticated, version of the 'treasury view' states that investment and savings are both functions of the real rate of interest (where $dI(r)/dr<0$ and $dS(r)/dr>0$). Now if aggregate investment demand increases due to, say, increase in government investment through deficit financing, then the rate of interest would increase, but there wouldn't be full crowding-out because the aggregate savings would also increase due to increase in rate of interest (since $dS(r)/dr>0$). As a result of this, the rate of interest would not increase to such a level that full crowding-out took place, but both ex post investment and savings would be higher and the rate of interest would also increase. This is called the theory of partial crowding-out due to increase in government investment financed by a fiscal deficit (via a higher real rate of interest).

Graphically, if the rate of interest is r_o – determined by the intersection of negatively sloped investment (I_oI_o) and positively sloped savings (S_0S_0) curves (at E_o), then due to increase in government investment financed by fiscal deficit, the I_oI_o curve shifts upward – right to I_1I_1 (say). The new interest rate (at E_1) would be r*, which is higher than r_o but lower than r_1 (i.e. the rate of interest corresponding to full crowding-out). This version of treasury view also says that if government investment increases, the rate of interest would necessarily rise and in turn cause crowding-out (though partial). But, in the above diagram, it is perfectly possible that the savings curve can shift rightward (from S_0S_0 to S_1S_1) with the increase in government investment (i.e. shift of investment curve from I_0I_0 to I_1I_1) at any given interest rate r_0. The initial savings–investment equality is at point E_o and the after-adjustment equality can be at point E_2, which implies that the increased aggregate investment demand results in both the ex post investment and savings increasing from X_0 to X_1 at any given rate of interest (r_0).

While this view allows savings to depend on the interest rate, it is still pre-Keynesian in the sense that it takes the level of income as given. However, once again, in the context of a demand-constrained economy, there is no valid reason to believe that increased government investment financed by borrowing would necessarily increase real rate of interest and cause crowding-out (not even partially) of private investors to maintain ex post savings–investment identity. Even if we believe that the rate of interest affects, *ceteris paribus* the level of savings, then it is obvious that the aggregate savings can also rise with a rise in aggregate investment demand through an increase in the level of activity even if the interest rate is kept unchanged. As savings are a positive function of income, if exclusive output adjustment takes place with an increase in aggregate demand (leaving prices in terms of the 'wage unit' unchanged), which is perfectly possible in an economy operating well below full employment, then savings will increase and ex post savings–investment identity can be attained at any particular real rate of interest in the economy. In fact, even in case of full employment, instead of output adjustment, price adjustment takes place; an autonomous increase in the level of aggregate investment demand reduces the real income of wage earners and increases the real profit share. Since a larger proportion is saved out of profit as compared to wages, the aggregate savings rises – which is called 'forced savings' in the literature of economics. The point is that the ex post aggregate savings can become equal to aggregate investment demand without increasing the real rate of interest. Therefore, it is clear that increased investment demand can always generate an equal volume of aggregate savings at any given level of the interest rate, so that attributing a rise in the interest rate to the higher investment demand is plain wrong.

Opposing pre-Keynesian understanding of savings-determined investment, Joan Robinson argued in 1970, 'the rate of interest, confused with the rate of return on investment, was the regulating mechanism which caused savings to be invested and secured equilibrium with full employment' (Robinson 1970, 507). One thing comes out quite clearly from this debate, that savings does not necessarily automatically get invested in the economy; that is, investment has an autonomous component for sure. Again, Kalecki (1954) argued '[…] the investment automatically brings into existence an equal amount of savings' (Kalecki 1954, 73). Therefore, it is the investment which determines savings under below full-employment level of activity for ex post savings–investment identity, and the causality is not the other way round. Keynes himself wrote, 'The investment market can become congested through shortage of cash (finance). It can never become congested through shortage of saving' (Keynes 1937b, 669). And also 'But, "finance" (I use the term "finance" to mean the credit required in the interval between planning and execution) has nothing to do with saving' (Keynes 1937b, 247). Pre-Keynesian economists regarded the rate of interest as the factor which brought the demand for investment and the willingness to save into equilibrium with one another. But according to Keynes, 'the rate of interest is not the "price" which brings into equilibrium the demand for resources to invest with the readiness to abstain from present consumption (that is, savings) and it (the rate of interest) is the "price" which equilibrates the desire to hold wealth in the form of cash with the available quantity of cash' (Keynes 1936, 168) (That is, the interest rate equilibrates the demand for and the supply of money.) This difference has serious consequences for macroeconomic policy decisions. In Keynes's own words, 'a decreased readiness to spend will be looked on in quite a different light if, instead of being regarded as a factor which will, cet. par., increase investment, it is seen as a factor which will, cet. par., diminish employment' (Keynes 1936, 185).

Let us now consider Dennis Robertson's loanable funds theory (as mentioned in Kahn 1954). In any given period the supply of loanable funds equals the sum of cash dishoarded and savings, while the demand for loanable funds equals the sum of investment and hoarding. Dennis Robertson differentiated between saving and hoarding and defines them by saying, 'A man is said to be saving if he spends on consumption less than his disposable income (of previous day). A man is said to be hoarding if he takes steps to raise the proportion which he finds existing at the beginning of any day between his money stock and his disposable income' (Robertson 1933, 399–400). Now, both the demand and supply of the loanable funds are taken to be functions of only the rate of interest and therefore the equality of demand and supply of loanable funds is supposed to determine the rate of interest in any given period. It follows from this that if the demand for loanable funds increases due to, say, deficit financing, then the rate of interest increases.

In Figure 13.3, if the fiscal deficit increases, the demand for loanable fund would also increase and the DLF curve would shift rightward (from DLF_0 to DLF_1), and as a result of that the rate of interest is bound to increase (from r_0 to r_1 at new equilibrium E_1) since the SLF curve is positively sloped (a positive function of rate of interest). But, starting with the initial equilibrium E_0, as the demand for loanable fund goes up (shift of DLF curve upward–right from DLF_0 to DLF_1), then supply of that can also rise (shift of SLF curve rightward from SLF_0 to SLF_1) due to a rise in income, and the interest rates can be unaffected (at r_0) at the new equilibrium E_2.

Figure 13.3. Demand for and supply of loanable funds and interest rate

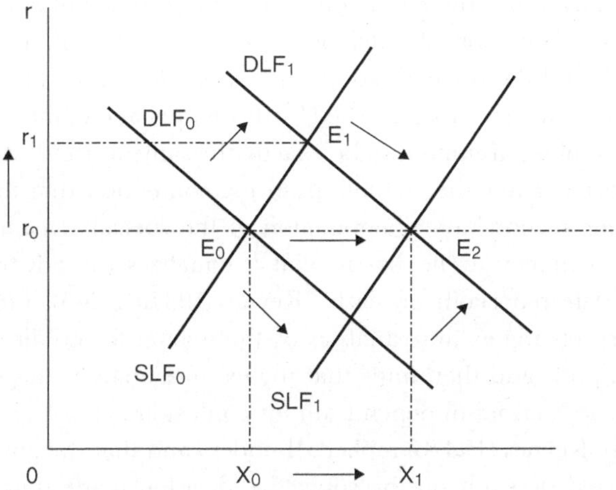

Any theory that draws a 'supply of loanable fund' (or supply of savings) curve as a function of interest rate only is implicitly assuming a given level of income. If it is not explicit, then that is only because of a lack of intellectual clarity. For every level of income there must be a different supply of loanable fund curve. One can think of a single supply of loanable fund curve only by assuming income to be given, and the level of income which is generally taken as given is the full-employment one. This assumption is crucial for the loanable funds theory, since once we recognize the fact that the supply of loanable funds depends on the level of output as well, we can have a new equilibrium with a higher fiscal deficit, higher income and an unchanged real rate of interest. Joan Robinson opined that '[...] Dennis Robertson confused an analysis of "the supply and demand of loanable funds" with an argument about "the real forces of productivity and thrift"' (Robinson 1970, 511). Thus the loanable funds theory shares with the treasury view the unrealistic assumption of a given level of income and hence fails to be relevant to the real world. Yet in a way it is an improvement over the latter in the sense that by explicitly taking into account the hoarding and dishoarding of cash, it presumably recognizes an inactive balance not used for circulation. However, this advance is not enough since without an independent theory of interest rate determination, the loanable funds theory, to be logically consistent, is still dependent on a full-employment assumption.

Regarding the determination of rate of interest also, there was an extremely interesting debate between Keynes and a group of economists. Keynes complained against a comparison of his theory of interest with 'a common-sense account of events in terms of supply and demand for loanable funds' (Keynes 1937c, 210). In reply, Dennis Robertson wrote, 'I remain of the opinion that our best course is to begin by describing the rate of interest as the price of the use of loanable funds' (Robertson 1937, 428). Keynes was in the process of abandoning the theory that the rate of interest is determined by the condition that it equalizes the supply and the demand for saving, or in other words, equalizes saving and investment. Ohlin argued that the net supply of credit, that is, the quantity of saving, depends on the interest rate, and the total supply of new claims minus the reduction in the outstanding volume of old ones gives the demand – also a function of rates of interest – for the different kinds of credit during the period, and the prices fixed on the market for these different claims – and thereby the rates of interest – are governed by this supply and demand in the usual way. Keynes criticized Ohlin's argument to be exactly the same as the classical doctrine and argued, 'The above is altogether remote from my contention that the rate of interest is, strictly speaking, a monetary phenomenon in the special sense that it is the own rate of interest on money itself, that is, that it equalizes the advantages of holding actual cash and deferred claim on cash' (Keynes 1937a , 245). Prof. Ohlin replied, 'Mr Keynes interprets my ex ante analysis of the market for credit, that is, claims, as if it had been ex post, and then finds that my ex ante analysis has disappeared. The whole of Mr Keynes's criticism depends on his confusion here of ex post and ex ante' (Ohlin 1937, 424). Keynes (1937b) replied, 'I understand that the amount of "ex ante" saving in any period depends on the subjective decision made during that period to make objective savings out of income which will accrue subsequently; and similarly, the amount of "ex ante" investment depends on the subjective decision to invest which will take objective effect subsequently' (663). And 'there will always be exactly enough ex post saving to take up the ex post investment and so release the finance which the latter had been previously employing' (669). Joan Robinson commented later, 'This episode confirmed Keynes's conviction that the rate of interest is a monetary phenomenon, not bound by "real forces"' (Robinson 1970, 507).

There exists another version of the theory of crowding-out due to financing larger government investment through borrowing. According to this theory banks can create only a certain amount of credit in any period (Patnaik 2001). Out of that if the government takes more, then banks would substitute government bonds for private bonds, or in other words the private investors would be rationed out because the government as a borrower is more attractive. This theoretical understanding is an improvement on the fixed-pool-of-savings or the loanable fund arguments in the sense that it does not assume that an increased investment demand via deficit financing cannot increase the savings or supply of loanable funds.

In the fixed-pool-of-bank-credit theory it is said that banks can create only a certain amount of credit in any period. For this to be at all true, it must be the case that the banks have no unutilized capacity to create credit. But in most developing countries it is seen that the commercial banks always have excess capacity to create fresh credit; for example, they are seen to hold more government securities, including low yield securities, than the minimum requirement under the statutory liquidity ratio, due to lack of adequate demand for credit. Let r and r′ be the rates of interest on government securities and on credit; then banks would get rid of excess holding of securities if 1/c times r′ exceeds r, where c is the cash reserve ratio, or in other words, banks would never hold excess government securities over and above the SLR requirements, as long as $r'/c > r$. Therefore if there is sufficient credit demand, excess holding of government securities will never be resorted to. In a situation like this, it is really erroneous to believe that since in a particular period the credit-creating ability of commercial banks is limited, if demand for credit increases due to increased fiscal deficit, the rate of interest would necessarily go up. Even if for the sake of argument we accept that banks cannot create extra credit given the existing stock of reserve money, if they can get additional reserve money when they need, credit cannot be seen as a constraining factor. Monetary policy, in other words, is the crucial factor here.

According to Keynes (1937a), the difference between finance and savings is one between a flow and a stock. Credit, in the sense of 'finance', looks after a flow of investment. It is a revolving fund which can be used over and over again. It does not absorb or exhaust any resources. The same 'finance' can tackle one investment after another. Each new net investment has new net saving generated by it. According to the Keynesian tradition the rate of interest is determined in the money market by the supply and demand for money. In the IS–LM framework (Branson 1989) (whether in its original closed economy version or for its extensions to an open economy as in the Mundell–Fleming model), the supply of money is taken to be exogenously given while the demand for money – taken as the aggregate of transaction and asset demand – is believed to be a function of aggregate output and the rate of interest (where $M_d = f[Y, r] : dM_d/dY>0$ and $dM_d/dr<0$). Now, if the fiscal deficit financed by borrowing increases demand (consumption and/or investment), and as a result of this if aggregate output of the economy increases, then the demand for money will also increase. Since the supply of money is exogenously given, the increased demand for money will cause the rate of interest to rise. This in turn would cause private investment demand to come down and the level of employment and output falls (though in magnitude it will have to be less than initial increase in output, otherwise the very reason for the increase in interest rate would have ceased to exist). According to these models, if fiscal deficit increases (in fact if employment and output increases anyhow for a given stock of money), the rate of interest increases, too. In the r–y plane the slope of the LM curve would be positive. If the IS curve (commodity market equilibrium condition) shifts rightward due to, say, increased government demand, then the rate of interest increases and partial crowding-out takes place, and ultimately we get a new equilibrium point at a higher level of output and definitely at a higher rate of interest.

In Figure 13.4, if y increases due to, say, increased government expenditure, then the commodity market equilibrium curve, that is, the IS curve, shifts upward right (from I_0S_0 to I_1S_1), the rate of interest increases from r_0 to r_1. In the money market, as y increases the transaction (and precautionary) demand for money increases, but since the money supply is exogenously given, the rate of interest rises, which in turn causes speculative demand for money to fall, and ultimately the money market comes to equilibrium at a rate of interest which is higher than the initial level. The new equilibrium point E_1, that is, the intersection point of I_1S_1 and LM, is situated upward right as compared to the initial equilibrium point E_0.

As the theory evolved (particularly after the Keynesian revolution), economists accepted the fact that the level of output is not given, and hence the dependence of savings on income became important. Simultaneously, theories of the interest rate depending on the investment–savings equality were replaced by theories which saw interest rates as

Figure 13.4. Rate of interest in a simple IS–LM framework

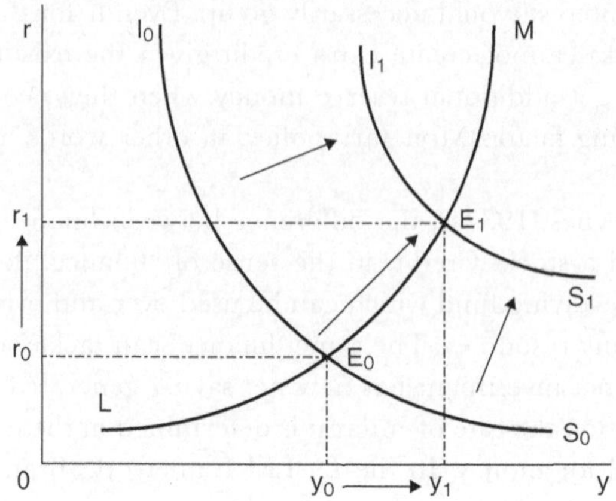

being determined in the asset market. Following exactly this line of thinking, models like IS–LM came into the literature of economics. But in the IS–LM framework (closed or open economy), the money supply (M_s or M_s/P) is taken as exogenously given. Given this assumption, any increase in the demand for money would, ceteris paribus, cause the rate of interest to rise. The proponents of endogenous money argued that money supply is not something which is exogenously given but is determined endogenously depending upon the aggregate demand for credit.

One of the major theoretical advancements in the literature of economics has been the development of the theory of money supply endogeneity; that is, demand for money or credit is the basic determinant both of money supply and of credit availability, as opposed to the simplistic neoclassical notion that the money supply grows strictly through Central Bank initiatives, that is, through exogenous processes. As the post-Keynesian literature has developed, it has also become clear that there are actually two distinct theories of money supply endogeneity within this tradition (Pollin1991). One perspective, called accommodative money supply endogeneity, argues that when banks and other intermediaries hold insufficient reserves, Central Banks must necessarily accommodate their needs. According to the other view, even if the Central Bank chooses to restrict the growth of non-borrowed reserves, then additional reserves are generated within the financial structure itself, and thus this perspective is referred to as structural endogeneity. Both approaches share a common starting point: the idea that the rate of money supply growth and, more importantly, credit availability is fundamentally determined by demand-side pressures within financial markets. Money is demand-determined and credit-led (Moore 1986 and 1988). The contributions of Minsky (1957), Kaldor (1978) and Joan Robinson (1970) to monetary theory are without question an important feature of the post-Keynesian theory of money supply endogeneity.

Figure 13.5 shows that if demand for money increases due to any expansionary measure on the fiscal front, then the M_d curve shifts upward right (from $M^{\circ}_d M^{\circ}_d$ to $M^1_d M^1_d$). Now the new demand for money curve cuts the old money supply curve at

Figure 13.5. Demand for and supply of money

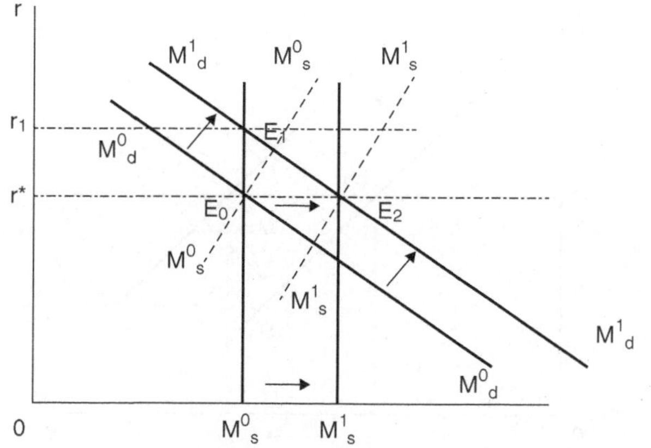

E, and the corresponding rate of interest becomes r_1, which is higher than r*. But an appropriate expansionary monetary policy can increase the money supply, and the M_s curve can also shift rightward from M°_s to M^1_s, and interest can remain the same (r*) in the new equilibrium E_2 as the initial situation (E_o). Even if we consider that money supply is a positive function of r, then the results also do not change. The dotted money supply curves imply money supply is interest responsive. Now, if the money supply happens to be endogenously determined and the rate of interest is a policy variable (which is fixed at a particular level though it can vary from period to period according to the monetary policy), then the money supply would always be equal to the demand for it at any given interest rate. Therefore, for any period, the LM curve would be horizontal in the IS–LM framework since money supply would be adjusted according to the demand for money, leaving the rate of interest unchanged (Das 2010). Then if government investment financed by a fiscal deficit increases, then the IS curve can shift upward-right (I_0S_0 to I_1S_1) and hence the level of employment and output may rise (Y_0 to Y_1), but the rate of interest would be unaffected (at r*) because of the horizontal LM curve.

Another very widely believed argument is that if the government has to borrow from the market to finance the budget deficit, then the supply of the government securities has to be increased, and as a result of that the price of government securities must fall in general and the rate of interest would rise, which will in turn cause crowding-out of private investors. For example, the Reserve Bank of India in its Report on Currency and Finance for the year 2002–03 expressed the fear that the demand for government securities reached saturation, and any further increase in the government borrowing would cause unwanted pressure on the interest rates and the commercial banks wouldn't be able to meet the demand for credit if it increased in the future. In other words, any further government borrowing would cause rates of interest to rise and in turn necessarily cause crowding-out. The belief that the increased supply of the government securities must lower security prices in general is based on an assumption that the total demand for securities is given (or more generally, the demand curve for securities as a function of

Figure 13.6. Increased government expenditure and horizontal LM curve

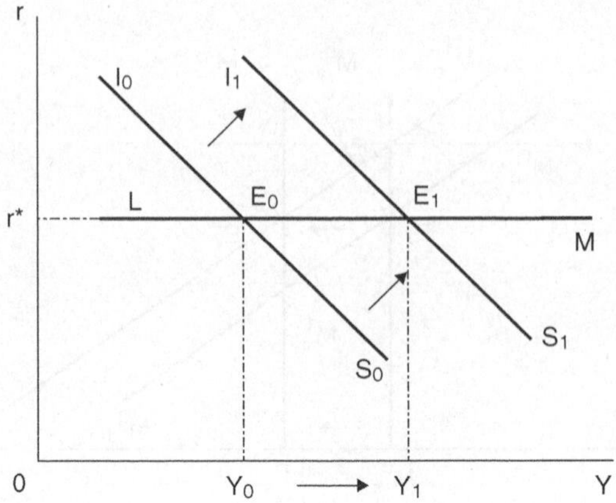

the interest rate, even if not vertical, is given). But a fiscal deficit not only increases the supply of securities but also their demand; that is, it shifts both the demand and the supply curve outwards. The demand for securities increases precisely because the fiscal deficit increases the level of private savings, which in turn have to be placed in various financial assets.

The identities (S – I) ≡ (G – T) and (S – I) + (M – X) ≡ (G – T) hold for closed and open economies respectively. A fiscal deficit always generates in a closed economy an amount of private excess savings (in case of open economy S + M) over private investment (in the case of an open economy I + X) equal to itself at any given level of rate of interest. In the case of a demand-constrained economy, it happens through output adjustment, and in the case of a supply-constrained economy, it happens through price adjustment via income redistribution and forced savings. Hence there is no reason that an increase in the supply of government securities would necessarily decrease the price of securities and in turn would increase the rate of interest in the economy in general.

In Figure 13.7, if the supply of the government securities increases, then the supply curve shifts from S_0S_0 to S_1S_1. If the demand for it does not increase, then the equilibrium point is E_1 and the corresponding price of the securities is P′, which is lower than P* (initial price). But if with the increase in the supply, the demand for government securities also increases as it must, then the demand curve shifts rightward from D_0D_0 and the price of securities rises. In Figure 13.7, D_0D_0 shifts to D_1D_1 and the new intersection point becomes E_2 and the corresponding price is P*, which is the initial price level corresponding to initial equilibrium E_0. This is a special case of security prices returning to their initial level either if the additional private savings are fully held in the form of government securities or if the money supply is endogenous so that the monetary system stands by to convert government securities to money to whatever extent required in order to maintain a constant interest rate. Still, there may be a possibility of change in portfolio choice and increase in demand for money. If aggregate demand for money increases for any given money supply, it could be argued that the rate of interest

Figure 13.7. Demand and supply of government securities

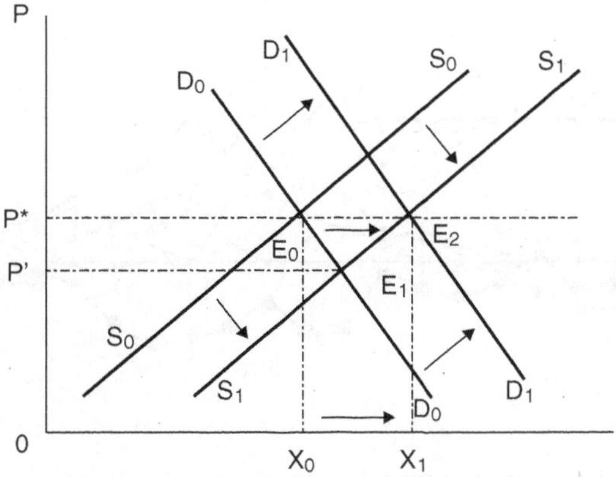

would go up. But, the money supply could always be adjusted according to its demand at any given interest rate.

Therefore, from the above arguments it is seen that there is absolutely no reason to believe that the fiscal deficit financed through market borrowing by issuing government securities necessarily raises the real rate of interest in the economy and in turn causes crowding-out. In a world where widespread unemployment and large-scale unutilized capacity exist, that is, where the level of actual output is less than the potential level of output, there the aggregate output is likely to increase with an increase in government demand through deficit financing, rather than price adjustment or inflation. Again, as the rate of interest is determined by the money market equilibrium condition, that is, by the equality between the demand for money and the supply of money, then if money supply is endogenously determined and adjusted according to its demand through appropriate monetary policies, the rates of interest become mere policy variables. According to the monetary policy of the government, it may be high or low irrespective of the level of fiscal deficit or government borrowings. The question however is: how empirically valid is this theory? In the next two sections, the empirical evidence from India, as well as from 82 other countries of the world economy, has been examined.

Empirical Evidence: India

In this section we shall look at the available empirical evidence on the Indian economy to try to find out whether the interest rates in India are in any way dependent on the fiscal deficit to GDP ratio. This section concentrates only on the experience of the Indian economy during the period 1980–81 to 2006–07; that is, the last two and a half decades. The data on fiscal deficit as percentage of Gross Domestic Product (GDP) and different real interest rates (i.e. $r - \Delta p/p$; inflation is calculated on the basis of GDP deflator) have been taken into consideration for the sake of our analysis. All the data used in this section are taken either from the Ministry of Finance, Government of India or from the Reserve Bank of India (RBI). For our empirical exercise we have considered the call money rates,

Figure 13.8. Movements of different interest rates and combined FD–GDP ratio in India 1980–81 to 2006–07

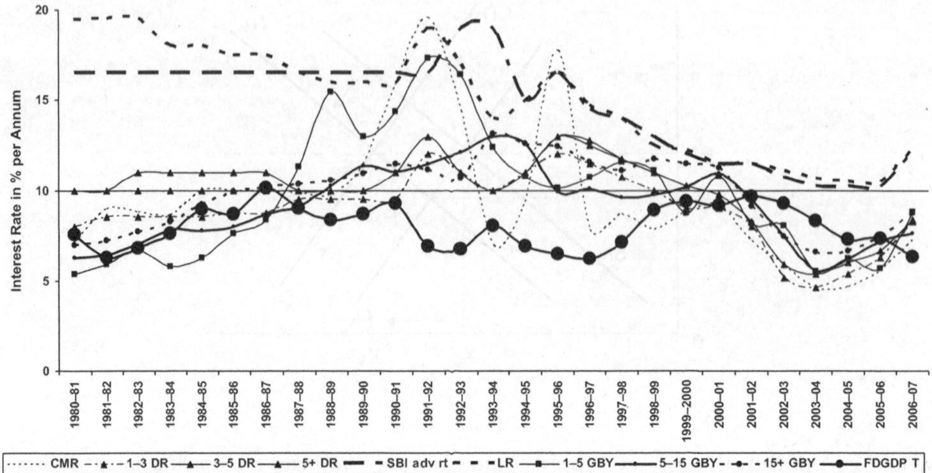

Source: Handbook of Statistics on Indian Economy, RBI, GoI, Economic Survey, Indian Public Finance Statistics, Ministry of Finance, Government of India.

1–3 years deposit rates, 3–5 years deposit rates, 5 years and above deposit rates, SBI advance rates, ceiling of lending rates, and rate of government bonds of 1–5 years and 5–15 years. In the case of lending rates and deposit rates, we have taken into account only the upper limits (provided by RBI) of the respective rates for different years because if crowding-out is caused by high interest rates, then the upper limits of rates of interest deserve much more attention. In Figure 13.8 the trends of different kinds of real interest rates and FD–GDP ratio are presented.

The SBI advance rate was fixed at 16.5 per cent throughout until 1991–92. Then there was a sudden jump up to 19 per cent in the early '90s, and then it gradually came down to 10.5 per cent until the recent increase to 12.5 per cent in 2006–07. The ceiling on the lending rate has also come down consistently, from 19.5 per cent in the early '80s to 10.5 per cent until 2005–06, excepting a little increase in the early '90s. The deposit rates remained slightly above or below 10 per cent during the '80s. During the 1990s, the deposit rates crossed the 10 per cent mark, and then they came down steadily from above 10 per cent in the late '90s to below 5 per cent during 2003–04. After that they have gone up slightly to 7.5 to 8 per cent in the recent past. The call money rate remained between 8.5 and 10 per cent until the late '80s. Between the late '80s and the mid '90s, we notice huge fluctuations and two peaks of 19.6 per cent and 17.7 per cent. In the second half of the '90s, the call money rate remained roughly between 8 per cent and 9 per cent. From 2000–01 onwards it came down consistently to below 5 per cent until the recent increase during the middle of the present decade. As far as government bond yields are concerned, the short-run (1–5 years) rate remained below 7 per cent during the first half of the '80s, then it went up to 12 per cent quite steadily by the mid '90s, and after that it came down to around 7 per cent again on an average by 2005–06. It rose quite sharply in 2006–07. The longer-run government bonds yielded interest rates that were a little higher but more or less followed similar trends.

Now, the combined fiscal deficit (of the centre and the states) to GDP ratio remained within 5 to 10 per cent throughout the period under consideration. It went up from 6.3 per cent in 1981–82 to 10 per cent in 1986–87. Then it came down slightly but again went up to 9.3 per cent during 1990–91. Then it came down again to 6.5 to 8 per cent until it went up again to 9.4 per cent in 1999–2000 and 9.6 per cent in 2001–02. Then it has been brought down on a regular basis by imposing the Fiscal Responsibility and Budget Management Act to 6.3 per cent during 2006–07. Inflation (not shown in the above graph), based on the GDP deflator, which has been used for calculating real interest rates, was 11.5 per cent in the beginning of the '80s, came down to 6.8 per cent in the mid-'80s, then again went up to 13.8 per cent in 1991–92, then came down consistently since 1994–95 to 3 per cent in 2001–02 and then rose to 5.5 per cent.

Now we wish to check whether there exists any definite positive linear relationship between real rates of interest and the fiscal deficit to GDP ratio on the basis of the above data by using some elementary econometric tools. First of all, the correlation coefficients are calculated for the first difference of both the variables to see whether the change in FD–GDP ratio significantly positively affects the real interest rates. The first differences are calculated simply by subtracting the previous year's values from the current year's values of each variable for different years during the time period 1980–81 to 2006–07. We have tested every series for the 'unit roots' or for the existence of 'random walk' by using the McKinnon p-value as well as the Dickey–Fuller test statistic. Any series is considered to be stationary if the McKinnon p-value (through Monte Carlo simulations) is less than 10 per cent (i.e. $Z(t)<0.1$) or the absolute value of the Dickey–Fuller test statistic is greater than its critical values (10 per cent); that is, if the null hypothesis that the series is non-stationary or there exist unit roots can be nullified (with 90 per cent level of confidence). Then we have made the time series stationary by taking appropriate differences (in all the cases here the series are stationary at their first difference level) for all the variables under consideration. Then we regressed every stationary series of different rates of interest, taking the fiscal deficit to GDP ratio as the explanatory variable. R^2, or the coefficient of determination, is a measure of how well the regression line fits the data. The adjusted R^2 is used sometimes depending on degrees of freedom. A function of sample observations whose computed value determines the final decision regarding acceptance or rejection of the null hypothesis is called a test statistic. Here we have used F or t (here these two are equivalent because in our regression model there is only one explanatory variable) as the test statistic. Here our null hypothesis is that the regression coefficient will be zero, and hence the alternative hypothesis is that the regression coefficient is non-zero; that is, if the null hypothesis cannot be rejected (with 90 per cent level of confidence), we cannot say that the alternative hypothesis will be necessarily true; that is, the real rates of interest necessarily depend positively on the fiscal deficit to GDP ratio. The results are listed in Table 13.1, considering combined fiscal deficit of the centre and the states, fiscal deficit for the centre separately and that for all the states taken together chronologically.

The fiscal deficit as a percentage of GDP has been stationary at the first difference level, and all kinds of real interest rates are also stationary at their first difference levels. As far as the real call money rates are concerned, the correlation coefficient with the combined fiscal deficit of the central government as well as the state government as proportion of GDP is –0.11, that with the central government's FD–GDP ratio is –0.25, and that with the fiscal deficit of all the states as a whole as percentage of GDP is 0.07. It could be concluded that there is no significant correlation between these two. As far as the regression analysis is concerned, the values of adjusted R^2 are –0.03, 0.02 and –0.04 respectively. The regression coefficients are also insignificant, which are –0.41 (–0.58), –1 (–1.28) and 0.50 (0.35) with probability of t-statistics being 0.56, 0.21 and 0.73 respectively. The terms in the parentheses represent the corresponding t-values of correlation and regression coefficients. We may say from this result that there is no direct dependence of real call money rate on fiscal deficit to GDP ratio in India between 1980–81 and 2006–07.

If we consider the short-term deposit rates of 1–3 years' duration, we see that the correlation coefficient with the combined fiscal deficit of the central government and the state government taken together as proportion to GDP is –0.12, that with the central government's FD–GDP ratio is –0.15, and that with the fiscal deficit of all the states as a whole as percentage of GDP is –0.07. It could be claimed that there is no significant correlation between these two. As far as the regression analysis is concerned, the values of adjusted R^2 are –0.03, –0.02 and –0.04 respectively. The regression coefficients are also insignificant, which are –0.20 (–0.57), –0.3 (–0.76) and –0.26 (–0.36) with probability of t-statistics being 0.58, 0.45 and 0.72 respectively. The terms in the parentheses represent the corresponding t-values of correlation and regression coefficients. Hence, the regression results suggest that there is no relation between the real short-run deposit rate with the FD–GDP ratio, neither of the centre nor of the states, nor the combined FD–GDP ratio in India during the period under consideration.

The change in real 3–5 years deposit rates has correlation coefficient of –0.04 with change in combined FD–GDP ratio, –0.13 with change in the centre's FD–GDP ratio and –0.02 with change in the states' FD–GDP ratio. Therefore, there is no significant correlation between the two. As far as the regression coefficients are concerned, these are –0.07 (–0.2) with adjusted R^2 –0.04 and probability of t-statistics 0.84 with the combined FD–GDP ratio. The regression coefficient of real medium-term deposit rate with the centre's FD–GDP ratio is –0.24 (–0.63) with adjusted R^2 being –0.02 and probability of t-statistics being 0.54. That with the states' FD–GDP ratio is –0.08 (–0.12) with adjusted R^2 being –0.04 and 91 per cent probability of null hypothesis being true. Hence, the null hypothesis is not being rejected (rather being accepted), so that we may say that there is a significant relation.

In the case of real deposit rates above 5 years the story does not alter much. The correlation coefficients are –0.01, –0.09 and –0.02 with combined, centre's and states' fiscal deficit to GDP ratio. The regression coefficients are –0.02 (–0.04), –0.19 (–0.45) and –0.08 (–0.11) with values of adjusted R^2 being –0.04, –0.09 and –0.04 and probabilities of t-statistics being 0.97, 0.66 and 0.92 respectively. Therefore, in general we may claim

Table 13.1. Regression of real interest rates on fiscal deficit to GDP ratio, India 1980–81 to 2006–07

Stationarity	Dependent Variable	Corr. Coeff.	Adj. R^2	Reg. Coeff.	t	P>t
Regression of Interest Rates on Combined FD–GDP Ratio						
1st Difference	Call Money Rate	–0.11	–0.03	–0.41	–0.58	0.56
1st Difference	1–3 Years DR	–0.12	–0.03	–0.20	–0.57	0.58
1st Difference	3–5 Years DR	–0.04	–0.04	–0.07	–0.20	0.84
1st Difference	Above 5 Years DR	–0.01	–0.04	–0.02	–0.04	0.97
1st Difference	SBI Advance Rate	0.16	–0.01	0.37	0.81	0.43
1st Difference	Lending Rate Ceiling	–0.15	–0.02	–0.28	–0.74	0.46
1st Difference	1–5 Years GBY	–0.18	–0.01	–0.42	–0.90	0.38
1st Difference	5–15 Years GBY	0.23	0.01	0.48	1.15	0.26
Regression of Interest Rates on Centre's FD–GDP Ratio						
1st Difference	Call Money Rate	–0.25	0.02	–1.00	–1.28	0.21
1st Difference	1–3 Years DR	–0.15	–0.02	–0.30	–0.76	0.45
1st Difference	3–5 Years DR	–0.13	–0.02	–0.24	–0.63	0.54
1st Difference	Above 5 years DR	–0.09	–0.03	–0.19	–0.45	0.66
1st Difference	SBI Advance Rate	0.15	–0.03	–0.19	–0.45	0.66
1st Difference	Lending Rate Ceiling	–0.27	–0.02	–0.40	–1.38	0.18
1st Difference	1–5 Years GBY	–0.06	–0.04	–0.17	–0.30	0.76
1st Difference	5–15 Years GBY	0.18	–0.01	0.42	0.87	0.39
Regression of Interest Rates on States' Fiscal Deficit to GDP Ratio						
1st Difference	Call Money Rate	0.07	–0.04	0.50	0.35	0.73
1st Difference	1–3 Years DR	–0.07	–0.04	–0.26	–0.36	0.72
1st Difference	3–5 Years DR	–0.02	–0.04	–0.08	–0.12	0.91
1st Difference	Above 5 Years DR	–0.02	–0.04	–0.08	–0.11	0.92
1st Difference	SBI Advance Rate	–0.06	–0.04	–0.29	–0.30	0.77
1st Difference	Lending Rate Ceiling	0.01	–0.04	0.05	0.07	0.95
1st Difference	1–5 Years GBY	–0.12	–0.03	–0.57	–0.58	0.57
1st Difference	5–15 Years GBY	–0.02	–0.04	–0.08	–0.09	0.93

Source: Handbook of Statistics on Indian Economy, RBI, Government of India, Economic Survey, Indian Public Finance Statistics, Ministry of Finance, Government of India.

Note: FD–GDP ratio has been calculated by dividing nominal fiscal deficit by GDP at current market price. Nominal interest rates are deflated by GDP deflator by deducting inflation based on the GDP deflator from the nominal rates. The total number of observations is 26 years in all the regressions. DR implies deposit rates, and GBY implies government bond yields.

that there is no empirical evidence in India during the period from 1980–81 to 2006–07 to suggest that the real deposit rates depend on the FD–GDP ratio.

If we consider the real advance rate of the State Bank of India, the correlation coefficients are 0.16, 0.15 and –0.06 with combined, centre and state FD–GDP ratios. The regression coefficients are 0.37 (0.81), –0.19 (–0.45) and –0.29 (–0.3) respectively. The adjusted R^2 values are –0.01, –0.03 and –0.04, and the probabilities of t-statistics are 0.43, 0.66 and 0.77 respectively. Therefore, changes in real SBI advanced rates are not significantly correlated with changes in FD–GDP ratio. The regression analysis suggests that the null hypothesis that the regression coefficient is zero cannot be rejected with sufficient level of confidence.

The ceilings of real lending rates, which are most directly related to the crowding-out hypothesis if at all (whether higher interest rate necessarily leads to crowding-out or not, that is a matter of separate debate and out of the scope of our present work), are not significantly positively correlated with FD–GDP ratio of either the centre (–0.15) or all states taken together (–0.27), or with combined FD as a percentage of GDP (0.01) in India. The regression coefficient of change in lending rate on change in combined FD–GDP ratio is –0.28 (–0.74), on change in the centre's FD–GDP ratio is –0.4 (–1.38), and states' FD–GDP ratio is 0.05 (0.07). The adjusted R^2 values are –0.02, –0.02 and –0.04 respectively, and P>t are 0.46, 0.18 and 0.95. Here we get empirical proof that the real lending rate has nothing to do with FD–GDP ratio in India, at least during the period under consideration.

The real short-run (1–5 years) government bond yields are not really significantly positively correlated either with the combined fiscal deficit to GDP ratio (–0.18) or with the fiscal deficit of the central government to GDP ratio (–0.06) or with the fiscal deficit of all the states taken together as a percentage of GDP (–0.12). As evident from Table 13.1, the regression coefficients are –0.42 (–0.9), –0.17 (–0.3) and –0.57 (–0.58) respectively with values of adjusted R^2 being –0.01, –0.04 and –0.03 and P>t being 0.38, 0.76 and 0.57. Therefore, real government bond yields do not depend on the FD–GDP ratio significantly in India.

As far as the longer-run (5–15 years) real government bond yields are concerned, the correlation and regression coefficients with combined FD–GDP ratio are 0.23 and 0.48 (1.15), with centre's FD–GDP ratio being 0.18 and 0.42 (0.87) and with states' FD–GDP ratio being –0.02 and –0.08 (–0.09) respectively. The probabilities of rejecting the null hypothesis are 0.26, 0.39 and 0.93 respectively. In this case also we are not getting any concrete evidence from India during the period from 1980–81 to 2006–07 that the real interest rate would necessarily depend on the fiscal deficit as a percentage of GDP.

Therefore, from the above observations, on the basis of available empirical evidence between 1980–81 and 2006–07 in the context of Indian economy, we can conclude this section by saying that there is absolutely no reason to believe that the rates of interest would necessarily rise if the fiscal deficit as a proportion of GDP is higher.

Questions might be raised about the limitations of our simplest bivariate framework of empirical analysis. First of all, the inclusion of an irrelevant explanatory variable is as dangerous as the omission of relevant variables, if any, because of the reduced precision of the estimates. 'We can view the omission of a set of relevant variables as equivalent to imposing an incorrect restriction' (Green 1997, 401–4). The covariance matrix in the short regression (excluding some relevant variable) is never larger than the covariance matrix for the estimator obtained in the presence of the superfluous variables. There is no loss if the explanatory variables are perfectly orthogonal or unrelated ($X'_1X_2 = 0$), which makes sense in terms of the information about X_1 contained in X_2; however, this is not likely to occur in practice. Now, if the interest rates are largely administered (at least within a band), it is conceptually difficult to firmly claim that they necessarily depend on some other relevant variable. In that case, if we incorporate some other explanatory variable, then the chance of inclusion of irrelevant variables would be higher to solve the problem than that of omitting variables. Moreover, there is no guarantee that the effects of fiscal deficit on real interest rates would become significant after inclusion of some more explanatory variables in the regression model.

Empirical Evidence: World

In this section we want to see the empirical evidence available for 82 countries other than India on the relation between the fiscal deficit as a proportion of GDP and the level of interest rates net of inflation. Here we wish to test whether the statement that 'the fiscal deficit to gross domestic product ratio necessarily affects the real rates of interest' is valid for different countries all over the world. Moreover, on the basis of the available information we want to examine whether or not a fiscal deficit is necessarily bad for the health of the economy in the sense that it necessarily raises the interest rates in the economy and hence causes a crowding-out of private investment.

We have used IFS (International Financial Statistics) data provided by the IMF (International Monetary Fund). We have taken the data of 25 years (1981–2005) into consideration. We have calculated the real rates of interest for five kinds of interest rates, namely Government Bond Yield (GBY), Treasury Bill Rate (TBR), Deposit Rate (DR), Lending Rate (LR) and Money Market Rate (MMR), by using the GDP deflator or wholesale prices (if these are not available, then CPI) of the respective years for each country for which data are available. If the nominal rate of interest is R per cent and the inflation rate is $\hat{u} = (dP/P)\times 100$, then the real rate of interest is calculated as $r = R - \hat{u}$. We have calculated the fiscal deficit to GDP ratio simply by dividing fiscal deficit in the national currency for each country by GDP in the national currency for the respective years. Exclusion of countries is dictated entirely by the non-availability of data (less than 15 observations have not been considered for time-series analysis). Using the same methodology, we get the following results as listed in the subsequent tables.

As far as the real government bond yields are concerned, we have data for all the required series for 21 countries all over the world. For five countries, both the real government bond yield series and the fiscal deficit as percentage of GDP are stationary at their levels and for the rest of the countries series are stationary at their first difference levels. The expected relationship is negative because the fiscal deficit has been considered to be negative and the surplus has been considered to be positive. Therefore, as the dependent variable decreases, that is, the fiscal deficit to GDP ratio increases, the real rate of interest is expected to rise according to the existing theory of crowding-out. Out of 21 countries, we get a negative significant (probability of t–statistics being less than

Table 13.2. Regression of real government bond yields on fiscal deficit to GDP ratio

No.	Order	Country	Obs.	t	P>F,|t|	Adj. R^2	Coeff.
1	1	Australia	21	1.46	0.16	0.05	0.43
2	0	Belgium	25	1.10	0.28	0.01	0.10
3	1	Canada	20	–2.20	0.04	0.17	–0.55
4	1	Denmark	19	1.03	0.32	0.00	0.49
5	1	Fiji	15	–1.55	0.15	0.09	–0.33
6	1	France	17	–0.03	0.98	–0.07	–0.01
7	0	Germany	18	0.38	0.71	–0.05	0.23
8	1	Honduras	22	–0.18	0.86	–0.05	–0.23
9	0	Korea	17	0.99	0.34	–0.00	0.57
10	1	Nepal	20	0.87	0.40	–0.01	0.70
11	1	Netherlands	18	0.29	0.78	–0.06	0.16
12	1	New Zealand	17	1.02	0.33	0.00	0.53
13	1	Norway	22	–0.65	0.81	–0.04	–0.06
14	1	Pakistan	21	–0.20	0.85	–0.05	–0.16
15	1	South Africa	24	–1.59	0.13	0.06	–0.57
16	1	Spain	18	–0.95	0.36	–0.01	–0.21
17	0	Switzerland	23	1.41	0.17	0.04	0.30
18	1	Thailand	22	0.47	0.65	–0.04	0.39
19	1	United Kingdom	18	–1.53	0.14	0.07	–0.26
20	1	United States	24	–0.69	0.50	–0.02	–0.11
21	0	Venezuela	18	–0.51	0.62	–0.05	–1.03

Source: Calculated from International Financial Statistics, July 2007, IMF by STATA.

0.10) relation between the real GBY and the FD–GDP ratio only in Canada (although the adjusted R^2 is very low, at only 0.17). Even if we allow the probability of null hypothesis of regression coefficient to be zero to be 0.20, that is, if we loosen the confidence interval to 80 per cent, then also we find there are only five countries out of which, for Fiji, South Africa and the United Kingdom (before formation of the European Union) the coefficients are negative, but for Australia and Switzerland, the coefficients are in fact positive.

For real treasury bill rates, out of a total 40 countries, only five countries, namely Barbados, Israel, Kenya, Sierra Leone and the United States, have shown significant (at 10 per cent level) regression coefficients. Both the series are stationary at levels in Barbados, Kenya and Sierra Leone, and they are stationary in their first difference levels in Israel and the US. The interesting part is that all the five significant coefficients are positive, which means that if the fiscal deficit increases, the real rate of interest will go down and vice versa. For 32 countries, the coefficients are insignificant even at 20 per cent level. Therefore, there is no empirical evidence until now of the necessary positive dependence.

Table 13.3. Regression of real treasury bill rates on fiscal deficit to GDP ratio

No.	Order	Country	Obs.	t	P>F,|t|	Adj. R^2	Coeff.
1	1	Australia	20	1.03	0.32	0.00	0.57
2	0	Barbados	24	2.02	0.06	0.12	0.48
3	0	Belgium	25	1.17	0.25	0.02	0.11
4	0	Bulgaria	12	–0.35	0.74	–0.08	–5.94
5	1	Canada	20	–0.47	0.64	–0.04	–0.18
6	0	Cyprus	21	0.70	0.49	–0.03	0.24
7	0	Ethiopia	19	1.17	0.26	0.02	1.04
8	0	Fiji	18	–1.37	0.19	0.05	–0.59
9	1	France	17	1.13	0.28	0.02	0.35
10	0	Germany	18	–0.50	0.62	–0.05	–0.31
11	0	Ghana	17	1.47	0.16	0.07	4.86
12	1	Greece	18	–0.60	0.56	–0.04	–0.11
13	0	Hungary	18	–0.63	0.53	–0.04	–0.23
14	1	Iceland	17	–0.30	0.77	–0.06	–0.10
15	1	Israel	17	4.36	0.00	0.53	4.90
16	0	Kenya	25	1.87	0.07	0.09	1.10
17	0	Lesotho	16	0.76	0.46	–0.03	0.22
18	1	Malaysia	18	0.25	0.81	–0.06	0.04
19	0	Malta	15	–0.84	0.42	–0.02	–0.13
20	1	Mexico	22	1.67	0.11	0.08	3.45
21	1	Nepal	22	0.89	0.39	–0.01	0.60
22	1	New Zealand	15	1.32	0.21	0.05	0.80
23	1	Nigeria	13	–0.72	0.49	–0.04	–0.70
24	1	Papua New Guinea	23	1.28	0.22	0.03	0.18
25	1	Philippines	24	–1.20	0.24	0.02	–1.49
26	1	Seychelles	17	–0.46	0.65	–0.05	–0.02
27	0	Sierra Leone	25	2.07	0.05	0.12	4.81
28	0	Singapore	25	–0.20	0.84	–0.04	–0.04
29	0	Solomon Islands	18	0.93	0.37	–0.01	0.17
30	1	South Africa	24	–0.49	0.63	–0.03	–0.29
31	1	Spain	18	–0.05	0.96	–0.06	–0.01
32	0	Sri Lanka	24	–0.03	0.98	–0.05	–0.03
33	0	St Vincent & Grens.	21	–0.92	0.37	–0.01	–0.24
34	0	Swaziland	23	0.74	0.47	–0.02	0.21
35	1	Switzerland	24	0.37	0.72	–0.04	0.14
36	1	Uganda	19	–0.68	0.51	–0.03	–3.71

(Continued)

Table 13.3. Continued

No.	Order	Country	Obs.	t	P>F,|t|	Adj. R^2	Coeff.
37	1	UK	18	0.65	0.52	–0.04	0.15
38	1	US	24	2.63	0.02	0.20	0.42
39	1	Zambia	15	0.35	0.73	–0.07	0.64
40	1	Zimbabwe	16	0.90	0.38	–0.01	0.54

Source: Calculated from International Financial Statistics, July 2007, IMF by STATA.

If we move on to the deposit rates now, we have significant regression coefficients after fulfilling the stationarity criteria only in 15 countries out of a total 75 countries for which data were available. Out of these 15 countries, the Kingdom of Bahrain, Chad, Ireland, Israel, Myanmar, Turkey and Uruguay have registered negative significant regression coefficients. However, Barbados, Bolivia, Indonesia, Korea, Mauritius, Mexico, Morocco, Sierra Leone and the United States have registered positive significant coefficients, which negates the proposition that higher fiscal deficit to GDP ratio leads to higher real deposit rates. Both the variables for seven countries are stationary at their levels, and for the remaining eight countries they are stationary at their first difference levels out of those countries for which the regression coefficients are significant at 90 per cent level of confidence or the probability of t-statistics is less that 0.10. Out of 74 countries, in 53 economies the null hypothesis in bivariate regression cannot be rejected even with 80 per cent level of confidence. In 14 countries, the regression coefficients are insignificant with more than 80 per cent confidence interval. In 40 out of 74 economies, the significance level is even less than 50 per cent. Therefore, a necessary relationship between the real deposit rates and the fiscal deficit to GDP ratio could be ruled out from this empirical evidence.

As far as the real lending rates are concerned, which are extremely important from the point of view of the crowding-out argument, we have data for a total of 70 countries. Out of these 70 countries, the regression coefficient is significant only for 11 countries. Out of these 11 countries only Hungary, Ireland and Myanmar have registered negative significant coefficients. And in Barbados, Ethiopia, Korea, Mauritius, Morocco, Peru, Sierra Leone and the United States the coefficient is significant and surprisingly positive. In 52 economies out of total 70, the regression coefficient is insignificant even at 80 per cent level of confidence. Therefore, at least this could be argued here that there is no necessary direct relation existing between real lending rates and the fiscal deficit to GDP ratio always.

As far as the real money market rates of interest are concerned, we have only three significant coefficients out of a total of 33 countries. In 27 economies, the probability of t-statistics is higher than even 0.20. Only Ireland shows the expected sign of the regression coefficient (i.e. negative) but in the case of the other two countries whose coefficients are significant, namely Mauritius and the United States, the coefficients are actually positive. In the case of Mauritius, both the series are stationary at their levels, but in the case of Ireland and the US, they are stationary at their first difference levels. However, here also there is no evidence that the real interest rates would necessarily depend on the

Table 13.4. Regression of real deposit rates on fiscal deficit to GDP ratio

No.	Order	Country	Obs.	t	P>F, |t|	Adj. R^2	Coeff.
1	0	Argentina	17	0.23	0.82	–0.06	160.71
2	1	Australia	21	0.62	0.54	–0.03	0.32
3	0	Bahrain, Kingdom of	20	–2.04	0.06	0.14	–0.27
4	0	Barbados	24	1.95	0.06	0.11	0.41
5	0	Belgium	23	0.29	0.77	–0.04	0.05
6	1	Bolivia	15	22.20	0.00	0.97	298.05
7	1	Botswana	14	–0.44	0.67	–0.07	–0.04
8	0	Bulgaria	15	–0.12	0.91	–0.08	–1.79
9	0	Burkina Faso	25	–0.18	0.86	–0.04	–0.12
10	1	Canada	20	–0.70	0.50	–0.03	–0.26
11	1	Chad	15	–1.95	0.07	0.17	–0.12
12	1	Chile	19	0.63	0.54	–0.03	1.76
13	1	Columbia	19	1.12	0.28	0.01	0.91
14	1	Costa Rica	20	–0.40	0.70	–0.05	–1.37
15	0	Cyprus	23	0.66	0.52	–0.03	0.21
16	1	Denmark	19	1.38	0.18	0.05	0.64
17	0	Dominican Republic	13	–1.40	0.19	0.07	–6.11
18	1	Ecuador	21	0.37	0.71	–0.05	0.26
19	1	Egypt	22	–0.01	0.99	–0.05	–0.00
20	0	Fiji	18	–1.43	0.17	0.06	–0.47
21	1	Finland	19	–0.65	0.53	–0.03	–0.23
22	1	France	17	–0.57	0.58	–0.04	–0.10
23	0	Germany	18	–0.56	0.58	–0.04	–0.32
24	0	Ghana	15	1.28	0.22	0.04	4.60
25	1	Greece	18	–1.27	0.22	0.03	–0.22
26	0	Guatemala	24	–1.38	0.18	0.04	–1.43
27	1	Honduras	23	–0.08	0.94	–0.05	–0.10
28	0	Hungary	25	–0.44	0.67	–0.04	–0.54
29	1	Iceland	23	0.46	0.65	–0.04	0.52
30	0	Indonesia	25	1.70	0.10	0.07	3.61
31	1	Ireland	17	–2.04	0.06	0.17	–1.35
32	1	Israel	18	–2.09	0.05	0.16	–3.50
33	1	Japan	12	0.32	0.75	–0.09	0.08
34	0	Kenya	21	1.30	0.21	0.03	0.67
35	0	Korea	17	2.92	0.01	0.32	1.75
36	1	Kuwait	20	–1.31	0.21	0.04	–0.06

(Continued)

Table 13.4. Continued

No.	Order	Country	Obs.	t	P>F, |t|	Adj. R^2	Coeff.
37	0	Lesotho	16	0.85	0.41	–0.02	0.26
38	1	Malaysia	18	0.10	0.92	–0.06	0.02
39	0	Malta	21	–0.58	0.57	–0.03	–0.12
40	0	Mauritius	25	1.91	0.07	0.10	0.34
41	1	Mexico	24	2.01	0.06	0.12	3.58
42	0	Morocco	19	6.17	0.00	0.67	1.30
43	1	Myanmar	21	–2.32	0.03	0.18	–6.15
44	1	Netherlands	18	0.33	0.74	–0.06	0.18
45	1	New Zealand	15	–0.39	0.71	–0.06	–0.14
46	0	Nicaragua	14	0.83	0.42	–0.02	0.09
47	0	Nigeria	25	–0.01	0.99	–0.04	–0.01
48	1	Norway	22	–0.76	0.45	–0.02	–0.28
49	1	Panama	14	0.50	0.63	–0.06	0.45
50	1	Papua New Guinea	23	–0.26	0.80	–0.04	–0.05
51	0	Peru	14	1.17	0.26	0.03	2.92
52	1	Philippines	24	–1.15	0.26	0.01	–1.59
53	0	Rwanda	21	–0.36	0.72	–0.05	–0.26
54	0	Seychelles	19	–1.47	0.16	0.06	–0.13
55	0	Sierra Leone	25	2.00	0.06	0.11	4.34
56	0	Singapore	25	–0.06	0.95	–0.04	–0.01
57	0	Solomon Islands	18	0.23	0.82	–0.06	0.04
58	1	South Africa	24	–0.35	0.73	–0.04	–0.19
59	1	Spain	18	–0.44	0.66	–0.05	–0.08
60	0	Sri Lanka	25	–0.62	0.54	–0.02	–0.50
61	0	St Vincent & Grens.	21	–0.40	0.69	–0.04	–0.11
62	0	Swaziland	23	1.05	0.31	0.00	0.29
63	1	Sweden	22	1.36	0.19	0.04	0.33
64	1	Switzerland	24	0.16	0.88	–0.04	0.05
65	1	Tanzania	18	0.55	0.59	–0.04	0.38
66	1	Thailand	22	0.71	0.49	–0.02	0.52
67	0	Togo	19	0.16	0.87	–0.06	0.25
68	1	Turkey	14	–5.65	0.00	0.70	–4.01
69	1	Uganda	21	–0.06	0.95	–0.05	–0.26
70	1	UK	17	0.31	0.76	–0.06	0.10
71	1	US	24	3.31	0.00	0.30	0.56
72	1	Uruguay	24	–2.52	0.02	0.19	–2.98

(Continued)

Table 13.4. Continued

No.	Order	Country	Obs.	t	P>F, |t|	Adj. R^2	Coeff.
73	0	Venezuela	18	–0.11	0.91	–0.06	–0.23
74	1	Zambia	14	–0.13	0.90	–0.08	–0.26
75	0	Zimbabwe	17	1.02	0.33	0.00	0.69

Source: Calculated from International Financial Statistics, July 2007, IMF by STATA.

fiscal deficit to GDP ratio and if that ratio increases, there would necessarily be upward pressure on the real rate of interest.

For the sake of argument one may point out that there might be a problem of 'endogeneity' in the sense that higher interest rates may also lead to higher fiscal deficit to GDP ratio by increasing the interest payment component of the government on its outstanding debt. However, there is a whole array of possibilities through which the fiscal deficit to GDP ratio may change. For example, other expenditure components (excepting the interest payment component) may change; tax and non-tax revenue of the government may also change for varying the gap, that is, the fiscal deficit. Again, the denominator of our independent variable (i.e. the GDP) may also vary for determining the ratio, etc. Hence, it would be too strong a proposition to point to only one single expenditure component – that is, only the interest payment component of the government as being responsible for changes in the ratio of fiscal deficit to GDP for so many countries and so many years. Rather, it would be safer to take fiscal deficit to GDP ratio as an exogenous variable broadly independent of the movements in rates of interest (government bond yield or treasury bill rate). Moreover, endogeneity is a problem when the regression coefficients are significant, but when they are insignificant, it becomes redundant.

In this section we have considered five kinds of rates of interest, namely real government bond yield, treasury bill rate, deposit rate, prime lending rate and money market rate of interest for a total of 82 countries all over the world. Our regression results of rates of interest on fiscal deficit to GDP ratio show that for very few countries the regression coefficients are significant as well as positive; that is, for very few countries it can be said that if the fiscal deficit as a proportion of GDP rises, the rates of interest will also rise. Again, when we regress (depending upon the stationarity of both the series) the change in real interest rates on change in fiscal deficit to GDP ratio, we get very similar results as before, in the sense that for very few countries it gives significant positive results; that is, for very few countries it is true that the changes in the fiscal deficit to GDP ratio cause the rates of interest to change in the same direction. Therefore, we can conclude from this section that it is not justified to say – at least as far as the empirical evidence from 82 different countries (excepting India) all over the world is concerned – that fiscal deficit as a proportion of GDP necessarily raises the rates of interest in the economy and hence in turn necessarily causes crowding-out. In bivariate regression, even if we get a positive significant relation between interest rate and fiscal deficit to GDP ratio, the causality might be opposite; that is, higher interest rate may lead to lower investment and growth, which in turn may lead to lower revenue receipt of government and higher fiscal deficit to GDP ratio and vice versa.

Table 13.5. Regression of real (prime) lending rates on fiscal deficit to GDP ratio

No.	Order	Country	Obs.	t	P>F,|t|	Adj. R^2	Coeff.
1	1	Australia	21	0.72	0.48	–0.02	0.38
2	1	Bahrain, Kingdom of	15	–0.40	0.70	–0.06	–0.04
3	0	Barbados	24	2.29	0.03	0.16	0.50
4	0	Belgium	25	0.96	0.35	–0.00	0.09
5	1	Bolivia	13	0.41	0.69	–0.07	0.40
6	1	Botswana	14	–0.53	0.61	–0.06	–0.04
7	0	Bulgaria	15	–0.53	0.60	–0.05	–7.47
8	0	Burundi	22	–0.44	0.67	–0.04	–0.18
9	1	Canada	20	–0.50	0.63	–0.04	–0.18
10	1	Chad	15	1.70	0.11	0.12	1.74
11	1	Chile	19	0.48	0.64	–0.04	1.38
12	1	Columbia	19	1.10	0.29	0.01	0.92
13	1	Costa Rica	19	0.27	0.79	–0.05	0.27
14	0	Cyprus	23	0.39	0.70	–0.04	0.12
15	1	Denmark	19	1.39	0.18	0.05	0.69
16	0	Dominican Republic	13	–1.49	0.17	0.09	–6.05
17	0	Ecuador	24	0.34	0.74	–0.04	0.34
18	1	Egypt	20	0.36	0.72	–0.05	0.13
19	0	Ethiopia	15	2.11	0.06	0.20	2.33
20	0	Fiji	18	–0.24	0.81	–0.06	–0.07
21	1	Finland	21	–0.66	0.52	–0.03	–0.22
22	1	France	17	0.79	0.44	–0.02	0.18
23	0	Germany	18	–0.98	0.34	–0.00	–0.66
24	1	Greece	18	–1.44	0.17	0.06	–0.24
25	0	Guatemala	24	–0.11	0.91	–0.04	–0.15
26	1	Honduras	23	0.02	0.99	–0.05	0.02
27	0	Hungary	17	–2.14	0.05	0.18	–1.14
28	1	Iceland	24	0.42	0.68	–0.04	0.45
29	0	Indonesia	20	1.26	0.22	0.03	3.69
30	1	Ireland	17	–2.24	0.04	0.20	–1.48
31	1	Israel	20	–0.40	0.70	–0.05	–1.92
32	1	Japan	12	0.69	0.51	–0.05	0.17
33	1	Kenya	24	1.23	0.23	0.02	0.92
34	0	Korea	17	2.03	0.06	0.16	1.27
35	1	Kuwait	20	–1.26	0.22	0.03	–0.06
36	0	Lesotho	16	1.14	0.27	0.02	0.33

(Continued)

Table 13.5. Continued

No.	Order	Country	Obs.	t	P>F, |t|	Adj. R^2	Coeff.
37	0	Malta	21	–0.61	0.55	–0.03	–0.14
38	0	Mauritius	25	2.72	0.01	0.21	0.73
39	1	Morocco	16	2.08	0.06	0.18	0.83
40	1	Myanmar	17	–2.90	0.01	0.32	–8.50
41	0	Nepal	16	–0.67	0.52	–0.04	–0.35
42	1	Netherlands	18	0.15	0.89	–0.06	0.07
43	1	New Zealand	14	–0.34	0.74	–0.07	–0.17
44	0	Nicaragua	14	–0.48	0.64	–0.06	–0.36
45	0	Nigeria	25	0.14	0.89	–0.04	0.12
46	1	Norway	22	–0.89	0.39	–0.01	–0.32
47	1	Panama	14	0.43	0.68	–0.07	0.38
48	1	Papua New Guinea	23	–0.80	0.43	–0.02	–0.16
49	0	Peru	16	4.75	0.00	0.59	198.2
50	1	Philippines	24	–0.91	0.37	–0.01	–1.29
51	1	Poland	15	0.09	0.93	–0.08	0.17
52	1	Seychelles	13	–0.56	0.59	–0.06	–0.03
53	0	Sierra Leone	25	1.97	0.06	0.11	4.50
54	0	Singapore	25	–0.18	0.86	–0.04	–0.04
55	1	South Africa	24	–0.57	0.57	–0.03	–0.33
56	1	Spain	18	–1.10	0.29	0.01	–0.32
57	0	Sri Lanka	25	–0.04	0.97	–0.04	–0.04
58	0	St Vincent & Grens.	21	–0.70	0.49	–0.03	–0.21
59	0	Swaziland	23	1.05	0.31	0.00	0.31
60	1	Sweden	22	1.39	0.18	0.04	0.34
61	0	Switzerland	25	–1.35	0.19	0.03	–0.61
62	1	Tanzania	20	1.49	0.15	0.06	0.98
63	1	Thailand	22	0.80	0.43	–0.02	0.62
64	1	Uganda	17	–0.59	0.57	–0.04	–3.39
65	1	UK	18	0.69	0.50	–0.03	0.16
66	1	US	24	3.70	0.00	0.36	0.59
67	0	Uruguay	25	0.86	0.40	–0.01	1.59
68	0	Venezuela	18	–0.39	0.70	–0.05	–0.87
69	1	Zambia	16	0.14	0.89	–0.07	0.26
70	1	Zimbabwe	16	1.21	0.25	0.03	0.93

Source: Calculated from International Financial Statistics, July 2007, IMF by STATA.

Table 13.6. Regression of real money market rates on fiscal deficit to GDP ratio

No.	Order	Country	Obs.	t	P>F,|t|	Adj. R^2	Coeff.
1	1	Australia	21	0.86	0.40	–0.01	0.48
2	0	Austria	16	–0.69	0.50	–0.04	–0.55
3	0	Bulgaria	15	–0.22	0.83	–0.07	–3.26
4	0	Burkina Faso	25	0.32	0.75	–0.04	0.22
5	1	Canada	20	–0.52	0.61	–0.04	–0.20
6	1	Denmark	19	1.00	0.33	–0.00	0.55
7	0	Fiji	17	–1.03	0.32	0.00	–0.49
8	1	Finland	24	–0.48	0.64	–0.03	–0.17
9	0	Germany	18	–0.89	0.39	–0.01	–0.55
10	1	Iceland	18	–0.54	0.60	–0.04	–0.21
11	0	Indonesia	24	1.43	0.17	0.04	2.24
12	1	Ireland	17	–2.29	0.04	0.21	–1.66
13	0	Korea	17	1.65	0.12	0.10	1.11
14	1	Kuwait	20	–1.08	0.29	0.01	–0.06
15	1	Malaysia	18	–0.17	0.87	–0.06	–0.04
16	0	Mauritius	25	1.86	0.08	0.09	0.37
17	1	Mexico	23	0.68	0.50	–0.02	1.31
18	1	Norway	22	–1.24	0.23	0.03	–0.44
19	1	Pakistan	24	0.29	0.77	–0.04	0.23
20	1	Philippines	24	–0.81	0.42	–0.01	–1.02
21	1	Singapore	24	1.10	0.28	0.01	0.31
22	1	South Africa	24	–0.37	0.72	–0.04	–0.23
23	1	Spain	18	–0.30	0.77	–0.06	–0.10
24	0	Sri Lanka	25	0.17	0.87	–0.04	0.15
25	0	St Vincent & Grens.	17	–0.39	0.71	–0.06	–0.07
26	0	Swaziland	15	1.21	0.25	0.03	0.29
27	1	Sweden	20	1.42	0.17	0.05	0.50
28	1	Switzerland	24	0.63	0.54	–0.03	0.24
29	1	Thailand	22	1.24	0.23	0.02	0.85
30	0	Togo	19	–0.25	0.81	–0.06	–0.39
31	1	UK	18	0.71	0.49	–0.03	0.16
32	1	US	24	3.44	0.00	0.32	0.57
33	1	Zimbabwe	16	0.36	0.72	–0.06	0.19

Source: Calculated from International Financial Statistics, July 2007, IMF by STATA.

Conclusion

Therefore, this work ends with the conclusion that the interest rates do not necessarily depend on the fiscal deficit as a proportion of GDP, which means that policies based on this understanding are also erroneous (Das 2004). There is neither any theoretical nor any empirical basis, either in India or in other countries around the world, to believe that a higher fiscal deficit to GDP ratio would necessarily cause interest rates to go up and result in crowding-out of private investment.

References

Branson, W. H. 1989. *Macroeconomic Theory and Policy*. New York: Harper and Row.

Das, S. 2004. 'The Effect of Fiscal Deficit on Real Interest Rates'. *Economic and Political Weekly* 39, no. 12: 1299–1310.

______. 2010. 'On Financing the Fiscal Deficit and Availability of Loanable Funds in India', *Economic and Political Weekly* 45, no. 15: 67–75.

Greene, W. H. 1997. *Econometric Analysis*. London: Prentice Hall International.

Kahn, R. F. 1954. 'Some Notes on Liquidity Preference'. Manchester School. Reprinted in Kahn 1972.

______. 1972. *Selected Essays on Employment and Growth*. Cambridge: Cambridge University Press.

Kaldor, N. 1978. 'The New Monetarism'. In *Further Essays on Applied Economics*. London: Duckworth.

Kalecki, M. 1954. 'The Short-Term Rate of Interest'. In *The Theory of Economic Dynamics*. London: Allen & Unwin.

Keynes, J. M. 1936. *The General Theory of Employment, Interest and Money*. London: Macmillan.

______. 1937a. 'Alternative Theories of the Rate of Interest'. *Economic Journal* 47, no. 186: 241–52.

______. 1937b. 'The "Ex-Ante" Theory of Rate of Interest'. *Economic Journal* 47, no. 188: 663–9.

______. 1937c. 'The General Theory of Employment'. *Quarterly Journal of Economics* 51, no. 2: 209–23.

Minsky, H. 1957. 'Monetary Systems and Accelerator Models'. *American Economic Review* 47, no. 6: 860–83.

Moore, B. J. 1986. 'How Credit Drives the Money Supply: The Significance of Institutional Developments'. *Journal of Economic Issues* 20, no. 2: 443–53.

______. 1988. *Horizontalists and Verticalists: The Macroeconomics of Credit Money*. Cambridge: Cambridge University Press.

Ohlin, B. 1937. 'Alternative Theories of the Rate of Interest: Three Rejoinders'. *Economic Journal* 47, no. 187: 423–8.

Patnaik, P. 2001. 'On Fiscal Deficit and Real Interest Rates'. *Economic and Political Weekly* 36, nos. 14–15: 1160–63.

Pollin, R. 1991. 'Two Theories of Money Supply Endogeneity: Some Empirical Evidence'. *Journal of Post Keynesian Economics* 13, no. 3: 366–96.

Robertson, D. H. 1933. 'Saving and Hoarding'. *Economic Journal* 43, no. 171: 399–413.

______. 1937. 'Alternative Theories of the Rate of Interest: Three Rejoinders'. *Economic Journal* 47, no. 187: 428–36.

Robinson, J. 1970. 'Quantity Theories Old and New: Comment'. *Journal of Money, Credit and Banking* 2, no. 4: 504–12.

Data Sources

Report on Currency and Finance, RBI, Government of India.
Handbook of Statistics on Indian Economy, RBI, Government of India.
Economic Survey, Ministry of Finance, Government of India.
Indian Public Finance Statistics, Ministry of Finance, Government of India.
International Financial Statistics, July 2007, International Monetary Fund.

Chapter 14

GOING, GOING, BUT NOT YET QUITE GONE: THE POLITICAL ECONOMY OF THE INDIAN INTERMEDIATE CLASSES DURING THE ERA OF LIBERALIZATION*

Matthew McCartney

Introduction

Mitra (1977), Jha (1980) and Bardhan (1984) are part of India's rich tradition of political writing and specifically a product of the debate about 'Industrial Stagnation' (1965 and 1980). There have been works of political economy since Varma (1998), Herring (1999), Chibber (2003), and Harriss-White (2003), but the volume of that output has declined notably, especially that related to class (Chibber 2006). This chapter marks a return to this tradition; specifically it is a response to the re-release of both Bardhan (1984) in 1998 as an expanded edition with an epilogue and Mitra (1977) in 2005 in a new edition with a freshly penned introduction. Mitra by 2005 was saying, 'The doubt persists. Is there much point in re-issuing a book which has disappeared from the market for nearly a quarter of a century?' and that 'Circumstances conspired to make mincemeat of what the book sought to say' (Mitra 2005, xi–xiii). Mitra does argue of a continued relevance, 'It wanted political economy to be put back on the agenda of conventional economics [...] what was said thirty years ago may possibly still have some relevance in today's world' (Mitra 2005, xvii). Bardhan was more optimistic: 'All these changes and realignments in the composition and attitudes of the dominant coalition have made some of the deregulatory reforms more acceptable than before. But [...] one should not underestimate the enormity and tenacity of vested interests in the preservation of the old political equilibrium of subsidies and patronage distribution' (Bardhan 1998, 132). In this chapter we complete this process and return to Jha (1980). We are doing so in an academic world which is not only bereft of much new thinking about class-based political economy but one in which the world to explain has changed dramatically. The industrial stagnation and commitment to state-led industrialization that prompted these writings

* This chapter draws on and updates a version previously published in 2009 as chapter 5 of the author's *Political Economy, Growth and Liberalisation in India, 1991–2008*. London: Routledge.

gave way to rapid economic growth after the early 1980s and extensive liberalization after 1991.

The theory of intermediate classes and regimes was originally developed by Kalecki (1972) in a general way as being relevant to many developing countries, recognized as being relevant to India by Raj (1973), critically contested by Namboodiripad (1973) and Byres (1997), but also refined as applied to conditions of stagnation by Jha (1980). This chapter seeks to explore the relevance of intermediate classes and regimes for a very different political and economic context, that of liberalization after 1991.

This chapter is organized as follows. The first section outlines the theory of the intermediate regime and intermediate classes. The second examines what the theory has attempted to explain. The third looks at the relation between big and small/intermediate business capital from a theoretical perspective, and the fourth discusses the reasons for the continued success of the latter. The fifth explores the changing role of the middle class as a possible alternative ruling alliance. The final section concludes by arguing that although the political economy of India has become more fragmented during the 1990s, the intermediate classes still represent a powerful social structure of accumulation.

What are the Intermediate Regime and the Intermediate Classes?[1]

The context of Kalecki's (1972) analysis of intermediate regimes is an economy and state in an incomplete transition to mature capitalism where most people are not wage earners. The distinctive characteristic of the intermediate classes (self-employed and small farmers) is the lack of a contradiction between labour and capital, and between labour and management.[2]

> Its earnings can neither be classified as a reward for labour, nor as a payment for risk taking (i.e. profit) but are an amalgam of the two. The self-employed thus lie midway between the large-scale professionally managed capitalist enterprises of the private sector, and the working classes. (Jha 1980, 95)

Preconditions for an 'intermediate regime'

Jha (1980) sought to integrate the theory of rent seeking (Kreuger 1974) with a political economy of Indian development during the years of stagnation (1965–80). His immediate influence was the analysis of intermediate regimes by Kalecki (1972) and its initial application to India by Raj (1973). The sole precondition identified by Jha to bind the intermediate classes into an intermediate regime is the existence of pervasive shortages. The response of the intermediate classes distinguishes them from the big bourgeoisie. From Kalecki, Jha observes, 'It is the rise to dominance of an intermediate class or stratum consisting of market orientated peasant proprietors, small manufacturers, traders and other self-employed groups which benefited from economic stagnation and had a vested interest in its perpetuation' (Jha 1980, vii). Within the context of 'shortages', the self-employed can engage in mark-up pricing. Small-scale business and traders can avoid central price controls by engaging in parallel trade and speculation and by siphoning resources into the black economy. The entrepreneur can easily gain directly from such activity, unlike the shareholder of a professionally managed company. Small farmers producing a marketed surplus likewise benefit from shortage during drought years. The bureaucracy are salary earners but also derive income from bribes, fraud and the private sale of state goods such as licenses and sanctions; they are de facto self-employed and earn a fee from the provision of a service. Jha offers examples from licensing and price control. Industrial licensing (anti-monopoly provisions and capacity constraints) in India, he argues, generated a specific bias against large-scale investment. Hundreds of goods and services were reserved exclusively for production in the small-scale sector. Credit and raw materials were targeted to the small-scale sector. The prices of 84 major commodities were controlled. Controls on steel, fertilizer, bulk drugs, shipbuilding and oil refining were based on 1971–2 prices and costs. Subsequent high inflation meant that by 1974 no single plant was capable of earning even a 10 per cent return on capital. Government policy, argues Jha, systematically favoured the intermediate classes and was subsequently subverted to their further benefit through organized and politicized corruption.[3]

The intermediate regime, intermediate classes and liberalization

The rationale of an intermediate regime is to subordinate 'the market' to a progressive reshaping of the social and economic environment to the benefit of its composite intermediate classes. The class objective is to guide and benefit from the process of development via state capitalism (according to Kalecki) and/or by the creation of shortage (according to Jha). McCartney and Harriss-White argued that 'Liberalization and deregulation systematically undermined the policy props upon which the edifice of the Intermediate Regime rested' (McCartney and Harriss-White 2000, 40).

Liberalization and Politics: The Orthodox Theory

Neoliberal economics argues that liberalization will allow resources to flow between different economic sectors in response to changes in profitability. Government intervention that prevents the free working of the market, such as minimum wages, hinders the allocation of labour (creates a shortage), allows a rent to be earned over and above a free market wage and so likely creates an interest group keen to perpetuate the intervention. This is exactly the argument made by Jha, albeit rooted in a bit more history. Jha suggests that the intermediate regime began in 1957 when the decline in the world prices of raw materials after the Korean War led to a balance of payments crisis for India. This was met with the imposition of trade and exchange controls, which in turn generated shortages. Hence, since 'this class has benefited from economic controls, it tried, not unnaturally to perpetuate and even strengthen the regime of shortages' (Jha 1980, viii).

From a bold attempt to place class at the centre of a political economy Jha seems to have stumbled, with a lot more fuss, into accepting neoliberal conclusions: that liberalization will end shortage and so undermine intermediate classes. The issue here is to make the important and neglected distinction between intermediate classes and the intermediate regime they may constitute. Jha is unclear on this point. In actuality intermediate classes exist *prior to* and independent of any regulatory structure and by extension will *continue* to exist in a liberalized environment. As we shall see later the 1990s may have seen the ending of the intermediate regime and a more fragmented political economy, but the intermediate classes have not disappeared. The intermediate classes are still commanding labour in the sweat shops, still ploughing their five acres and still earning corrupt commissions in the bureaucracy. Even if the intermediate classes now have less influence at the apex of policymaking and formulation, they have a profound influence on the day-to-day implementation of policy.

Big and Small-Scale Capital

This section explores the role of one fraction of the intermediate classes – the self-employed business class. A large body of opinion does not accept the thesis of a rising relative influence of intermediate business class capital and criticizes Jha and Raj for ignoring the role of the big bourgeoisie (Bardhan 1984; Byres 1997, 67).

In 1976–77 Annual Survey of Industries (ASI) data showed that Indian manufacturing was more large-size[4] orientated (in terms of the employment share of large enterprises) than the US or Japan (Little, Mazumdar and Page 1987, 86, 92). The output share of 'monopoly houses' showed no decline between 1951 and 1975 (Chandra 1979, 1261). Policy intervention by the state in many cases directly benefited the large-scale sector. Nationalized industry complemented big business by providing industrial inputs at low prices and social overhead capital. The fixed costs of license application (both legal and illegal) were better borne by big business and served to prevent entry and protect monopolistic profits. Capacity controls, intended to divert marginal output growth to the small-scale sector, were rarely actually enforced. Illegal excess capacity in the large-scale sector was eventually regularized ex post in various amnesties. This view is most convincingly critiqued by an examination of time-series data.

According to the 1971 census, 45 per cent of secondary sector workers were employed in the household sector and another 32 per cent in the non-factory, non-household sector (Little, Mazumdar and Page 1987, 72). The typical pattern for developing countries was a sharp decline in the employment share of small enterprises and a rising share of larger enterprises (Little, Mazumdar and Page 1987). Employment patterns in India showed a distinct difference from this norm. Growth rates of employment were consistently higher in small-scale (0–9 workers) than large-scale enterprises (50+ workers) especially in urban areas (Little, Mazumdar and Page 1987, 99). Between 1956 and 1977 small- (0–100) and medium-sized (100–500) enterprises more than doubled their share of employment at the cost of large firms (500+) (Kashyap 1988). Between 1981 and 1991 almost the entire addition to manufacturing employment came from the non-household, non-factory segment (Ramaswamy 1994). The relative growth of small-scale enterprises is reflected in changes in the average size of firms. The average size of the factory at the all-industry level declined from 109 workers per factory in 1951 to 73 in 1970 and for textile firms from 598 to 249 (Sandesara 1979). Within the small-scale sector, average firm size declined from 12 to 6 employees between 1972 and 1987–88. Medium-sized industries in 1972 such as food products (average of 20 employees) were by 1987–88 typically characterized as small-scale (average of 5 employees) (Sandesara 1993, 225). The striking output share and influence of the large scale sector noted by authors such as Chandra and Byres did not imply a negligible small-scale sector; rather it was medium-sized enterprises that were strikingly absent in India relative to East Asia and the US (Little, Mazumdar and Page 1987, 92).

In 1971 the household and non-factory non-household (census data) fractions of capital were responsible for 38 per cent of manufacturing value added (Little, Mazumdar and Page 1987, 86). The aggregate industrial sector grew by around 4 per cent in the 1970s. Between 1973–74 and 1979–80, village and small-scale enterprises grew at a rate of 6.8 per cent. By the late 1980s the small-scale sector accounted for more than half of total manufacturing in terms of value added, employed more than three-quarters of persons engaged in manufacturing and provided more than one-third of total exports (Kashyap 1988). An extreme example was the textile sector. Between 1951 and 1981 production of cotton and non-cotton cloths declined from 3727 million to 3147 million metres in the (large-scale) mill sector; in the (small-scale) decentralized handloom and powerloom sectors it increased from 1013 million to 4913 million metres (Mazumdar 1984, 36).

Some small-scale business will be professionally managed, and some of the small-scale sector was fictitious, being in fact fragmented components of large enterprises seeking the benefits from preferential regulations and taxes – in neither case intermediate classes. There was evidence of a rise of multiple ownership by the mid-1970s (Harriss 1980, 951; Tyabji 1984, 1427). Other evidence points to the fact the dominant portion of small-scale businesses are a part of the intermediate classes (Harriss 1980, Nagaraj 1984, Harriss-White and Sinha 2007). Between 1989–90 and 1999–2000 within non-manual middle-class occupations the share of self-employed remained at 16 per cent. In urban areas the share of self-employed remained stable at just over 30 per cent. In 1999–2000 the self-employed totalled 70 million or 24 per cent of broad definitions of the middle class (Sridharan 2004, 415).

Small-sector promotional policies

For those accepting the high and rising relative position of the small-scale sector, the most obvious culprits were the policies that sought to promote small-scale industries. This is the argument of both neoliberal economists who argue such supports have propped up an inefficient small-scale sector (Panagariya 2007) and of Jha (1980), who argued that the structure of regulation thrown up by dominant intermediate classes led to a relative expansion of the small-scale sector.

Small-scale promotional policies date back to the first two five-year plans (1951–1961). Reservation of goods for exclusive production by the small-scale sector was introduced in 1967 and extended in the 1970s and 1980s (Guhathakurta 1993). The only consistent criteria in choosing products to reserve was whether small-scale firms were physically capable of producing them (Little, Mazumdar and Page 1987, 26; Mohan 2002, 220). This was irrespective of production costs, technological progress, international competitiveness or long-term comparative advantage. Reservation was supported by numerous other measures, including fiscal (investment allowances, tax holidays, additional depreciation, sales tax exemption) and financial incentives (interest rate, capital, water, electricity and land acquisition subsidies). After banking nationalization in 1969 there was a sharp increase in the share of bank lending going to small-scale sectors (Eastwood and Kohli 1999).

No evidence production was a function of reservation

There is no strong evidence to show the relative increase of small-scale production was a direct consequence of small-scale sector reservation. The first hypothesis is that reservation induced entry for firms producing reserved products. There is no relation between levels of production and whether the item was reserved, though there is some sign that reservation helped the entry of some small-scale enterprises (Katrak 1999). Reservation and its expanding coverage bore little correlation to the pattern of small-sector growth. The output share of reserved items in industries with larger shares of reserved items has not increased (Ramaswamy 1994). Of 200 products classified as leading products in the small-scale sector (production exceeding Rs 400 million in 1987–88), only 48 were in the reserved category (Mohan 2002). Output growth in the small-scale sector tended to be higher for unreserved items between 1985–86 and 1987–88 (Bala Subrahmanya 1995; Nair 1995, 2211). The second hypothesis is that reservation encouraged incumbents to expand capacity. Units producing mainly reserved items did have higher levels of productive capacity (Katrak 1999). The third hypothesis is that reservation stimulated capacity expansion in technically less adept small-scale enterprises or through investment in capital equipment with scale indivisibilities leading to capacity underutilization. Some find capacity utilization lower in reserved sectors (Katrak 1999; Mohan 2002), while others disagree (Nair 1995). The fourth hypothesis is that reservation helped small enterprises in reserved sectors to stay in business. There is no relation between exiting production and reservation (Katrak 1999).

The small-scale sector and liberalization

Kalecki argued that international capital will tend to restore the role of big capital at the expense of the small. It is an implicit argument of Jha that as liberalization undermines the structure of regulation (shortage) supporting the Intermediate Classes the normal role of large capital will be progressively restored. There is, however, good evidence to show that the small-scale firms of the Intermediate Classes have been resilient throughout the 1990s.

There has been steady attrition of the coverage of small-scale sector reservation. In 2000–01 the government de-reserved ready-made garments; in 2001–02 the investment limit that classified industries as small was raised and another 14 products de-reserved; in 2002–03 51 items were removed from reservation (Chakraborty 2005). Trade liberalization has undermined the bite of small-scale reservation. Even if still subject to domestic reservation reserved items can be produced by large overseas enterprises and imported into India. Almost 75 per cent of all reserved items were importable after the removal of quantitative restrictions on consumer goods in April 2001 (Mohan 2002).

Contrary to the pessimistic views about the prospects for the small-scale sector in a liberalized regime, the growth in number of units, net value added, fixed capital, invested capital and employment was faster for small-scale industries between 1990 and 1998 relative to the previous decade. For all these indicators, except growth in the number of units, the balance of advantage shifted from the large- to the small-scale sector in the liberalization decade (Chakraborty 2005, 25).

Liberalization over the 1990s has allowed much greater freedom for international capital. Kalecki argued its unfettered access would lead to the restoration of the 'normal' role of big business, at the expense of the small. Foreign Direct Investment (FDI) did contribute to some concentration; between 1997 and 1999, for example, nearly 40 per cent of FDI inflows into India took the form of Merger and Acquisition (M+A) activity by MNCs of Indian enterprises. Between August 1991 and December 2005 the top five recipients of FDI were electrical equipment, including computer software and electronics (16.5 per cent), the transportation industry (10 per cent), the services sector (10 per cent), telecommunications (10 per cent), and power and oil refinery (8 per cent) (Panagariya 2008). There has been minimal FDI in areas in sectors dominated by the intermediate classes, notably agriculture and retail. Domestic firms have continued to dominate in metallurgical industries, sugar, cement, textiles, chemicals and paper. These later sectors, as we shall see, are those that are typically dominated by intermediate class capital.

More generally there is limited evidence on the impact of liberalization on patterns of concentration in industry. The data focuses on the apex of the industrial economy. Athreye and Kapur (2006) find that concentration (1970 to 1999) increased in the sugar industry and cement, declined in brewing and distilling, dyes and pigments, and drugs and medicinal preparations, and showed no trend in woollen textiles, automobiles, machine tools and fertilizers. These later fractions of declining or stable levels of concentration are the sectors more typical of intermediate class capital.

An Explanation for the Success of the Intermediate Business Classes

So far the chapter has two main arguments. The first is that the relative importance of the small-scale business sector increased in the post-independence period. The second is that contrary to the implicit implications of the first argument the small-scale thrived during the liberalization era. This section examines how the intermediate business classes have managed to thrive, both in an era of regulation and also in an era of liberalization.

A limitation of many studies is the uncritical acceptance of the view that scale is entirely determined by technical production requirements and only in sectors with few economies of scale production will take place in the small-scale sector (e.g. Gang 1992, Nair 1995). Under such circumstances liberalization will remove the bias in favour of the small-scale sector, and the relative share of the large scale will increase. The evidence discussed previously does not support this proposition. We need to move away from this limited perspective to explain the relative success of the small-scale and intermediate classes.

Can exploit liberalization

Jha (1980) argued that the intermediate classes are systematically better able to avoid regulations, price controls and taxation. There is good case study evidence that this continued into the era of liberalization. The import of watches and clocks, for example, was moved to Open General License (OGL) in April 2000, subject to a total import duty of 67.08 per cent. Small-scale units adapted to the new situation in a manner not possible for large-scale units. 'All tiny and small-scale factories [...] have given up all manufacturing activities and instead they have switched over to importing (smuggled) 'watch movements', fixing glasses on them, encasing them and selling them in the grey market' (Krishna 2000, 2).

Subcontracting

In Kalecki's original formulation of the intermediate regime he argued that small business was at risk of being displaced by large business. In the Indian context small capital has consistently proved to be of use to large capital. Subcontracting refers to a type of inter-firm relationship where large firms procure manufactured components, sub-assemblies, and products from a number of small firms and in some cases supply them with raw materials. Such arrangements are prevalent in industries in India producing consumer goods and durables like electronic appliances, metal products and food, and clothing and leather products (Nagaraj 1984). These are also sectors commonly associated with production by intermediate class business.

The fundamental basis of industrial subcontracting is that small firms have relatively lower labour costs (Nagaraj 1984). The relation between the parent and subcontractors is usually unequal. The parent can pass the burden of market fluctuations on to the subcontractors through delaying payments and refusing to take delivery of goods. Management can also use subcontracting as a means of containing the power of trade unions (Nagaraj 1984). There is ample case study evidence of such motivations for subcontracting in India (Harriss 1980; Shaw 1990; Tewari 1998; Neetha 2002; Harriss-White 2003). Service sector growth in India in the 1990s and 2000s has been intimately linked with the growth of outsourcing and linkages from software firms to the rest of the economy (Banga and Goldar 2004).

Exploitation and profitability in the small-scale sector

Small firms are less productive and face constraints in terms of output prices but manage to offset these factors with considerably lower wages than large-scale firms. Small intermediate class firms survive because they are more profitable. A more relevant political economy fault-line is not that between big and small capital as suggested by Kalecki, but rather between capital and labour within the small-scale sector. We discover that the intermediate classes are capitalists after all. A clue is the wide and widening gap between productivity and wages in the small-scale sector. This is not just a temporary aberration from free market wages but reflects a deeply rooted structural characteristic of the Indian labour market, the much weaker bargaining position of labour in small firms.

Protection of the small-scale textile industry dated from the early years of independence and included reservation for small producers and a ban on the installation of new looms by large factories. The share of cotton cloth produced in the small-scale sector increased from 16 per cent of total output in 1956 to 55 per cent in 1981. Almost all of the increase in production was provided by powerlooms (Mazumdar 1984, 13). This argument is an example of Jha's thesis that the structure of regulation was responsible for the growth of the small-scale sectors. There is good reason to doubt this conclusion. The small-scale (handloom) sector experienced rapid growth pre-dating protection, between 1900 and 1939 (Mazumdar 1984, 7). This is supported by evidence on relative profitability: 'It is possible that even in the absence of physical restrictions on mills, given the cost structure and in particular the wage differential between mills and powerlooms, the latter would have been the favoured sector' (Mazumdar 1984, 47). A survey of handloom and powerloom units in the textile town of Mau in Uttar Pradesh found powerlooms to be very profitable, some with profit rates as much as 50 per cent (Little, Mazumdar and Page 1987). Earlier this section suggested that low wages (exploitation) in the small-scale sector was a strong candidate to explain its higher profitability. There are numerous case studies showing that wages are lower in the small-scale sector (Little, Mazumdar and Page 1987; Shaw 1990; Cawthorne 1995; Dupont 1998; Tewari 1998; Neetha 2002). Survey evidence confirms this general pattern and also has evidence for productivity and profit levels by firm size. There is a steady increase in capital and output per worker as the size scale of production increases; this is offset by a strongly positive correlation between wages and scale of production. Together these trends imply that profitability is lower among large-scale producers. Output–capital ratios are higher in small-scale enterprises indicating that they work capital more intensively. This would be consistent with the 'intensification of labour' hypothesis (Little, Mazumdar and Page 1987, 117). These patterns are also apparent when firms are ordered by the size of their capital stock rather than employment (Little, Mazumdar and Page 1987, 121).

The driving force behind the growth in the relative share of the small-scale sector was profitability. Between 1955 and the 1970s the largest firms (5000-plus employees) changed from being the most to the least profitable (Nagaraj 1985, M30). Profitability in the 1970s and 1980s was not due to promotional policies but because the gap between wages and productivity in the small-scale sector had been widening relative to the large-scale sector (Ramaswamy 1994, M21). This trend cannot be reconciled with the neoclassical productivity theory of wages, which holds marginal productivity to determine wage levels. It is possible, however, if we focus on the contradiction of the intermediate classes with landless labourers and urban workers and suggest this, rather than a contradiction with large-scale capital, is the true political economy fault-line. Local producers can undercut big capital by super-exploiting labour, compromising health and safety, casualization, and family labour (Harriss-White 2003). The small-scale sector is in a position to organize the off-seasonal supply of agricultural labour/raw materials to achieve higher capacity utilization.

Intermediate classes have a long history. Harriss-White (2003) notes that over the previous century India underwent a 'process of decentralised agro-industrial mercantile accumulation' and that this gave rise to 'a numerically powerful stratum of small-scale capitalists with low management costs and flexible labour practises' (Harriss-White 2003, 17). Such trajectories of accumulation have varied enormously across India but are characterized in the main by their small scale and informality.

In Kheda, central Gujarat, (Rutten 1995) surplus farmers raised the capital intensity of agriculture in the 1960s and 1970s through the application of new inputs, then in the 1980s started to invest output agriculture in related activities such as dairy farming, trade and cold storage capacity. This process saw the emergence of a class of 'agrarian capitalist entrepreneurs', certainly capitalist and entrepreneurial, basing their investments on a surplus accumulated in agriculture or a related activity and retaining strong agrarian roots. Typically accumulation was based on the opening of new enterprises rather than re-investing in the expansion of existing enterprises. In part this was because of many of the factors highlighted by the orthodox view (as discussed previously), evading compliance with labour legislation, gaining access to state subsidies for the small scale, and paying lower taxes (Rutten 1995, 212). In part this pattern of diversification reflected the social structures of Kheda. Diversification and multiplication of small enterprises enabled labour to be controlled and fragmented across locations – the typical form of labour hiring was through contractors. The intermediate classes in Kheda were predominantly members of the Patidar caste, who retained very close managerial links through the joint family system and business partnerships (Rutten 1995, 349). As well as providing a corporatist structure for management to relate to labour, this enabled firms/individuals to mobilize the financial and managerial resources needed for various business operations in agriculture, trade and industry. In Tiruppur, Tamil Nadu, the Gounder caste emerged from peasant origins – again a form of decentralized capitalism from below – to become small-scale knitwear capitalists. The Gounders had worked alongside labourers in agriculture as former peasant-workers and retained their skills in labour control as they moved into small-scale industrial knitwear production. The idiom of 'family' remained important and was central to the control of labour power. The need to closely supervise labour in an industry relying on long hours and sweated labour would keep production small-scale and hinder accumulation and innovation (Chari 2000). In coastal Andhra Pradesh the Naidu caste utilized the high productivity and profits in agriculture to fund urban migration and economic diversification that produced a new urban (intermediate) business class. Agricultural profits became first trading capital and then industrial capital. Again there was a tendency to a multiplication of small businesses (Upadhya 1988). Elsewhere, such as Northern Tamil Nadu, the landlord–merchant–moneylender class has been dominated by a small single-caste elite, and mercantile and agricultural profits have been sunk into unproductive trading and moneylending. Small-scale mercantile capital has reproduced itself and perpetuated agrarian stagnation (Harriss 1982).

The intermediate classes are of longstanding provenance, rooted in decentralized, small-scale accumulation going back a century. The process pre-dated the regulation of the post-independence period and continued into the liberalizing era of the last few decades. Throughout, Indian capitalism has been marked by its small scale and informality. It is a characteristic of Indian capitalism: accumulation is marked by the establishment of new small enterprises rather than the re-investment in and expansion of existing enterprises – a process called by one 'amoebic capitalism' (Cawthorne 1993).

Throughout, intermediate classes have thrived as their smallness has permitted firms to keep labour costs low and pursue market access rather than innovation.

The Intermediate Regime and Alternative Class Alliances

Liberalization and the BJP

McCartney and Harriss-White (2000) suggested that the BJP were the refuge of threatened intermediate classes and the Hindutva and Swadeshi projects were ideological covers behind which these classes challenged a homogenizing globalization, liberalization and marketization. Such ideas have a long genealogy.

> The lower middle class, the small manufacturer, the shopkeeper, the artisan, the peasant, all these fight against the bourgeoisie, to save from extinction their existence as fractions of the middle class [...] they are reactionary, for they try to roll back the wheel of history. (Marx 1967, 91)

The spectre haunting the intermediate classes in India, it was argued, was the growth of the middle classes (McCartney and Harriss-White 2003). The middle classes *are* distinct from the intermediate classes, despite the careless manner in which some scholars conflate the two. Intermediate classes as theorized here are defined by reference to the means of production, rather than to income. The middle classes are defined by lifestyle, education, employment and attitude (Bardhan 1984, Fernandes and Heller 2006, 500).

A strong prediction of McCartney and Harriss-White (2000, 29) was that any attempt to undermine the intermediate regime by policy change was not enough. An effective challenge required a new alliance with the power to replace the numerically dominant class coalition. The rise of the middle class did offer a potential counterweight to the intermediate classes. This next section shows that the tensions between the two class alliances were reflected *within* the BJP ruling alliance during the 1990s.

The rise of the middle classes

The three dominant proprietary classes theorized by Bardhan (1984) are inching towards homogenization; the sons of farmers and small shopkeepers are becoming professionals. The middle classes have invested in the stock market, creating a structural link with corporate capital. All fractions of Indian society are now represented in the middle classes, including large numbers of farmers (Corbridge and Harriss 2000). The ideological importance of the middle class is even more extensive than its numbers suggest manifestation. The *urge* to become middle-class is now widespread, cutting across religions, language and caste (Fernandes 2006).

Some authors have gone as far as to argue this re-orientation towards the middle classes was complete by the 1990s, that the increase in growth in the 1980s was driven by middle-class consumption (Baru 1985; Patnaik 1986; Harriss 1987; Kurien 1989). The liberalizing economic reforms in India, argue some, are characteristic of this new political economy and 'have been prosecuted by or on behalf of social elites which have been in revolt against an earlier model of state directed economic development' (Corbridge and Harriss 2000, 145).

Problems with this model/perspective

There are a number of problems with this argument. Growth in the 1980s was more clearly linked to public investment, not middle-class consumption (McCartney 2009). Middle-class consumption is import-intensive, so it would generate few linkages with the domestic economy (Kumar 1986). The consumer durables sector is too small to explain a turnaround in aggregate economic growth. The weight of the consumer durables sector in the indices of industrial production in the 1980–81 series was only 2.55 per cent. Fieldwork shows that in the most developed states in the late 1980s, the proportion of total expenditure not spent on basic wage goods was only 11 per cent in rural areas and 14 per cent in towns (Harriss-White 2003, 10). In 1998–99 the middle class in its most elite form covered only 6 per cent (55 million people), and by an extended definition only 12 per cent (115 million) of the population (Sridharan 2004). There are large fractions of the middle class who have clearly not benefited from nor supported liberalization. Liberalization led to job losses for traditional fractions of the middle class in public sector banks while subcontracting recruitment and payroll calculation to specialized companies has casualized elements of white collar work (Fernandes 2006, 107). Approval of reforms has consistently borne no relation to patterns of voting. In both 1996 and 1998 more voted for left parties who approved of than disapproved of reforms. The Congress Party despite initiating reforms in 1991, continued to attract a greater proportion of support from groups disapproving of than approving of reforms in both 1996 and 1998. Even though it opposed reforms until entering government in 1998, more supported the BJP, who approved of than disapproved of reforms in both 1996 and 1998 (Kumar 2004, 1623).

Conclusion: The Intermediate Classes in the 1990s: Decentralization and Accumulation

The strong implication of McCartney and Harriss-White (2000) was that the intermediate regime formed a 'political economy equilibrium'. Given the balance of class interests prevailing in the period of stagnation (1965 to 1980), a new structure of objective class interests would be necessary to implement reforms such as liberalization. This chapter doesn't go so far as to suggest there is now a realistic alternative to the intermediate regime. Rather, the conclusion here is that the political economy of India has become more fragmented and contradictory. In particular the middle classes, backward castes and agricultural (kisan) interests are increasingly influencing without succeeding in determining the structure of policymaking and implementation (McCartney 2009, Chapter 5). Reports of the death of the intermediate classes, however, continue to be greatly exaggerated.

The role of the centre in resource allocation has declined with deregulation and an abolition of industrial licensing. Liberalization of FDI has set state against state in a competition to host foreign capital that has compelled further erosion of state interventionism (Weiner 1999). Decentralization has also occurred as part of the effort of the centre towards fiscal consolidation. The average level of central government transfers (grants and shared taxes) fell after the mid-1980s. The centre has decentralized the burden of fiscal adjustment.

Local states have larger deficits and are more corrupt, less stable and less efficient than the central government (Weiner 1999). The revenue to GDP rate in the states declined over the 1990s and beyond. This revenue loss was marked in the case of taxes on land and agriculture, stamps and registration, state excises and state sales tax. It originates in the inability of the state to tax informal business, agriculture, trade and property transactions (Roy 1996).

A major source of the fiscal imbalance was not reflected in budgets. Outstanding state guarantees, implying significant contingent liabilities accumulated by state-owned financial corporations and utilities, grew by 40 per cent between 1993 and 2000. All-India transmission and distribution in losses of electricity from State Electricity Boards (SEBs) reached between 30 and 45 per cent of total generation in 1999–2000. This was due both to the theft of power and failure to collect bill payments from customers (Panagariya 2008). This vast fiscal transfer (equal to 1 to 2 per cent of GDP) is largely captured by intermediate classes. Formal sector business pays among the highest rates in the world; agriculture gets near free electricity. Much of this electricity is sold by local mafias on well-organized markets linking up with informal small-scale industrial capital.

Policy measures initiated by the central government have set the pace for industrial liberalization, but the implementation of these policies takes place at state level (Bhargava 1995). Despite the abandonment of industrial licensing at the centre, licenses and permits are still required for access to land, water and power. Environmental, labour, company and tax laws have to be complied with, which entails numerous inspections on industrial enterprises. The local state engages directly in production and storage of commodities, and in provision of transport and credit services. Indirectly, the state influences the local economy through regulative laws and institutions. The local state regulates technology, trade and price ceilings for some essential commodities (basic food, drugs and freight) and sets safety and quality standards. Local state intervention is implemented in a manner that distorts officially intended aims. Both direct state intervention and regulation are arenas of political contestation. The interface between the local state and local capital has become an avenue for primitive capital accumulation. Evasion of laws by powerful traders and their selective imposition on weak ones, fraud, corruption, adulteration and exploitation of labour, and customers are used to obtain resources (Harriss-White 2003). Intermediate classes have also created informally regulated niches to protect economic rents: 'Collective action by traders or producers ensures the collective ownership and maintenance of sites, insurance, protection of property, economies of scale, the reduction of transaction costs and the resolution of disputes' (Harriss-White 2003, 67). Intermediate classes have shown resilience at the local level unexpected by Kalecki or Jha. The local state has in some respects been informally privatized, state employees and politicians earning income through self-employment and the informal provision of private law enforcement, enforcing black market contracts, acquiring environmental clearance, land allocations, factory inspections, license renewal or utility connections. Kalecki observed the creation of employment for the sons of the intermediate classes to be an important function of state capitalism under an intermediate regime. Predictably, with the demise of the intermediate regime, the central state has progressively withdrawn from its role in creating employment for the educated lower middle class. Little changed at the local level despite fiscal rot; between 1984 and 1994 state level employment increased from 6.1 to 7.3 million (Weiner 1999).

A reading of Jha would suggest the solution to be simple: liberalization should have permitted market forces to remove shortages and deregulation remove opportunities for state rent-seeking. Such reforms 'ignore the effective radical privatisation, informalisation and now mafianisation that south Asian states have been undergoing for much longer than the era of liberalisation of the 1990s' (Harriss-White 2003, 101).

Notes

1 This section draws from McCartney and Harriss-White (2000).
2 Agricultural intermediate classes are not discussed here for reasons of space; see McCartney (2009).
3 The shortage model has a number of weaknesses and sought to explain a wide variety of phenomena in 1960s and 1970s India (such as inflation paranoia). These are discussed more fully in McCartney and Harriss-White (2000).
4 Firms of 500-plus workers, though this data does not include small firms with less than 10 or 20 workers.

References

Athreye, S. and S. Kapur. 2006. 'Industrial Concentration in a Liberalising Economy: A Study of Indian Manufacturing'. *Journal of Development Studies* 42, no. 6: 981–99.

Bala Subrahmanya, M. H. 1995. 'Reservation Policy for Small-Scale Industry: Has It Delivered the Goods?' *Economic and Political Weekly* 30, no. 21: M51–M54.

Banga, R. and B. Goldar. 2004. 'Contribution of Services to Output Growth and Productivity in Indian Manufacturing: Pre and Post Reforms'. ICRIER Working Paper no. 139. New Delhi: ICRIER.

Bardhan, P. 1984. *The Political Economy of Development in India.* New Delhi: Oxford University Press (reissued 1998).

Baru, S. 1985. 'The State in Retreat?' *Economic and Political Weekly* 20, no. 16: 703–6.

Bhargava, S. 1995. 'Industrial Liberalisation: Policy Issues at State Level'. *Economic and Political Weekly* 30, no. 234: M117–M123.

Byres, T. J. 1981. 'The New Technology, Class Formation and Class Action in The Indian Countryside'. *Journal of Peasant Studies* 8, no. 4: 405–54.

_______, ed. 1997. *The State, Development Planning and Liberalisation.* New Delhi: Oxford University Press.

Cadene, P. and M. Holmstrom. 1998. *Decentralised Production in India: Industrial Districts, Flexible Specialisation and Employment.* New Delhi: Sage Publications.

Cawthorne, P. 1993. 'The Labour Process under Amoebic Capitalism: A Case Study of the Garment Industry in a South Indian Town'. DPP Working Paper. Milton Keynes: The Open University.

_______. 1995. 'Of Networks and Markets: The Rise of South Indian Town, the Examples of Tiruppur's Cotton Knitwear Industry'. *World Development* 23, no. 1: 43–56.

Chakraborty, D. 2005. 'Small-Scale Industries – An Overview'. In *Small-Scale Industry in India: Large Scale Exit Problems* edited by B. Debroy and L. Bhandari. New Delhi: Academic Foundation.

Chandra, N. K. 1979. 'Monopoly Capital, Private Corporate Sector and the Indian Economy: A Study in Relative Growth, 1931–76'. *Economic and Political Weekly* 14, nos. 30–32: 1243–5, 1247, 1249, 1251, 1253–5, 1257, 1259, 1261, 1263–5, 1267, 1269–72.

Chari, S. 2000. 'The Agrarian Origins of the Knitwear Industrial Cluster in Tiruppur, India'. *World Development* 28, no. 3: 579–99.

Chibber, V. 2003. *Locked in Place: State-Building and Late Industrialisation in India*. Princeton: Princeton University Press.

Corbridge, S. and J. Harriss. 2000. *Reinventing India: Liberalisation, Hindu Nationalism and Popular Democracy*. London: Polity Press.

Debroy, B. and L. Bhandari (eds). 2005. *Small-Scale Industry in India: Large Scale Exit Problems*. New Delhi: Academic Foundation.

Dupont, V. 1998. 'Industrial Clustering and Flexibility in the Textile-Printing Industry of Jetpur (Gujarat)'. In *Decentralised Production in India: Industrial Districts, Flexible Specialisation and Employment* edited by P. Cadene and M. Holmstrom. New Delhi: Sage Publications.

Eastwood, R. and R. Kohli. 1999. 'Directed Credit and Investment in Small-Scale Industry in India: Evidence from Firm-Level Data 1965–78'. *Journal of Development Studies* 35, no. 4: 42–63.

Fernandes, L. 2006. *India's New Middle Class: Democratic Politics in an Era of Economic Reform*. Minneapolis: Minnesota University Press.

Fernandes, L. and P. Heller. 2006. 'Hegemonic Aspirations: New Middle Class and India's Democracy in Comparative Perspective'. *Critical Asian Studies* 38, no. 4: 495–522.

Gang, I. N. 1992. 'Small Firm Presence in Indian Manufacturing'. *World Development* 20, no. 9: 1377–89.

Guhathakurta, S. 1993. 'Economic Independence Through Protection? Emerging Contradictions in India's Small-Scale Sector Policies'. *World Development* 21, no. 12: 2039–54.

Harriss, J. 1980. 'Character of an Urban Economy: "Small-Scale" Production and Labour Markets in Coimbatore'. *Economic and Political Weekly* 17, no. 23: 945–54.

______. 1982. *Capitalism and Peasant Farming: Agrarian Structure and Ideology in Northern Tamil Nadu*. Oxford: Oxford University Press.

______. 1987. 'The State in Retreat? Why Has India Experienced Such Half Hearted "Liberalisation" in the 1980s?' *Institute of Development Studies Bulletin* 18, no. 4: 31–8.

Harriss-White, B. 2002. 'India's Informal Economy: Facing the 21st Century'. Paper for the Indian Economy Conference, Cornell University, 19–20 April.

______. 2003. *India Working: Essays on Society and Economy*. Cambridge: Cambridge University Press.

______. 2007. *Trade Liberalisation and India's Informal Economy*. New Delhi: Oxford University Press.

Herring, R. J. 1999. 'Embedded Particularism: India's Failed Developmental State'. In *The Developmental State in Historical Perspective* edited by M. Woo-Cumings. Ithaca: Cornell University Press.

Jha, P. S. 1980. *India: A Political Economy of Stagnation*. New Delhi: Oxford University Press.

Kalecki, M. 1972. *Essays on the Economic Growth of the Socialist and the Mixed Economy*. London: Unwin.

Kashyap, S. P. 1988. 'Growth of Small-Size Enterprises in India: Its Nature and Content'. *World Development* 16, no. 6: 667–81.

Katrak, H. 1999. 'Small-Scale Enterprise Policy in Developing Countries: An Analysis of India's Reservation Policy'. *Journal of International Development* 11, no. 5: 701–15.

Krishna, S. 2000. 'The Impact of Phasing Out of Import Licensing on Small Scale Industries'. Working Paper No. 60. New Delhi: ICRIER.

Krueger, A. O. 1974. 'The Political Economy of the Rent-Seeking Society'. *American Economic Review* 64, no. 3: 291–303.

______. (ed.) 2002. *Economic Policy Reforms and the Indian Economy*. New Delhi: Oxford University Press.

Kumar, A. 1986. '1986–87 Budget: Signs of Growth Pains Without Growth'. *Economic and Political Weekly* 31, no. 15: 662–4.

Kumar, S. 2004. 'Impact of Economic Reforms on Indian Electorate'. *Economic and Political Weekly* 39, no. 16: 1621–30.

Kurien, C. T. 1989. 'Indian Economy in the 1980s and On to the 1990s'. *Economic and Political Weekly* 24, no. 15: 787–9, 791, 793–5, 797–8.

Little, I. M. D., D. Mazumdar and J. M. Page. 1987. *Small Manufacturing Enterprises: A Comparative Analysis of India and Other Economies*. Washington, DC: Oxford University Press.

Marx, K. 1967. *The Communist Manifesto*. London: Penguin.

Mazumdar, D. 1984. 'The Issue of Small Versus Large in the Indian Textile Industry: An Analytical and Historical Survey'. World Bank Staff Working Paper no. 645. Washington, DC: World Bank.

McCartney, M. 2009. *Political Economy, Growth and Liberalisation in India, 1991–2008*. London: Routledge.

McCartney, M. and B. Harriss-White. 2000. 'The "Intermediate Regime" and "Intermediate Classes" Revisited: A Critical Political Economy of Indian Economic Development from 1980 to Hindutva'. Queen Elizabeth House Working Paper no. 34.

Mitra, A. 1977. *Terms of Trade and Class Relations*. New Delhi: Frank Cass (reissued 2005).

Mohan, R. 2002. 'Small Scale Industry Policy in India: A Critical Evaluation'. In *Economic Policy Reforms and the Indian Economy* edited by A. O. Krueger. New Delhi: Oxford University Press.

Nagaraj, R. 1984. 'Sub-contracting in Indian Industries: Analysis, Evidence and Issues'. *Economic and Political Weekly* 19, nos. 31–3: 1435–7, 1439, 1441, 1443, 1445, 1447, 1449–53.

______. 1985. 'Trends in Factory Size in Indian Industry, 1950 to 1980: Some Tentative Inferences'. *Economic and Political Weekly* 20, no. 8: M26–M27, M29–M32.

Nair, K. R. G. 1995. 'Reservation Policy for Small Industry'. *Economic and Political Weekly* 30, no. 35: 2210–11.

Namboodiripad, E. M. S. 1973. 'On Intermediate Regimes'. *Economic and Political Weekly* 8, no. 48: 2133, 2135–40.

Neetha, N. 2002. 'Flexible Production, Feminisation and Disorganisation: Evidence from the Tiruppur Knitwear Industry'. *Economic and Political Weekly* 37, no. 21: 2045–52.

Panagariya, A. 2007. 'Why India Lags Behind China and How it Can Bridge the Gap'. *World Economy* 30, no. 2: 229–48.

______. 2008. *India: The Emerging Giant*. New York: Oxford University Press.

Patnaik, P. 1986. 'New Turn in Economic Policy: Context and Prospects'. *Economic and Political Weekly* 21, no. 23: 1014–19.

Raj, K. N. 1973. 'The Politics and Economics of Intermediate Regimes'. *Economic and Political Weekly* 8, no. 27: 1189, 1191–8.

Ramaswamy, K. V. 1994. 'Small-Scale Manufacturing Industries: Some Aspects of Size, Growth and Structure'. *Economic and Political Weekly* 29, no. 9: M13–23.

Roy, R. 1996. 'State Failure in India: Political-Fiscal Implications of the Black Economy'. *Institute of Development Studies Bulletin* 27, no. 2: 22–30.

Rutten, M. 1995. *Farms and Factories: Social Profile of Large Farmers and Rural Industrialists in West India*. Oxford: Oxford University Press.

Sachs, J. D., A. Varshney and N. Bajpai, eds. 1999. *India in the Era of Economic Reforms*. New Delhi: Oxford University Press.

Sandesara, J. C. 1979. 'Size in the Factory and Concentration in the Factory Sector in India, 1951 to 1970'. *Indian Economic Journal* 27, no. 2: 1–34.

______. 1993. 'Modern Small Industry, 1972 and 1987–88: Aspects of Growth and Structural Change'. *Economic and Political Weekly* 28, no. 6: 223–9.

Shaw, A. 1990. 'Linkages of Large Scale, Small Scale and Informal Sector Industries: A Study of Thana-Belapur'. *Economic and Political Weekly* 25, nos. 7–8: M17–M19, M21–M22.

Sridharan, E. 2004. 'The Growth and Sectoral Composition of India's Middle Class: Its Impact on the Politics of Liberalisation'. *India Review* 3, no. 4: 405–28.

Tewari, M. 1998. 'Intersectoral Linkages and the Role of the State in Shaping the Conditions of Industrial Accumulation: A Study of Ludhiana's Manufacturing Industry'. *World Development* 26, no. 8: 1387–1411.

Tyabji, N. 1984. 'Nature of Small Enterprise Development: Political Aims and Socio-economic Reality'. *Economic and Political Weekly* 19, nos. 31–3: 1425–7, 1429, 1431, 1433.

Upadhya, C. B. 1988. 'The Farmer-Capitalists of Coastal Andhra Pradesh'. *Economic and Political Weekly* 23, no. 27: 1376–82.

Varma, P. V. 1998. *The Great Indian Middle Class*. New Delhi: Viking.

Weiner, M. 1999. 'The Regionalisation of Indian Politics and Its Implications for Economic Reform'. In *India in the Era of Economic Reforms* edited by J. D. Sachs, A. Varshney and N. Bajpai. New Delhi: Oxford University Press.

Woo-Cumings, M., ed. 1999. *The Developmental State in Historical Perspective*. Ithaca: Cornell University Press.

CONTRIBUTORS

Uma Basak: Associate Professor, Department of Economics, Malda Women's College, Malda.

Amit Bhaduri: Professor Emeritus, Jawaharlal Nehru University, New Delhi.

Sudipta Bhattacharyya: Professor, Department of Economics and Politics, Visva-Bharati, Santiniketan.

Terence J. Byres: Professor Emeritus of Political Economy, School of Oriental and African Studies, University of London, London.

C. P. Chandrasekhar: Professor, Centre for Economic Studies and Planning, Jawaharlal Nehru University, New Delhi.

Surajit Das: Assistant Professor, Centre for Economic Studies and Planning, Jawaharlal Nehru University, New Delhi.

Anthony P. D'Costa: Professor and Chair, Contemporary Indian Studies, Australia India Institute and School of Social and Political Sciences, University of Melbourne, Carlton.

Jayati Ghosh: Professor, Centre for Economic Studies and Planning, Jawaharlal Nehru University, New Delhi.

Surajit Mazumdar: Associate Professor, Ambedkar University, Delhi.

Matthew McCartney: Director, South Asian Studies and University Lecturer in the Political Economy and Human Development of India, University of Oxford, Oxford.

R. Nagaraj: Professor, Indira Gandhi Institute of Development Research, Mumbai.

Parthapratim Pal: Associate Professor, Economics, Indian Institute of Management, Calcutta.

Prabhat Patnaik: Professor Emeritus, Centre for Economic Studies and Planning, Jawaharlal Nehru University, New Delhi.

Utsa Patnaik: Professor Emeritus, Centre for Economic Studies and Planning, Jawaharlal Nehru University, New Delhi.

Ashok Rudra: Late Professor, Department of Economics and Politics, Visva-Bharati, Santiniketan.